LIBERTY SHIPS

THE UGLY DUCKLINGS
OF WORLD WAR II

The *Stage Door Canteen*, named for the World War II social and recreational club for service men in New York, slides down the ways at Baltimore on 12 October 1943. Built by the Bethlehem Fairfield Shipyard, she was christened by stage star Ilka Chase. The ship was scrapped in 1961.

LIBERTY SHIPS

THE UGLY DUCKLINGS
OF WORLD WAR II

by

John Gorley Bunker

NAVAL INSTITUTE PRESS

Annapolis, Maryland

Library of Congress Catalog Card No. 72-80211
ISBN 0-87021-340-7

PRINTED IN THE UNITED STATES OF AMERICA

. . . all ships, all oceans. . . .

FOREWORD

Sailors believe that ships are living things, and most sailors consider that their own particular ship, no matter what type she may be, is the best ship of that type that ever lived. Sailors who were at sea during World War II felt, understandably, that the type of ship in which they served contributed most to victory, and whether they served in carriers, submarines, destroyers, or LSTs, each of them had good right to that partisan viewpoint. And so did the men of the American merchant marine who spent the war in Liberty ships, those unforgettable "ugly ducklings" that proved so beautiful in their simplicity of design and function. But the work of the Libertys, built to serve only so long as the war lasted, did not end when the war was over. For a quarter of a century afterward they did their part in helping to rebuild the wartorn world and aiding the progress of commerce and industry.

The Libertys were built to carry cargo, but they were more than just another cargo type. Like the LSTs, their simple design made them adaptable for many uses by both the Army and the Navy: troop transports, hospital ships, repair ships, net tenders, even mule carriers. Later, some performed radar picket duty during cold war operations. The Navy's last Liberty ship hauled down her flag early in 1972.

During World War II it was my good fortune to be one of the few regular Navy officers who served at sea in these ships. I worked with the Libertys when they were supplying the hard-pressed defenders of Guadalcanal, and had the opportunity to know and respect their crews and those of other merchant ships, as they performed their hazardous duty. The merchant marine sailors, be it remembered, were the only American civilians who faced the enemy and learned the fury of his attacks launched upon, above, and beneath the sea.

Most merchant marine sailors were young, like their contemporaries in uniform, but not a few were what are now politely called "senior citizens," many of whom had returned to sea after long years ashore. In all the Liberty ships from which I flew my commodore's pennant, the one which was best officered and disciplined had a master who might have been thirty years old, but did not look it. His mate had left the sea some eighteen years earlier to become a San Francisco policeman; and the chief engineer had, for a similar period, cared for the refrigeration plant at the University of California in Berkeley.

Now, thirty years after Guadalcanal, one of my neighbors in the small Texas town where I live is a former Liberty ship sailor. William J. Grady had had years of service with Lykes Brothers, Inc., and in World War II went back to sea in another Lykes ship, the *J.L.M. Curry* (EMC2 Hull No.1).

The action off Guadalcanal was tough, but nothing compared to the ordeal of the Murmansk run, where the *J.L.M. Curry* met her end. After making the hazardous voyage to Murmansk, she spent six months in that bleak port, subjected to frequent air raids against which her best defense was the deckload of Sherman tanks awaiting unloading. Having fought off the enemy all that time, the *Curry* finally started home, only to break up and sink in a 40-knot gale. Today, in all Russia, there is no memorial to the *Curry* or the many other ships lost helping to save the Soviet Union—and precious few memorials to the Liberty ships anywhere else in the world.

The Liberty ships were discussed, but only objectively, in the comprehensive *Ships for Victory* by Frederick C. Lane, which the author described as an account of shipbuilding under the U.S. Maritime Commission. That excellent British official publication, *Merchant Shipping and the Demands of War* by Miss C. B. A. Behrens of Cambridge University, does discuss ship operations rather than shipbuilding, but from the viewpoint of overall crisis requirements and without emphasis on any particular ship type.

It is a satisfying and happy task to introduce this book on Liberty ships, by an author who sailed in them in World War II. The book is long overdue because, while the contributions to victory by the Liberty ships have been recognized and appreciated, their story has never been completely told.

Nearly three thousand Liberty ships took to the seas during World War II. Sad to relate, they are now nearly all gone, but their achievements in war and peace, ably detailed here by John Bunker, will keep them living on as all good ships do, in the memories of old sailors. From this old sailor, to all the Libertys and all their crews: *Well Done.*

JOHN D. HAYES
Rear Admiral, U.S. Navy (Retired)

PREFACE

Ships beyond all numbering have been the subjects of numerous books. In setting out to write one book about almost numberless ships—the great fleet of Liberty ships that sailed in World War II—it became apparent that the exploits of many ships which served faithfully and well would remain unrecorded, in part for lack of space and in part because some of the records no longer exist.

The usual scholarly sources were of small help in this project because, while there are plenty of books about World War II, very few of them mention Liberty ships. If there was to be one footnote on a primary source for this book, it would have to name the SS *Jonathan Grout*, a Liberty ship. If anything made me an expert on Libertys, it was the ten months spent aboard that ship on a global voyage which included the invasion of Sicily on 10 July 1943. Service on another Liberty, the *William B. Giles*, plus time spent in a round half-dozen "Hog Islanders" and other merchant types as coal passer, fireman, oiler, deck engineer and purser, all provided me with essential background information not readily available in reference libraries.

The published works consulted were chiefly the account of the Royal Navy in World War II, *The War At Sea* in three volumes, by Captain Stephen N. Roskill, RN, published by Her Majesty's Stationery Office; and the *History of U.S. Naval Operations in World War II* in fifteen volumes, by Samuel Eliot Morison, published by Atlantic, Little Brown. The various wartime memoirs of that "former naval person," Winston Churchill, were also consulted.

Among the records that do exist, I searched the voluminous Armed Guard voyage reports and survivor interviews in the Classified Operational Archives of the U.S. Naval History Division in Washington, D.C., and the hundreds of voyage log books now maintained by the U.S. Maritime Administration in the

Federal Records Center, New York City. The wartime editions of various maritime union newspapers, the news releases of the U.S. Maritime Administration and the U.S. Shipping Administration, and the house organs and records of many shipyards and shipping lines were also useful in compiling the story of the Liberty ships.

Turning to less official sources, I drew on the memories and experiences of numerous seagoing men. Some of these were contained in letters, jotted down in diaries, and narrated in personal interviews, and some were merely bits of information sifted out of casual conversations. None of this lends itself to rigid bibliographic classification, but without it the book would not have been possible.

Actually, the book is the result of the interest and contributions of a great many people in government, industry, the merchant marine, the Navy, and the various maritime unions. The names of those who appear in the text are included not only because they were contributors but because they were active participants in Liberty ship operations. It was impractical to name them all, just as it was impossible to list all the documentary sources. The one person who does deserve mention here is Lieutenant Commander Arnold Lott, U.S. Navy (retired), the Naval Institute Press editor whose enthusiasm over this book, during several years, carried it through from conjecture to completion. He helped with the original organization, kept the project on course where content and style were concerned, and made certain that the finished book was all ship-shape and Bristol fashion.

To the masters and crews of those ships whose deeds should have been described here but were not, my apologies; to all those who should have been named here but were not, my sincere regrets; to everyone who helped build, sail, or write about the Liberty ships, my heartfelt appreciation.

JOHN GORLEY BUNKER

CONTENTS

ILLUSTRATIONS

All photographs are official Navy Department or Coast Guard releases
unless otherwise noted

LIBERTY SHIPS
THE UGLY DUCKLINGS
OF WORLD WAR II

Photograph courtesy of the Henry J. Kaiser Historical Library.

Quitting time! Three times a day, at eighteen shipyards across the United States, this scene was repeated as shift workers laid down their tools and started home. This is the main gate of the Henry J. Kaiser plant at Vancouver, across the Columbia River from Portland, Oregon.

1

THE
BUILDING
PROGRAM

On Saturday, 27 September 1941, a new ship was ready for launching at the Bethlehem-Fairfield shipyard in Baltimore, Maryland. Her hull and superstructure were bright with fresh gray paint. Gay bunting draped her bow. Signal pennants fluttered from stem to stern in the warm fall breeze.

Thousands of spectators filled every vantage point around the launching area. Roads leading to the yard were lined with automobiles. The Baltimore and Ohio Railroad had run a special train from Washington with government officials and representatives of industry, labor, and the press. Extra streetcars had been put into service for the occasion.

Obviously, this was not the launching of just another ship. That day, 27 September, had been designated Liberty Fleet Day, and throughout the United States the Maritime Commission had scheduled 14 ship launchings in what was hailed as "the largest launching of merchant vessels that this country has seen since World War I."

For a homely, unromantic freighter, the launching of the first of the Liberty fleet had attracted a distinguished party. Rear Admiral Emory S. Land, the principal speaker and head of the United States Maritime Commission, shared the ceremonial platform with government officials, representatives of the yard, and Mrs. Henry A. Wallace, wife of the vice-president of the United States, who would christen the ship.

In his speech, Admiral Land reported that the nation's emergency ship-construction program was many months ahead of schedule—that instead of two Liberty ships being delivered in 1941, as originally planned, at least 20 ships would be completed and in service by the end of the year.

"As long as America faces the crisis and challenge of Hitlerism," he concluded, "there will be a continuous and increasing flow of ships from this and other American plants." Then there was a loud crack as a cutting torch burned through the steel "anchor" plating just below the speaker's platform. The bow of the ship moved ever so slightly. An official handed the bottle of champagne to Mrs. Wallace and shouted "Smash it!" She swung the bottle against the bow and, as it burst into foam, said, "I christen thee *Patrick Henry*."

The Baltimore Civic Band struck up the "Star Spangled Banner" as the first of all the Libertys slid into the waters of the Patapsco and a flock of homing pigeons darted from a cage beneath the speaker's platform and circled above the cranes and scaffolds. Then they headed homeward to the Naval Air Station at Lakehurst, New Jersey. They carried messages to be transmitted to President Roosevelt in Washington, informing him that the *Patrick Henry* had been launched.

□

Patrick Henry was only the first of 312 ships to be turned out by the Bethlehem yard alone. And they were only a fraction of the Libertys that were eventually to slide down American shipways in the most stupendous building program the world will probably ever see. No one, whether in Rome, Berlin, Tokyo, or Washington, could anticipate that *Patrick Henry* was to be followed by more than 2700 sister ships that would carry American troops and their fighting gear around the world.

Even as the *Patrick Henry* was towed to a fitting-out dock, shipyard workers prepared to lay the keel of another Liberty ship. And thus it was to be until the end of the war, as a score of shipyards launched an armada of ships so vast that the Axis powers would be overwhelmed by a flood of men, guns, and machines.

The *Patrick Henry* slid down the launching ways none too soon. Although

Pearl Harbor was still three months in the future, the United States, for all intents and purposes, was already in the shooting war. On 4 September, the USS *Greer*, a World War I destroyer, was attacked by a German submarine 175 miles southwest of Iceland. Within another month the destroyer *Kearny* was torpedoed near Iceland and the destroyer *Reuben James* was sunk by a German U-boat. Actually, the U. S. Navy became involved in the Battle of the Atlantic on 17 September 1941, when five U. S. destroyers were assigned to escort convoy HX150, bound from Halifax for the British Isles. This naval assignment short of an official declaration of war was occasioned by Britain's desperate need for convoy protection. Merchant ship losses were reaching the point where Hitler's hope of winning the war with submarines, of strangling Britain by severing its ocean supply lines showed every sign of success.

The decision to augment American merchant ship tonnage and to accelerate construction of new ships had been made during a period when German submarines and surface raiders were sinking more than 500,000 tons of Allied shipping each month in the North Atlantic alone.

The Allies needed ships by the hundreds to replace such losses and increase the flow of supplies to Britain and Russia. The Libertys, slow but capacious, were the ships. With the launching of the *Patrick Henry*, they were on their way.

Patrick Henry went into service just 23 days after the attack on Pearl Harbor, the interval between launching and commissioning being the time required for installation of machinery and the myriad other aspects of making her ready for sea.

Chief Engineer Leonard Whaley took the ship out of the shipyard, stayed with her all during the war, and finally left her at the end of her twelfth voyage in April, 1946. "She ran like a charm," he said. "I hated to get off and turn her over to someone else. She was a great ship—the greatest."

The *Patrick Henry's* master on the first few voyages was Captain Richard G. Ellis. Captain Erling Olmstead, who succeeded him, said, "I am proud to be the master of the first Liberty. No one picked a soft trip for this veteran. She made all the tough runs and always delivered her cargo. I, among thousands of men who have sailed these ships, am in a position to know best the wonderful job they have done. I know their ruggedness and untiring character. I know how tough they are and well able to hold their own in any weather."

The *Patrick Henry* backed her master up all the way. On a voyage to the Middle East the ship steamed 7,633 miles at an average speed of 11.6 knots and delivered 11,028 tons of cargo. Her fuel-oil consumption was a nominal 193 to 194 barrels a day.

Liberty ships soon became the workhorses of World War II, more famous perhaps than the sleek American clipper ships that preceded them by about 100 years. During the war, and afterward, there was hardly a port anywhere in the world, from Chicago to Chittagong, where the Libertys were not a familiar sight. No other single type of merchant vessel has ever sailed the seas in such vast numbers.

□

What, exactly, was a Liberty ship? Designated an EC2 in the Maritime Commission's nomenclature of vessel types (E for Emergency, C for Cargo, 2 for large capacity), the *Patrick Henry* differed very little in any respect from her hundreds of sister ships. The Liberty was the product of a standardized design, and each ship was a blueprint copy of the others, except that each varied by a few tons in gross tonnage.

The Liberty ship design was adapted from that of an old and time-proven British tramp ship. Any doubts about the origin of the design were dispelled by a statement from Admiral Land, printed in the U. S. Naval Institute *Proceedings* for December, 1960:

> "The contract plans and many others for the Liberty ship were obtained from the British. Detailed plans were prepared by Gibbs & Cox, a firm of naval architects in New York, and by the U.S. Maritime Commission. The design came from Sunderland and originated in 1879. Various claims for the Liberty ship design have been made by U. S. Citizens, even a gold medal was awarded for one, but they were erroneous and no award was deserved. The Liberty was based on an old tramp ship design."

Plans for the Liberty designs were shown to President Roosevelt in 1941, when Admiral Land spread out some blue prints on the President's desk in the White House. Roosevelt was a lover of ships and had an eye for a ship, but it must not have been in good focus that day. As the President leafed through the prints, Land recalled, "He came to the profile sheet, backed away from it and said, 'Admiral, I think this ship will do us very well. She'll carry a good load. She isn't much to look at, though, is she? A real ugly duckling.' "

The press picked up this comment and from then on that's how Libertys were known. Later, in 1943, after Admiral Land so described them, the "ugly duck-lings" became "the expendables." They were much maligned and misunderstood by a misinformed public. Headline-hunting critics added to this misinformation. But the *Patrick Henry* and the hundreds of ships that followed justified the fondest hopes of those who designed and built them, confounded their critics, and helped to defeat the Axis powers.

The standard Liberty was 441 feet 6 inches over all, with a beam of 56 feet, 10¾ inches and a loaded draft of 27 feet, 9¼ inches. The deadweight tonnage was 10,920, gross tonnage about 7,500, and displacement tonnage 14,257. Libertys carried 9,146 tons of cargo with a full load of fuel. It was quite common, however, for them to haul more, and most of them sailed with holds filled and a deckload of planes, tanks, crated aircraft, trucks, heavy machinery, or locomo-tives, holding them down to their Plimsoll marks or deeper with a 10,000-ton payload.

The ship had five holds; three forward of the engine spaces and two aft. Cargo capacity was equal to that of 300 railroad freight cars. A Liberty could carry 2,840 jeeps, 440 light tanks, 230 million rounds of rifle ammunition, or 3,440,000 C-rations.

The Maritime Commission specified a reciprocating steam engine for power, partly because of its simplicity of operation and ease of procurement, and partly because turbines and complicated electrical equipment were slated for warship use.

These three-cylinder "up-and-down" engines were fed by two oil-burning boilers and produced 2,500 horsepower and a speed of 11 knots with the ship fully loaded, although many engineers were able to get 11.5 knots when boilers and hull were clean and the machinery was in good order.

Officers had private rooms, but crewmen slept two or three to a room. The ships provided showers, a luxury to many prewar seamen who were accustomed to the traditional bathtub for merchant seamen, a bucket.

Officers ate in the "saloon" on the main deck in the forward part of the mid-ships house. Crewmen and the armed guard had separate dining areas and were served by messboys in separate sittings, as there was not enough room for all hands to eat together. A galley on the main deck adjacent to the crew's mess was usually fitted with oil-burning ranges, but some had coal ranges.

Some Armed Guard men lived amidships, six or eight to a room, one room on the starboard side and the other on the port side adjacent to the officer's saloon. About half of the complement bunked in the most uncomfortable part of the ship, the after deckhouse. The stern moved violently in rough weather, tossing, bucking, and shaking every time the propeller came out of water in a heavy sea. This was one reason why many a gunner experienced chronic seasickness and had to be transferred.

☐

The Liberty ship program was actually preceded in 1940–41 by the construction of 60 *Ocean*-class vessels for the British Ministry of War Transport, based on plans originally used at Newcastle-on-Tyne in 1879. The simple design was well adapted for emergency production in large numbers. The first of these ships, the *Ocean Vanguard*, was the first all-American-made vessel for the British. She was also the first ship built by the new Todd-California yard (a Henry Kaiser operation) in Richmond, California. The ship was launched just seven months after ground was broken for construction of that shipyard. Sixty such ships were built for the British, by Kaiser, half at the Portland, Maine yard, which had been constructed for this purpose, and half at the Richmond yard. The American-built British Libertys were similar to the U. S. type, but with a different silhouette because of the split deckhouse, which followed the general design in British tramp ships. They burned coal and had Scotch boilers. Crew accommodations were not as good as in the American ships. Chain rails were used on deck instead of bulwarks, and there were other minor differences. Construction of these ships accelerated the decision of the Maritime Commission to build an emergency-type freighter. The Commission, even as late as 1941, had little relish for such vessels, believing they would be a detriment to American shipping in later years and holding to the idea that the standard C-types should be constructed in larger numbers. America's fast drift into the shooting war and huge Allied shipping losses combined to focus thinking on the emergency-ship concept.

The EC2 design was selected because of its simplicity and adaptability to mass-production methods. Mass production of shipping had first been used successfully in the U. S. during the emergency ship program of World War I, when America startled the maritime world by using prefabrication techniques to turn out ships of standardized design. The best known ships were called "Hog Islanders," so named because they were constructed at the 900-acre Hog Island emergency shipyard in Philadelphia. Hog Island had 50 shipways and was the first yard ever built especially for mass production of ships. It launched its first ship, the SS *Quistconck*, on 5 August 1918, and the last of 122 ships on 29 January 1921.

None of them were ready before World War I ended, but many served the merchant marine for over 20 years afterward. The Navy had several—stores ships *Capella, Sirius, Spica, Vega;* transports *Chaumont, St. Mihiel, Chateau Thierry;* and tenders *Wright* and *Argonne*—when World War II began.

Standard "Hogs" measured 380 feet overall, with a 54-foot beam, 24-foot draft, and 2,500-horsepower steam turbines. Some were 58 feet longer and had 6,000 horsepower. The American merchant fleet, between the two world wars, found them handy in size, fairly fast, and economical. Many of them served through World War II; 58 were sunk by submarines or were casualties of the war through other types of battle action, groundings, or accidents. "Hogs" were known as good seaboats, giving a comfortable ride in stormy weather. The 448-foot "Hogs"—*Wright, Chaumont, Argonne, St. Mihiel,* and *Chateau Thierry*—were strange-looking ships that appeared, when viewed broadside, to be sagging at the bow and stern. They also, at a quick glance, appeared to be going both ways at once. This was the result of being designed without sheer, deadrise, or tumble home to simplify fabrication and to speed construction.

Besides the legendary "Hog Islanders," the World War I emergency program produced everything from turbine-powered cargo freighters to tankers, tugs, and barges. In fact, one World War I U. S. Shipping Board emergency type of freighter, the *Los Angeles*-class, was seriously considered for reproduction as the World War II Liberty ship. This 11-knot vessel with triple-expansion steam engines and watertube boilers had construction features suitable for speedy production and economical steel consumption. The British design won out for various reasons, one of the most important being that the firm of Gibbs and Cox, New York naval architects, was already well along in preparing detailed plans from the British design.

☐

The Maritime Commission never considered the Liberty ship as an ugly duckling. "The Liberty ship," said a press release of 1941, "will present a trim, seagoing appearance. Riding low in the water, with its long, slender prow and its simple, straight-lined superstructure, it will knife its way through the waves as gracefully as any vessel afloat." Liberty ships at sea fulfilled the prediction. They were neither ugly nor ungainly.

As the German submarine campaign became more effective, and business and government in the United States voiced dismay over mounting ship losses, hundreds of suggestions, plans, and proposals for new ships or shipping schemes were pressed on the President and members of Congress. All of them eventually were referred to Admiral Land, many with powerful sponsorship from politicians and influential industrialists.

Among plans for replacing ship losses was one for building a large fleet of sailing ships, similar to the government-sponsored sailing ship construction of World War I, which had been a great waste of time, money and materials. The proponents wanted to build hundreds of two- and three-masted schooners with gasoline or diesel engines to carry coastal and Caribbean commerce. The idea was discarded as impractical, but not before it had received some important support. One Caribbean nation even applied for a million-dollar loan to build its own fleet of such ships.

Still more impractical, as seen in the perspective of later years, but vociferously advocated at the time by President Roosevelt and others, was a small, freight-carrying vessel called the Beaver or Sea Otter. Designed for propulsion by gasoline engines, this craft lay so low in the water that it looked more like a Great Lakes whaleback or a submarine. Its low freeboard and wave-top silhouette, claimed the backers, were advantages, presenting a small target for a submarine.

Proponents of this ship could hardly have had practical experience in a North Atlantic gale; nor could they have envisioned the long trips that wartime freighters would make to distant fighting fronts. And how these little ships could have transported locomotives or Sherman tanks would have been an interesting problem, too. Nevertheless, in October of 1942 the Commission was pressured into awarding a contract for a ship of this type. It became a subject of controversy in Administration and shipbuilding circles for more than a year; opponents of the craft saying it was a waste of money and proponents claiming it would be an answer to the submarine menace.

The theory behind the Sea Otter was to provide a type of ship that could be produced in such a number that the enemy couldn't keep up with them. They would carry a small crew—perhaps 20 or so—and 1,500 tons of cargo at a speed of 12 knots. The argument seemed so logical that the Senate started an inquiry into why the Maritime Commission didn't jump "whole hog" into the project.

Whatever type of ship was to be built, it would have been impossible without the rejuvenation program provided by the Merchant Marine Act of 1936. Without the building stimulus of that legislation, construction of the vast Liberty fleet might well have been impossible and would, even at best, have been greatly delayed. Had this building program not been well underway by 1941, the nation's shipyard capacity would not have been able to handle the emergency shipbuilding efforts. The Act of 1936 set up the U. S. Maritime Commission, which replaced the old Shipping Board, and asserted a bold new maritime policy for the United States.

The preamble to this legislation, often called the Magna Carta of the modern U. S. Merchant Marine, stated:

> It is necessary for the national defense and the development of its foreign and domestic commerce that the United States shall have a Merchant Marine (a) sufficient to carry its domestic waterborn commerce and a substantial portion of the export and import foreign commerce of the United States and to provide shipping service on all routes essential for maintaining the flow of such domestic and foreign waterborn commerce at all times; (b) capable of serving as a Naval and Military Auxiliary in the time of war or national emergency (c) owned and operated under the United States flag by citizens of the United States in so far as may be practicable, and (d) composed of the best equipped, safest and most suitable types of vessels, constructed in the United States and manned with a trained and efficient citizen personnel. It is hereby declared to be a policy of the United States to foster and encourage the development of such a Merchant Marine!

The first ship built under this new policy was launched on 22 April 1939. She was the freighter *Donald McKay,* named for the famous Boston designer and builder of clipper ships, and was the first of 20 high-speed steel cargo ships built on the well-known C2 design. The *McKay* and ships of her class were in prime demand as high-speed transports when the war started. The C2s were 435 feet long, measured 8,875 deadweight tons, and were turbine-powered for a speed of 15½ knots fully loaded.

Increasing tension in Europe in the summer of 1939 indicated a need for accelerating the shipbuilding program. On 14 September 1939, the SS *Sea Arrow*, the first oceangoing merchant ship to be launched on the Pacific Coast since World War I, slid down the ways of the Moore Dry Dock Company in Oakland, California. She was a 492-foot, 16½-knot freighter of the Maritime Commission's C3 design. Other C3 hulls followed.

In 1937 there were only ten shipyards in the entire country capable of turning out a vessel the size of a Liberty. Under the Maritime Commission's shipyard construction program, the number of yards was increased to 40 by 1941. These yards had a total of 275 shipways capable of handling vessels of 400 or more feet in length. By VE Day (7 May 1945) the United States had more than 50 active shipyards, of which 18 built the Libertys.

In his speech at the launching of the *Patrick Henry*, Admiral Land predicted that experience gained with that ship, plus the *Star of Oregon, John C. Fremont,* and several others nearing completion, showed that the EC2 could be delivered in from four and a half to six months, compared with ten to twelve months for the famous "Hog Islanders" and other emergency types built during World War I. Land at that time had no idea how American mass-production ingenuity would meet and exceed these expectations.

□

The Oregon Shipbuilding Corporation built a shipyard out of a swamp and compiled an outstanding record on its eleven shipways. The keel of its first ship, the *Star of Oregon*, was laid 19 May 1941. This ship was launched on 27 September and delivered on 31 December, a total of 253 days. Building time at this yard was rapidly reduced: the tenth ship was delivered in 154 days, the nineteenth in 86 days, the thirteenth in 73 days. The *Thomas Bailey Aldrich*, from keel laying to delivery, was completed in a total of 46 days.

The Kaiser yard took 197 days to build and deliver its first Liberty ship in Richmond, California. By August, 1942, Kaiser's Portland, Oregon, yard launched and delivered the *Pierre S. DuPont* in 31 days. His yard at Richmond, California completed the *Joseph N. Teal* in 16 days.

The keel for Liberty ship hull number 440 was laid at Richmond on 8 November 1942. The completed vessel, containing more than 250,000 different items, was completed in four days and 15 hours and was launched on 12 November as the *Robert E. Peary*. In 24 hours the hull had taken shape and 1,450 tons of steel —all prefabricated sections—and the 135-ton engine were in place. By the end of the second day, the upper deck was finished. On the third day, deckhouses, masts, and deck equipment were installed. Final welding, wiring, and painting was completed on the fourth day, and the *Robert E. Peary* was ready for launching. She went into operation three days later.

To work this shipbuilding miracle, construction time was cut from months to weeks by rigid uniformity in design, specifications and procurement. Sixty-one percent of the ship was prefabricated, with more than 152,000 feet of weld performed on the assembly line. A total of 97 prefabricated sections were trucked from the prefab plant to the ways. The hull was assembled in huge 250-ton "chunks" swung into place with all interior fittings—even mirrors, bunk ladders, portholes, washbasins, and radiators—already installed. Seventeen banks of welding machines were used on each side of the hull. As the magazine, *Ships*, of the Shipbuilders Council of America explained it, the EC2 was "standardized to the last small gasket, to the final door hinge." Libertys were turned out like automobiles, and so fast that sometimes painters were still at work on them when they slid down the ways.

Building hulls was only part of the ship-construction story. While shipyards won headlines for launching Libertys in a matter of days, the ships they built would have been useless if subcontractors all over the country had not made scheduled deliveries of the vast variety of machinery and equipment that went into them. For every Liberty ship launched, industry had to supply a three-cylinder reciprocating engine, standing all of three stories high and weighing 135 tons, a propeller shaft, two watertube boilers, one condenser, one steering engine, two anchors, two propellers (each ship carried an emergency spare), at least ten antiaircraft guns, six generators, and six steam pumps. Each ship also required booms, winches, fans, beds, ventilators, hatch covers, life rafts, lockers, compasses, chairs, gauges, ladders, stoves, and other equipment, thousands of miles of wiring and pipe (from $\frac{1}{4}''$ to $12''$ in diameter), hundreds of valves, and a storeroom full of spare parts and fittings. The construction of one Liberty ship required 3,425 tons of hull steel, 2,725 tons of plate, and 700 tons of shapes, which included 50,000 castings.

Every EC2 carried at least four lifeboats; those converted into troopships were equipped with two or more additional boats. These were 24 feet long and certificated for 25 passengers. One boat out of four was fitted with a gasoline engine.

Even with this vast expansion of shipyard facilities, wartime ship production would never have reached such monumental goals had it not been for mass production know-how and the all-out use of prefabrication techniques. The Maritime Commission made a bold and courageous decision in replacing traditional riveted construction with welding for speed and economy of steel and manpower. Welding was still a fairly new process and still unaccepted by many naval architects, shipbuilders, and shipowners in 1941. Insurance firms, too, were still wary of welding.

□

But selecting a simple design, perfecting mass-production techniques, and building the necessary shipyards were only part of the job. There were not enough qualified shipyard workers in the United States for all the new yards. Many men who could have built ships were going into the armed forces. So thousands of men and women who had never seen a ship in their lives were recruited and trained to work in the new yards.

All shipyards organized schools to train welders, shipfitters, electricians, joiners, and others needed to meet an anticipated peak requirement of 700,000 workers by 1943. By comparison, the usual peacetime labor force in all U. S. shipyards was less than 100,000 in the busiest years.

"Rosie the Riveter" became a wartime byword as women moved into the shipyards by the thousands, donning goggles, overalls and welding masks and looking as grimy as any male by the end of a working day. "Rosie" became such a part of the national scene in those years that she was immortalized by Norman Rockwell in a cover painting for *The Saturday Evening Post.*

At one time, women made up more than 30 percent of the work force in West Coast shipyards. By October of 1942, more than 400 of them were at work in Kaiser's Richmond yards alone, where Hazel Phillips repaired pneumatic drills, Kay MacAdams was a shipfitter, and Elizabeth Norden, five times a grandmother, was a burner. Esther Clark was a rigger's helper, Pearl Smith was a boiler maker's helper, and Mrs. Art Bjorhus worked alongside her husband as a shipfitter's helper. Jillian Tyrell-Feltham, an Englishwoman who lost her soldier-husband at Hong Kong and escaped from Manila just before it fell, worked for Kaiser as a weld checker—probably the first woman ever to hold down that job in a shipyard.

"Women," said Admiral Land, "make excellent welders. To the women it was like a sewing machine job."

On the whole, "Rosie" and her fellow workers "sewed a fine seam." Otherwise, the EC2 would never have survived its wartime rigors and gone on to serve over 20 years in peacetime operations.

But because of the press of work, lack of training, inadequate inspection, and other reasons, there was some careless and sloppy work in the shipyards. Such work was not always found out before a ship sailed, and probably accounted for the loss of some ships that had to drop out of convoy to make repairs. The *Henry Wynkoop* fractured her decks and side shell while loading in New York on 17 February 1943. The *George P. Garrison* developed cracks up forward and in her deckhouse during a North Atlantic crossing. In the Alaskan theatre, the *John P. Gaines* broke up and was lost, the *Alexander Baranoff* broke in two and was welded together again, and the *Chief Washakie* developed extensive cracks that were then welded. The *Thomas Hooker* and *J. L. M. Curry* were lost because of structural defects. There was no evidence of sabotage in these ships.

The *John Philip Sousa* had continual trouble on her first voyage because grease was fouling up the boiler water. The ship was unable to sail on her second voyage until 13 buckets full of grease were removed from one boiler. This was a clear case of failure of shipyard personnel to clean away the protective grease used in shipping the boiler from factory to shipyard.

□

On 6 September 1943, with more than a thousand of the "ugly ducklings" in the water, President Roosevelt had this to say about the nation's shipbuilding industry and its 700,000 workers, most of them war-recruited men and women who wouldn't have known a keel from a hatch cover before the war began:

> They have delivered on or ahead of schedule every ton of every ship they were called upon to build. They have smashed every production quota set for them so that today, less than two years after our entry into the war, the total deadweight tonnage of their ships more than doubles that of the entire American merchant marine before Pearl Harbor. By the end of 1944, new ships delivered by American yards will equal the combined pre-war merchant fleets of the United States, Great Britain, Germany, Japan and Norway.

The President had called for eight million tons of merchant shipping—"a great bridge of ships"—to be built in 1942. The astronomical figure staggered officials in the Maritime Commission and the nation's shipyards. But instead of deciding it couldn't be done, they accepted the challenge and vowed to give the President more than he had asked for.

By the end of 1942 they had turned out 746 ships of 8,089,732 deadweight tons. But this was only a beginning. The 1943 record was 1,896 ships of 19,238,646 deadweight tons, and of this number, 1,238 were Libertys. By 1944 the emphasis was on the faster turbine-powered Victory ships, but even at that the 1944 schedule still called for 800 Libertys.

In 1941 the estimated base construction cost of a Liberty was $1,500,000 and contracts were written on this assumption. Contractors' fees contributed an additional $60,000 to $140,000 for each ship, this being contingent on whether the yard could claim a bonus for fast delivery or was penalized for not meeting a schedule. The price of a complete Liberty ran around $1,600,000, although construction costs from yard to yard varied from a low of $1,543,000 to a high of $2,099,000. Rising costs of labor and materials also contributed to higher-than-estimate totals, although the spread between estimates and actual cost was negligible compared to the differences in many other procurement projects.

In almost every phase of wartime operations, there was some particular use that could be made of a Liberty ship. In fact, as Admiral Land said in 1943: "The Liberty ship is a product for war use. It can be classed with the tank, the fighting planes and other materials of war. It was produced to be expendable if necessary. If expended, it had served its purpose. Its production was necessitated because of a definite limitation on the amount of propulsion equipment, available for our higher type ships."

In the wartime use to which the Admiral referred, Libertys steamed to every port of the world where ships had to deliver supplies for Allied forces or load raw materials for war plants at home. They may have been "ugly ducklings," but President Roosevelt had been right when he said ". . . this ship will do us very well." Most of them had done better than that. Considering the hazards of wartime operations, losses were not excessive. A total of 195 Libertys were lost to torpedoes, mines, explosions, collisions, strandings, or other hazards of the sea.

As the powerful U. S. Navy beat the Japanese fleet into submission in the last days of World War II—using in the process considerable bombs, bullets, and beans carried in Liberty ships—the last of a long line of EC2s came off the ways. On 14 August 1945 Japan agreed to accept the terms of the Potsdam Declaration and surrender. On that same day the Liberty ship *J. Howland Gardner* was delivered. Six days later the U. S. Maritime Commission cancelled $425 million worth of contracts for 135 ships, including some Libertys under conversion for special uses, and the great U. S. wartime shipbuilding boom was over.

□

But the *Howland* was not the last Liberty ship. There was a last Liberty ship, obviously, because suddenly no more of them were being built, although there is considerable difference of opinion as to which ship was the last one. The final ship on the Liberty list, hull number 3148, was the *Ora Ellis*, whose keel was laid on 23 July 1945. The *Ora Ellis* was delivered on 16 October 1945. But the *Walter F. Perry*, whose keel was laid several days ahead of the *Ellis*, was delivered on 20 October, four days after the *Ellis*. To complicate matters, the *Albert H. Boe*, laid down and launched with the *Perry*, was delivered on 30 October, still ten days later.

For some unknown reason, on 30 June 1945 the Maritime Commission issued a press release heralding the *Stanley R. Fisher* as being the last of the Liberty fleet. Built by the New England Shipbuilding Corporation and named for a merchant seaman lost when his ship was torpedoed, the *Fisher* was delivered on 1 July 1945. Actually, 16 keels were laid and 16 ships were delivered after the *Fisher*. So, the *Ellis* was the last ship laid down, *Perry*, *Boe*, and *Ellis* were the last ships launched—all on the same day—and *Boe* was the last ship delivered.

To the question as to how many Libertys were built, there are almost as many answers as to which one was last. It all depends on whose tabulations are used. Liberty hulls were numbered in consecutive order, with *J. L. M. Curry* being 1, and *Ora Ellis* being 3148, but nothing like 3000 ships were built. Many blocks of hull numbers were cancelled for one reason or another. Frederick Lane's *Ships for Victory*, published by Johns Hopkins Press in 1951, the most detailed and comprehensive report of the U. S. shipbuilding program, sets the Liberty total at 2,708. The Maritime Commission, on whose records the book was based, issued a 1 July 1945 press release stating the Liberty fleet total was 2,580, not including some military versions still under construction and not yet delivered. The Maritime Commission's official construction report set the total at 2,751. The American Bureau of Shipping, which surveyed all ships for insurance purposes, established the total as 2,742. This included 2,580 regular EC2 hulls (the Commission's Liberty Fleet of 2,580), 60 *Ocean*-class Libertys for Britain, 20 aircraft transports (ZEC2-S-C5), 12 colliers (EC2-S-AW1), 8 tank carriers (ZEC2-S-C2), and 62 tankers (Z-ET1-S-C3).

No matter which total is used, the Libertys still comprised the greatest standardized fleet the world had ever seen. No one who helped design, build, or sail them in World War II could have foreseen that some of them would still be doing well, plodding the seas as an important segment of world merchant marine fleets nearly twenty years later. The wartime expendables had become nearly indestructible.

The usual Liberty ship crew consisted of about 50 men, of which a dozen were licensed, if not experienced, officers. The others, deck-hands, firemen, oilers, wipers, and messmen, were usually youngsters who needed plenty of instruction. Here the mate of the Liberty tanker *Thomas F. Cunningham* puts his men through lifeboat drill.

2

MANNING
THE
SHIPS

Building a huge fleet of Liberty ships was one thing, but finding men, especially trained officers, to sail them was another matter. People who had never seen a ship could be trained to make the pieces with which to build one, but once the ship was in the water, loaded with ten thousand tons of cargo, and ordered half around the world, it took men with experience to get her there. Without crews, the ships would have been absolutely useless. Supplying trained men for the emergency fleet was a highly important but little appreciated achievement of World War II.

In 1940 the entire United States merchant marine, from ocean liners to towboats, included some 65,000 men (and a few women). By June of 1943 this seagoing force had increased to 85,000. A year later it numbered 175,000 and when the war ended in August, 1945, it had reached a high of 250,000.

Who were these men? Where did they come from? How did they acquire the training necessary to take the ships where they were going and bring them home again?

Wartime merchant seamen came from all parts of the United States and from some Allied nations. Boys too young to be drafted joined the merchant marine.

Men too old for the draft, or who for one reason or another were not accepted by the armed forces, found in the merchant marine an opportunity to take an active part in the war effort.

Some few men went to sea for what in those days was good pay and some did so to escape military service, but these were not the overriding attractions for most wartime volunteers. A man could make good pay in shipyards and war plants without any of the risks of seafaring. And as for escaping the draft, many thousands of young men who were attracted to sea by wartime recruiting posters had little if any concept of what life in the merchant marine was like—or what pay or danger was involved.

Captain Hollie J. Tiedemann, superintendent of the St. Petersburg training station of the U. S. Maritime Service, believed that relatively few of the thousands of boys who passed through the government training schools were attracted by the promise of high wages. "Most of them," he said, "came with a desire to have a part in the war. Money was a secondary consideration. The many I had occasion to talk to had little idea when they arrived at the school just what the pay would be. They had heard that the merchant marine was a good place to see action in a short time and they were eager to get in it."

Early in the war, ships sailed with a nucleus of old-timers among the crew, but later there were so many new ships that there were not enough veterans to go around. Many new ships were fortunate if they had a dozen men in the unlicensed crew who had more than a voyage or two behind them.

An early Liberty would have a crew of seagoing men from the prewar merchant marine, plus a handful of newcomers. The boatswain might be a tanned and brawny Dane; some of the able seamen might be Norwegians or Swedes who had spent most of their lives in sail and steam. The firemen were probably veterans of the old coal-burners; and oilers might be old-timers who could squirt oil from a can into a thimble-sized oil cup with the engine doing 70 revolutions a minute and never spill a drop. Cooks might have been Filipinos, wiry little men who traveled together from ship to ship; spoke Tagalog, and gambled their earnings away at cards long before the ship had reached its first port.

Such typical prewar merchant sailors knew no home but a ship—they were conscientious, hard workers at sea and hard drinkers in port. They made good shipmates, for they did their jobs and expected others to do the same. They were the kind of men who went down with the *Catahoula*, the *Selma City*, the *Norlindo*, the *Afoundria*, the *Marore*, and a hundred other ships in the early days of the war. It is an eternal tribute to the quality of these men, rough, tough and unpolished as they were, that ships never lacked crews or missed a sailing date in the days when many of them had no guns or armed escorts to protect them.

Such quality was highly diluted later in the war, of course. The merchant marine took in thousands of men who had never seen a ship before they arrived at one of the Maritime Service training centers for a quick course of indoctrination before shipping out. Some of them were newcomers who knew little about the job and cared less.

And, of course, there were the vociferous few seeking the fast buck; the kind for whom, as the saying went, there were only three kinds of time on board ship: sack time, coffee time, and overtime.

The ships kept sailing despite a critical shortage of key personnel, but it took almost superhuman efforts on the part of the War Shipping Administration (WSA) to juggle crews. Often a ship arriving from a foreign voyage would be tapped for an engineer, radio officer, boatswain, or perhaps even her master so that another ship that had completed loading its cargo could join a convoy on schedule.

Some ships met their sailing dates by collecting the rag, tag, and bobtail of the waterfront. One ship of 1921 vintage left New York in 1944 with three Brazilian firemen who had signed on because the shipping agent promised them the vessel would go to Rio for a cargo of coffee. One of the oilers was an Army veteran who had lost some of his fingers in the Aleutians. The chief cook was a middle-aged German-American who had walked out of his bakery in Wisconsin because he "couldn't stand to be readin' about the war and not doin' anything." The chief engineer was a 72-year-old retired Navy captain who had come back to sea to help the war effort. The second engineer was a Yugoslav who tried to convert the men on his watch to communism. The crew included an Englishman, a Dane, and a Jamaican.

The amazing thing was that with such hodgepodge crews, the ships left port, for the most part maneuvered according to convoy plan, arrived at their assigned destination, and came home again.

Finding and training enough engineers, navigators and ship handlers was a far different matter from filling the required unlicensed billets aboard a ship. Handling a ship in convoy, especially in fog, dark of night, or evasive maneuvers; or taking it to a port halfway around the world was not something that could be left to novices.

□

Crewing the ships was a joint effort by the various maritime unions, government and steamship company hiring halls, and the government training schools, including the United States Merchant Marine Academy and the state maritime academies operated by Maine, Massachusetts, Pennsylvania, New York and California.

The War Shipping Administration conducted a nationwide recruiting drive in 1942 to find former seamen who had left the merchant marine for jobs on shore. More than 16,000 men with prior experience returned to sea by November of 1942, a time when the shipping industry was still experiencing heavy losses. In New York alone, 30,000 men applied for berths in a ten-day period. About 5,000 of these were immediately dispatched to waiting ships. A number of states aided the recruiting program by allowing Civil Service employees to return to sea without loss of seniority.

A training division, the U. S. Maritime Service, was set up within the War Shipping Administration in July of 1942 under Captain Edward Macaulay, with Telfair Knight as director of training. Commander Richard D. McNulty was assistant director and supervisor of cadet training.

The Maritime Service operated seven training ships, but their activities were considerably curtailed by the dangers of wartime cruising. One of the ships, the *American Mariner*, an EC2 especially altered during construction to serve as a schoolship, helped to give at least a modicum of actual shipboard experience to thousands of men before they shipped out for the first time. Built by the Bethlehem-Fairfield yard at Baltimore, she accommodated 400 trainees and a crew of 132 and operated out of Staten Island, New York, making week-long trips in the protected waters of Long Island Sound. After the war, she became a missile-tracking ship for the Army, then was used as a bombing target in the Chesapeake Bay. Her hulk is still there.

The largest of the training establishments for unlicensed seamen was the one at Sheepshead Bay, Brooklyn, New York. Occupying the site of a former amusement park, this base was intended to process 30,000 men a year in short indoctrination courses. Other schools were located at St. Petersburg, Florida, and at Avalon on Catalina Island off the Southern California coast.

Officer training schools were established at Fort Trumbull, Connecticut, and Alameda, California. There was an acute shortage of radio operators when the mass production of ships commenced and schools to train them were located at Gallup's Island in Boston harbor and at Hoffman Island, New York. In addition, there were emergency cadet officer schools at Pass Christian, Mississippi, and San Mateo, California.

The WSA schools for unlicensed men and officers, plus upgrading and refresher courses, turned out 270,000 graduates, including 10,000 officers from the U. S. Merchant Marine Academy and the state maritime academies. The short courses for upgrading unlicensed men to officer status produced 23,000 mates and engineers. Basic schools trained 155,000 men for shipboard jobs. More than 7,500 radio officers were trained as well as 5,300 pursers, who also served as pharmacist's mates.

☐

During the summer of 1943 there were times when as many as 600 deck officers had no licenses, sailing on temporary emergency endorsements issued by the Coast Guard. There was always a greater shortage of engine-room personnel, and at the same time, as many as 1,000 engineers had no licenses. Hundreds of seamen who had sufficient sea-time requirements but lacked the official license were moved up into officer positions, and the ships went out, usually on schedule.

Every possible scheme was tried to find qualified people. Employers were asked to release men with prior sea experience, and veteran merchant seamen who had been drafted into the armed forces were released for service in the merchant marine. Hundreds of men were added to the merchant marine in this way. In addition, shoreside employers were warned not to hire merchant marine personnel who might come ashore looking for jobs, regardless of age or draft eligibility.

The age limit for enlistment in the Maritime Service was lowered to 16 years in May, 1944, as a further expedient toward getting men. During the following week more than 7,000 adventure-minded youngsters volunteered at some 40 recruiting offices throughout the nation.

But it was not only the youngsters who showed up and wanted to go to sea. Men who were old enough to be their grandfathers, and who could have stayed at home and listened to war reports on the radio, chose to be back where the action was.

Percy P. Evans was 70 years of age when he signed on as engineer for the *Joseph R. Drake*. William Mallett had been chief engineer on the transport *America* in World War I; he returned to sea in World War II as chief engineer of the *John Davenport*.

Otto Preussler, better known as "Lucky Uncle Otto," had gone to sea in the Russo-Japanese War and again in World War I; in World War II, he sailed as a cook on several Liberty ships. James A. Logan, 76 years old when he signed on as a cook for the *Joshua Hendy*, had 49 years of sea service up until that time. Another old-timer, Henry Jones, went to sea in England at the age of 14 during the Boer War and had been 40 years at sea when he signed on the *Abraham Lincoln* as second mate in 1944.

Among the many seamen lured to the convoy routes was Thomas Cavely, skipper of a New York harbor ferryboat; his longest voyage in years had been between Sixty-ninth Street in Brooklyn and St. George on Staten Island. Cavely shipped out as first mate on the *Waigstill Avery* on a voyage to the Persian Gulf, and when the *Avery's* captain died there, he took over and brought the ship safely home. Cavely wasn't a complete stranger to deep water, having acquired a master's license in the British merchant marine in World War I.

Along with the old graybeards, men of youthful years commanded many of the wartime Libertys and proved themselves equal to any of the hardy young mariners who sailed in the famous American clipper ships. William Travers, 22 years old, was captain of the *James Ford Rhodes*. His brother, the first mate, was 21; the third mate was only 20.

Harold H. Niss, barely 24 when he took command of the *John W. Gates*, felt it necessary "to assume all the bravado possible, especially as the first and second mates were sea dogs in their sixties." To temper his exaggerated self-confidence, he wore his cadet hat from the New York State Maritime Academy. "It always confused the customs and immigration people. The boarding officials always went to the third mate, only to be referred to the kid master in the cadet's hat." But, as the kid master could proudly point out, he took the ship everywhere with never a casualty. The *Gates* reached Constanza, Rumania, in July of 1945, probably the first American ship into the Black Sea after VE Day.

There could be a wide spread in ages among crews of Liberty ships. When the *Oliver Wolcott*, left New Orleans "for ports of the world" in October of 1944, Chief Engineer Frank Aiken, and Chief Mate Hugh Young, were both 67 years old. Radio Operator Herman Stone Jr. was 19, and Acting Second Mate John Shuttleworth was only 20. A dozen of the 44-man crew were under 20 and several were only 16. This was truly an all-American crew, from 15 different states.

While high-school lads and old granddads were going to sea on the Libertys, a good many mascots went to sea with them, although there was a general rule against pets on ships. The crew of the *Robert Newell* included two mongrels, Sparks and Snafu. Sparks had a broken leg when the ship's radio operator, Moe Preskell, then a Maritime Service trainee, found him on a Boston street and took him to a veterinarian to have the leg set. The cost of the operation was shared by fellow trainees at the Gallup's Island Radio School. When Preskell shipped out on the *Robert Newell*, Sparks signed on, too.

The *Jonathan Grout* had a mongrel dog named Brownie, picked up in Puerto Rico. Brownie jumped into an open hatch at Khorramshahr in the Persian Gulf and died a few days later as the ship steamed down the Arabian Sea. Brownie was sewed up, sailor style, in a canvas bag and given a farewell salute with a burst of 20-millimeter fire as he was dropped over the side.

Even some women wanted to go to sea. Most of the larger passenger ships in prewar service carried women as stewardesses, hairdressers, and in some other capacities. When the ships were taken over by the government, they lost their jobs. One of them, Betty Jackson, wrote to President Roosevelt about it: "I am one of the many seafaring women. . . . We are not afraid of the dangers and we are willing to put up with any inconvenience as long as we can be reinstated and go back to sea."

Admiral Land replied for the President, telling Miss Jackson that her request was praiseworthy, that women were quite capable in the jobs thay had been doing at sea, but that there were no provisions on wartime ships for women crew-members.

Despite the Admiral, some women did get to sea, and at least three of them were authorized to wear the merchant marine combat bar after their ships were torpedoed.

□

On 17 November 1941 Congress authorized the use of Navy guns and gunners for the defense of American merchant ships. The first vessel so protected was the SS *Dunboyne*, which received several .50 caliber machine guns and a seven-man Armed Guard detachment under a coxswain on 2 December, just before she sailed for Murmansk. The SS *Expositor* sailed for Murmansk early in 1942 with an armed guard crew of four seamen and a signalman under Lieutenant (junior grade) Robert B. Hicks.

By the end of December, 1941, 14 American merchant ships had naval Armed Guard crews. By the end of 1942, there were Armed Guard units on 1,000 American ships, almost all of them commanded by junior grade lieutenants or ensigns of the Naval Reserve. In addition, there were Armed Guard contingents on some American-owned vessels under Allied colors, primarily Panamanian.

The gun crews at first numbered from 12 to 15 men. They were increased to as many as 27 later in the war. Merchant crewmen also had battle stations, serving as ammunition passers or assisting at the 20-millimeter guns.

On the *J. H. Drummond*, six of the Armed Guard lived in a cabin on the main deck, forward, port side, and three on the starboard side. Their commander had a cabin on the bridge deck. Sixteen gunners lived in the after deckhouse. This berthing arrangement, with slight variations, was used for the Armed Guard complement on hundreds of ships.

There was, undeniably, frequent friction between Navy gunners and civilian merchant seamen, often a discontent nurtured by the disparity in pay. Navy men shared the same ship and the same dangers but saw their civilian crewmates paying off at the end of the trip much more handsomely than they did.

There was friction, but there was also cooperation and good feeling. The merchant crew on the *Smith Thompson* sent a letter to Secretary of the Navy Frank Knox lauding the action of their Navy gunners in repelling air attacks on 4 October 1943.

Ensign Leon Robinson, the Armed Guard officer on the *Button Gwinnett*, commended the "splendid cooperation of Captain E. W. Braithwaite and his crew. "Your men," he wrote in a letter to the captain, "were of invaluable assistance in hoisting and passing of ammunition, and in relaying the 20-millimeter magazines."

An unusual incident of camaraderie and mutual respect between merchant crew and Armed Guard men occurred in April of 1944 when the Boatswain on the *Harry A. Garfield* died during an Atlantic crossing. Members of the Armed Guard acted as a guard of honor in dress blues with their merchant marine shipmates as the captain read the traditional service for burial at sea.

Most Armed Guard officers were intensely proud, and rightly so, of their commands. Lieutenant James M. Gatling of the *Henry Ward Beecher* reported, after the ship took part in the invasion of Southern France: "Heavy shrapnel has fallen on this ship and in the gun tubs on numerous occasions and 20-mm shells have been fired into it point blank by wild gunners, but this [gun] crew has never given an inch."

Many young Armed Guard officers felt it was their duty to evaluate the competence and behavior of the ship's officers, especially the master. One even went so far as to report to naval intelligence that the ship's captain behaved "most suspiciously," and suggested that he was probably a spy. He attached a list of "suspicious incidents" that had occurred during the trip. Reports by Armed Guard officers contained many comments on the navigational ability of the ship's officers.

On the other hand, thoughtful shipmasters were frequently appreciative of the hard work and devotion of sincere, young naval officers and their men. Captain Kingdom S. Thomas of the *Uriah M. Rose* wrote to the Bureau of Naval Personnel:

> It has been my pleasure to have with me Ltjg. F. J. Szemala as Armed Guard commander . . . This voyage has been long and trying and during the entire period I have had the complete cooperation of Lt. Szemala and his men. Due to his energy and ability there has been no friction between the Armed Guard and the merchant crew.
>
> I also wish to commend him and his men for aid given the ship during a serious fire which occurred at Townsville, Australia, on March 29, 1944. This fire was discovered in the bottom of number four hold and in the immediate vicinity of some 200 cases of land mines.
>
> The naval authorities insisted on moving the ship into the stream in case there should be an explosion aboard and the merchant crew being unable to shift the ship and fight the fire at the same time, Lt. Szemala and his men took over the fire fighting under the master's direction and successfully aided in controlling the fire.

Not all men in the merchant marine were heroes, at least not any more than they were in the military services. Out of several thousand men who commanded Liberty ships, there were sure to be some who became befuddled in emergencies, who panicked when torpedoes hit, or who were just plain unfit for command. One group of Liberty ship survivors complained to United States naval intelligence at an East African port that their captain was "incompetent as a ship handler and navigator and was emotionally unstable." A report from Durban said his actions "indicated that he is neither normal nor reliable and it is doubtful if he is in a fit condition to command a ship." A dire wartime need for licensed master mariners provided jobs for many men who no steamship company would have considered for command in peacetime.

In contrast, when Captain George R. Bickford of the SS *Waigstill Avery* died at sea, his crew collected $166 to buy a silver plate for his widow. "The old man was a skipper of the old school," said a report from the ship to union headquarters. "We all were sorry to lose him."

There was, unfortunately, more than one instance of a captain losing his head and forgetting to order "stop" for the engines or give official commands to abandon ship, causing confusion and loss of life. But such derelictions of duty were overshadowed many times by instances of heroism and service "far and beyond the call of duty," as indicated in the official Navy report of the sinking of the *Walter Q. Gresham:* "The master was highly commended by all of the crew for his coolness, ability, assistance and general good conduct. All survivors agreed that by his action and good judgment a panic was averted. He is directly responsible for the orderliness in abandoning ship."

The Armed Guard officer on one ship that made a voyage to Russia in 1943 said that relations between Navy and merchant marine personnel were most congenial and that the captain went out of his way to meet their requests.

"The merchant crew on this ship is about average," the report continued. "As it is inevitable under a set up where there are two such entirely different systems of discipline and standards of performance, there has been friction. Nothing of great importance, but at times most annoying. The center of most disturbance seems to have been the union (NMU) representative on board. This man, holding a dishonorable discharge from the Navy, is a constant agitator."

□

The merchant marine was a strange paradox of a peacetime industry operating under wartime conditions. Crews, in fact, came under the Articles of War and one Liberty ship at Alexandria lost half her deck crew to a prison camp when they refused to rig booms for loading tanks before the invasion of Sicily in a dispute over whether the job should be done by the shoreside stevedores or the crew. Army officials stepped in, read the Articles of War to the crew and escorted six of them ashore for months of rigorous road building in the Egyptian desert.

The maritime unions, quite naturally, were fearful that the merchant marine would be taken over by the armed forces and resisted any move in this direction. They pointed out, with considerable justification, that a Liberty ship under a civilian crew operated with less than 50 men, plus armed guard, while the same ship with a Navy crew would need 150 men or more.

At the end of each voyage a union patrolman would board ship and receive the complaints of crewmen about the trip, complaints which the patrolman would usually work out to the satisfaction of the crew with representatives of the operating company.

The *Pilot*, official newspaper of the National Maritime Union that reflected the whimsies, dangers, and vagaries of wartime sailing in the merchant marine, carried typical complaints from union delegates aboard ship, which, when considering that GIs were dying in jungle foxholes and beachheads, might seem trivial and incongruous.

On the other hand, the unions were guarding the better working and living conditions won for seamen during the hard-fought strikes of the thirties and saw no reason why their hard-won gain should be set aside on the excuse of "war emergency" when steamship operators were making handsome profits.

Among typical complaints, or requests, were these. From the *George Leonard:* "Crew wants a larger radio and electric ice cream mixer; also a helmet and gas mask for every man." From the *Horace Williams:* "The black gang wants a modern pop-up toaster for use in the engine room." From the *Charles Goodyear:* "The crew requests drinking water piped to the engine room and a better quality of breakfast cereal and a separate refrigerator for the Armed Guard messroom." Men on the *Theodoric Bland* wanted a large ice cream freezer, more library books, and a radio for the crew messroom, while the crew of the *Elisha Mitchell* asked for an oilskin locker and a radiator for the ship's hospital.

These were not unreasonable requests, but they were the basis for exaggerated reports about demands for linen tablecloths, more varieties of ice cream, or steaks for every meal.

The crew of the *George Cleeve* wrote a very practical request to the War Shipping Administration: "We feel that laundries should be installed on all Liberty ships. The quarters aboard these ships are necessarily cramped and the addition of a laundry room would add greatly to the comfort of all hands." As merchant sailors and Navy men had done since steam went to sea, the men on most Liberty ships washed their clothes in a bucket, using live steam to heat the water. And as saltwater was much more plentiful than freshwater, saltwater was what they frequently used.

Men in the merchant marine did not usually wear uniforms, although khaki uniforms similar to those worn by the Navy were later authorized for use by officers. The standard "uniform" for seamen was a blue shirt and dungarees, and a newcomer often towed his dungarees astern of the ship for a day or two, then bleached them in the sun to give them that well-faded look that bespoke an old hand. When officers of the prewar school wore a uniform, it was invariably khaki pants and a khaki shirt open at the collar, with a well-battered cap bearing the company insignia.

Union newspapers carried many letters from the ships against proposals that came out from time to time to uniform the merchant marine, Navy style. Typical was a letter in the *Pilot* of December, 1943:

> "We don't need any fancy high pressure suits. The only thing they're good for is half price rail fares and a chance to get served quick at restaurant counters or a second look from a uniform-conscious girl. Let's keep the merchant marine on the side where it belongs and fight it out in dungarees and blue shirts."

There was no television, no movies, and few radios, so the Navy furnished an entertainment kit for every Armed Guard gun crew. That for the *Dan Beard* was typical: a punching bag, boxing gloves, and medicine ball, and games—Chinese checkers, chess, cribbage, acey-ducey, checkers, and dominos—plus darts, playing cards, a phonograph, and records. All ships received books, usually from the American Merchant Marine Library Association, and the purser acted as librarian.

Some ships, such as the *Felix Riesenberg*, produced mimeographed newspapers. They were usually, but not always, the work of the purser. A 1945 issue of the *Riesenberg Weekly*, definitely not written by the purser, reported that "His Majesty the purser, has . . . opened the slop chest." Another issue noted that "our two ace wipers have been trying to camouflage the ship with red lead. They've even got it into the soup." It also reported that the boatswain was distributing beeswax to those with fancy mustachios.

Men with no desire to run a seagoing newspaper, but with plenty of spare time, found other ways of expressing themselves and penned numerous poetic tributes to the Libertys. Since few poets were sailors and fewer sailors were poets, their lines sometimes had a few extra feet and the rhyme scheme frequently fell apart, but after all, no one needed to understand the sonnet form to tell how he felt about a Liberty ship.

The *Seafarers Log* of the Seafarers International Union carried such a tribute, attributed to a Captain Betto;

Yes, she's a Liberty ship built in 20 days
One of the hundreds that slipped the ways,
A champagne bottle, an unknown name
And no design on future fame.

She was laden deep with goods of war
Below her marks both aft and fore
And as if to tempt the hand of fate
Her decks were piled with plane and crate.

Why, there's not a cargo great or small
But a Liberty tramp has carried them all,
High test gas and TNT
From Guadalcanal to Tripoli.

We've trod your decks, we're proud to tell,
You've sailed us in and out of hell,
We've cursed you and we've praised you, too
As Sailor men so often do.

We'll drink a glass in Barney's bar
To you, good ship, so there you are,
A Merchant Ship, a Liberty,
Another tramp upon the sea.

There were poets on almost every ship, including a Liberty torpedoed in the Indian Ocean in 1943. Her crew spent 17 days in a lifeboat; time enough for the ship's poet to observe on their chances of rescue:

There's a troopship leaving Bombay
But we don't think it's coming our way . . .

A sailor, obviously suffering from a bad case of "channel fever," wrote:

Oh, if I had the wings of an angel,
Off this bloody ship I would fly
I would fly to the Rock of Gibraltar
And get one more beer 'for I die.

One Liberty ship bard evidently had a higher regard for the silver cartwheels issued by Secretary Morgenthau's Treasury Department in Washington, D.C., than he did for certain pronouncements which came from that big white house a block down the street:

> I'm a hero, this I know
> 'Cause Franklin Roosevelt told me so.
> I gather that is what he means.
> By 'unsung heroes of the merchant marines'
> Yes, we'll sail the ocean, we're not afraid
> At one twenty five per airplane raid.
> And tin-fish can not our courage dent
> But we still want our hundred percent.
> And at the end of the voyage when they
>   hand out the medals
> Just give us the kind that Morgenthau peddles.

Before it was all over and the Libertys went the way of the galleons and clippers, the *Pilot* printed: "To the Liberty Ship on VE Day," from which a few verses are sufficient to complete a discussion of the literature of Liberty ships:

> From Murmansk to Salerno and the Persian Gulf
> In hot or cold, in calm or rough,
> You've been seen here, there and everywhere
> The goods were delivered through your tender care.
>
> In every invasion you've taken part
> You've been there plugging since the start,
> You've been used as carrier, troopship and tanker;
> Have been used and misused in every manner.
>
> You've carried cargoes where they were needed most
> To you, staunch Liberty, we give a toast
> Though tomorrow on high seas you may not be seen
> Yet today and till all the war is done you are the queen.

The poem had probably as many faults as any Liberty ship that ever sailed, but like the Libertys it described, it did the job. The man who wrote it was proud of his ship, pleased with his poem, and signed it—John J. Harmata. Keats could have been no more sincere.

□

An average Liberty carried a crew of 41 men. Deck officers included the master, chief mate, second and third mates; engine officers included the chief engineer and first, second and third assistants. The deck crew included a boatswain, six able seamen, three ordinary seamen, and a carpenter. Unlicensed engine room personnel included three firemen, three oilers, two wipers, and a deck engineer who took care of the deck winches, steam lines, radiators, and other equipment outside the engine spaces. The steward's department, always an important part of a Liberty ship's complement, included a chief steward, chief cook, second cook, night cook and baker, six messmen, and a galleyman. Each ship also carried a radio operator and a purser to take care of ship's business.

There were variations in manning, depending partly on contracts between the operating company and the unions manning the ship. Some vessels had no carpenter but did carry a deck maintenance man, a dayworker in the deck force. Many Libertys with Army cargo also carried a cargo security officer, a representative of the Army and not part of the crew. Libertys carrying troops had additional cooks and messmen. Many carried from two to four deck and engine midshipmen from the U. S. Merchant Marine Academy at Kings Point, New York. These cadets spent at least a year aboard ship as part of their four-year training program and served with distinction throughout the war.

Typical of the fine type of young American selected for the Merchant Marine Academy were Cadets P. B. Moran and W. J. Kutney, assigned to the *Francis Scott Key* for a voyage to North Russia in 1943.

Moran was in a hotel at Murmansk when it was hit by a German bomb. He escaped uninjured but went back into the burning building and brought out an injured Russian officer. He was cited for this and for later saving the life of a Navy gunner who had been knocked overboard by the concussion from a bomb hit.

Kutney was wounded while manning a 20-millimeter gun in an air raid but refused to leave his post until the raid was over. He was commended for this action and for another described in a report by the ship's Armed Guard officer, Lieutenant D. T. Broderick, Jr.

"His presence of mind," said Broderick, "and his quick action without regard for personal safety in leading an emergency detail to extinguish a large number of incendiary bombs which had fallen on deck saved the vessel from possible serious consequences."

Pay scales in the prewar merchant marine were moderate at best. From 1940 on, the government approved special, additional compensation for crews on ships subject to enemy attack. This compensation was finally standardized, effective 24 February 1943, in the form of voyage, area, and attack bonuses.

A seaman was paid an additional 40 to 100 percent of his total wages, including overtime, during the time his ship was transiting certain areas considered subject to enemy action. There was no bonus at all for voyages between Pacific coast ports and some other sections of the Pacific.

Pay was further boosted by an "area bonus" of five dollars per day for each day the vessel spent in any of three specified areas:

Murmansk—the Atlantic and Arctic Oceans east of the Greenwich Meridian and west of 60 degrees east longitude and north of 60 degrees north latitude.

Mediterranean—east of a line from Cape Spartel to Cape Trafalgar, including the Adriatic and Aegean Seas.

South Seas—the area bounded on the north by 20 degrees north latitude, on the east by 170 degrees east longitude, on the south by 20 degrees south latitude, and on the west by 120 degrees east longitude.

Finally, there was a bonus of $125 paid to each man if a vessel was under enemy attack at any port or anchorage.

It was no wonder that Armed Guard gunners, sharing the same dangers, felt that they were coming out on the short end and expressed their resentment against the better-paid merchant crew.

The merchant marine had never been known as a kid-glove profession; the very nature of life at sea attracted the adventurer, the homeless, the restless and, in short, the kind of man who loved freedom and hated routine or restraint. For many men who had no family or shoreside ties, a ship was a home. For others it was an argosy to adventure. For some, it was something to be endured until the next payoff, after which they would "live it up" until their money was gone, and then they would look for another outward-bounder.

Along with the professional seaman on prewar ships, many of them veterans of basic training in windjammers, there were "characters" or "performers," as sailors called them, men who were emotionally unstable, alcoholics, or just plain hard cases who loved trouble. The tremendous wartime expansion inevitably brought a larger share of laggards, misfits, and performers aboard ship. They served only to provide the number of "bodies" required by law before the ship could sail, contributed nothing to the success of the voyage, and often turned an otherwise happy ship into a trouble ship.

In January 1943 the War Shipping Administration established a committee on crew disciplinary affairs, and from January through November of that year a sampling of log books were examined to see the extent and seriousness of disciplinary problems. In 302 logs that were inspected, there were 56 recorded infractions of shipboard discipline, of which 32 went to Coast Guard hearings and resulted in disciplinary action. It should be remembered that the merchant marine has traditionally been more tolerant in matters of shipboard conduct than the Navy, and many cases of bad conduct that would have resulted in disciplinary action on a naval vessel went unrecorded on a merchantman or were dealt with in such fashion that the incidents were not remembered officially. Also, a merchant ship captain had to reckon with a union official when the ship returned to port and often considered it easier to forget bad conduct than argue the merits of the case with the accused man and his union representative.

Typical of incidents involving Coast Guard action were these from the log of a Liberty ship in European waters in July of 1944:

> Fireman ——— ——— caused disturbance by throwing another man's clothes out of the focsle port. He was insubordinate and refused to obey a lawful command. He threatened an officer.
>
> Captain called to quell fight in crew's messroom. Cook ——— ——— and Able Seaman ——— ——— threatening each other with fire axe and knife. Cook bleeding profusely. Seaman accused of attack and chained to bunk.

One of the worst breakdowns in discipline occurred on the *Richard Henry Dana* in the Persian Gulf in 1943. Almost like that of an old Nantucket whaler, the ship's log for 23 April read:

> 8:15 p.m. Part of the ship's crew rushed the Captain's deck, threatening to kill the chief engineer, steward and third officer. Gun crew and officers were armed and stood by in case of attack while the chief officer talked to the men and tried to quiet them down. Signalled to guard vessel for assistance in order to prevent bloodshed. Part of the

crew not involved told to stay in their rooms and report to Captain's room for protection.

The log named the men involved and noted that "the mutineers were discharged to the British patrol ship." It did not, of course, give the crew's side of the story or the eventual disposition of the case by the Army and Coast Guard. The "mutineers," as the log called them, were left behind when the ship sailed.

In contrast to this incident, a boat crew from the same ship rescued 13 native longshoremen from a burning cargo barge in the Shatt-el-Arab near Khorramshahr.

Fights were not infrequent on long trips, and could erupt over such a minor event as a game of cards. A few drinks on shore often resulted in trouble when men returned to the ship, such as this incident aboard a Liberty discharging cargo at London's Tilbury docks in 1943. "Ordinary Seaman ———— ———— cut in right hand by knife by ———— ————, messman. Taken to hospital for treatment." The log noted later that a Coast Guard officer came aboard to investigate the incident.

"The principal cause of difficulties on board ship," said a WSA report of August, 1945, were "clashes of personalities, intransigence, incompetence and negligence."

Charges made against crewmen by masters were taken up by Coast Guard Merchant Marine Hearing Units, with the accused having the right to review or appeal. Coast Guard Hearing Units were found to be much more effective than the old custom of fining to maintain discipline. They could take away a seaman's papers, without which he could not obtain a job at sea—a much greater deterrent for "performers" than loss of pay, although they could also uphold fines levied by the captain.

Failure to join a ship on sailing day or being absent without leave were the major reasons for disciplinary action, providing close to 40 percent of the total number of cases. Negligence or incompetence on the job accounted for 27 percent of the disciplinary actions, with misconduct, including drunkenness and assault, contributing 14 percent. Censorship violations, pilferage, theft, and a variety of other offenses accounted for the rest.

Considering the stress and strain of wartime operating conditions, infractions of good order and discipline were probably no more common afloat in the merchant service than they were ashore in civilian life. The merchant marine was essential in winning the war, and in looking on the bright side of things, Admiral Land paid this tribute to the merchant seamen:

> Patriotism, courage and devotion to duty are among the outstanding attributes of the seamen who man our merchant marine. During the first part of the war, a lack of sufficient armament on board merchant ships, inadequate escort vessels, slow convoys and insufficient safety devices all made the seamen's life one of almost constant peril. Nevertheless, experienced seamen have continued to go back to sea while courageous, red-blooded young Americans have flocked to fill our training stations, determined that our ships shall be kept sailing. High wages and war bonuses are not the essential inducements which lead these men voluntarily to go to sea ... ships, valuable war cargoes, and lives have been saved through the resourcefulness and perseverance of American crews. Ships have been ... repaired, salvaged and brought limping into port by their merchant crews ... seamen have stuck of their posts with only a slim chance for survival ... and in the end have won out over the enemy.

For devotion to duty, such as described by Admiral Land, many men in the merchant marine received commendations, awards, and decorations. In addition to the Distinguished Service Medal for heroism or distinguished conduct and the Mariners Medal for wounds or physical injury received in action with the enemy, area ribbon bars were issued for service in the Atlantic, Mediterranean-Middle East, and Pacific theatres. The U. S. merchant marine combat bar was issued for service on a ship that had been attacked or damaged by the enemy; among those authorized to wear that bar were three women who were serving on American ships as stewardesses when their vessels were torpedoed.

Distinguished Service Medals were awarded to 130 merchant marine officers and men for "service far and beyond the call of duty." A total of 5,099 Mariner's Medals were given for death or injury in action and 103,052 combat bars were awarded to men whose ships experienced enemy attack. More than 125,000 men received war zone bars.

Members of the Armed Guard detachments aboard the Libertys won more than their share of high decorations, including several Navy Crosses, Silver Stars, and Navy and Marine Corps Medals. The Navy named a number of destroyer escorts for Armed Guard men who lost their lives in such actions, and some Liberty ships were named for merchant seamen who lost their lives in the early part of the war.

Every launching required a woman sponsor who christened the ship, champagne for the ship, and flowers for the sponsor. The *Louisa M. Alcott*, launched by the Bethlehem Fairfield Shipyard at Baltimore on 28 May 1943, was christened by WAVE Ensign Regina Flanigan. The attendants included WAVES, Marines, and SPARS.

3

NAMING
THE
SHIPS

In all history there could never have been a more unlikely group of people than *Big Foot Wallace, Button Gwinnett, Betsy Ross, Abner Doubleday, Pocahontas, Sun Yat-Sen, Moses Brown, Billy Sunday, Bernardo O'Higgins, Johnny Appleseed, F. Scott Fitzgerald, Hans Heg,* and *Hawkins Fudske*. The mind boggles at the thought of them all seated at dinner together. Neither Sherlock Holmes nor Nero Wolfe at their finest could ever have deduced a logical connection between 13 such characters. Yet in World War II it should have been elementary enough for even Dr. Watson—they were all Liberty ships.

When the Liberty ship program began, the job of naming 300 ships seemed simple enough. The ships were to be named for outstanding Americans, heroes and leaders in American history. There were certainly enough of these, even without counting the founding fathers and revolutionary patriots, to make up a list of 300. But when the Liberty fleet continued to grow to 500, to 1,000—and even twice that—the naming process became much more than a matter of skimming through a grade school history book.

Oddly enough, although plans and specifications for the Liberty ships were detailed right down to the last washbowl, there was no such care given to naming them. Eventually somewhere within the Maritime Commission a committee was set up and given the job of establishing likely categories and selecting names from them. Eventually, some 60 name lists included authors, athletes, abolitionists, painters, historians, political and social reformers, scientists, college presidents, feminists, merchant marine heroes, railroad builders, diplomats, explorers, Indians, and pioneers. Names given to ships included those of 493 senators and congressmen, 157 cabinet members, 248 state and territorial governors, 208 regional heroes and pioneers, 63 doctors, 11 Negroes prominent in national history, 14 musicians, and 7 American philosophers.

In selecting names, there was an attempt to avoid duplication on the well-founded assumption that three or four ships with the same name or very similar names could cause considerable confusion in the handling of sailing orders, cargo loading, and communications. For example, if a *Mary Brown* sent out an SOS while another *Mary Browne* happened to be in the same general area, it might be nearly impossible to untangle the resulting confusion.

However, by the time the Liberty name list was complete, it was not without possibilities of confusion.* It provided a good cross-section of American proper names and as might be expected, Smith, Jones, Brown, Johnson, and Williams led the parade. The *Smith* fleet included *Alfred E., Charles E., Delazon, E. Kirby, Erastus, Francis M., Hugh M., James, Jedediah, Joseph, Junius, Milton H., William L.,* and *Winfred L. Smith.* The *Jones* boys were represented by *John Paul,* who was well known, plus *Anson, Charles C., C. J., Jerome K., Paul David, Russell R., William A.,* and *Willie Jones.* The *Browns* followed with *Albert G., Alexander E., Henry B., Joseph A., Moses, Noah,* and *Tarleton Brown.* Even the mere half dozen Johnsons were capable of confusion. *Allen, John A., Thomas,* and *Reverdy Johnson* were easy enough to handle, but the difference between *William W. Johnson* and *Willard R. Johnson,* written with a scratchy pen or on a smudged carbon copy, might be difficult to see on a dark night.

There was a slight chance that a man with literary inclinations but a poor memory might confuse *Zane Gray* with *Zona Gale* and a much bigger chance that someone who read the first name of a ship as *John* but missed the last name would have trouble in finding it again, as there were 222 ships with *John* for their first

* The name Samuel Gompers appears twice, through no error. The first ship so named, hull number 640, was sunk on 1 January 1943. The second ship with that name, hull number 2699, was completed in July, 1944.

name. There were also 193 ships with *William* for their first name and, to complicate matters, there were eleven ships with either *William*, *Williams*, or *Williamson* for a last name, and as a final touch, one with both—*William Williams*.

☐

The idea was to name ships for people who were dead, as the Navy did. "That way," said Admiral Land, "we couldn't get into any hassles with VIPs who wanted ships named after themselves or members of their families." Even so, Admiral Land discovered plans afoot to name a ship after him, but being very alive, he soon squelched the idea, although he permitted one to be named after his father, *Scott E. Land*.

The names selected by the Commission's public relations and personnel divisions read like a "who-was-who" of American history, but a certain regional flavor was shown in some cases: the *Sam Houston*, *Davy Crockett*, *James Bowie*, and *Winfield Scott* were all built in Texas; the *Virginia Dare* and *William Moultrie* were built in Wilmington, North Carolina; and *Luis Arguello*, *Gaspar de Portola*, and *Sebastian Vizcaino* were built in California.

The men who painted names on ships had a snap with *John P. Poe*, *John Jay*, and *Pio Pico*. At least a couple of dozen ships had short, eight-letter names such as *John Hart*, *John Penn*, *John Wise*, *John Page*, *John Bell*, *John Muir*, *John Lind*, *John Ross*, *John Owen*, *John Reed*, *John Ball*, *John Drew*, and *John Hope*; and, for the ladies, *Mary Lyon*, *Jane Long*, *Mary Ball*, and *Zona Gale*. By contrast, it was an all-day job to lay out *Joseph-Augustin Chevalier*, a name seldom mentioned in biographical dictionaries but famed for being the longest ever given a Liberty ship. Runners-up were *Richmond Mumford Pearson*, *Frederick Jackson Turner*, *George Washington Carver*, *Jeremiah Van Rensselaer*, and *Charles Brantley Aycock*. Fortunately, whoever decided to name the *F. T. Frelinghuysen* settled for initials instead of the full Frederick Theodore.

The Commission received some letters from people asking to have Liberty ships named for one of their ancestors, and some complaints from those who didn't like a name given to one or another of the ships. A prominent West Coast politician wrote: "I hear you have named a Liberty ship after me. I am not dead, I'm not in dry dock and I don't need my bottom scraped. Please change the name." He was told that the naming was a coincidence; that the ship actually honored another person of the same name who had been dead for years.

The names of many women—writers, artists, and those famous in the nation's history—were given to Liberty ships. The first "lady Liberty" was the *Amelia Earhart*, named for the woman flyer lost on a Pacific flight in 1937. The one whose name was probably most familiar to World War II sailors was the *Carole Lombard*, named for the film star who died in 1942. Out of the school books came *Priscilla Alden*, *Molly Pitcher*, *Betsy Ross*, *Virginia Dare*, *Barbara Fritchie*, *Pocahontas*, and, perhaps, *Annie Oakley*. Women authors were represented by *Sara Teasdale*, *Helen Hunt Jackson*, *Amy Lowell*, *Louisa M. Alcott*, and *Emily Dickinson*, among others.

The *Jane Swisshelm* honored a pioneer fighter for women's rights who was also a newspaper editor and one of the first women to volunteer for nursing service in the Civil War. The *Virginia Dare* honored the first white child born in colonial America, at Roanoke Island, in 1587. Wine made from grapes grown on Roanoke Island was used in christening the ship. The *Sara Bache* honored Benjamin Franklin's only daughter, who was a nurse during the Revolutionary War. The *Juliette Low* honored the founder of the Girl Guides and Girl Scouts. The *Mary Cullom Kimbro* was named for the first woman member of the U. S. merchant marine to be killed at sea in World War II. She was lost when the *City of Birmingham* was torpedoed on 30 June 1942. The *Anne Bradstreet* honored the wife of an early governor of Massachusetts and one of the country's first women authors. When her son sailed for England, a dangerous journey three centuries before the Battle of the Atlantic, she wrote:

> Thou mighty God of Sea and Land,
> I here resigne unto thy hand
> The son of prayers, of vowes and teares,
> The child I stayed for many yeares.
> Preserve, O Lord, from stormes and wrack,
> Protect him there and bring him back.

The poignant lines could have been written for her namesake as she steamed across the Atlantic and into battle with German torpedo-bombers in the Mediterranean.

Of the 114 Libertys named for women, ten were lost through enemy action: the *Virginia Dare*, *Anne Hutchinson*, *Julia Ward Howe*, *Molly Pitcher*, *Lydia M.*

Child, Phoebe A. Hurst, Flora Macdonald, Alice F. Palmer, Cornelia Spencer, and *Penelope Barker.*

□

A few Libertys were named for merchant marine heroes of World War II. The *Oscar Chappell* was named for the heroic helmsman of the tanker *Dixie Arrow,* which was torpedoed by a U-boat the morning of 26 March 1942, off Cape Hatteras. Eleven of the ships crew of 33 were lost, and many of those who were saved could attribute their rescue to shipmate Oscar Chappell.

"Chappell was at the wheel," reported Paul Myers, who was on the forecastle head after the tanker burst into flames. "Fire was shooting up all about him. He saw several men trapped by the flames that the wind was blowing around them. He turned the ship's head hard right, which took the flames off the bow but threw them directly upon himself. He lasted only a few minutes after that. He died at the helm."

Later in the war, a number of ships were named for men who had lost their lives at sea, though not necessarily for acts of heroism. A few of those so honored were *Michael J. Monaghan,* machinist on the tanker *Gulfamerica; Frederick Austin,* second mate on the tanker *R. W. Gallagher; Robert J. Banks,* a messboy on the *Gulfamerica; William Cox,* fireman on the coastal collier *David Atwater; George R. Poole,* first assistant engineer on the tanker *Gulfstate; Harold O. Wilson,* oiler on the Liberty ship *Flora Macdonald; William J. Jerman,* master of the tanker *Cities Service Empire; Carl Zachary Webb,* wiper on the tanker *Allan Jackson; Benjamin Fisher,* chief engineer on the freighter *Alcoa Guide;* and *William McKee,* able seaman on the freighter *Biennville.*

Several war correspondents who lost their lives during World War II were honored by having Liberty ships named after them. The ships, and the papers or services who employed their namesakes, were: *Robert F. Post (The New York Times), Ralph Barnes* and *Byron Darnton (New York Herald Tribune), Jack Singer (International News Service), Melville Jacoby (Time-Life), Edward H. Crockett (Associated Press), Webb Miller* and *Harry Percy (United Press), Carl Thusgaard (Acme News Pictures), Ben Miller (Baltimore Evening Sun),* and *Ernie Pyle (Scripps-Howard Newspapers).*

When the *Jean Nicolet* was sunk by a Japanese submarine in the Indian Ocean in 1944, many of the crew were shot or drowned. One of the missing men was the purser, Francis J. O'Gara, who had been a sports writer for the Philadelphia

Inquirer. A new Liberty was named for O'Gara and delivered on 30 June 1945. The *Francis J. O'Gara* was less than four months old when the real Francis J. O'Gara, like Enoch Arden, came home. He had been captured by the submarine that sank the *Nicolet* and spent 15 months in a Japanese prison camp. The only man ever to see his own name on a Liberty ship, Francis J. O'Gara was later presented with the builder's plaque from the *Francis J. O'Gara*. The ship joined the U. S. Navy after the war as the radar picket ship *Outpost*.

□

Liberty ship names ran the gamut of Americans, famous or forgotten, who had contributed something to the achievements of their time. The *Moses Cleveland* was named for a soldier and lawyer who founded the city of Cleveland, Ohio. *Myron T. Herrick* was named for a former governor of Ohio and later American ambassador to France. *William Gray* was named for the first colonial merchant shipper to trade in the Columbia River. The *Hugh Young* was named for a Confederate general; the *Robert L. Vann* for one of the nation's pioneer Negro newspaper publishers; and the *Arthur M. Huddell* for a prominent labor leader of the early twentieth century. *William E. Borah* was named for a senator from Idaho; and *Royal S. Copeland* for another senator who helped write the Merchant Marine Act of 1936.

Among ships honoring men who had made significant contributions to agriculture in the United States were the *Clarence Roberts*, named for the editor of the *Stockman-Farmer; Otis E. Hall*, named for a leader in the Kansas 4-H Club program; and *Cyril G. Hopkins*, named for a researcher in problems of soil fertility.

Religious, ethnical, and patriotic groups suggested many Liberty ship names. The *Andreas Honcharenko* honored the first known Ukrainian immigrant to the United States. The *Nachman Syrkin* was named for a longtime American worker for a Jewish national homeland in Palestine and a founder of the American Jewish Congress.

School children who took part in a national scrap-metal salvage campaign were invited to suggest names for Liberty ships. Their first choice was *Lou Gehrig* of the New York Yankees. Others on the so-called "children list" of names were *Daniel Webster; John A. Dix*, governor of New Hampshire; *John Burke*, governor of North Dakota; *Robert M. LaFollette; William E. Borah;* Admiral *David G. Farragut;* Confederate General *Leonidas Polk;* and *Pocahontas*.

Many Liberty ships were named for foreigners. *Eloy Alfaro* was named for a statesman and president of Ecuador who was, like many Latin American patriots, killed by assassination. *Mello Franco* was named for a Brazilian representative to the League of Nations and a judge on the Permanent Council of International Justice at the Hague from 1923 to 1929. *Nicholas Labadie* honored a Canadian and an ex-priest who fought in the Texas War for Independence and later moved to Texas and practiced medicine there. *Rueben Dario* was a poet and writer who lived at various times in Nicaragua, Chile, and Argentina. *Filipp Mazzazi* was named for an Italian who came to the United States at the suggestion of Benjamin Franklin and Thomas Jefferson to experiment with the cultivation of grapes and olives. *Frederick von Steuben* was the Prussian officer who served with General Washington, turning raw recruits into disciplined troops, and who later had a hand in planning the U. S. Military Academy at West Point. *Pierre L'Enfant* was the French architect who laid out the nation's capital. *Frederick Barthaldi* was the French sculptor of the Statue of Liberty.

The *Alf Lindeberg* was named for a Norwegian merchant marine officer executed by the Germans. When the ship sailed from New York for England early in 1944 she carried a crew of Norwegians who had sailed together since 1939. After their original ship was torpedoed in the North Atlantic late in 1943, they asked the Norwegian Shipping and Trade Mission in New York to send them out together again, but no Norwegian ship was available that could use a full crew. Hearing that the United States was launching Liberty ships by the hundreds and that some of them were being transferred to Allied flags, they then asked the Mission to help them sail on one of the new ships. But their Captain, Mons Augestad, suggested that they ask President Roosevelt himself, and sent a telegram: "Seamen just saved from a torpedoed Norwegian motor ship. Stand ready to go to sea again immediately. Be so kind as to help us get a new ship."

Roosevelt, intrigued by the idea of a crew sailing the hazardous Atlantic sea-lanes together for four years, asked the War Shipping Administration to see what could be done. The result was that Captain Augestad and his crew got a brand new Liberty ship, the *Alf Lindeberg*. Their "thank you" to Roosevelt and Admiral Land, sent via the Norwegian Shipping Trade Mission, ended with "Long live Uncle Sam."

Presidents and patriots rode the seas, as it were, on the bows and sterns of Liberty ships. There was the *Thomas Jefferson, James Monroe, James K. Polk, Zachary Taylor, Abraham Lincoln, Benjamin Harrison, Woodrow Wilson,* and *Calvin Coolidge.* Not so well known were *William B. Giles,* U. S. senator and governor of Virginia from 1827 to 1830; *Lucretia Mott*, nineteenth century social reformer who worked for woman suffrage and world peace; *Ralph Izzard*, U. S. senator and member of the Continental Congress from South Carolina; *Elisha P. Perry*, first governor of the state of Washington; *Timothy Pickering*, George Washington's secretary of state; and *William Hooper*, a signer of the Declaration of Independence from South Carolina.

Liberty ships were named for *José M. Morelos*, a national hero of Mexico who was captured and shot while serving with rebel forces under Hidalgo; *Silvester Escalante*, a Spanish priest who explored the southwest in 1768–69; and *Juan Pablo Duarte*, who founded the Dominican Republic.

Two names that rode proudly on the bows of Liberty ships were in a sense foreign, but truly as American as *Billy Sunday* or *Sam Jackson;* the *Amerigo Vespucci* honored the Italian navigator and explorer who made four voyages to the Americas and for whom the Western Hemisphere is named; and the *Leif Ericson* honored the Viking who is credited with reaching North America almost 500 years before either Vespucci or Columbus.

Other explorers commemorated were *Sebastian Vizcaino*, the seventeenth-century Spaniard who explored the West Coast; his predecessor, *Juan Cabrillo*, the Portuguese who discovered California for Spain; and *Gaspar de Portola*, *Pierre Marquette*, *Ponce de Leon*, *Victor Bering*, and *Samuel de Champlain*. The names of many inventors were carried by Liberty ships, and some of them, of course, contributed directly or indirectly to the ships that honored them. *John Fitch*, *James Rumsey*, *Robert Fulton*, and *John Stevens* all developed early steam engines. *Samuel F. B. Morse* invented the telegraph and the Morse code, which was used by the radio operator aboard every Liberty ship. *Elias Howe* invented the sewing machine without which no tarpaulin could have been made. Much of their electrical equipment stemmed from the work of *George Westinghouse*. *Alexander Graham Bell* gave them their phones, *Thomas Edison*, their electric lights, *Elmer A. Sperry* their gyro compasses, and *Isaac Babbit* the metal that kept their shaft-bearings from running hot.

A few Libertys were not named for any individuals at all. The *Pearl Harbor*, in a way, was named for nearly 2500 men who lost their lives there on 7 December 1941. The *Houston Volunteers* so honored the hundreds of young men from Houston, Texas, who volunteered en masse for naval service after the cruiser *Houston* was lost in the Battle of Sunda Strait. The ship with what must have been the shortest name in the world was the *U. S. O.*, honoring the wartime

United Service Organizations, which provided hospitality and entertainment centers for servicemen. The *U. S. O.* sailed the seas under a variety of other names in the postwar years, being known, consecutively, as the *Columbella, Ekali,* and *Loyal Fortunes.* She ended up on Pratus Reef about 165 miles southeast of Hong Kong, driven on the shoals by a typhoon in November of 1967. In the same category was the *Stage Door Canteen,* named for that famous servicemen's center in New York that was operated by the city's theatrical fraternity. The hyphenated *Am-Mer-Mar,* obviously, was named for the entire American Merchant Marine as was the *American Mariner.*

□

In the latter stages of the building program, many ships designated for use by the Navy as cargo ships were renamed, following the Navy system, with names of stars. The names ran from *Acubens* to *Zaniah* and were somewhat better suited to a life at sea than those bestowed on ships turned over to the British Ministry of War Transport. The British choice of names commencing with *Sam* could be understood (for Uncle *Sam* or Superstructure *A*ft of *Mid*ships, depending on the point of view), but many an American sailor would have been put off, if not downright gagged, by names such as *Samfairy, Samnid,* and *Samshee.* All in all, there were 88 "Sam" ships, commencing with *Samadang* and ending with *Samythian.*

Another group of Liberty ships carried somewhat unusual and, to the uninformed observer, completely baffling names such as *Jagger Seam, Bon Air Seam, Jewell Seam, Pocahontas Seam,* and *Glamorgan Seam.* Twenty-four ships all carried the same "family" name. They were colliers—built to carry coal—and each was named for a notable coal deposit, or seam, in the United States.

Except for a few ships mentioned in official news releases, most Libertys spent their wartime careers in complete anonymity as far as the public was concerned. Names were known to crews and shipping companies, shipping commissioners, and convoy commodores, but in convoys the names on bow or stern were obscured by wartime gray paint, and it was possible to sail with another ship for hundreds of miles and never know who she was unless a name board was hoisted for routing or convoy organizational purposes.

Selecting a name for a ship was only a small part of a ceremony whose traditions are as old as antiquity. The ship was christened at the launching ceremony, when she slid down the ways into saltwater for the first time. Launching was attended with all the festivity that time, and the budget, would permit: band music, speeches, colored bunting, flowers for the sponsor who broke the bottle of champagne over the bow, a present afterward, and sometimes an elaborate reception.

The problem of who was to christen a capital ship, such as a battleship or cruiser, could become fraught with political and social implications. The wife, or daughter, of the governor usually christened the battleship named for his state. With Liberty ships, there were so many that almost everyone got a chance at one of them. Even the wives of grimy shipyard workers christened ships their husbands helped build. When Mrs. Martin Staley, wife of a reamer, was selected for the honor of christening the *Nathaniel Hawthorne,* she took no chances on muffing the job. For several weeks ahead of time she practiced by smashing milk bottles against the barn at their farm home in Yault, Washington, and when the moment for launching came, and she had a bottle of champagne to work with, she performed in fine style.

A ship would probably sail as well whether she was properly christened and launched or not, but one could never be certain of this. When the *Timothy Pickering* was to be launched, and while the dignitaries were still gathering for the ceremony in which Mrs. George Havas was to christen the ship, the steel anchor plate broke, and the ship slid down the ways 15 minutes ahead of schedule, injuring several workmen. The ship never received her traditional baptism with champagne, nor the traditional words of the sponsor, "I christen thee. . . ." As the ship approached Sicily the following year with an invasion force, the *Pickering* was hit by a bomb and vanished completely as her ammunition blew up.

The *Rufus King* almost missed being christened at her launching on 11 March 1942 at the California Shipbuilding Company yard in Los Angeles. Just as the ceremony commenced a rainstorm drenched the official party, and then to make matters worse the air raid alarm sounded, but everyone stood their ground and the ship went down the ways, properly named and splashed.

□

The woman who christened a ship was usually presented with a suitable memento of the occasion. The value of the sponsor's gift varied greatly from yard to yard, and after the war, the Senate's Mead Committee looked into the matter of christening gifts. The committee found that five women, all relatives of government officials, received gifts totaling $6,457 for smashing the traditional champagne bottles against the bows of five ships. Sun Shipbuilding and Drydock Company, which did not build Libertys, gave its sponsors lavish gifts with a minimum value of $750 each. Eleanor Roosevelt's gift was worth $553. Actress Greer Garson received a $75 silver cigarette box. Liberty ship sponsors usually received more modest presents. When the *Ernie Pyle* was named for the famous war correspondent who was killed on Okinawa near the end of the war, the ship was christened by Mrs. Pyle, who received a $25 souvenir.

Possibly it was due to wartime rush, but after a name was chosen and given to a ship, there was no procedure for placing a memorial plate on the ship with a brief biography of the person whose name it carried. Destroyers in the U. S. Navy always carried such a plate, but many a merchant seaman spent a year or more on a ship without having the slightest idea as to whom it had been named for. Most men would recognize *Knute Rockne* or *James J. Corbett*, but who was *J. C. Osgood*? *Johnny Appleseed* and *Paul Bunyan* would have been encountered in a schoolbook at one time or another, but *George H. Price* would not have been. Men might be expected to know *Mark Twain* and *Jack London*, but not many of them would know *Victor Herbert* or *Simon Bolivar*. *Wiley Post*, *Floyd Bennett*, and *Billy Mitchell* had been names in the news recently enough to be remembered, but *Brander Matthews* wasn't, and it was very likely that men who had heard of *Billy Sunday* and *John J. Ringling* would not have heard of *Grant Wood* or *Mary Cassatt*.

Almost every Liberty that was sold to American or foreign interests after the war was renamed, and the original name was soon forgotten. But no matter what flag a Liberty flew—Greek, Italian, or Lebanese—she still carried evidence of her American origin. The brass identification plate mounted on the forward end of the midships deckhouse showed her first name, hull number, and the name of her builder. A similar plate was usually affixed to the bulkhead in the engine-room fidley at the entrance to the engine spaces on the main deck. The original name frequently appeared on the profile and hold plans that were framed and mounted in the passageway leading to the navigation bridge near the captain's cabin.

And no matter what her current name might be—*Amsteldiep*, *Kolkhoznik*, *Saint Nazaire*, *African Princess*, or *Thunderbird*,—there was no doubt about her hull lines. Nothing else afloat looked like a Liberty.

More than 80 different steamship companies operated Liberty ships during World War II. One of these, the Stevenson Lines, had 19 Libertys at sea. The *T. J. Stevenson*, shown here about 1947 in peacetime colors, was built as the *Raymond Clapper*. Renamed *Elias Dayfas II*, she was abandoned and sank off Yucatan in 1966.

4

GENERAL
OPERATIONS

The next step after a ship was built, christened, and launched, was "delivery," which depended on how long fitting-out took. As an example, the *Richard Henry Dana,* hull number 45 of the California Shipbuilding Corporation and number 294 in the Maritime Commission list, was launched on 12 July 1942. Fitting-out was completed on 31 July, and then the ship was ready for delivery by the shipyard. It was turned over to the U. S. Maritime Commission and then to the general agent—in that case the American Mail Line—assigned by the War Shipping Administration to operate the ship for the government.

The brief, unceremonious delivery usually accounted for the first entry in a new ship's log, as it did for the *Dana* on 31 July 1942: "4:30 p.m. *Richard Henry Dana* officially delivered by the California Shipbuilding Corp. to the American Mail Line. Hull number 45, Calship. Hull number 294 Maritime Commission."

Loading began on 2 August. Guns were mounted three days later. Carpenters were completing the catwalks over the deckload on 10 August when Pilot Maland

came aboard and the crew made preparations for getting underway. The ship
began her maiden voyage, out of San Pedro, the next afternoon.

From the moment that the American Mail Line, as general agent, took delivery,
it handled the myriad details of loading, provisioning, fueling, manning, and
obtaining port clearance for the ship. Most general agents were well-known steamship owners and operators with long experience in the shipping business. But as
wartime shipping increased tremendously, it strained the facilities of "old line"
operators and new, lesser known firms were appointed as agents by the WSA.
It was a policy to appoint only firms with a background of deep-sea operations.
Great pressure was put on the WSA and the Maritime Commission to grant
general agency status to ill-equipped firms or to those set up as wartime ventures
ready to assume an overnight corporate status for the prospect of a "quick buck."
Many such applicants for general agency appointment were turned down for lack
of sufficient experience, resources, and personnel, and because their appointment
would serve only to pirate trained men from existing organizations.

In November of 1943 WSA issued a policy statement on general agents:

> The demands of war require the full utilization of the American ship-
> ping industry in the operation of the American merchant fleet. Accord-
> ingly, the policy of the WSA has been to appoint as general agents
> qualified and experienced American operators of vessels who are willing
> to undertake the duties and responsibilities relating to the activity and
> who qualify with respect to financial and other requirements, including
> a history of pre-war operating experience.
>
> Priority both as to appointments and vessel allocations has been
> given to organizations which actually owned American flag vessels be-
> fore the war, with priority between the various shipowners being
> granted to those who constructed or purchased new American flag ves-
> sels in the Maritime Commission's long range program.

In some cases, firms that were agents for shipowners before the war were also
appointed as general agents. In other words, if they qualified in ship-operating
know-how, they did not necessarily have to be shipowners. Many applications for
general agent status were denied to new organizations "promoted solely for the
purpose of acting as general agents."

A total of 84 such agents operated freighters for the WSA; 10 of them operated
tankers. Each agent had to show a minimum net worth of $150,000, of which
$100,000 had to be working capital. The following served as general agents:

A. H. Bull Co.
A. L. Burbank
Agwilines
Alaska Packers
Alaska Transportation Co.
Alaska S.S. Co.
Alcoa S.S. Co.
American-Hawaiian S.S. Co.
American Export Lines
American Foreign S.S. Co.
American Mail Lines
American President Lines
American Range Liberty Line
American Republic Line
American South Africa Line
American West Africa Line
Barber Asphalt Corp.
Bernuth-Lembcke
Black Diamond Line
Blidberg-Rothschild
Boland and Cornelius
Bulk Carriers Corp.
Burns S.S. Co.
Calmar S.S. Co.
Coastwise S.S. Co.
Cosmopolitan S.S. Co.
De La Rama Co.
Dickman, Wright and Pugh
Eastern S.S. Co.
Grace Line
General S.S. Co.
Hammond Shipping Co.
International Freight Corp.
Inter-Ocean S.S. Co.
Isbrandtsen S.S. Co.
Isthmian S.S. Co.
James Griffiths and Sons
J.H. Winchester Co.
Los Angeles Tankers Operators
Luckenbach S.S. Co.
Lykes Brothers
Marine Transport Lines
Matson Navigation Co.

McCormick S.S. Co.
Merchants and Miners Transportation Co.
Mississippi Shipping Co.
Moore-McCormack S.S. Co.
Mystic S.S. Co.
North Atlantic and Gulf Co.
Northeast Transportation Co.
Norton Lilly Co.
Oliver J. Olson Co.
Olympic S.S. Co.
Overlakes Freighting Corp.
Pacific Atlantic S.S. Co.
Pacific Tankers Corp.
Parry Navigation Co.
Polarus S.S. Co.
Prudential S.S. Co.
R. A. Nicol Co.
Republic Oil Refining Corp.
Seas Shipping Co.
Smith and Johnson
South Atlantic S.S. Co.
Spencer and Kellogg
Sprague S.S. Co.
Standard Fruit Co.
States Marine Corp.
Stevenson Lines
Stockard S.S. Co.
Sudden and Christensen
Tankers Co.
Union Oil Co. of California
United Fruit Co.
United States Lines
U. S. Navigation Co.
Union Sulphur Co.
Waterman S.S. Co.
Wessel Duval Co.
Weyerhaeuser S.S. Co.
William J. Rountree Co.
West India S.S. Co.
Wilmore S.S. Co.
W. R. Chamberlain

From June 1942 until December 1943, general agents were paid on the basis of total deadweight tonnage of ships assigned to an operator. The scale of monthly payments under this system was as follows:

First 50,000 tons .... 50 cents per ton
Next 40,000 tons .... 40 cents per ton
Next 40,000 tons .... 30 cents per ton
Next 40,000 tons .... 25 cents per ton
Next 50,000 tons .... 20 cents per ton
Over 250,000 tons .... 15 cents per ton

General agents were also paid for the amount of tonnage handled by their ships at United States and foreign ports.

As of 31 December 1943 the system of payment was changed to a flat rate of $65 per day for each dry-cargo ship, tanker, or collier under general agency operation, plus an additional $15 per day per ship to cover accounting costs. Fixed rates per ton of cargo handled by each ship were also paid.

Recapture provisions were set up whereby the government could reclaim a percentage of a general agent's profits above a certain amount. There was also an arrangement whereby the government contributed substantially toward making up any losses incurred by an operator, such as excessive costs in obtaining and transporting crews to a vessel's departure port, buying supplies at places where American foods were more expensive, and other factors.

As of 1 January 1944 the recapture provisions and the payment system were changed again. Ninety percent of any profits in excess of $15 per ship per day were subject to recapture. The provision for helping to make up losses was cancelled. The recapture provisions were set up to prevent an operator who had low overhead from making exhorbitant profits, since the rates were based on the average cost of the large operators.

A steamship company acting as a general agent for the WSA experienced a meteoric increase in operations and personnel. Alaska Steamship Company, as an example, operated 17 ships before the war, only between Seattle, the Alaskan mainland, and Aleutian ports. By the end of 1943 the company was agent for 82 WSA vessels engaged in worldwide operations.

Steamship company staffs had to be enlarged many times to handle the vast amount of detail connected with such far-flung operations. Operators had lost some of their best people, in many cases, to the Army and Navy and had to make up for it by working their staffs long hours, seven days a week. "It got so, later in the war," said one official, "that we were glad to have anybody. As long as it was a warm body we put it to work." Ships would never have been loaded and dispatched had it not been for the hard work put in by steamship company staffs.

A general agent had to supply stores and fuel for the ship and arrange for tugs, pilot, and customs clearance at the time of sailing. They arranged for berthing the ship and for cargo handling through a stevedoring firm. They arranged for signing on a crew, prepared payrolls, and paid-off the crew when the voyage was ended.

A large part of the general agent's staff work involved compiling and submitting detailed voyage accounts to the WSA for every trip made by every vessel. Even the smallest expenditures during the trip had to be itemized and accounted for. All such expenditures were double-checked by WSA auditors who worked in the agent's own offices.

The general agent also had to arrange for representation in any foreign port where ships under its control might call, by appointing subagents, either American or foreign firms with experience in ship operation. Fees charged by subagents were added to bills submitted to the government by the agent.

The captain of a ship operating under agency agreement usually carried about $10,000 in cash for advances to the crew in foreign ports and for purchase of emergency supplies. Additional money could be obtained from subagents or from overseas offices of the WSA.

☐

After a ship was delivered, the next event was her departure on a maiden voyage, which might well be an around-the-world trip. For example, the *William B. Giles,* delivered on 29 August 1942, sailed from New Orleans in September, cleared the Canal Zone on 10 October, and headed for Cape Horn, via the Pacific. She reached Cape Town on 14 November and on 15 December was in Bombay to discharge cargo. More cargo was discharged in Colombo, Calcutta, and Madras. She loaded at Vizagapatam on 22 January 1943, crossed the Indian Ocean to Hobart, Tasmania, then sailed via Panama to Guantanamo Bay, Cuba and New York where she arrived on 17 April. The *George Gipp* began her maiden voyage at Oakland, California, on 15 June 1943, sailed to Hobart, Tasmania, through the Suez Canal to Alexandria, Egypt, and completed her voyage at Philadelphia on 17 October, having logged 21,739 miles.

During her wartime career the *William A. Richardson* made nine voyages. She was underway in the Atlantic en route to Malta on her tenth voyage when VJ Day ended the war. By that time she steamed 102,000 miles and loaded some 64,000 tons of cargo. A summary of her nine voyages follows:

Voyage No. 1. Sailed from San Francisco 27 November 1942 with 7,600 tons of British Lend-Lease cargo for Wellington, New Zealand, and Melbourne, Australia. At Melbourne loaded 5,500 tons of cargo, mostly lead, wool, and hides. Voyage ended 8 March 1943 at New York; total miles steamed, 13,107. Captain W. H. Baylis.

Voyage No. 2. Sailed from Brooklyn 18 March 1943 with 3,546 tons of Army cargo and mail. Touched at Bermuda for orders; arrived at Algiers 14 April 1943 in convoy. Sailed from Algiers and arrived New York 9 May 1943. Captain H. R. Clark.

Voyage No. 3. Sailed from Hoboken, N. J., 28 May with 3,784 tons of Army cargo. Arrived Casablanca 16 June. Discharged cargo and loaded 320 POWs. Sailed 7 July, in convoy. On 21 July collided with escort ship; no serious damage to either. Arrived Newport News, Virginia, 23 July; disembarked POWs, sailed to Baltimore. Captain O. F. Ahlin.

Voyage No. 4. Loaded 3,700 tons of cargo in Baltimore, took on troops at Newport News, sailed 5 September for Algiers. Arrived 25 September in Algiers and discharged troops and cargo. Touched following Mediterranean ports: Oran, Nemours, Malta, Augusta, Taranto, Bizerte, Palermo, and Naples. Returned to Baltimore 25 January 1944. Captain O. F. Ahlin.

Voyage No. 5. Loaded cargo in Baltimore, troops at Newport News, sailed 23 February. Arrived Oran, North Africa, 12 March. Discharged cargo there and at Arzew and took on more troops and cargo. Sailed for Oran 25 March. Touched at Augusta, Naples, Salerno, Naples, Augusta, Oran, Mers-El-Kebir, where took on 500 POWs. Sailed from Oran 24 April in convoy. Voyage ended at Norfolk, Virginia, 13 May. Captain O. F. Ahlin.

Voyage No. 6. Sailed from Norfolk 20 May for Philadelphia to discharge ballast; loaded 6,713 tons of Army cargo. Sailed from Lynhaven Roads 12 June, in convoy, en route to Persian Gulf. Arrived at Khorramshahr 23 July; arrived at Bahrein Island 10 August. Loaded cargo at Aden and Suez; sailed from Port Said 2 September. Arrived New York 28 September. Miles steamed, 19,058. Captain Frank DeLuca.

Voyage No. 7. Sailed from New York 17 October; loaded 4,160 tons of cargo in Baltimore. Sailed from Lynhaven Roads 1 November. Arrived at Augusta,

Sicily, 23 November. Touched at Naples, Leghorn, Oran. Sailed from Oran 7 January 1945; arrived Baltimore 24 January. Captain Frank DeLuca.

Voyage No. 8. Loaded 3,750 tons of Army cargo in Baltimore; sailed from Lynhaven Roads 17 February in convoy for Naples. Arrived Naples 12 March. Arrived Oran 23 March; departed 28 March for Manzanilla, Cuba, and loaded 3,500 tons of sugar. Arrived New York 5 May 1945. Captain Edward J. Elliot.

Voyage No. 9. Sailed from New York 8 June, loaded 3,750 tons of Army cargo in Philadelphia. Sailed 20 June for France; arrived Le Havre 5 July. Loaded 751 troops; sailed 23 July for New York. Arrived New York 4 August. Captain Frank DeLuca.

□

By the fall of 1944, ship operators working for the War Shipping Administration were supervising the use of more than 3,500 ships—20,000,000 tons of shipping—and dispatching loaded ships from U. S. ports on an average of one every 30 minutes. And every pound of cargo cleared from American ports, as well as most of the imports brought back from overseas, had to be cleared by the ship operators. Most of the WSA fleet was carrying Army cargo, with the next largest portion carrying Lend-Lease cargo. The rest of it was transporting essential raw materials and civilian commodities—everything from bauxite to salt and coffee—and some material for the Navy.

Besides the system of general agents and their subagents all over the world, ship operations were expedited by WSA offices, staffed by experienced shipping men, in major American and foreign ports serving the war zones. They were specialists in avoiding bottlenecks and scheduling docking and cargo-handling. While the merchant marine officers and crews won most of the praise—and rightfully so—for moving wartime cargo around the world, their work would not have been possible without the unsung workers in the offices of the general agents. Their dedicated efforts enabled the ships to sail, as a WSA news release in 1944 pointed out:

> Without the paper work and supervision of the ship operators, the great steel hulls of the merchant fleet might lie in harbors, rusting out their bottoms, or end in an unsolved tangle of misdirection and confusion. Thousands of workers for the ship operators keep long hours over typewriters, adding machines, manifests, declarations, insurance policies, war-complicated ship payrolls, and a thousand and one complex details to see that the planes, tanks, food and men reach the right place at the right time.

At least 800 ships, carrying everything from shoes to steam engines, sailed on the hazardous Murmansk Run. Storms, ice, mines, collisions, fire, U-boats, and the Luftwaffe all took their toll; 97 ships never reached their destinations. One of them was this unidentified merchantman, victim of an aerial torpedo.

5

THE
MURMANSK
RUN

As long as men write about the dangers of the seas and the heroic deeds of those who take their ship into battle against long odds, they will tell tales of the "Murmansk Run" in World War II, when merchant ships steamed into the stormy Arctic with supplies for the Russian front. It was then that the new Libertys went into battle for the first time and, along with their older companions, faced a relentless enemy as they fought through to the Barents Sea and the White Sea to reach the distant Russian supply ports of Archangel and Murmansk.

This supply route was absolutely vital to the Russians if they were to hold out against the Nazi offensive. Without the Allied ships that made the voyage with products from the American war arsenal, the Russians may well not have beaten back the German invasion.

The only other deepwater route to Russia terminated in the Persian Gulf ports, but the rail lines and roads that ran from the Gulf to the interior of Russia would, because of their length and their limited capacity, have been unable to carry the vast amount of munitions and food needed by the Russians. All other supply routes were under German control. Ships had to make the Murmansk run to keep Russia in the war.

A voyage to North Russia was never a routine affair, for there was always the hazards of storms and arctic ice, whether or not the ship faced enemy attack. From a day or two after leaving the points of departure—Loch Ewe in northern Scotland, or Reykjavik in Iceland—ships could expect submarine surveillance or attack while they steamed 1,600 miles from Scotland to Murmansk or 1,500 miles from Reykjavik to the same port.

Convoys, and in a few cases unescorted merchantmen, sailed within easy striking distance of German air bases spaced strategically along the coast of Norway from Bodo, just above the Arctic Circle, to Banak, a short distance from North Cape. Added to the threat of planes and submarines was the constant possibility of a foray by German capital ships or destroyers based at Trondheim and various fjords along the coast. The battleships *Tirpitz* and *Scharnhorst* and the battlecruisers *Admiral Scheer* and *Admiral Hipper* were a force in being that, while never attaining its potential for destruction on the convoy routes, did serve effectively to tie down a powerful segment of the British Home Fleet through a good part of the war. The Allies failed to realize that the principal purpose of this fleet was not to harass the Russian convoys, but to defend Norway against what Hitler believed was an inevitable Allied invasion.

Admiral Sir John Tovey, Commander-in-Chief of the British Home Fleet, told the Admiralty that the Germans would do everything in their power to stop the Russian convoys. This prediction certainly proved true. Although the German capital ships spent most of their time hiding in Norwegian fjords, waiting an expected invasion, submarines and aircraft pressed their attacks against the convoys until the end of the war. German destroyers were able adversaries, too, accounting for a number of merchantmen and convoy escorts when they accompanied the larger combat craft on convoy-hunting expeditions.

These were by no means the only threats to ships making the Murmansk run. During the short northern summer, 24 hours of daylight made it possible for German aircraft to attack continuously from the time ships came within striking range. Throughout the rest of the year, the merchantmen and their hard-worked escorts, especially the destroyers and smaller craft, had the world's worst weather to contend with: spray that froze on topside surfaces, blinding snow, driving sleet, and violent storms that tossed ships about and hopelessly scattered convoys.

Careful and well-planned convoy protection was often disrupted by storms. From 24 to 27 March 1942, convoy PQ13 was scattered over 150 miles of ocean by a storm. Pack ice made matters even worse. In those four days of trouble off

North Cape, five merchant ships were sunk by submarines and aircraft, and the British cruiser *Trinidad* was damaged in a battle with German destroyers.

In the winter and spring of 1942, President Roosevelt and Harry Hopkins, as well as Premier Josef Stalin, continually pressed the English to step up the number and the size of convoys to Russia, despite protestations by Winston Churchill and the Admiralty that their naval forces, especially in the matter of destroyers, were stretched to the limit.

Stalin sent an urgent message to Churchill in May of 1942 in which he said, "I am fully aware of the difficulties involved and of the sacrifices made by Great Britain in the matter (the Russian convoys). I feel, however, incumbent upon me to approach you with the request to take all possible measures in order to ensure the arrival of the above-mentioned materials in the USSR in the course of May as this is extremely important for our front."

The situation reached a climax that month. Dozens of Russian-bound ships were waiting in Iceland, and Churchill approved a much-debated plan to sail a convoy—PQ16, of 34 ships—in the latter part of that month. "The operation is justified," he said, "if half gets through."

There was Stalin's own assessment of the importance of these convoys to Russia's ability to hold back the German invader. It is no exaggeration, in the light of history, to say that the convoys kept the Russians in the war. The Russian front was no less important to the winning of the war than the Normandy landings or the invasion of Okinawa.

The understandable British reluctance to accept the heavy losses to merchantmen and escorts on this run, and the continued Russian and American insistence that the convoys should move regardless of losses, was a matter of contention that created bitter feelings and suspicions despite the polite wording of official communiqués.

The British viewpoint was expressed by Captain S. W. Roskill, R.N., who wrote in *War at Sea* that "the Russians never relieved the Home Fleet of any appreciable share of responsibility for defending the Arctic convoys." Neither, for that matter, did the United States, where ardent protestations of the need to sail the ships was not accompanied by any offer of escort craft to help see them through. Indeed, the U. S. Navy was so woefully short of escorts and trained personnel that it couldn't even protect Allied ships along the Atlantic seaboard.

☐

Forty convoys, with a total of more than 800 ships, including 350 under the U. S. flag, started on the Murmansk run from 1941 through 1945. Ninety-seven of those ships were sunk by bombs, torpedoes, mines, and the fury of the elements. Were the Murmansk convoys instrumental in keeping Russia in the war? They carried more than 22,000 aircraft, 375,000 trucks, 8,700 tractors, 51,500 jeeps, 1,900 locomotives, 343,700 tons of explosives, a million miles of field-telephone cable, plus millions of shoes, rifles, machine guns, auto tires, radio sets, and other equipment.

The first convoy to Russia—six English ships and one Russian—sailed from Scotland in August of 1941 and delivered 15,000 tons of cargo without incident. The first Liberty ships to make the Russian run were the *R. H. Lee, Zebulon Vance, John Randolph,* and *Francis Scott Key,* which set out for Murmansk in the early convoys of 1942.

"From Philadelphia to Murmansk," the deck log of the *Francis Scott Key* began, when the voyage commenced in Philadelphia on 29 January 1942. But many months passed before the ship reached her destination.

By March the *Key* was in Halifax, Nova Scotia, ready to join a ten-knot convoy across the submarine-infested North Atlantic.

> March 3, 1942, 11:00 a.m.—Stand by engines 12:00 noon. Anchor aweigh. Standing out the river. 1:00 p.m., half ahead, pilot away. Overcast and raining. Vessel pitching moderately. Shipping heavy spray over all.

They were routine comments from a ship's log, but for vessels outward bound on the Russian run they signalled a departure from safe haven into a hazardous and stormy unknown; and for many a ship and crew, a voyage of no return.

For anyone who has sailed in a freighter on the wintry North Atlantic, these entries in the log will recall the sight of angry, mountainous spray-topped seas and the sound of wind howling and screeching through the stays.

> March 4. Vessel rolling heavily. Overcast and heavy fog.
> March 7. Sighted convoy and rejoined. Easterly gale.
> March 9. Overcast. Fog banks. Vessel rolling heavily. Heavy N. E. swells.
> March 12. Ship pitching and rolling and shipping water over the deck.

The *Francis Scott Key* was some 13 days reaching Greenock, Scotland, a distance of 2,712 miles at a little better than 8 knots. There she joined a convoy to Iceland, but collided with a destroyer en route and missed the Murmansk convoy she had originally been scheduled to join.

She sailed from Reykjavik on 26 April in convoy PQ15 of 23 ships, which encountered intermittent air and submarine attack during the nine-day run to Murmansk. The convoy lost only one freighter, blown up and sunk by an aerial torpedo.

Five gangs of 40 men worked night and day, unloading the ship in seven days. There were numerous German air raids at Murmansk but no ships were damaged and the *Francis Scott Key* left on 21 May. She reached Iceland on 29 May after a 1,615 mile run. The ship was back in New York on 31 July, still lucky. But only two weeks out of New York the *Seattle Spirit,* an old World War 1 Liberty-fleet ship sailing with her, was torpedoed and sunk.

Long voyages and the constant danger of being sunk, especially in winter weather, were hard on crews both physically and mentally. By the time the *Francis Scott Key* arrived in New York, tempers were raw. There were numerous fights among the men and one of the Armed Guard detachment threatened to "blow the first mate's brains out" for inadvertently showing a light while taking a nighttime bearing on the bridge.

The *John Randolph* and *Richard Henry Lee* were the only Liberty ships in convoy PQ16. On 24 May, the *Lee* reported floating mines while the convoy was steaming through patches of thick fog. The mine warning instantly put everyone on the alert and made it especially tough for the black gang going on watch below. As soon as the fog lifted, German bombers hit the convoy.

On the morning and forenoon watches of 25 May, about a dozen bombers and torpedo-bombers attacked. One plane was shot down by the *Lee*'s Navy gun crew. Like most ships making the run at that time, the *Richard Henry Lee* was armed only with light machine guns.

That evening the log recorded: "Air battle on again. All driven away. This is no child's play. Battling is furious. Fog banks save the day. Convoy fighting ice, mines, bombs, torpedoes and submarines."

Next day a sub attack was followed by an air raid in which one ship was sunk. "More blessed snow equalls," read the 1600 log entry.

On 27 May, a stick of bombs landed within 20 feet of the *Richard Henry Lee* with no visible damage. The machine gunners ran out of ammunition and had to broach the cargo for more. "During the attack," the log noted, "our ship's carpenter died. J. Thompson—a fine man. The raid was so heavy we only had time to cover him up with some blankets."

At 1100 on 28 May a funeral service was conducted. Before the Scripture reading was over, bombers roared in again and the crew had to run for the guns. And at 2000 that night: "Here they come again. Four bombs landed about 20 feet off the starboard side. Bomb fragments all over the deck." Next day: "Rain and fog. This is the kind of weather we like."

Courage and determination were bywords in the Murmansk run.

"I had little hope for her survival," said Commodore Onslow, senior officer of the escort for convoy PQ16 after his ship, the *Ocean Voice*, had been hit and set afire during mass air attacks. "But this gallant ship maintained her station, fought the fire and, with God's help, arrived at her destination. We were all inspired," he added, "by the parade-ground rigidity of the convoy's station keeping, including the *Ocean Voice* and the *Stari Bolshevik* (Russian), who were billowing smoke from their foreholds."

A few convoys delivered their cargoes without incident, but for most of them the Murmansk run meant either going down in battle or fighting through with guns, seamanship, and devotion to duty. Almost every ship that traveled this route gave her crew plenty of thrills to remember. The first-trip Libertys shared adventures with ships that were old before the ugly ducklings were hatched. All of them had one common fault: they were too slow to outrun submarines.

Ships of the early convoys were usually too lightly armed to put up much fight against air attack, but they fought valiantly with what they had. The *Michigan* in PQ16 shot down two planes with her meager armament. Gunners on the *Expositor* blew the conning tower off a submarine. The *Steel Worker* struck a mine in Kola Strait. The ammunition-laden *Syros* was torpedoed and disintegrated in one terrifying blast. The *Bateau* was sunk in a running fight with German destroyers. During convoy operations, merchant ships and escorts shot down many enemy planes, but there was no way of establishing a final score. Escorts sank the German submarines *U88*, *U589*, and *U457*.

□

Of all the convoys that made the Murmansk run, PQ17 has become the most famous—and with good reason. It consisted of 33 merchant ships when it left

Reykjavik, Iceland, on 28 June 1942, headed for the Denmark Strait, Archangel, and Murmansk.

Of the 21 U. S. ships, six were new Libertys: *Christopher Newport, William Hooper, John Witherspoon, Daniel Morgan, Samuel Chase* and *Benjamin Harrison,* all fresh from the yards. The others were American ships under the Panamanian flag, plus British, Russian, and Dutch ships.

At that time Russia was reeling before the German blitzkrieg, so PQ17 was loaded with strategic materials urgently needed by the Soviets—armor plate, steel, flour, canned goods, nickel, oil stills, aluminum, cordite, TNT, aircraft parts, guns and planes. Every ship carried a cargo worth a rajah's ransom.

For protection against attack by the German surface fleet, PQ17 had a heavy escort: the British cruisers *London* and *Norfolk,* and the U. S. cruisers *Wichita* and *Tuscaloosa,* a gesture of aid to the British and a token of camaraderie for the doubting Russians. The immediate convoy patrol included destroyers, corvettes, two antiaircraft ships, several armed trawlers, three rescue ships for picking up the crews of sunken vessels, and two submarines. A covering force, battleships HMS *Duke of York* and USS *Washington,* the carrier HMS *Victorious,* three cruisers and numerous destroyers, had been assigned to the general area over which the convoy was to travel, but they remained well beyond the 300-mile flight range of German aircraft.

This formidable escort did not deter the enemy. At 0230 on 4 July, a Heinkel torpedo-bomber eluded a hail of fire from the corvette *Palomaris* and torpedoed the *Christopher Newport.* The explosion blasted a big hole in the engine room, and the men on watch drowned. The survivors abandoned ship.

That evening, at suppertime, a flight of 24 twin-engine bombers attacked, winging in no more than 20 to 30 feet above the sea. Despite a curtain of fire, five planes managed to get in among the convoy to torpedo the British freighter *Navarino,* the American Liberty ship *William Hooper,* and the Russian tanker *Azerbaijan.* The *Navarino* and *Hooper* sank.

Soon after that the convoy commodore hoisted an astonishing signal: "Scatter fanwise. Proceed to destination at utmost speed." Some of the captains could not believe the order and requested a repeat, but there had been no mistake. The escort had been ordered to abandon the merchant ships and their precious cargoes. Each vessel was to proceed independently and the devil take the hindmost.

Long afterward, the mystified skippers learned the reason for their abandonment. The British Admiralty believed that the German battleship *Tirpitz* and battlecruiser *Scheer* had left their Norwegian bases to intercept PQ17. Scattering the convoy was the best, but tragic, alternative to having the Germans pounce on all the ships in one compact group, a target which their big guns would have eliminated in short order. The cruisers were withdrawn to keep them from being part of the expected sacrifice. The USS *Washington* and HMS *Duke of York*, with the *Victorious* and the cruisers, were not brought forward for fear they might be sunk by planes or submarines, thus freeing the German fleet for raiding operations in the North Atlantic. Since the main hope of eliminating the German battleship threat was through a decisive surface action, such timidity in refusing to employ *Duke of York, Washington,* and *Victorious* has been questioned in the years since. But cold facts at the time dictated the necessity of hazarding merchant ships rather than battleships and cruisers. The scattered convoy, as it turned out, only became easier victims for planes and submarines, and by 7 July, 18 freighters and 100,000 tons of cargo had been sent to the bottom.

The *Daniel Morgan* and the American freighter *Fairfield City* were making for Nova Zembla when Junkers bombers attacked and sank the latter. During this attack, nine sticks of bombs fell around the *Morgan*. Despite the fact that her 3-inch gun crew had been at battle stations for more than 24 hours without rest, they splashed two of the attackers. But many near-misses ruptured a number of hull plates and the *Morgan* was taking water fast. The crew abandoned ship, after which a submarine torpedoed her and she went down. The U-boat surfaced and gave the crew a course to steer to the nearest land. They were soon picked up by the Russian tanker *Donbass* and helped man the guns on that ship, shooting down one more bomber before they reached the White Sea.

As the remnants of PQ17 limped on, German attacks continued. On the afternoon of 5 July, the radio operator of the *Samuel Chase* logged these transmissions on the progress of the battle:

> Unidentified ship: "Two subs attacking."
> SS *Washington*: "Being dive bombed."
> Unidentified ship: "Have just been torpedoed."
> Unidentified ship: "Attacked by seven planes."
> SS *Daniel Morgan*: "Under heavy attack."
> SS *Pan Kraft*: "Under attack by aircraft."

On 10 July, while making a last-leg dash from Nova Zembla toward the White Sea, the *Chase* was attacked by six Junkers 88s. According to her log not all the fighting was done by the Germans:

Received six near misses within 60 yards of the ship. Snapped steam lines to main engine and auxiliaries. Ship lay dead in water. Compass knocked from the binnacle. Taken in tow by corvette at 1534 hours. Planes over again. Dive bombers driven away by ack-ack. Two shot down.

Of PQ17's original 33 ships, only 11 finally delivered their cargoes. Of the six Libertys, only *Samuel Chase* and *Benjamin Harrison* reached Murmansk. As Churchill so aptly put it, PQ17 was "one of the most melancholy episodes in the whole of the war." Regrets over errors in judgment could not bring back the ships, the men, or the vast amount of cargo sent to the bottom with the unprotected ships of this unfortunate convoy, but the Admiralty vowed that no such disaster would befall the next convoy—PQ18—to make the Murmansk run.

That fleet of 39 merchantmen left Loch Ewe, Scotland, on 2 September with one of the heaviest escorts ever assigned to any convoy of comparable size throughout the war. The convoy included Liberty ships *Esek Hopkins, Nathaniel Greene, Oliver Ellsworth, Virginia Dare, William Moultrie,* and *Patrick Henry.* In addition to merchant ships, there were two fleet oilers, a rescue ship, and an oiler and three minesweepers assigned for transfer to the Russians.

For defense against submarines there were two destroyers, two submarines, four corvettes, three minesweepers, and four trawlers. Two antiaircraft ships steamed along inside the convoy columns for defense against air attack. Further protection against air attack or a sortie by capital ships was provided by the aircraft carrier HMS *Avenger,* escorted by four destroyers.

Fearing, and yet halfway hoping, that the Germans might hazard an attack on the convoy by a battleship or battle cruiser, the Admiralty had also given PQ18 an independent force of 16 destroyers accompanied by the cruiser *Scylla,* their prime mission being to attack and torpedo the *Tirpitz, Scharnhorst,* or *Scheer.*

Further protection against a heavy ship attack was a cruiser covering force that included the *Norfolk, Suffolk,* and *London.* Also available, in case of emergency, were the cruisers *Sheffield* and *Cumberland* and one destroyer, which were accompanying a convoy on a supply mission to Spitzbergen. The battleships *Anson* and *Duke of York,* escorted by the cruiser *Jamaica* and five destroyers, were deployed to the westward, safely beyond German bomber range.

As an added precaution, the Admiralty had ordered submarine patrols off the Lofoten Islands and the coast of Norway to spot any foray by the *Tirpitz* or her companions and, if possible, to torpedo them as they sortied.

Such formidable protection did not discourage the enemy. The German submarine *U589* torpedoed the *Oliver Ellsworth* on 13 September, and from then on the ships of PQ18 kept their men constantly at battle stations as they fought off day and night attacks by bombers and submarines.

Most ships on the Murmansk run carried TNT or ammunition, so their crews knew full well that a torpedo or bomb hit could send a ship and all aboard her to Kingdom Come in one terrible, all-consuming blast. So it was on 14 September. Every ship in the convoy was busy that day. One attack by 40 bombers sank eight ships. The American freighter *Mary Luckenbach*, carrying 1,000 tons of TNT, was hit by an aerial torpedo. Little was left of the vessel except a pillar of smoke when rescue craft arrived to look for survivors. According to the *Esek Hopkins*, the torpedo was dropped by a burning plane and the explosion of the *Luckenbach* destroyed that plane and another as well.

The blast effect shook the nearby American ship *Scoharie* as though she had been torpedoed, throwing men flat on the deck and hurling fragments of steel from bow to stern. On the *Nathaniel Greene*, the blast threw gunners from their stations, smashed crockery in the galley, broke doors, and showered the vessel with debris, including shell casings from the *Luckenbach*'s guns.

Captain George Vickers of the *Nathaniel Greene* had just swung his ship away from one of several aerial torpedoes when the *Luckenbach* blew up. He thought at first that his ship had been hit and ordered the crew to lifeboat stations.

Captain Richard Hocken of the *William Moultrie*, steaming in the same column immediately astern of the *Luckenbach*, said that when his ship passed over the spot, "there was nothing left of her at all—not even a raft—no wreckage, not even a match box; hardly a ripple on the surface of the sea."

With more luck than some and thanks to her captain's leadership and a courageous crew, the *Moultrie* came through the voyage safely. Hocken received the Merchant Marine Distinguished Service Medal and this citation:

> His ship, the S.S. *William Moultrie*, in a convoy which suffered heavy losses, fought through a week of continuous attacks by enemy bombers and submarines to deliver her cargo of war material to a North Russian port. In the course of the long, running battle, the ship was directly attacked 13 times and was credited with downing eight planes and with scoring hits on 12 others. During the first attack on the convoy, the *William Moultrie* distinguished herself by shooting down three torpedo planes and assisting in the destruction of six more. The

following day her guns shot down four more of the attacking planes and damaged five. Later, after successfully repelling another attack by planes, four torpedoes were sighted heading for the ship. The guns fired on them, exploding one and the other three were eluded by skillful seamanship.

Captain Hocken, master of a gallant ship and a gallant crew, exhibited qualities of leadership and high courage in keeping with the finest traditions of the U. S. Merchant Marine.

The *Virginia Dare* was a new Liberty ship on her maiden voyage, yet her green crew was credited with shooting down or assisting in the destruction of seven bombers. The *Nathaniel Greene* shot down several planes that day. Her Armed Guard officer, Lieutenant (junior grade) R. M. Billings, described the action:

> Upwards of 25 torpedo planes attacked the port flank of the convoy and some of them went for the aircraft carrier. At about 1355 a swarm of torpedo planes were sighted near the water in front of the convoy on the starboard side ... the planes circled and came in directly at us, and we opened fire with everything we had ... one plane crossing our bow received a direct hit from our three inch gun and crashed in the water. Two more planes were shot down by our machine gun fire as they went down the port side and another plane was shot down on the starboard side. The planes were so close you couldn't miss with a machine gun.

Convoy PQ18, after fighting nearly all the way, arrived at its destination on 21 September with 20 ships. Planes and U-boats had sunk 13. Eight American ships went down—the Liberty *Oliver Ellsworth,* and the *Kentucky, Mary Luckenbach, Oregonian, Wacosta, John Penn, Africander,* and *Macbeth,* an American ship flying the Panamanian flag. The convoy paid a heavy price in ships and cargo, but it also exacted a heavy toll from the enemy that, along with urgent demands upon the Germans for more aircraft elsewhere, discouraged further mass air attacks against heavily protected Murmansk convoys.

□

Getting to Russia was only part of the job. Some ships spent so much time waiting to unload in the crowded ports that the crews began to feel like Soviet citizens. The crew of the *Yaka,* at Murmansk, sweated out 156 air raids while off-loading cargo. The *Ironclad* ran aground at Archangel and was given to the Russians. The Libertys *Thomas Hartley, Francis Scott Key,* and *Israel Putnam* spent nearly eight months unloading, and endured many air attacks. *Hartley* was credited with three kills. The *John LaFarge* and *John Ireland* also shot down enemy bombers. Men learned enough Russian to ask, "How about the next dance?" or "Do you have a husband?" They hitchhiked around the forbidding countryside and some managed to get as far as 200 miles inland before being escorted back to their ships. Finally, in September 1943, the five Libertys steamed down Kola Strait and headed for home.

After the heavy losses of convoys PQ17 and PQ18, it was decided to try to sneak some ships through unescorted. The Liberty ships *Hugh Williamson, John H. B. Latrobe, John Walker, Richard B. Alvey,* and *William Clarke* were dispatched from Iceland in this fashion in October and November of 1942.

The *William Clark,* with a cargo of planes, tanks, auto tires, ammunition, and a crew of 71 men, was an easy mark for a waiting U-boat shortly after noon on 4 November. The sky was overcast, with a moderate sea running. Visibility was seven miles. The first torpedo hit amidships, flooding the engine room. The order was given to abandon ship, and after the lifeboats pulled away, two more torpedoes broke the vessel in two and sent her to the bottom. The *St. Elstan* and the *Cape Pallister* picked up the 41 survivors.

Of 13 ships that were sent off independently to Russia in the fall and winter of 1942, three turned back, four were sunk, one was wrecked, and five arrived safely at Murmansk. Out of 23 ships that sailed independently from Murmansk for Iceland, only one was sunk.

Another epic voyage was made by the *Richard Bland,* a new Liberty that sailed from Philadelphia on 1 May 1942. She left Halifax on 14 May in a 42-ship convoy for the United Kingdom, but with nine other ships, broke off from the main convoy ten days later enroute for Iceland, assembly point for the Murmansk convoys.

In Iceland the *Bland* swung at anchor for a full month until the high command had made up its mind about sailing another Murmansk fleet. On 27 June she left with PQ17, ran into fog, hit some heavy ice, stove in the forepeak, then ran aground on rocks. Towed to Reykjavik, she spent several weeks discharging cargo and undergoing temporary repairs. Then she sailed to Loch Ewe, Scotland, to discharge cargo, have her hull repaired, and load the cargo again. She finally reached Murmansk on 27 December.

On 1 March 1943, the *Bland* left Russia in convoy JW51A, which included

J. L. M. Curry and *Richard Bassett.* At 0927 on the morning of 5 March, the American freighter *Executive* and the *Bland* were both torpedoed by a submarine. *Bland* dropped out of the convoy but for some reason the U-boat failed to finish her off and she rejoined just in time to help fight off an attack by a dozen Heinkel 111s. A stick of four bombs missed the *Bland* by a few skips and a jump.

The next night a heavy gale with 40-knot winds scattered the convoy and by dawn *Bland* had lost it completely. The bridge steering gear went out and crewmen struggled to keep on course with emergency steering from the after steering platform. The heavy weather continued for several days.

On 10 March, in intermittent snow squalls, poor visibility, and heavy seas, lookouts sighted a submarine periscope astern and seconds later a torpedo exploded in number four hold. Before the stern gun could be swung onto the target, thick snow obscured it. Another torpedo just missed the stern.

Expecting the submarine to try again, the captain decided to abandon ship by lowering the two boats on the windward side, and bringing them along the leeward side. But in the heavy wind and sea the men lost control and the boats, each with four men on board, disappeared in the driving snow.

There were not enough boats left for the 60 men still aboard ship, so the captain announced that some would have to remain aboard with him, hoping that the convoy escorts would answer their SOS. "I don't think she'll sink unless they put another torpedo into us," he said. A few minutes later the German submarine did exactly that.

Navy Lieutenant William A. Carter, a passenger, saw the torpedo coming.

> When it hit we were surrounded by flames and water poured down on us. We [Carter and Ensign E. J. Neely, the Armed Guard commander] made our way to the boat deck and I ran through a sheet of flame to the port side, then down a ladder to the main deck. The boat [lifeboat] came past and I jumped in and managed to hang on, though I had my leg caught between the ship's side and the boat.
>
> I struggled to get the boat clear of the ship in heavy seas. Two men were holding on to the side of the boat by me and I tried to get them into the boat but their clothing was so heavy and the boat was so crowded that three of us were unable to haul them over the side. We held on to them as long as there was any use to hold on to them.
>
> Ensign Neely jumped over the side. The third mate and the third engineer reached for him and grabbed him but he was unconscious and couldn't help himself. They lost him.

Soon after this, the ship broke in two just forward of the bridge; the stern section sank in a few minutes, the forward half floated free.

Carter's lifeboat was so crowded there was only a few inches of freeboard—too crowded even to row. The third mate put out a sea anchor and organized a bailing squad that kept the half-swamped craft afloat until the wind and seas began to abate.

The men bailed all night, although several of them were nearly inert, apparently from shock. They signalled with flashlights, and after about ten hours they were picked up by the British destroyer *Impulsive*. Twenty-seven men were rescued from this lifeboat. Both of the boats that had been carried away from the ship prematurely were also picked up, with their eight occupants. The captain's boat was never found.

The *J. L. M. Curry*, which sailed from Russia with the *Richard Bland*, got caught in the same gale, on 6 March, and as she smashed into a heavy head sea there was a report like gunfire: the hull had cracked. An inspection showed ominous looking fissures in the deck forward and aft of number three hatch and at the after end of number four hatch. Captain Johnson decided to keep going but asked the convoy commodore to assign an escort to stand by.

Their situation was dismal at best. "Thick snow squalls. Heavy westerly sea," said the log. "Ship rolling and plunging." Shortly after midnight there was a new break on the starboard side of the afterdeck. The forward deck was opening up all the time, and the sea condition was becoming more serious.

Captain Johnson still hoped to get the ship to Reykjavik, but in order not to risk the lives of all on board, he decided to send away all but a skeleton crew and so signalled to the *St. Elstan*, a small British escort ship.

The next morning a new split ran through the starboard deep tank at the bottom of number three hold. By 0830 the *Curry* was "working very badly in all breaks."

The rest of the story was in the log of HMS *St. Elstan*, which picked up the narrative of events from the log of the sinking freighter.

> 0830 a.m. *J.L.M. Curry* prepared to abandon ship.
> 0915. First boat away. Picked up boat's company and proceeded to screen *J.L.M.C.*
> 1000. Two more boats picked up.
> 1100. Motor boat making three trips with remaining crew. Last boat alongside at 1112 with master on board.

> 1115. Opened fire on *J.L.M.C.* with four inch, using S.A.P. and H.E.
> Three shells in engine room on starboard side. Holes below water line.
> Spurted oil from fuel tanks. Three shells in number two hold; under
> forward gun and under master's accommodations, setting fire to latter.
> 1204. Opened fire on port side of *J.L.M.C.*, setting fire to bridge and
> midships accommodations. Ceased firing after dropping depth charges
> from starboard thrower to a position on port side amidships Ship last
> seen listing 30 degrees to starboard and sinking.

If Johnson had not decided to abandon ship when he did, it would have been too late, for in another twelve hours the storm had grown to a full gale, with violent snow squalls and high swells, conditions that might have made it impossible to get lifeboats away from the sinking ship.

Soon after the *St. Elstan* had picked up the *Curry*'s crew, the American freighter *Puerto Rican*, in the same convoy, sent an SOS. She had been torpedoed and was sinking fast. The *St. Elstan* was ordered to search for her, and passed through an extensive oil patch; found an empty and waterlogged lifeboat, but no survivors. It was learned later that the *Puerto Rican* had straggled from the convoy during the storm and was 25 miles astern when she was torpedoed. Only one boat could be lowered because the davits and ropes were coated with ice, but it could not be released from the falls and capsized, throwing its occupants into the sea. Eight men swam to a small raft, which was found by the *St. Elstan* two days later. By then, only one man was alive.

When the ship was hit, he had taken time to don one of the neck-to-toe rubber survival suits with which American ships on the Russian run were equipped. The suit saved his life, but his feet were frozen and had to be amputated in a hospital in Iceland.

While searching for survivors of the *Puerto Rican*, the *St. Elstan* took time to shepherd the Liberty ship *J. H. B. Latrobe,* straggling from the convoy with steering-engine trouble and a damaged propeller. That made a second close call for the *Latrobe*; running alone from Iceland toward Murmansk on 5 November 1942, she had been attacked by eight German torpedo planes. All eight torpedoes missed, because, perhaps, of a stream of fire from the Liberty's guns. After the planes left, the officers decided that, since their position was known, there would be another and probably heavier attack and that it would be folly to go on. The *Latrobe* returned to Reykjavik to await a convoy, a decision that saved some

7,000 tons of trucks, planes, heavy machinery, food, and guns worth many millions of dollars.

Another ship nearly done in by weather on the Russian run was the *James Bowie*, whose crew learned what it meant to fight for survival against the fury of the sea. The ship left Loch Ewe on 15 February 1943 in a convoy bound for Murmansk but had to change course four days later when "mountainous seas and strong winds" loosened the lifeboats and shifted the deck cargo.

Four days later there was "a loud jarring report" and the engine room reported an 18-inch-wide crack in the hull. Water was pouring into the engine spaces. All bilge pumps were cut in to handle the flood.

An inspection showed that the break extended from the main deck through the store room above the engine spaces and down into the engine room. According to the voyage report they were from then on their own:

> Convoy out of sight. Master ordered all ships personnel out on deck at lifeboat stations with lifejackets on. Deck department rigged heavy wire cables drawn taught with turnbuckles and winches to hold the break. Cable was drawn from bitt at number three hatch to bitt at number four hatch. We proceeded with all possible speed to Loch Ewe for temporary repairs.

A piece of steel was welded over the split and the *James Bowie* later went to Newcastle-on-Tyne for a complete repair job.

□

The German battleship *Scharnhorst*, which had lurked in Norwegian fjords for years threatening convoys, was finally lured to her destruction off the north coast of Norway in December of 1943. The bait was the 19-ship convoy JW55B, including *Will Rogers* and eight other Libertys, bound from Loch Ewe, Scotland, to Murmansk and heavily protected by cruisers, destroyers, and the *Duke of York*. This mighty battleship was screening both northbound convoy JW55B and southbound convoy RA55A, one or both of which, in the opinion of the Admiralty, would be spotted by German submarine or air reconnaissance and would be too tempting, under conditions of the winter Arctic darkness, for the Germans to resist.

Unaware of the presence of *Duke of York* and eager to smash convoy JW55B, the Germans dispatched the *Scharnhorst* from Altenfjord on Christmas Day.

U-boats and bombers shadowed the convoy in advance of the sortie but did no damage. The log of the *Will Rogers* for 23 December noted: "General quarters. All men to battle stations. Two enemy aircraft approaching on the port quarter. Escort vessels sent up effective barrage, driving planes off."

On 26 December, the British cruiser *Belfast* made radar contact on the *Scharnhorst* and alerted the *Duke of York*, still 125 miles away. The *Belfast*, *Sheffield*, and *Norfolk* and escorting destroyers stayed between the raider and the convoy, hoping *Duke of York* would close the gap before the *Scharnhorst*'s destroyer scouts sighted the merchantmen. The British cruiser fired on the *Scharnhorst* briefly, but the Germans, for some unknown reason, did not return the fire, and the cruisers were undamaged.

The *Duke of York*, making top speed in heavy seas, was headed on an intercept course for the *Scharnhorst*, although neither ship was aware of the fact at the time.

On the evening of 26 December, the *Duke of York* made radar contact on the *Scharnhorst*, returning to Norway after failure to find the convoy. Her protecting German destroyer had already gone home. Soon after this *Scharnhorst* was illuminated by a parachute flare from the *Duke of York* and the battle began.

For once Liberty ships were not in the fight, but some of them saw it. Ensign John W. Broderick, armed guard officer on the *Will Rogers*, watched from a distance, and saw gunfire and parachute flares on the port beam. He knew that he was seeing a surface battle between the escorts and enemy warships.

Aboard *Will Rogers* and the other merchantmen, sailors watched the distant flashes of the guns, hoping the enemy ships would not break through and run rampant through the "sitting ducks." For two hours the orange-red streaks of flame lit the sky, while the freighters rolled and plunged onward toward Murmansk and the *Scharnhorst* tried to evade the 14-inch shells of *Duke of York*. After 77 rounds had been fired, British Admiral Fraser ordered the battleship to cease fire and sent the cruisers *Belfast* and *Jamaica* and four destroyers in to finish off the crippled *Scharnhorst* with torpedoes. Only 36 men of her crew of 1,940 were picked up by the British. Not one of her officers survived.

☐

Although the *Scharnhorst* was gone, there was no pause in German attempts to break up the Murmansk convoys. A submarine put two torpedoes into the *Penelope Barker* enroute from Iceland to Murmansk with convoy JW56A on 25 January 1944. The second explosion blew the 20-millimeter guns out of the tubs, knocked down the stack, blew two lifeboats overboard, and partially destroyed the bridge. The ship was loaded with tanks, locomotives, and flat cars, and went down in ten minutes. Survivors were picked up by HMS *Savage*. Eleven men were killed.

The British Liberty *Samsuva*, in convoy RA60 from Archangel to Scotland on 29 September 1944, swerved to avoid hitting the *Edward H. Crockett* when she was torpedoed by a German submarine. A minute later the *Samsuva* was also torpedoed, and all the black gang on watch were killed. The ship was then sunk by the HMS *Corsica*. Survivors were taken aboard the *Rathlin* which, with the *Zamalek*, rescued hundreds of men from torpedoed ships in the North Atlantic and Arctic. The *Crockett*'s crew, except for one man killed in the engine room, were also picked up by the *Zamalek*; the ship was sunk by friendly gunfire.

Planes and submarines haunted the convoys almost to the last days of German participation in the war. The *Horace Gray*, carrying 7,500 tons of potash, was torpedoed on 14 February 1945 at the entrance to Kola Inlet. She was beached at Tyuva Bay, a total loss, but with no casualties. The *Thomas Scott* was torpedoed shortly after leaving Kola Inlet en route to Scotland in convoy RA64. The 40 Norwegian refugees on board, together with the merchant crew and armed guard, were picked up by a British destroyer and were landed at Vianga, Russia. A Russian destroyer attempted to tow the ship but it broke up and sank.

A Russian salvage tug was successful in saving the *Horace Bushnell* after she was torpedoed near the White Sea on 20 March 1945, in convoy JW65. The engine room was demolished by the explosion, and five men were killed. The *Bushnell* looked more like a submarine than a ship by the time the tug beached her at Tereberski, and she probably did not sail again, although there was one report the Russians had salvaged and repaired her.

In the same convoy the *Thomas Donaldson*, carrying ammunition and locomotives, was torpedoed with the loss of four men. Escorts took her in tow, but she sank a few hours later.

□

The story of the Russian run had a fitting finale in the last voyage of the *Henry Bacon*, which left the White Sea in February of 1945 in the 34-ship convoy RA64. On board were 35 Norwegian refugees—men, women and children—who had fled to Russia during the Nazi invasion and were being sent to England.

The convoy cleared North Cape and started down the Norwegian coast. On 18 February a violent storm with 60-mile winds whipped up turbulent seas and completely scattered the ships. By the time the escorts had rounded up the strays, several freighters had been torpedoed by U-boats. The British escort sloop *Bluebell* was sunk by *U711*, with only one survivor.

Four days later another storm scattered the fleet again. Some ships hove to, while others ran before tremendous seas that rolled a British escort carrier 45 degrees and nearly sent her aircraft over the side.

Again the escorts rounded up all the strays except the *Henry Bacon,* which had lagged some 50 miles behind because of trouble with the steering engine. It took the engineers several hours to make repairs, and by the time the ship resumed her course she was a tempting target for planes or U-boats. Captain Alfred Carini back-tracked up the course for an hour hoping to find the other ships, but with no luck. By that time he had not slept for 45 hours and kept awake by pacing the bridge and drinking black coffee.

At 1415 on the afternoon of 25 February, the lookout in the crow's nest reported: "Airplanes. Sounds like a lot of them."

Even against the whine of the wind, Carini could hear them and sounded the general alarm. Men tumbled out of bunks and grabbed helmets, lifejackets, and extra clothing for protection against the wintry blasts of wind on the open deck. The steward mustered his cooks and messmen to break out bandages, splints, and anesthetics, covering the wardroom tables with blankets in preparation for battle casualties. Below decks, all the black gang could do was listen— and wait.

Gunners jerked the canvas covers off the guns none too soon. Big, black Junkers 88s broke out of the overcast, flying 30 feet above the wave tops. There was no need for the Armed Guard officer on the bridge to give the order to fire. Every gun that could bear went into instant action.

Carini counted 23 planes. Twenty-three bombers against one ship. Heavy odds for even a cruiser or a battleship. Aircraft carriers had been sunk by fewer planes than this. There was no nearby ship the *Henry Bacon* could call for help.

A bomber dropped a torpedo 500 yards away on the port quarter, and Carini yelled, "Hard a port!" The helmsman spun the wheel hard over and the torpedo just missed.

Another plane started a torpedo run several hundred yards off the bow and the 3-inch gun blew it to bits. Pieces of flaming aircraft fell into the sea just off the bow.

Another plane flew into a wall of 20-millimeter shells which sliced it in two and sent the pilot's compartment cartwheeling into the sea.

So many planes had only to persist to be successful against one ship. A torpedo finally hit the *Henry Bacon* in number three hold on the starboard side, forward. The vessel shuddered as a 50-foot column of water shot up above the bulwarks. The spray was still falling along the deck when the second torpedo hit. Carini ordered abandon ship. If he waited any longer, a third torpedo might send the vessel down without a chance to launch the boats.

"Refugees first," he called to the mate. "Get the passengers on the boat deck as fast as you can. Tell them to bring lots of clothes."

The German bombers, seeing that their target was doomed, broke off the attack and withdrew, with one skimming the wave tops as black smoke poured from an engine.

The *Bacon* carried four lifeboats, plus a number of rafts, but men on a raft would have little chance of survival in winter seas. Carini maneuvered the ship to provide a lee for lowering the boats. They would be lucky to get even two boats safely into the water.

The first boat lowered away successfully and pushed off. When the second boat was safely overside, Third Mate Joseph Scott counted the passengers. "I can take six," he shouted. "Six more . . . and hurry." Several merchant crewmen and Navy gunners climbed down into the boat as it rose on the crest of a wave. The ship was settling and waves were breaking over the bulwarks.

Chief Engineer Donald Haviland looked up at a young Navy gunner on deck. The boy couldn't have been more than 17 years old. "Put me alongside," he said to the third mate. "Let that kid have my place. It won't matter so much if I don't get back."

Haviland climbed back to the deck while the sailor scurried down the scramble-nets into the boat, which pulled quickly away. The ship was going down soon, and they didn't want to be sucked under with her. A raft with several men on it bobbed some distance away. The wind and waves were taking the lifeboats away from the ship, and no pullling on the oars would bring them close enough to pick up the men on the raft.

Men in the boats saw Haviland, Boatswain Halcomb Lammon, and several other seamen on the foredeck, probably making a raft out of dunnage. Captain Carini waved from the bridge. The boats drifted off into the mist as the *Henry Bacon*, her ensign snapping proudly at the gaff, settled slowly beneath the sea.

By the time convoy escorts arrived to look for survivors there were only a few boards and crates to mark where the *Henry Bacon* and 22 of her men went down.

Said the Maritime Commission: "It was a splendid defense by a merchant ship against overwhelming odds and of discipline of the highest order amongst the ship's company." The men of the *Henry Bacon* had added a gallant chapter to the history of the American merchant marine.

But the heroic deeds of ships and men that braved the hazards of the convoy routes to carry aid to Russia in World War II were soon forgotten in Murmansk. Twenty-five years later, there is not a single testimonial there to the Allied merchant seamen and their naval comrades who died to keep supplies flowing to the Russian front. The Murmansk museum contains many relics of World War II, but no remembrance whatsoever of the wartime convoys or of the 97 ships and countless men lost in making the hazardous Murmansk Run.

A black funeral pyre of burning fuel oil marks the end of another merchant ship, hunted down by a German U-boat in the 68-month long Battle of the Atlantic. This was the *Byron D. Benson*, sunk off the Chesapeake Capes on 8' April 1942, one of 23 ships torpedoed that month.

6

THE
BATTLE
OF THE
ATLANTIC

The Battle of the Atlantic was the longest and most bitterly fought battle of World War II. It started on 3 September 1939, when a German submarine torpedoed the British liner *Athenia* less than 12 hours after the outbreak of hostilities between England and Germany; and it ended on 5 May 1945 when Grand Admiral Carl Doenitz sent a signal ordering all U-boats to cease combat operations and return to Germany. For Britain the message ended 68 months of unremitting warfare on the North and South Atlantic sea-lanes.

With England a besieged island completely dependent on ships for all imports of food, oil, and U. S. aid, it was apparent that the Atlantic was to be the battleground on which the war could be won or lost. Doenitz declared in 1940 that "the U-boat alone can win the war." His prophecy came close to fulfillment. Mass production of American Liberty ships, plus the development of antisubmarine weapons and tactics such as hedgehogs, hunter-killer groups, and radar, which the Admiral had not foreseen, were the factors that decided this sea war in favor of the Allies. But for many months in 1942 and 1943 it was "touch and go." The disasterous month of May, 1942, marked the peak of Germany's war on Allied shipping when U-boats sank 125 ships of 600,000 gross tons in all areas of the Atlantic.

"The Battle of the Atlantic," according to British Prime Minister Winston Churchill, "was the dominating factor all through the war. Never for one moment could we forget that everything happening elsewhere, on land, sea, or in the air, depended ultimately on its outcome, and amid all other cares we viewed its changing fortunes day by day with hope or apprehension."

In his book, *Grand Alliance*, Churchill wrote that American presidential adviser Harry Hopkins, in summing up the feeling of American war leaders, predicted that the Battle of the Atlantic would be the "final decisive battle of the war." It was the only battle in World War II, except for a brief foray by Japanese submarines against the West Coast, that brought the fighting to U. S. shores.

□

The initial U-boat onslaught in American waters was made by the *U66*, *U130*, *U106*, *U103*, and *U123*. Lieutenant Hardegen's *U123*, which had already sunk more than 100,000 tons of shipping before joining other subs for the American incursion, opened the offensive by sinking the British freighter *Cyclops* on 11 January 1942, about 160 miles south of Nova Scotia, with a loss of 87 men. The battle off the Atlantic Coast began 14 January when *U123* torpedoed the Norwegian tanker *Norness* 60 miles southwest of Montauk Point, Long Island. She next sank the British SS *Coimbra*. The tanker *Gulftrade* was sent down just 20 miles off Southampton, Long Island. The *U123* also sank the freighter *City of Atlanta* and tanker *Allan Jackson* off Cape Hatteras with large loss of life.

In ten days these five submarines torpedoed 25 ships of 200,000 tons between Long Island and Cape Hatteras while meager sea and air defensive forces scouted the coast in a vain hunt for the enemy. Such unpreparedness would have been laughable were it not costing so much in ships, lives, and cargoes. The U-boats soon grew so daring that people on shore could see the smoke and flame of burning ships. Oil and flotsam from U-boat victims littered Atlantic beaches from New Jersey to Key West.

One of the first Liberty ships sunk by a U-boat was the *Thomas McKeen*, sailing, unaccompanied, from New York to the Persian Gulf, loaded with planes, tanks, machinery, and ammunition. She was torpedoed some 1,200 miles east of

Jacksonville, Florida, on 29 June 1942. The torpedo merely set her on fire, so the U-boat surfaced and put 57 shells into the vessel before she finally sank. Five men were killed. The survivors abandoned ship in three boats, all of which arrived safely at various Caribbean ports.

A good many ships went down in the battle of the Atlantic before the last Liberty was sunk. That was the *Cyrus H. McCormick*, torpedoed at noon on 18 April 1945, 68 miles off the coast of France. The *McCormick*, carrying 8,400 tons of locomotives, cranes, trucks, and other heavy equipment, sank in a few minutes with a loss of four merchant crewmen and two Armed Guard sailors.

Within a few weeks, after German submarines began operations on the U. S. East Coast, they moved into the Gulf of Mexico and the Caribbean, where crowded shipping lanes made for good hunting. Before the war ended, the count of American merchant ships sunk in the wide-ranging battle of the Atlantic reached 141 in the North Atlantic, 78 along the American coasts, and 27 off the Normandy beachhead. An additional 122 were lost in the Caribbean area. The submarine war ended nearly three years later when the last American victim, the Boston collier *Black Point*, was sunk by *U853* on 5 May 1945, just a few miles off Newport, Rhode Island. The collier lost a number of crewmen; the *U853* was hunted down and depth-charged by a large fleet of vessels and sank with the loss of her entire crew. The action was quite a contrast to the time in 1942 when coastwise colliers were torpedoed and there was no attempt made to find or sink the enemy.

Unlike other battles of World War II where opposing naval forces slugged it out with heavy guns, aircraft, and bombs in definite short, furious engagements, the Battle of the Atlantic was a never-ending series of minor skirmishes between hunter and hunted. And all too often, the victim never knew she was being hunted until it was too late.

The *Alexander Macomb* was on her way from New York to join a trans-Atlantic convoy at Halifax when a submarine sent her down the morning of 3 July 1942, with a cargo of tanks, planes, plane engines, and ammunition destined for the Russian front. Ten men were lost.

Despite an escort of two Free French frigates, the *George Thacher* was sunk by a U-boat on 1 November while en route from Charleston, South Carolina, to Freetown and Takoradi, West Africa. She carried a load of trucks, ambulances, road-building equipment, and gasoline in drums. Two torpedoes hit forward and aft, exploding the gasoline and setting the ship ablaze. Casualties included the captain, first mate, and the Armed Guard officer, plus 18 gunners, merchant crew men, and Army passengers.

Such heavily loaded ships went down fast. The *Julia Ward Howe*, headed for North Africa with a high priority cargo of 60 medium tanks, straggled from convoy UGS4 on 27 January 1943, southwest of the Azores. A U-boat fired two torpedoes at her, missed with one but broke her in two with the other, and in five minutes the ship was gone, taking her captain and chief engineer with her. The submarine surfaced, questioned survivors in the two lifeboats and gave them a course to steer to the Azores. The U-boat's crew were in high spirits and the executive officer, in good English, told them they were the thirtieth ship this raider had sunk. The two lifeboats were picked up by the Portuguese destroyer *Lima* and taken to Ponta Delgada in the Azores.

At Ponta Delgada the second mate, who had been taken aboard the submarine for questioning, saw a familiar face on the street. It was, he later swore to American authorities, the U-boat skipper, in the uniform of a Portuguese Army officer.

The *Jeremiah van Renssalaer* was hit by three torpedoes and set afire early in the morning of 2 February 1943, en route from New York to England in convoy HX224. Two boats capsized on launching, and 46 out of the merchant crew and armed guard contingent of 70 men were lost. The *Renssalaer* burned and had to be sunk by gunfire from a convoy escort.

The convoy rescue ship *Accrington*, seeing distress signals astern of the convoy, raced back and found the *van Renssalaer* ablaze. In strong wind and heavy seas, the little British ship, with Captain A. W. R. M. Greenham in command, searched and found a lifeboat and two life rafts carrying the 24 survivors. Too exhausted and cold to grab lines thrown to them, these men owed their rescue to Captain Greenham's expert seamanship and the bravery of Able Seamen McIntyre and Thomson, who went overboard and secured lines to the survivors so they could be hoisted aboard.

□

March, 1943, was one of the worst months of the war with 120 merchant ships being sunk in the Atlantic, mostly by U-boats. Of this total 82 went down in the North Atlantic—a loss of 470,000 tons of shipping, a vast amount of food and war material, and hundreds of merchant seamen.

One of the March casualties was the *Wade Hampton*, which had dropped behind convoy HX227 in heavy weather when a U-boat torpedo blew off her stern. Most of the survivors were picked up by HMS *Vervain*, but Able Seaman Rexford Dickey and Boatswain John Sandova were not seen in the darkness and drifted off in the night on board a small raft. Sandova died of exposure but Dickey, water-soaked and half-frozen by wind and spray, was determined to live. He kept moving his arms and legs while he clung to the tumbling craft, rubbing his feet when they became numb, talking, singing, and shouting to keep himself awake when he felt the pleasant drowsiness that presages death from the cold. His determination to live was rewarded three days later when HMS *Beverly*, the former American four-stack destroyer *Branch*, spotted what looked like a U-boat conning tower and was ready to open fire on it when it was identified as a raft. Dickey soon was picked up, wrapped in warm blankets, and given a shot of hot rum. Sandova was buried at sea.

The *Meriwether Lewis*, carrying ammunition and automobile tires, disappeared from the same convoy four days after the *Wade Hampton* was hit. "Torpedoed and presumed sunk at 62 degrees ten minutes north, 28 degrees, 25 minutes west," said the official report. A convoy escort searched for two days in an attempt to locate survivors, but found only a 30-mile-long line of floating tires.

Convoy HX228 was bound from New York to Liverpool in March, 1943, when submarines attacked. There ensued a battle within a battle that contained all the elements of exciting sea fiction, considerable general confusion, and a mass panic that was near comedy but ended in tragedy. On the dark, moonless night of 10 March, submarines were about and HMS *Harvester* managed to ram and sink *U444* but was badly damaged in the collision. Next, another submarine put torpedoes into the *William C. Gorgas*, which carried 900 tons of TNT. Amazingly, both torpedoes missed the TNT, but the engine room watch were all killed.

Fifty-one survivors from the *Gorgas* were picked up by the *Harvester*, which was then attacked by the *U432*. Damaged in her battle with the *U444*, the *Harvester* was unable to take evasive action and was torpedoed. She went down so fast that many men were unable to get topside and go overboard. This put the survivors of the *Gorgas* in the unenviable position of having been torpedoed and sunk twice in one evening.

The *U432*, which had been depth-charged by the Free French corvette *Aconit* during her attack on the *Harvester*, then suddenly surfaced. The *Aconit* opened fire at 7,000 yards, ran the submarine down as she dived again, dropped more depth charges, forced her to the surface once more, and then opened fire again and sunk her. Then she rescued the survivors of the *Gorgas* once more. The score for the evening was two German submarines and two merchant ships sunk. Only 12 men from the *Gorgas* survived.

The next day, as waves ran 30 feet high, the *Henry Wynkoop* collided with an unidentified submerged object. The ship rolled far over to starboard and crewmen heard "a rumbling and roaring sound under the keel." Nothing was sighted afterward to account for the collision; it was just possible the ship had unwittingly added another U-boat to the roster of those that never returned from patrol and were listed as "lost from causes unknown."

As the *Wynkoop* slowed down while she was inspected for damage, some of the crew assumed she had been ordered abandoned. Disregarding the fact that there had been no such order from the captain, 33 of them lowered lifeboats in the stormy sea for a precipitous departure that was successful but left the ship drastically short handed. The *Wynkoop* got underway again and recovered eight of her men from one boat but had to go on without the rest. The corvette *K58* picked up 16 but went on about her duties without returning them to the *Wynkoop*. The British steamer *Stuart Prince* rescued five. The corvette *K57* picked up one man who had not waited for the boats but had jumped overboard and was still swimming. Three men lost their lives in the panic.

Astern of convoy HX228 came HX229 and HX122, eastbound on parallel courses and numbering 100 ships between them. In one of the most powerful and determined U-boat wolf-pack attacks of the war, at least 40 submarines harassed the convoys and sank 21 ships, including four Libertys, before they reached the protecting cover of antisubmarine aircraft 600 miles off the English coast.

The *Walter Q. Gresham*, carrying 9,000 tons of powdered milk, sugar, and other supplies, took a torpedo hit in number five hold, which blew off the propeller and left her helplessly out of control. Two lifeboats capsized in heavy seas. An unnamed but courageous Armed Guard sailor swam from the overcrowded raft on which he had taken refuge to an empty raft and helped to transfer ten men to it. This saved 20 who might otherwise have been lost.

The *James Oglethorpe* went down with a load of planes, tractors, and trucks and many of the crew and Armed Guard detachment. About two hours later, a submarine torpedoed the *William Eustis* but did not sink her. It was impossible to attempt a tow while the battle was in progress, so one of the escorts sank the *Eustis* by dropping depth charges close alongside. There were no casualties.

Convoys were often trailed by U-boats looking for "lame ducks,"—ships that had dropped behind because of engine trouble—or for stragglers separated from the brood by fog or stormy weather, a frequent occurrence in the North Atlantic.

The *William Pierce Frye,* a lame duck in convoy HX230 from Halifax to England on 28 March 1943, was hove-to making engine repairs when two torpedoes missed her by a matter of feet. Repairs were hastily concluded and the *Frye* started off at top speed, with the submarine paralleling her course several thousand yards away. Heavy seas were running and this, plus evasive action, enabled the *Frye* to evade the U-boat, but the next night two more torpedoes hit her and set off the cargo of explosives. She sank so quickly there was time to launch only one lifeboat. Some men jumped overboard, climbed into an LCT that was being carried on deck and floated off when the ship sank and were picked up five days later by HMS *Schikuri.* Only seven men out of 64 survived.

The commodore of convoy HX230, on 31 March, radioed to Commander-in-Chief, Western Atlantic: "*W. P. Frye* torpedoed when straggling. Do not intend detaching ships to search unless situation improves. U-boats shadowing all last night in spite of sweeps. Straggler *John Eaton* rejoined." Stragglers and lame ducks had to take their chances; *Eaton* won, *Frye* lost.

On 5 April 1943 the *Joel Roger Poincett* helped to pay back the debt that many an American owed to the little British rescue ships which accompanied the North Atlantic convoys to save torpedoed seamen. The *Poincett* assisted HMS *Loosestrife* in picking up 129 survivors from the British *Waroonga.* The torpedo that sank *Waroonga* hit many hungry Englishmen right in their pantries, for she was carrying 8,360 tons of butter, cheese, and meat.

□

Another chapter in the Battle of the North Atlantic began on 11 April 1943. The brand new Liberty ship *James W. Denver* had straggled from her convoy in a heavy fog, then stopped when overheated engine bearings made it necessary to shut down for repairs.

While the black gang labored with sledges, calipers, and scrapers to repair the bearings and get going again, two torpedoes sent the ship down as though she had been scuttled. In the excitement, one lifeboat overturned and the men were spilled into the sea, but were hauled out again.

Somehow or other, all the deck officers wound up in the same boat, with the result that two of the boats had no one with any knowledge of navigation. To complicate matters, all the boats were soon separated by heavy seas and never sighted one another again, but resourcefulness and determination carried all of them through their ordeal with the loss of only one life.

Deck Engineer Dolar Stone was in a boat carrying 18 engineers, stewards, and Armed Guard gunners, only two of whom knew anything at all about small boat seamanship. Although he knew more about deck winches and ship's gear than he did about small boats, Stone took command as being the man aboard with the most seagoing experience.

Captain Everett W. Staley gave each boat a course to steer toward the nearest land, and a last command: "Hoist sail and let's get going."

"There was some light-hearted joking at first," said Stone, "but all in all it was a solemn leave taking from the *James W. Denver*. We hated to lose our ship and especially to see her go down without ever having fired a shot from all those beautiful new guns."

On the third night out, the bow lookout on Stone's boat sighted a vague shape in the dusk and someone yelled "Destroyer dead ahead!" To attract attention, they switched on their life jacket lights. Almost before they realized what was happening, a submarine appeared directly across their course.

"It was a big one," Stone recalled, "and we were careening right down on to it." The lifeboat grated against the hull and a German officer shouted at them from the conning tower.

"Where are you from?"

"Brooklyn!"

The German laughed. "That's where the baseball comes from," he said in good English.

As *Denver* was stencilled on the lifeboat equipment, they answered up readily enough when the officer asked the name of their ship: "*James Denver*." The German laughed again so the men guessed this was the submarine that had sunk them.

"Well, well," he said. "You are from one of the new Liberty ships." A German sailor handed them a carton of cigarettes. From the bridge, the officer shouted a course for them to steer, and the U-boat moved off into the night on the hunt for more victims.

In another boat, some unidentified man, probably First Mate Andy Del Pro-posto, kept a log of their 23 day ordeal. Such chronicles are rare. This one is well worth reading because it fittingly describes the fortitude and patience of men who waited out their fates for more than three weeks, and won:

April 11: Ship hit at 5 p.m. Second explosion 9:40 p.m. Rough and large, choppy sea. Wind northeasterly all night.

April 12: Lost sea anchor 11 a.m. Rig up new one and put over side 12:05. Mounting sea. Sea anchor out all night. Men living on one cracker, two ounces water.

April 13. 6:00 a.m. Hoist sails. 6:30 a.m. Take sails down. Sea too rough. Put sea anchor out again. Boys feeling fair. Still living on two crackers, four ounces water. Found out had no flares. Cans empty. No chocolate in food containers. Drifting southwesterly. Out 48 hours.

April 14. 5:30 a.m. hoist sail, heading south. Wind NNE. Medium sea and swell. Men living on two crackers, four ounces water. Sun came out for first time today. 9:45 a.m., chop sail. Sea too large. Put out sea anchor. Wind force 6. Lost sea anchor at 6:53 p.m. Had to rig up another from two oars. 9:45 p.m. cleared up a little. Hoisted sail. Head south. Wind during night. All men have wet clothes now four days.

April 15. Day started clear. Sea moderate with westerly winds. Force 3. 7 a.m. set sail heading south by east. North wind. Sun out again and feels good. 11:30 pm. wind died down. Everything calm, put out oars. 3 p.m. wind sprung up from northwest. Force 3. Put up sail and made good time. Raining. Everything wet.

Friday. April 16. Raining. All calm. Try to catch water. No luck. Went to three ounces of water, two crackers and pemmican also one malt milk tablet. 12 noon approximately 600 miles from coast. Try fishing. No luck. Fish all around. Won't bite. Air stirring a little. 5 pm. Breeze freshing to NNE. Making a little time. Sun out. Maybe we'll dry out. Everyone's clothes damp. Getting on everyone's nerves. All snapping at one another. Set regular watches. Five men to watch. 5:30 a.m. Men talking of food and water and what they like to have. Also talking of religion. Rain during night. Try to catch water. No luck.

Saturday. April 17. Eight miles south of yesterday's position. Calm sea. Air stirring slightly. Might have to row. Back to two ounces of water. Havn't seen a thing in six days now. 10 pm started to row. Men got extra two ounces of water. 11 pm wind freshing to northwesterly. Quit rowing. Getting small sea. Up speed. Continued sailing all night on easterly course.

Palm Sunday. Clear NWly breeze. Continued sailing easterly course. Men got four ounces of water but not eating much. 12 N. Still sailing easterly course. Small following sea. Making good time. 3 pm gave men extra two ounces water. Wind change to westerly. Have not see a thing yet. Men feeling pretty good. Doing a little singing. Now and then a man is a little seasick. Have not eaten since in boat. Given extra two ounces of water. First ass't. and lieutenant pretty sick. Given extra water. Deck cadet feet swelling. Can't get in shoes. Clothing starting to dry out a little now, but with night everything wet and cold again. 11 pm continued on easterly course. 4 am rain squalls. Still heading easterly. Wind westerly. Following small sea.

Monday, April 19, Fresh westerly breeze. Force 3. Large following sea. Occasional squalls. Men growling now and then. Sea getting worse. Shipping water. 8 pm Took in sail. Wind change to northerly. Can only make leeway. 12 M. Cold and damp. Full moon. Jib up only makes leeway. Saw few birds today. Men got 4 ounces water. Must have 450 miles to go.

Tuesday, April 20. Bob has birthday. 27 years old today. Gave men six ounces of water. 6 pm moderate northerly sea and swell. Put up main sail. Can't seem to get clothes dry and makes men cold and snappy. Can't get civil answer anymore. 8 pm small northerly Sea and swell heading easterly. Second assistant pretty sick. Made 75 miles today.

Wednesday, April 21. Clear and calm. Wind mod. northerly. Heading southeasterly. Making fair time. App 400 miles to go. 6 pm. Clear, full moon. Occasional rain squalls. Making fair time.

Thursday, April 22. 6 am clear and bright. NW wind and mod. sea. Quite a sharp current southerly. Men singing a little and hoping to be picked up soon. 12 M. Wind NE and mod sea. Cold damp. Overcast.

Friday, April 23. Overcast. Beam sea. Fresh NE breeze. Not making any time. Men pray now before breakfast and after supper. Not a thing sighted as yet. Still have hope. Body starting to ache. Damp clothing. Can't keep them dry.

Saturday, April 24. Overcast and cloudy. Cold NE winds. Heading south. Tide to west. Large, rough, choppy, quarter seas. Shipping sea occasionally. Must bale frequently. Everybody's nerves on edge. Still living on six ounces of water, crackers and pemmican. Now and then men will talk of home and what they would like to be doing or different food and wine. Worst part is you can't lay out straight. Always cramped up. No wonder we ache.

Easter Sunday, April 25. First time and hope it is the last I ever spend Easter in a life boat. Not sure of your position or anything. Day started clear. Put up sail. Wind from east, force 3. Large swell. Shipping water occasionally. Heading south. 12 noon. Men got treat. Half can of pemmican, ten ounces water. Nothing in sight. Still have hope.

Monday, April 26. Heading south. Drift to west. Large mountain sea and swells. 7 am lower sail. Shipping too much water. Drifting to west. 12 N wind much same. Hoist sail, head south again. Can't seem to get any easting at all. Dear God, how we pray for a ship to pick us up or for the sight of land. Men starting to lose hope now. Second assistant talking out of his head regularly now. Cut down on rations. Have enough to last 11 days reduced ration. Cold and damp. Can't seem to get warm, Most of men joints swelling. Rough beam sea all night. Force 3.

Tuesday, April 27. High mountainous beam sea. Wind northeasterly. Force 4. Shipping water. Temperature 72 degrees. Everything damp. 12 N. Cut down on rations again. Can't see anything. Must make food and water last. Try fishing. Nothing bites. Have no bait. Let's hope we see something soon. Men's feet swelling at joints and every word a complaint. Hoping to hit mainland or Cape Verde Islands. Strong westerly winds and sea. Small swell. Making fair time. Heading SE.

Wednesday, April 28. Daybreak clear. Nothing in sight. Hurley thought saw submarine but did not surface. Wind NE. Force 2. Small swell. Heading SE. Must have app. 150 miles to mainland. Taking one box crackers, two cans pemmican, eight ounces water for 11 men now. Making mash. Lets hope what we have left lasts till picked up.

Thursday, April 29. Daybreak clear. Had prayer and breakfast. Small sea. Easterly swell. Wind NE heading SE. Made app. 50 miles yesterday. Men starting to break. Sure wish I was in my ap't, with my wife and baby. Hope I can keep up my courage and stop thinking of home too much. Made fair time last night.

Friday, April 30. Daybreak clear. Plenty of hope left yet. Cut down to one can of pemmican, one box of crackers, eight ounces of water. Expect to see land sometime this week yet. Wind from E. Heading SE, small sea and swell. 12 N Took sight for latitude. Everything looks all right. About 75 miles to go if calculations right. Bound to hit coast this week. Wind change NEly. Second assistant very low. Small sea and swell.

Saturday, May 1. Second assistant passed away during night. Gave burial at sea this morning 7:20 am. Men feel bad. 12 N went in swimming for a bath. Water felt good. Wind force 3. Making good time.

Sunday, May 2. Daybreak cloudy. Wind force 2. Small sea and swell. Force 1, making little headway. 11:25 a.m. sighted plane. Sent out smoke bomb. Think we were seen. Sure felt good after 21 days to see something. Will know within 24 hours whether we were or not. If not, expect to see land tomorrow if calculations right. Wind from E. Making little headway.

Monday, May 3. Daybreak clear and calm. Drift SW. Losing quite a bit of distance covered. Small sea and swell. Sight seven whales at 10:05 am. Close enough we could have hit them with a stone. Sighted raft at noon. Boarded it to look for food and water. No luck. Found some marine growth so ate that. No sign of life yet. Looks like plane did not see us yesterday.

Tuesday May 4 (position 21 degrees 55 minutes north. 17 degrees, ten minutes west). Sighted smoke on horizon, but too far away to signal. Makes one feel low to see help so near yet so far. Daybreak clear. Wind strong NE. Heading SEly. Sighted fishing vessel 10 pm. Sent up flare. They sighted us and picked us up. We were 30 miles from African coast. Fed us and wined us in style. Now heading for Lisbon. Will be there in five days. Treat us like gentlemen. Gave us clothes and washed ours. Fed us again, Gave up their bunks so we may sleep. They keep feeding us everytime we open our eyes. They really are wonderful people. They just can't seem to do enough for us.

Wednesday, May 5. Aboard the *Albufeira*. Daybreak clear. Making ten knots. Had fish for breakfast and soup and wine. Then a nap. Feel like a million. Now supper. Cabbage and beef noodle soup, beef and potatoes. Abeam Canary Islands now. Only three days to Lisbon. Had spot of tea before going to sleep. These men give you their bunks and sleep on deck. Too bad there is nothing we can do in return.

Friday, May 7. Breakfast coffee and sea biscuit. Had bath. Dinner fried fish and potatoes bread and wine. Supper fish chowder and rice, baked fish wine and bread. Tea before retiring. Eat, sleep.

Saturday May 8. 4 pm Casablanca abeam. 8 pm today ends clear.

Sunday, May 9. Passed Cabo de Sae Vicente.

Monday, May 10. Passed pilot boat at mouth of Tagus River and proceeded up river to Lisbon where we disembarked at the pier about 5 am amid many officials, police and a large crowd. After clearance with local officials proceeded at once to the British Hospital.

In the Captain's boat, there was a sextant but no mathematical tables, so he relied on dead reckoning, steering with a compass held between his legs. Several men tried to jump overboard—a phenomenon of human behavior in almost every lifeboat trip of any duration—but were restrained. When food ran out, they wondered if they would live to sight land again or if some passing steamer would eventually find only their mute skeletons.

The captain had a chart and each day's dead reckoning position provided a constant reminder of their progress and was a great morale builder. Sometimes the captain would strike up a song, and most of them would join in. He would dole out the water with: "It's only water now, boys, but keep your spirits up and you'll be drinking champagne one of these days soon."

Finally, on 5 May, the twenty-fifth day after leaving the ship, they made land —the beach at Rio del Oro, West Africa.

They were so weak no one could walk. They crawled up the beach on hands and knees, exulting in just being on dry land, but their joy was considerably mitigated by the discovery that they had landed on a desert—no water, no signs of human life; nothing. After five days of blinding sandstorms and unrelenting bright sun, intensified by the burning sands, they might have died there had it not been for another German submarine.

In a strange paradox of war, a U-boat had been sighted and depth-charged offshore by British planes a few days before and on 10 May a plane hunting for evidence of this marauding German sighted the *Denver*'s lifeboat. Some hours later a patrol vessel, which was also hunting for the U-boat, landed several armed men who thought at first that the *Denver*'s crew might be German survivors. They were soon aboard ship and headed for a hospital, where all of them recovered from their ordeal. Hardy sailors, most of them went back to sea when they returned to the United States.

☐

As Convoy HX332 was making a trans-Atlantic crossing in April of 1943, Seaman John W. Welch of the *James Jackson* saw a submarine surfacing about 5,000 yards astern. Gunners opened fire within seconds. Seven shots from the *Jackson* were short, but the eighth was seen to hit squarely at the base of the conning tower. Other merchant ships, as well as the escorts, were firing by that time, and some of the submarine's crew were seen crawling out of the conning tower and jumping overboard. The gunners of the *James Jackson* claimed credit for the kill—the *U175*—but credit for it was later given to the convoy escort, the Coast Guard cutter *Spencer*.

As convoy ON202 made its way from England to New York in September, 1943, the *Frederick Douglas* was lead ship in the port column. The morning of 20 September, a torpedo exploded in number five hold and the *Douglas* began to settle by the stern.

Seconds later, a torpedo struck the *Theodore Dwight Weld*, exploded the boilers, blew the lifeboats overboard, and broke the ship in two. Survivors jumped overboard; the good swimmers found rafts to cling to. The stern section sank within a few minutes.

The rescue ship *Rathlin*, hurrying up to help, reached the *Douglas* first, but seeing that she was in no immediate danger of sinking, sped on. From the floating bow section of the *Weld*, she rescued 38 men, choking and half-blinded by fuel oil from ruptured tanks.

Next the *Rathlin* picked up all hands from the *Douglas*, which carried a part Negro crew and—unknown until then—a Negro woman stowaway. Then she went back to check the bow section of the *Weld* to determine whether a destroyer escort should be called up to sink it with gunfire. There one more man was seen waving from the hulk; *Rathlin* launched a boat and picked him up.

Tobacco, fertilizer, and a deckload of P47 fighter planes nearly went down when the *James Nesmith* was torpedoed on 7 April, almost within sight of the British Isles. She was towed to Holyhead, beached, refloated, then towed to Liverpool, unloaded, and finally repaired.

Fortunately, not all Atlantic convoys were harassed by U-boats. Many a lucky crew never saw a submarine or a torpedo or witnessed the awesome sight of a ship sinking beneath the waves. As a result, most log entries were uneventful watch-by-watch and day-by-day accounts of courses run, speed, wind, weather, and fuel consumed, such as a 12-to-4 deck-log entry for the *Cyrus W. McCormick*, bound from Charleston, South Carolina, to Belfast in June 1943: "Observing convoy regulations. Watch uneventful. Weather fine and clear."

But crews never knew when an "uneventful" watch might suddenly be shattered by the call to battle stations. The next day the *McCormick*'s log read: "June 30. 2:50 p.m. Sounded general alarm. Sighted what appeared to be a periscope forward of the port beam. Guns fired at the object, which disappeared."

□

The thrills and uncertainties of convoy life when U-boats were on the prowl were tersely reported by Lieutenant (junior grade) Earl G. Hardt, Armed Guard commander on the *John Jay*, which sailed in USG6. As usual, stragglers were picked off by submarines.

> March 4. Two ships in convoy collided and returned to port. Two depth charges dropped by destroyer on forward port side of convoy. General alarm sounded. Destroyer on port side of convoy firing machine guns.

March 6. Sighted life raft on port beam. Notified destroyer.

March 7. Two 45 degree turns to port. Submarine alert. Two white rockets fired from ship on starboard side of convoy. Sounded general alarm.

March 12. 1600 hours. S.S. *Keystone* dropped out of convoy.

2117 hours. Bright white light on port side of convoy. Two 45 degree turns to starboard. Two rounds fired from large gun from ship on starboard side of convoy. Three depth charges dropped. More gun fire. Two emergency turns to port.

2118 hours. General alarm sounded.

2315 hours. About 15 depth charges dropped in 15 minutes.

March 13. Received message, S.S. *Keystone* torpedoed.

March 15. 0300 hours. Eight flashes of gunfire on starboard quarter. Red glow appeared on horizon.

0330. Depth charges dropped ahead of convoy. Alarm sounded.

1854. S.S. *Wyoming* hit by torpedo. then by second torpedo, both from starboard side.

1907 hours. *Wyoming* sunk.

March 16. 1900 hours. Ship torpedoed on starboard side of convoy. Sounded general alarm. Heavy gun fire began on starboard side of convoy. Ship in vicinity of number thirty three position fired large aft gun at object which broke water on its port quarter. Following each shot, black oil substance splashed about five feet out of water. Probable hits. Range 1500 yards.

1920 hours. Twenty millimeter gun number three on *John Jay* fired thirty rounds at object breaking water on starboard beam.

1934 hours. Three inch fifty gun opened fire on object trying to surface one point on port bow. Range 700 yards. Eight rounds expended. Destroyer pulled into convoy on starboard quarter of *John Jay* and then made sharp turn to port and dropped two depth charges on starboard bow at 100 yards.

1937 hours. Conning tower (identified as object at least six feet in diameter) broke water three points forward of port beam at 200 yards. Three fifty opened fire immediately. All 20 millimeters on port side also fired at surfacing object.

1945 hours. Port side 20 mm. jammed during firing. Francis Spencer, Gunner's mate third class, had three fingers on left hand cut off trying to clear the jammed gun.

March 17. 1829 hours. Aircraft dropped flares two points forward of port beam indicating submarine.

1932 hours. Paul Kirsh, S1c, spotted torpedo wake. Reported torpedo one point forward of port beam and fired. Sixteen rounds expended. Gun number four fired twenty rounds at same object. Captain and first mate gave orders "hard right" and blew two series of six short blasts on whistle.

1934. Torpedo crossed ahead of bow of *John Jay.*

1935. Ship in center of convoy hit by torpedo.

2020. Number six gun fired at object on port beam at 200 yards. Porpoise hit."

March 18. 2008 hours. Periscope sighted two points abaft port beam, traveling 90 degrees true, same course as convoy. Port side 20-millimeters opened fire immediately. Convoy made 45 degree emergency turn to starboard.

☐

The danger was not always from submarines. A ship on the Grand Banks of Newfoundland logged: "Dense fog. Sounding whistle signals. 7:12 p.m. Sighted large iceberg abeam, port side." And one on a North Atlantic passage noted: "Wind from Northwest, increasing. Ship rolling heavily. Taking spray fore and aft. Called out the watch to secure lifeboats."

Rough seas could be expected at any time in the unpredictable North Atlantic. The *Richard Henry Lee* met heavy weather on a springtime crossing in April, 1942, and labored so heavily that the forward cargo booms went adrift. All hands were called out, and the booms were finally secured after several hours of extremely hazardous work on the forward deck, which was being swept by boarding waves.

At 10:30 a.m. that day the ship ahead of the *Lee* signalled "man overboard" —the shortest description of a tragedy at sea that can be written. With mountainous seas running, there was little chance of rescue for anyone under those conditions.

Although submarine activity in the Atlantic reached a peak in late 1942 and the first half of 1943, U-boats were a menace to a lesser extent up to the end of the war. The *Martin Van Buren* was en route from Boston to Halifax on 14 January 1945, when a U-boat put a torpedo into the ship just ahead, the *British Freedom*. Fifteen minutes later, the *Van Buren* was hit by a torpedo that blew off the rudder, flooded the shaft alley, and knocked the stern gun into the sea.

Three Armed Guard gunners, blown off the after gun platform, were lost. Unable to maneuver, the helpless vessel was abandoned.

When the submarine did not follow up this attack, the crew tried to reboard the ship but were prevented by rough seas. The ship drifted ashore on Lobster Claw Ledge near Sambro Lightship, Halifax, and became a total loss. If a skeleton crew had remained on board, the *Van Buren* could have been towed to port and her cargo of food, trucks, and locomotives saved.

The wreck was a bonanza for fishermen and anyone else who could beg or borrow a boat big enough to get to Lobster Claw Ledge. None of the local citizens had any use for a locomotive, but they helped themselves to the 350,000 cases of canned food, dehydrated potatoes, cigarettes, and truck tires. Before representatives of the U. S. War Shipping Administration took charge of the hulk and its load, a goodly portion of the $3 million cargo had disappeared.

A crew of calm, cool sailors were aboard the *Ruben Dario* in convoy HX332, out of New York for the Mersey, when she was torpedoed on 27 January 1945. Although two holds were flooded and the vessel was far down by the bow and could make only 8 knots, the crew stayed on board and took her into Liverpool with her 8,000 tons of grain and gliders. Why gliders were still being shipped to Europe long after all invasions were past is one of those unexplained mysteries of wartime cargo movements.

☐

Submarine attacks and storms made life hazardous for sailors, but sometimes sailors themselves managed to create havoc. Wartime operations being what they were, some of the most spectacular catastrophies of the North Atlantic were the result of ships in a convoy colliding with each other. The *J. Pinckney Henderson* was making her maiden voyage from the East Coast to England in August of 1943. Six hundred miles east of Halifax, late at night and in dense fog, she collided with the American tanker *J. H. Senior*, which was carrying high-octane aviation gasoline and a deckload of aircraft and plane parts. The *Henderson* had a highly inflammable load of 10,000 tons of cotton, magnesium, magnesite, glycerine, resin, wax, oil, and other combustibles. Deliberate planning could not have brought together two more dangerous cargoes. Only nine men on both vessels survived the explosion and fire that followed.

The night of horror was described by Messman Karl O. Ruud of the *Senior* in

Ships of the Esso Fleet in World War II, an official history of the wartime
tankers operated by the Standard Oil Company of New Jersey.

> Sometime after 10 p.m., I was in the messroom playing cards with
> Messman Eskild Lundsgaard, Able Seaman Sixten Johansson and
> Junior Engineer Levi Eliassen. I felt a terrific jar. Someone said the
> ship was on fire, so I ran to my room, grabbed a life jacket and went
> up on the poop deck ... the galley and messroom were ablaze ... I
> forced myself through the fire and jumped overboard on the port side,
> aft.
> The flames were like a torch and burning oil had spread on the
> water to 100 feet or so from the vessel's side. I swam underwater away
> from the flames, coming to the surface only to breathe. I was severely
> burned about the face and hands, but I continued swimming around
> in the water. Then I ran into Junior Engineer Frank Freundlich, who
> was badly burned, and we stayed together. Second Engineer Harry
> Sondergaard finally drifted along on a small life raft and picked us up.
> Later, one of the lifeboats passed by with Navy gunner Walter A.
> Gawlick, Slc, and Fireman Sture Wihlborg. I jumped from the raft and
> they pulled me in.

The other lifeboats were destroyed in the flaming oil when the fire burned the
the falls, and they dropped into the water. Gawlik and Wihlborg had pulled themselves into a burning boat and, with Ruud's help, managed to put out the flames
before the fire reached cans of gasoline stored for use in the outboard motor that
it carried.

After an hour or so, the men were picked up and taken to St. Johns, Newfoundland. Five men survived from the *Senior*, four from the *Henderson*. Despite
the raging fire, neither ship sank. The *Senior* was towed to St. Johns and the
Henderson to Halifax, where she burned for several weeks. Marine surveyors
who inspected the ship said it was the most completely gutted hulk they had ever
seen.

Collisions were by no means uncommon; it is surprising that there were not
more of them, especially in nighttime maneuvers in convoy when course changes
had to be made on whistle signals. The fires and explosions that sometimes followed made such collisions spectacular, yet despite such dangers many ships
survived midocean crashes. Two such fortunates were the coal-laden *Howard
Gibson* and the British tanker *George W. McKnight*, which collided near the

Azores in October of 1944. The tanker's cargo ignited and swept both ships with searing flame. The *Gibson*'s crew abandoned ship. The USS *Holton*, a destroyer escort, put fire fighters aboard the ship despite the intense heat and smoke and exploding ammunition, and the fire was brought under control in an all-night battle.

According to a Navy report the *Gibson*'s forward section "looked like a Swiss cheese from the effect of exploding shells." After the fires were put out, the *Gibson*'s crew reboarded their vessel, sailed her to Casablanca, discharged cargo, and returned her to the United States. But there it was found that repairs were impractical, and she was sold for scrap.

With the *Gibson*'s fire under control, the fire fighters from the *Holton* and the *Ahrens*, another destroyer escort, next headed for the *McKnight*, which was blazing fiercely several miles away. Volunteers clad in asbestos suits and armed with foam extinguishers boarded the ship by a dangerous climb up lifeboat falls that were hanging over the side and swaying with each roll. They poured foam onto the flames through the tank hatches and extinguished the fire. The *McKnight*, too, was able to make port.

Some collisions might be caused by inexperienced crews and new ships, but they happened to even the biggest and most experienced ships at times. The giant British liner *Queen Mary*, veteran of numerous Atlantic crossings, and the Royal Navy's antiaircraft cruiser, HMS *Curacoa*, collided on 2 October 1942 in the eastern Atlantic.

The "*Mary*," making 30 knots with 15,000 American troops on board, sliced through the *Curacoa*, which sank in five minutes with a loss of 313 men.

□

Shipwreck was always a possibility in the Atlantic. The wreck of the *William Welch* was as harrowing as anything in fiction. The ship had delivered her cargo to the British Isles in 1944 and was on her way to join a homeward convoy when she ran into a howling blizzard off the bleak northern coast of Scotland where the retreating Spanish Armada had been wrecked hundreds of years before. Wind and seas put her on the rough and rocky shore. Huge waves smashed against the ship flooding the deck with cold, green water that swept everything before it. Boats and life rafts were carried away. They probably would have been useless anyway in that cauldron of breaking seas. The crew were forced to the flying bridge. It was impossible for British rescue vessels to reach them.

Then the pilot house was smashed, and all hands were washed off the ship. Men drowned or were flung to their death by powerful seas that broke against the cliffs in a terrifying fury. Hardy Scot farmers risked their lives to climb down rocky cliffs to the boiling surf and recover bodies. Those men found still alive were warmed by driftwood fires, then carried to their homes to be revived.

Second Assistant Engineer George L. Smokovitch was one of the survivors. Two women carried him four miles to the nearest farmhouse. Out of a crew of 60 merchant seamen and Navy gunners, only 12 survived.

The routine tasks of delivering cargoes across the North Atlantic, involved excitement and thrills, but such events were recorded only in the daily logs of the ships involved. A typical instance was a masterful display of seamanship and ship handling by Commander Irvin S. Stephens of the Coast Guard-manned destroyer escort *Merrill* and Captain Ralph M. Lill, Jr. of the *Benjamin Holt* during an Atlantic storm in 1945.

Carpenter Norris Wainwright, on the *Holt*, had his arms crushed when a heavy steel hatchcover fell on him. A request for medical aid was sent to the convoy commodore, who dispatched the *Merrill* to give assistance.

Both ships maintained a parallel course rolling and pitching in the stormy seas until the *Merrill*, after two unsuccessful attempts, finally put a breeches-buoy line across to the *Holt*.

Then the injured man was inched over 200 feet of tumbling waters to the *Merrill*. Had there been faulty seamanship—bad judgment in steering or ship handling—the line would have carried away and the injured man would have been lost.

More than once in the North Atlantic the safety of ship and cargo depended on the ingenuity and quick action of officers and crew, many of whom, on the basis of age, hardly qualified as old sea dogs.

When a boiler-room blower shaft broke on the *Charles Tufts* during a North Atlantic crossing in 1944, Captain Herbert N. Simmons, 26, faced the prospect of dropping out of the convoy while engineers took the fan apart, welded or replaced the shaft, and assembled it again, a task that might take many hours. In the meantime, the ship would be a sitting duck for lurking U-boats. Simmons and Chief Engineer Robert Hargis, 36, decided to try a novel expedient. Working at top speed, crewmen ripped out 12 porthole fans and installed them in the engine room to replace the regular blower. Every man on the ship had his fingers crossed when power was turned on for the makeshift blower, but the jury rig worked like a charm, and the *Charles Tufts* rejoined the convoy and reached England without further difficulty.

☐

Although the worst of the Atlantic battle was in the northern latitudes, German submarines ranged over thousands of miles of ocean, from the Arctic Circle into the lonely reaches of the Atlantic south of the Equator. No vessel was safe merely because she was far from the heavily travelled shipping lanes.

The *Star of Oregon*, second Liberty ship to be launched, was on the homeward leg of her maiden voyage—Durban to Trinidad with 4,000 tons of manganese ore —when a submarine torpedoed her off the coast of South America on 30 August 1942. The crew abandoned her, but when she showed no signs of sinking, the U-boat surfaced and put 17 shells into her. All hands were picked up by an American patrol boat and landed the next day at Port of Spain.

Another ship with a short life was the *Gaspar de Portola*. On the last leg of her maiden voyage, from Bombay and Calcutta to New York, she ran aground on Quena Suene Bank in the Caribbean. Crewmen jettisoned 1,500 tons of ore and unloaded another 1,600 tons of jute, burlap, and hides into the SS *Florida* before the Navy tug *Arsiz* and the salvage tug *Killerig* could budge the *Portola* from the reef. She continued on to Key West, where she was condemned for active service and was turned over to the Coast Guard for use as a fire-fighting school.

On the evening of 6 October 1942, the crew of the *William Gaston*, running alone from Takoradi to Baltimore with manganese, mahogany logs, and cocoa beans, heard distant gunfire and saw gun flashes on the horizon. At the same time the radio operator received an SOS from the *John Carter Rose*. The *Gaston* changed course immediately and at 12 knots put as many miles as possible between herself and the supposedly ill-fated *John Carter Rose*.

That ship was headed from New York toward Freetown, Sierra Leone, when lookouts spotted a U-boat several miles away running on a parallel course. The captain immediately changed course to bring the 5-inch stern gun to bear, and while the radioman got off an SOS, the gunners got off five shots, one of which appeared to hit the raider's after deck. At least, the submarine disappeared and the *Rose* continued on, with frequent changes of course and with from ten to twelve lookouts on duty at all times. The ship had no more trouble from submarines that night.

Shortly after midnight on 8 October, two torpedoes hit in quick succession, starting a gasoline fire in two holds. The radio operator sent out another SOS and the ship steamed on, but the fire became so intense that the crew had to leave her. A third torpedo hit after the lifeboats had been lowered and pulled away.

Soon after this, the submarine surfaced and her officers questioned the survivors. One man still in the water was picked up by the Germans and transferred to a lifeboat, but not before they showed him a piece of paper with the names, *John Carter Rose* and *William Gaston*. "Which is yours?" he was asked.

The submarine's conning tower bore a red shield with a golden lion's head and a quarter moon. She seemed to have a mixed German-Italian crew. As in numerous other sinkings, the Germans gave the men cigarettes, brown bread, and first aid supplies, and told them what course to steer toward the nearest land, in this case, Venezuela.

The American SS *West Humhaw* picked up 18 men of the *Rose* crew on 13 October and landed them in Freetown. The Argentine tanker *Santa Cruz* found two lifeboats with 35 survivors and took them to Recife. Five merchant crewmen and three of the Armed Guard were killed.

There was a clear, moonlit sky and a rough sea when the *Reuben Tipton* was torpedoed near Trinidad on 23 October 1942 while bound from Colombo to New York with 3,000 tons of chrome ore, 2,000 tons of rubber, 600 tons of cocoanut oil, and 3,000 tons of other freight. The torpedo blast put her down by the bow and she slowed to three knots, but kept her course. An SOS was broadcast, and the confidential papers were thrown overboard as a precaution against her sinking so suddenly there would not be time to dispose of them properly. That was a good move. Four hours later two more torpedoes completely wrecked the midships section of the ship. She went down so fast that the crew swam off the main deck to life rafts. Most of them were picked up three days later by a British motor torpedoboat and taken to Barbados. The captain and one seaman were rescued from a raft by a U. S. Navy Catalina aircraft.

The following month the *Jeremiah Wadsworth*, en route from New Orleans to Bombay with 8,000 tons of assorted cargo and a deckload of trucks, was 270 miles south of Cape Agulhas and almost in the Indian Ocean on 27 November, when the *U146* attacked her. Two torpedoes hit the ship. As the *Wadsworth*'s crew prepared to abandon ship, a jammed engine throttle valve made it impossible to turn off the steam. The *Wadsworth*, out of control, sailed around in circles at seven knots and swamped one of the four lifeboats before she finally went down by the bow with the propeller still turning. The three surviving lifeboats were soon separated by a storm, during which one disappeared. The others were picked up by the American *John Lykes*.

Everyone on the *Marcus Whitman* was lucky when a torpedo blew off her rudder and propeller on 9 November as she was en route from Cape Town to Dutch Guinea. After the crew abandoned ship, a second torpedo hit in the engine room, but still the *Whitman* did not sink. The submarine then surfaced and fired 20 shells into the ship before she finally went down. The four lifeboats reached the African coast within a few days, and there were no casualties.

It frequently took more than one torpedo to do in a Liberty. Then either the submarine, or an escort ship, had to sink the hulk by gunfire. The *Molly Pitcher*, en route from New York to Casablanca in convoy USG6, was torpedoed by a U-boat, but she finally had to be sent to the bottom by gunfire from the USS *Champlain*.

□

One of the longest open-boat trips of World War II began in the South Atlantic on 9 February 1943, after the *Roger B. Taney*, under Captain Tom Potter, was hunted down by a U-boat one night. The first torpedo was seen as a white streak that missed by 20 feet or so. "There wasn't time to change course or maneuver," said Donald Zubrod, the purser, ". . . just time enough to sing out 'torpedo off the port bow.' "

All hands immediately went to general quarters. Zubrod, while he wondered what it would be like to catch a piece of shrapnel or go over the side into a lifeboat on such a rough night, kept repeating to himself: "Remember to get the ship's papers and throw the confidential material overboard. Don't forget. Don't forget."

The sound of big diesels soon let the crew know that the submarine had surfaced in the darkness and was chasing them. The chase continued for an hour but the *Taney* could not outrun the raider, and at 2200 a torpedo hit the starboard side in the engine room, killing the third assistant engineer, the oiler, and the fireman on watch.

Zubrod was on a wing of the bridge when the ship was hit. "I looked overside and saw flames. It was the oil from our fuel tanks on fire. All the 20-millimeter guns started firing at once at imaginary targets but it was quite impossible to see anything. The bo'sun reported that the two lifeboats on the starboard side had been knocked overboard by the explosion."

Captain Potter ordered the crew to stand by the port boats and soon afterward gave the order to abandon ship. The machinery spaces were ruined and the *Taney* was a virtual derelict, a real sitting duck for another shot.

Getting the ship's papers and throwing confidential codes overboard took longer than Zubrod had anticipated. When he reached the boat deck the two lifeboats were pulling away in the black of the night. He shouted for them to wait, clutched a bag of ship's papers against his chest, took a deep breath, and jumped. Fortunately, one of the boats returned for him, and as he was being hauled aboard a second torpedo hit the *Taney* and within a few minutes she went down.

An hour or so later the submarine came within a few yards of the boats and put a searchlight on them. An officer shouted in excellent English: "What was the name of your ship?"

When no one answered, he said, "It doesn't matter. We know all about your ship." He offered them a tow but the offer was refused and the U-boat disappeared in the night.

After a conference, the officers decided to strike out for the southeast trade winds and the coast of Brazil, but the boats were soon separated by rough weather. The first mate's boat was picked up 21 days later. The captain's boat, in which Zubrod was riding, sailed through everything from flat calm to half gales to a violent tropic storm in which winds were close to hurricane force for a brief period.

There was no room for a man to stretch out or get even a minimal amount of exercise during long days and cold nights. The wind whipped the spray over the men as they hunched their backs and bent their heads trying to escape the salty blast.

Worst of all was the confinement. "Try sitting in a chair for a full day at a time without getting up," Zubrod said. "That will give you some idea of how it is riding an overcrowded lifeboat. Sometimes you get so nervous you want to yell or scream or just stand up and jump out of the boat."

The men talked about food—steaks, ham and eggs, mountains of ice cream, and good old American hot dogs and hamburgers—but their biggest worry was water. No rain fell for 30 days. Then, just when the water beakers went dry, a rain squall gave them a chance to spread the sail and fill the beakers again.

After 33 days they saw several birds and knew that land must be near. Two days later, Coxswain Sam Lo Presti speared a dolphin. They drank its blood and cooked the meat in a bucket over a fire made out of an extra oar.

After 40 nights they saw a distant glow of lights. The glow was brighter the next night. The following day they shipped their oars and began to row. For the first time in 42 days they saw a distant ship, then several more. Finally a Brazilian passenger ship spotted them, changed course, and picked them up.

Despite their cramped condition, all hands were able to climb up the Jacob's ladder and reach the vessel's deck unaided. Captain Potter had brought his men safely through a 42-day ordeal during which they sailed more than 2,600 miles.

□

The survivors of the *Stephen Hopkins* may not have sailed so long and so far after their ship went down, but their battle against overwhelming odds ranks as one of the truly great epics of the sea, which should have been told by Joseph Conrad or Stephen Crane.

On 27 September 1942 the *Stephen Hopkins* was eight days out of Cape Town en route to Dutch Guinea. The trip had been routine and the sea was calm. At 0930 two strange ships broke out of a bank of haze off the starboard bow and Third Mate Walter Nyberg called Captain Paul Buck to the bridge.

The captain took one look at the strangers and ordered the general alarm sounded. "I don't like the looks of this," he said "Two ships wouldn't be stewing around here like that if they were freighters. They're up to something." The crew of the *Stephen Hopkins* did not learn until much later that the ships were the German commerce-raider *Stier* of 4,800 tons and the blockade-runner *Tannenfels*. The *Stier* carried six 5.9-inch guns—enough for a destroyer—and two torpedo tubes. The *Tannenfels* had a lighter armament. Both had machine guns, and both used incendiaries, shrapnel, and contact fuses. The *Stephen Hopkins* had one 4-inch gun on her stern, two 37-millimeter guns on the bow, four .50 caliber and two .30 caliber machine guns.

As merchant marine sailors and Armed Guard gunners dashed to their stations, Captain Buck ordered First Mate Richard Woyhoski to break out the ensign and check all boats. Woyhoski hoisted the U. S. flag; it was larger than the usual ensign and had never been flown before. Almost at the same time the strangers ran up German flags and opened fire, and a shell splashed into the sea within a hundred yards of the *Stephen Hopkins*. The next shell hit amidships, killing Gus Tsiforos and Charles Fitzgerald just as they hurried on deck with helmets and lifejackets. Two more shells hit as the Captain ordered a port turn and George Papas put the wheel hard over to swing the ship and give the stern gun a chance at the enemy.

As the Armed Guard officer, Ensign Kenneth Willet, ran across the boat deck toward the stern platform, shrapnel from one of the shells knocked him down. Despite a severe stomach wound, he staggered on and took charge of the gun as it returned the German fire. The first shot from the *Hopkins* threw spray over the foredeck of the *Stier* and the next made a solid hit, with smoke and a plume of fire to prove it had done damage. Navy gunners and merchant seamen yelled and cheered.

"Aim low and make every shot count," Willet told the gun captain, who did exactly that. The gun crew urged Willet to go for medical aid, but he leaned against the ready ammo box and kept saying, "I'm all right. I'm all right." Between shots he yelled down the ammunition hoist, encouraging men who were passing up shells and powder from the magazine under the steering-engine room.

When the German ships closed the range to a thousand yards or so they opened up with small guns. Hot lead chattered and pinged against gun tubs and deck-houses. In the first excitement of battle, everyone around the stern gun was talking at once, but as machine-gun bullets sent a sailor reeling against the splinter shield with blood streaming from his chest they fell silent. A few moments later he died without saying a word.

In the engine room, boiler fires sputtered with the concussion of the stern gun, the electric lights shattered and went out, and the emergency lamps were switched on. Fireman Mike Fitzpatrick stood between the boilers watching the water in the gauge glasses jump with each shell burst. When a shot hit amidships the glasses broke and hot water dripped onto the deck. Shock knocked insulation from the steam lines, and asbestos covered the floor plates like snow.

Hemmed in by a maze of pipe and steel Third Assistant Kenneth Vaughan and Oiler Andy Tsigonis could only wonder what was going on topside and wish they were on deck. The chatter of machine guns came down the ventilators like the racket of riveting hammers. They never knew what happened when a salvo of 5.9-inch shells from the *Stier* smashed through the thin hull plates, and the engine room filled with live steam, water, and choking cordite fumes. After that hit, the bridge rang the engine room but there was no answer.

With the boilers wrecked, the engine slowed down and stopped. The ship lost headway, but the guns kept firing, and as the raiders swung around for broadside fire on the *Hopkins*, her 37-millimeter guns got in some telling hits on the *Stier*. The bow guns, under the direction of Second Mate Joseph Lyman, kept on firing until the gun tub was filled with empty cartridges, the platform was a mass of twisted metal from enemy hits, and finally every man there was killed or wounded.

It was evident that the engagement would soon end, but in the last few moments *Stier* and *Tannenfels* moved in close enough for the *Stephen Hopkins* to use her machine guns, and they swept the decks of both enemy ships until many of their guns were silenced and the gunners killed or wounded. On the stern gun of the *Hopkins*, with all shell handlers and gunners dead or wounded, Ensign Willet tried, in vain to lift one more shell into the breach. Edwin O'Hara, a U. S. Merchant Marine Academy cadet, fired the last five shells left in the ready box. As he rammed the last one home—the fortieth fired by that gun in the action—the after magazine blew up, rocking the ship and sending flames up the ammunition hoist.

Two more hits by the *Stier* wrecked what remained of the midships deckhouse, demolished the radio shack, and killed Hudson Hewey as he tapped out the SOS that was never heard. Twenty minutes after the battle began, the *Stephen Hopkins* was on fire in a dozen places fore and aft and was going down by the stern. Captain Buck gave the order to abandon ship, and seconds later a shell hit the bridge where he stood with a weighted box containing the ship's confidential papers. He was not seen again.

Woyhoski was wounded by the same explosion, but when Steward Stilson and Seaman James Burke tried to carry him to a boat he refused to go. "Get into the boats yourselves," he said. "Get off before it's too late. I'm done for. Don't bother with me."

Carpenter Hugh Kuhle and Ensign Willet, now so weak he could hardly stand, dropped a life raft alongside the ship. As they crossed the deck to release a second raft, both were cut down by machine-gun fire. O'Hara, who had fired the last shell from the stern gun only moments earlier, ran to help with the raft and he, too, was killed. As Second Engineer George D. Cronk helped lower a boat, a shell hit just above it, killing Andy Yanz and Bill Adrian and wounding four others. Cronk jumped overboard, took command of the boat, and stuffed blankets into the shell holes. It was no boat for an ocean voyage of hundreds of miles with wounded men, but the survivors manned their oars and pulled away just as the gallant *Stephen Hopkins*, ablaze from bow to stern, went down with her new American flag still flying.

The *Stephen Hopkins* was gone, but her gunners had done well. Prior to that day the *Stiers* had sunk four ships, a total of 29,000 tons, but the *Hopkins* left her a flaming wreck, and the *Tannenfels* moved in to take off the survivors. As the survivors of the *Hopkins* searched among wreckage to pick up several more men who had gone overboard and were clinging to planks or rafts, they rowed within 500 yards of the *Stier*, with smoke billowing out of her, but the Germans made no effort to intercept them. Perhaps they admired the spirited battle put up by the *Hopkins*, for she was merely a freighter although she had fought like a cruiser. Outnumbered and outgunned, the *Hopkins* could, in all honor, have surrendered without firing a shot, but her crew chose to do battle against superior odds in a manner befitting the *Jervis Bay* or the *Essex* and fought one of the great ship-against-ship battles of World War II.

The lifeboat finally held 19 men, five of them painfully wounded, all that were left of 60 Armed Guard and merchant sailors. As they sailed away under a freshening wind, the Germans were soon obscured by mist and rain. Some time later a thunderous blast reached them as the *Stier* finally blew up and sank.

□

Late that afternoon the lifeboat party sighted six more survivors on a small raft, some distance away, but couldn't recognize them, although they thought Jean Zimsel, the second cook, and one of the Navy gunners were among them. The wind blew the raft out of sight in the mist before the boat could overtake it. Then they saw Third Mate Walter Nyberg in the wreck of another lifeboat, that also disappeared in the drifting mist before they could reach it.

The next day two rafts were sighted—the sign of another ship gone down—but no survivors were aboard. They took food and water from the rafts, but even so, by 1 October they had to cut their rations to six ounces per day so as to have more for the wounded men. All they could do for them was to soak their bandages in saltwater.

In the days that followed, the survivors of the *Stephen Hopkins* had plenty of time to recount the battle as each one had seen it and to fully detail the fate of their shipmates. Second Mate Lyman had been killed at one of the bow guns, along with Herbert Love, messboy. Boatswain Allyn Phelps was last seen clearing away the wires of the shattered aerial so Hewey could send an SOS. The chief engineer had picked up Pedro Valez, a wiper who had been hit by a shell, and carried him to the messroom for first aid. They reached the messroom just before a salvo landed amidships and demolished the place. The steward found Henry Engle crawling along a passageway toward the messroom and ran to get bandages, but it was too late. "I couldn't do anything for him . . . nothing at all."

Eugene McDaniels, a cook, died on 6 October and Leonardo Romero, a steward, died two days later. Gunner Wallace Breck had a bad wound in his shoulder, and they operated on him without any anesthesia and removed a piece of shrapnel. He survived. But during the next two weeks Demetrades and Gelagates, firemen, died.

Finally, on 27 October, the lifeboat pulled up on a Brazilian beach 22 miles north of Rio with 15 survivors from the Liberty ship whose lone battle against two heavily armed raiders will long remain an epic of the sea. The United States Maritime Commission honored the *Stephen Hopkins* by naming her one of the "Gallant Ships" of World War II and commending "the stark courage of her valiant crew in their heroic stand." The Royal Navy's Captain Stephen S. Roskill in *The War at Sea*, which described British and German actions, wrote of the men of the *Stephen Hopkins* that "They fought an action of which all the Allied Navies and merchant marines would be proud. . . ."

The last word came years later, and from a German. Vice Admiral Friedrich Ruge in *Der See Krieg*, described how the *Stier* met her end when ". . . she encountered the U. S. Liberty ship *Stephen Hopkins* which bravely used her guns, and to good effect."

It was merchant seamen such as these and their naval comrades who fought— and finally won the Battle of the Atlantic. In paying well-deserved tribute to those whose vigilance was never relaxed in that long battle, Winston Churchill wrote:

> Especially was this true in the North Atlantic, where even the daily routine of ship operation was often an ordeal testing the determination and fortitude of stout hearts. "Dire crisis might at any moment flash upon the scene with brilliant fortune or glare with mortal tragedy. Many gallant actions and incredible feats of endurance are recorded, but the deeds of those who perished will never be known. Our merchant seamen displayed their highest qualities, and the brotherhood of the sea was never more strikingly shown than in their determination to defeat the U-boat."

Air attack was a constant threat in the Mediterranean, where ships always operated within striking distance of enemy air bases. When German bombers hit a convoy near Algiers the night of 20 April 1944, one of the victims was the ammunition ship *Paul Hamilton*, destroyed in a spectacular blast that killed 504 men.

7

THE

MEDITERRANEAN

No theatre of operations in World War II was more violently contested than the Mediterranean, where at one time or another British, French, Italian, American, and German forces were involved. Nowhere in that long, narrow sea, broken up as it is by islands, headlands, and peninsulas, were ships ever out of reach of land-based air attack. As soon as ships passed the "Rock" at Gibraltar, the ancient Pillars of Hercules, they were in waters where invasion and battle had gone on since the days of Ulysses.

The action in the "Med," for Liberty ships, began with the invasion of North Africa—Operation Torch—in November, 1942, and went on through landings that made history: Sicily, Salerno, Anzio, Southern France. Ships faced every known hazard of war at sea—submarines, shore batteries, aircraft, mines—and even a few new ones: frogmen under water and radio-controlled glide bombs in the air. Much of the action took place in sight of land and frequently while ships were tied up at a dock and unable to get away.

One of the first Libertys to see action was the *Thomas Stone*, which sailed from New York prior to the North African landings and reached Oran in convoy KMS3, one of the big follow-up supply groups that lost several ships to torpedoes.

On 6 February 1943, as the *Thomas Stone* sailed from Oran to Bougie in convoy KMS8, her gunners knocked down a German bomber. Early on 7 February a plane dropped flares over the convoy and two submarine torpedoes barely missed the *Stone*. A third hit but did not explode. When a submarine surfaced 500 yards away gunners on the *Stone* got in several hits before it crash dived. Several hours later a periscope was sighted and again her gunners hit it before it disappeared.

Convoys in the Mediterranean were subjected to the same harassment they got on the Murmansk run. Typical was that of a 13-ship convoy bound to Philippeville, Algeria, in January 1943. On 7 January German reconnaissance planes shadowed the convoy but were chased away by British Hurricanes. Two hours later Junkers 87s started torpedo runs on the convoy, and at the same time a flight of dive bombers attacked. The *William Wirt*, carrying 16,000 cases of aviation gasoline, was the first ship in the convoy to open fire and before the attack ended had sent four bombers into the sea. One of the planes shot down by the *Wirt* put a bomb into a hold filled with drums of gasoline, but it failed to explode. Another one shot down by the *Wirt* flamed into a Norwegian freighter astern of her and set it on fire. That ship exploded and sank. At the same time the British ship *Benalbanach,* carrying American troops, was torpedoed. She exploded and sank within a few minutes. Many soldiers jumped overboard from the burning ship only to be killed by depth-charge concussion. Another plane set on fire by the *Wirt*'s fighting gunners pulled out of a dive and stalled just above the bridge of the ship, then crashed into the water. Two bombs near-missed the ship and a third hit and flooded number four hold, but she stayed with the convoy.

On 19 January, the *Wirt* was in convoy only six miles from Philippeville when three waves of torpedo-bombers and high-level bombers staged a 70 minute attack. Again the *Wirt* escaped damage. Several hours later a submarine was forced to the surface by depth charges, and the *Wirt*'s gunners opened up on it, along with an escorting destroyer. They saw its bow point skyward, then slip back into the sea.

That night as the convoy neared Algiers, torpedo planes and bombers attacked again, and the *Wirt* knocked one down. Two hours later there was another air attack. The *Walt Whitman* was hit but made Algiers under her own power. Again the *Wirt* was lucky. The ships sailed from Algiers that night under another air attack in which one ship was bombed and sunk. The attack was so intense that three of *Wirt*'s gunners had their ear drums ruptured. The *Wirt* was undamaged.

Finally, as the *Wirt* steamed past Gibraltar on 7 February, homeward bound, the Germans tried once more. That time the concussion of near-miss bomb hits knocked the propeller shaft out of line and the ship had to go to Liverpool for repairs.

□

The North African landings were merely a prelude to the long-awaited invasion of Europe, the first direct attack on the Axis Powers. The Allied toehold in Africa simplified the matter of staging the greatest military amphibious operation the world had seen up to that point, as two huge invasion armadas moved across the stormy Mediterranean toward the island of Sicily. This was Operation Husky, under the Supreme Command of Lieutenant General Dwight D. Eisenhower.

One of the fleets carried the British 8th Army, battle-hardened veterans of the long and hard-fought desert war in North Africa. Their objectives were Pozalla, Pachino, and Avola. The other fleet carried the American 7th Army to landing beaches at Licata, Gela, and Cape Sparmania.

Helping to lift these great armies and their vast impedimenta were scores of Liberty ships that had assembled in African ports over a period of many weeks. Most of them had temporary accommodations for about 200 troops.

The crossing from Africa was made in rough and windy weather—a miserable night for seasick soldiers. Ships rolled and pitched and some lost the barrage balloons towed as a protection against dive-bomber attack.

In the early morning of 10 July, the *Matthew Maury* was torpedoed but did not sink and was towed back to Bougie. The American tanker *Gulfprince*, torpedoed at the same time, returned to Oran for repairs. Later that morning, the weather improved and there was little evidence of war as ships carrying units of the 8th Army approached Avola. The day seemed idyllic for a Mediterranean cruise until HMS *Frebus*, a stubby, low-decked monitor, let go a salvo from her 12-inch guns that raised clouds of smoke and dust on the high hills. A cruiser and two destroyers joined in to silence coast defense batteries.

As they approached their designated anchorages, ships of the eastern contingent passed shattered pieces of airplane wings and fuselage. A tug had tied on to one tail section of a half-submerged plane and was trying to pull it ashore. Bodies could be seen floating in the water; they were airborne troops from gliders that had been mistakenly shot down by Allied guns in the early morning hours.

The ships approached their anchorages with booms rigged and invasion barges ready to lower. Except for the occasional shelling by warships, it was too peaceful to be real—more like a dress rehearsal than the real thing. But that afternoon Avola was raided by high-level bombers and dive-bombers in the first of more than 50 air attacks to come in a week.

During an air attack most men were too busy to really see the planes diving or flaming down, shrapnel bursts in the air, bombs falling like glittering tinfoil, and the fires and explosions on ships. A Navy gunner on the *Colin Kelly* wrote, understandably, that "the stark terror of the sight is indescribable." The nonchalant third mate on that ship, Mr. Wonson, merely sang "Praise the Lord, and pass the ammunition," inspiring the crew even as hot shrapnel bounced around them on deck. In the same attack, red-hot shrapnel started a fire in a gasoline-filled hold on the *Jonathan Grout* but two seamen climbed down and put it out. The Dutch freighter *Baern* alongside the *Grout* was sunk.

Because of the coastal terrain, it was possible for enemy planes to sneak in over the surrounding hills and attack before anyone knew they were coming. In such an attack, two Stuka dive-bombers hit the Avola anchorage before the alarm could be given. The *Will Rogers*, which had just arrived, got in a few bursts of 20-millimeter fire, as did some other ships, but the planes were gone within a minute. One plane put two bombs into a hold full of ammunition on the *Timothy Pickering*, which had arrived with the *Will Rogers* and still had most of her troops aboard. The *Pickering* vanished in a mushroom-shaped cloud of smoke and fire that towered a thousand feet into the air. Some of the burning wreckage hit a nearby tanker, which also blew up, and bits of that ship killed several men on the *O. Henry*. Of 192 men aboard the *Pickering*, the only survivors were 23 men blown overboard in the initial explosion.

At Gela, during the landing of the American 7th Army, the *Robert Rowan*—another ship loaded with ammunition and carrying a total of 421 merchant sailors and Army troops—took three direct hits from what was thought to be an Italian bomber. The ship began burning, and the captain ordered her abandoned. In what must have been an outstanding example of well-ordered confusion, every last man got off before the ship blew up 20 minutes later.

It was a busy day for the *Nicholas Gilman* when she reached Gela; she was shelled by German tanks, hit by a bomb, set on fire, and still managed to shoot down three planes out of the estimated 30 German and Italian aircraft that staged the attack. Gunners on the *Tabitha Brown* got one dive-bomber, definite, and another "probable."

A couple of hours after the *Robert Rowan* sank, four German planes attacked with fragmentation bombs, one of which wounded eight men in the *Joseph Pulitzer*'s 3-inch gun crew. The *Pulitzer* had a former Navy gun pointer in her civilian crew, so Captain Kingdon S. Thomas made him gun captain of a merchant seaman gun crew which "did some fine shooting." The new gun crew was drenched by water that night when raiding dive-bombers gave them some near misses. The third mate merely ended the log for the 8-to-12 watch with, "Army stevedores discharging cargo between bombs, bullets and barges."

☐

The invasion of the Italian mainland began with Operation Avalanche, the Salerno landings, on 9 September 1943. The invasion price was high: 5,000 American and 7,000 British dead. The U. S. Navy lost the destroyers *Rowan* and *Buck*.

Among the many Libertys taking part in the Salerno operation were the *George Matthews, Charles Pios, Lewis Morris, William Dean Howells, James Woodrow, John Howard Payne, Daniel Webster,* and *David Caldwell,* whose crew helped to unload a high priority cargo of tanks, antitank guns, and ammunition needed to beat off German tanks.

The *James W. Marshall* arrived at Salerno on 11 September and was immediately hit and set on fire by a 250-pound bomb, but the fire was extinguished and the ship continued unloading. Two days later, she was hit by another bomb that killed 13 of the crew and many Army cargo handlers. In the holocaust, Cadet John Herbert showed rare courage and presence of mind by cutting loose a burning landing craft full of ammunition, after which he flooded the after magazine.

At Salerno the *Winfield Scott* had her baptism of fire when she blasted two German bombers out of the sky and drove others away before they could attack. Corporal Charles A. Hughes, a passenger, wrote to his father, a shipyard worker in Houston, where the *Scott* was built: "She not only can take it, but she can dish it out. . . . The only thing I hope is that the rest of the ships you worked on do as good as she did."

Just before the *Bushrod Washington* was launched at Baltimore in April, 1943, her first captain, John W. Wainwright, son of the famous defender of Bataan, General Jonathan Wainwright, scratched his initials in the fresh paint on the bow and said, "That's for good luck." The ship needed it at Salerno, where she arrived with 7,000 drums of aviation gasoline, 75 tons of bombs, and some 105-millimeter shells. On 14 September, after three days of continuous attack, a bomber made a direct hit with a 500-pound bomb that started a gasoline fire in number four hold. The resulting explosion destroyed the entire forward section of the vessel, but only four men lost their lives.

The *William Bradford* was also lucky. In four days she had one bomb explode 25 feet off the port bow, one missed by 30 yards, another exploded close enough to splash water on deck—was strafed, had her lifeboats riddled by machine-gun fire. She also shot down two aircraft. No one was injured.

The controversial landings at Anzio, which began 22 January 1944, were intended to bypass strong German resistance blocking the Allied advance up the Italian peninsula. In Operation Shingle, six divisions—more than 70,000 men and 18,000 vehicles—were landed along a 14-mile beachhead in the first few days. Again, as at Salerno, the anchorages and beachheads were within range of German 88s in the nearby heights, and air raids were a constant hazard.

German radio-controlled glide bombs were also a menace at Anzio. They carried a 660-pound explosive warhead, were fantastically fast—better than 600 miles an hour—and could be launched at altitudes above three miles. First seen at Salerno, they had near-missed the cruiser *Philadelphia* and badly damaged the *Savannah*. About the best defense against them was to pray that they missed. Or, as the *Lawton B. Evans* did, make a lucky hit.

That ship, with 4,000 tons of ammunition and gasoline, arrived at Anzio on D-Day and was immediately shelled by the much-feared 88s. Shells fell within 50 feet of the ship, peppering the hull and deckhouse with jagged pieces of hot shrapnel.

Captain Harry Ryan shifted the ship to another spot, but the German shells followed. Time after time during the next week the ship would move to gain a few hours respite before German gunners got the range again. During that time the gunners knocked down four planes and a glide bomb. They also got the bomber that dropped it; the plane blew up and left nothing but a carburetor, which landed on deck and was hung in the Armed Guard messroom as a symbol of their marksmanship. Soon after that, a glide bomb hit the *Samuel Huntington*, which was loaded with gasoline, bombs, and TNT. The bomb went into the engine room and killed four men; if it had hit a hold the ship would have disintegrated.

Another glide bomb hit the water some 15 yards astern of the *John Banvard*. The concussion cracked frames and gear on the deck, sprung doors in passageways, and broke steam and water lines. There were no casualties, and the *Banvard* made it to Naples under her own power.

A glide bomb got the *Elihu Yale* on 15 February. The *Yale* was loading artillery shells into LCT-35 at the time, and both ships were a complete loss.

During an air raid on 24 January, a hospital ship, *St. David*, was sunk. The armed guard gunners of the *Bret Harte* fired 745 rounds of 20-millimeter and got one of the two planes. At dusk that day the Germans came back. One just missed the *Hilary Herbert* and three more missed the *Bret Harte*. Eight planes were shot down, one of them by the *Bret Harte*. The *Herbert* had already gone through 26 raids, and her gunners had shot down two planes. In that raid they got a dive-bomber—it crashed into the hull just forward of the bridge and scattered itself all over the deck. Its two bombs exploded in near-misses which so damaged her engine that the *Herbert* had to be towed to Naples for repairs.

The *F. Marion Crawford*, during nine days at Anzio, logged more than 200 near misses from German 88s and shifted anchorage every few hours to disrupt the German range-finders. When fires were started by a shell hit on a hatch coaming just above a hold filled with 75-millimeter ammunition, the merchant crew put them all out in 15 minutes.

Attempts to smash the Anzio supply line cost the enemy many planes, and the Libertys got a few of them. A partial box-score for Liberty-ship gunners showed the *Samuel Ashe*, *James W. Nesmith*, *Tabitha Brown*, and *William Mulholland* with one each; *Bret Harte* and *Hilary Herbert* with three each.

A frequent last line in the obituaries of merchant ships in the Mediterranean and elsewhere was "Torpedo hit in the engine room. All men on watch were killed." Submarines and torpedo-bombers aimed for the engine room. If a ship could be crippled, there was always a chance to finish it off later. The black gang —firemen, oilers, wipers, and engineers—were marked men, but in no case during the war was there ever any evidence that they missed a watch in time of attack. Many men went below knowing there was a 50-50 chance they might not come back up again.

The *Richard Henry Olney* was torpedoed in the engine room but lost only two men. She was towed to a North African port and beached; cargo was transferred to the *John Fiske* and eventually reached Italy. The *Olney*'s master, Captain Erick Richter, then assumed command of the *John Dickenson*, whose captain had taken sick.

The *William Woods*, bound for Anzio with 400 troops and war supplies on 10 March 1944, was torpedoed barely 50 miles out of Palermo. Cadet Richard Stewart heard the torpedo blast and got on deck in time to see parts of hatches and life rafts still falling. Fifty-six soldiers and one Navy gunner were killed. Cadet Midshipman Myles Clark was credited with rescuing a number of soldiers by lashing mattresses together and throwing them to men in the water. Survivors were bitter at the lack of action on the part of a nearby Italian escort ship which made no effort to rescue them.

□

It could be expected that in the strain and stress of battle and the shock of frightening explosions and fire, men sometimes made on-the-spot decisions to abandon ships that under normal, peacetime conditions would have been saved. Time and weather permitting, ships that appeared badly damaged could still have been taken in tow and moved to a dry dock for repairs. This was especially true for some cargo ships that stubbornly refused to sink despite tremendous damage.

The *Matt Ransom* was an outstanding example of a ship being able to take terrific punishment and still remain afloat. The ship was nearing a North African port when a violent explosion tore a hole in the bow large enough for a truck to drive through. Moments later, there was a second blast, after which she began to settle, on fire in several places. Captain John Metsall ordered his men to abandon ship. All hands got away safely, but when the *Ransom* refused to sink, Metsall took six volunteers and reboarded her. Despite the fact that the vessel might plunge to the bottom, they started boiler fires, got her underway, and took her into port.

As the crew abandoned ship the falls of one lifeboat had fouled, and men were thrown into the sea. They swam to other boats, but the chief engineer, who had only one arm, was caught in the life net hanging down the ship's side. Ordinary Seaman George S. Baker, who was awarded the Merchant Marine Distinguished Service Medal for his actions, ". . . climbed down the net [from the deck] released the engineer, swam with him to a lifeboat and assisted him into the boat."

The *Alexander Graham Bell* hit a mine off Naples, but despite a gaping hole in the hull, she was towed in, repaired, and then returned stateside for another cargo. The *James Guthrie*, which hit a mine at the same time and place, was also saved by being towed in and beached.

Daniel Webster was torpedoed on 10 January 1944 and went down so far by the head that fish could have swum across the foredeck, but stayed afloat long enough to be beached on the coast of North Africa. Then she was abandoned.

Two more ships that refused to sink were the *Peter Skene Ogden* and *George Cleeve*, both torpedoed in Convoy GUS21 on 22 February 1944. Captain William P. Magann of the *Ogden*, with ten volunteers, sailed the crippled ship to the nearest port and beached her. The *Cleeve* had to be towed in and beached. Both ships were complete losses.

When the *Virginia Dare* struck a mine in the Bay of Tunis in March of 1944, the explosion severed the forward part of the ship just a few feet ahead of the deckhouse and engine room, but the rest of the vessel was towed to port and salvaged.

The *Thomas B. Masaryk* caught fire after being torpedoed off Algiers in 1944 and was purposely sunk in 28 feet of water as the best means of putting out the fire. Some weeks later, the *William T. Meredith* moored beside the wreck and her crew with the *Masaryk*'s began salvage operations, aided by a contingent of British soldiers and sailors. They saved millions of dollars worth of P39 and P47 fighter planes, as well as trucks, tires, canned goods, weapons, and other material.

Such salvage, with makeshift equipment, represented a great deal of ingenuity and long hours of gruelling labor under the most difficult conditions. In the *Masaryk*, to make matters worse, hundreds of tons of rotten egg powder and flour created an "unholy stench" which men had to endure 16 hours a day, seven days a week, until all the useable cargo had been removed.

The highly inflammable nature of many cargoes—gasoline, ammunition, bombs, and TNT—meant that even a short run of a couple of hours could be as hazardous as a trip half around the world with a load of canned food or bagged cement.

The *Daniel Huger* was discharging her load of 6,000 tons of gasoline at Bone, Algeria, on 8 May 1943, when 17 bombers attacked the port. Shrapnel killed Third Mate Bernard Golden and Gunner Myles Panek, wounded several others, and started a fire in a hold partly filled with barrels of gasoline.

A gallant attempt to stop the fire was made by Captain James Adams, Oiler Tom O'Leary, Cadet Midshipmen Method Medved, Elmer Donnelly, and Phil Vannais, who took a hose and sprayed water on the gas-filled drums. Flames were soon shooting hundreds of feet into the air, and Adams ordered his fire-fighters ashore. One of the last to leave was Ensign Edward P. Gilman of the Armed Guard, who braved flames and cascading gasoline to flood the after ammunition magazine.

When the British SS *Fort Lamontee* caught fire beside the *Howard A. Kelly* at Algiers, the Liberty's crew fought fire until ordered to move to keep the *Kelly* from burning. As the British destroyer *Arrow* towed the *Fort Lamontee* into the outer harbor, the burning ship exploded, with much loss of life on both ships.

Captain Amos B. Beinhardt, 27, of the *John C. Carlisle*, directed fire-fighting efforts that saved a British ship loaded with ammunition in an Algerian port.

When the British vessel caught fire and requested help, Beinhardt organized a fire-fighting crew from his ship, ran hoses to the burning ship, and fought the flames until they were finally extinguished with the help of shoreside apparatus.

Heroism and quick thinking saved the *John H. Eaton* under similar circumstances in July, 1943, as she loaded at a North African port for the invasion of Sicily. *Eaton* was moored between a British ship loaded with gasoline and a Norwegian ship carrying mines when bombers raided the harbor. Shrapnel started fires on the one side and exploded mines in the other. Remarkably, only one man was injured.

☐

One of the strangest aspects of the sea war in the Mediterranean was the surprisingly successful efforts of Italian frogmen to sink or damage Allied merchant ships by attaching mines to their hulls in the harbor of Gibraltar, where vessels put in to await convoys.

Shortly after midnight of 4 August 1943, the deck watch on the *Harrison Gray Otis* spotted a man in the water who appeared exhausted and about to drown. Fished out by a cadet engineer, he was found to be an Italian and was turned over to the British, who soon learned that he had attached a mine to the hull of the *Otis* and that it was set to go off anytime after an hour. "Turn the engine over slowly," said the British—the propeller wash might dislodge it. Although there was a good chance that the mine might blow up beneath them, the black gang kept up steam and kept the propeller turning. As predicted, but three hours later rather than one, an explosion just forward of the engine room ruptured the bulkhead and flooded the engine spaces. The *Otis* was beached, a total constructive loss. The British ship *Stanridge* and the Norwegian ship *Thorshovdi* were mined the same night.

In another frogman attack at Gibraltar, the Liberty ship *Pat Harrison* had a mine explode beneath the engine room with force enough to throw men out of their bunks. There were no fatalities, but the ship was beached as a complete loss. Two British ships, the *Mahsud* and *Camerata*, were damaged by mines at the same time.

☐

There was action and excitement enough for anybody during the hour that convoy MKS21 beat off an air attack the evening of 13 August 1943. The ships were crawling along peacefully a little south of Almeria, Spain, when an estimated 20 to 50 planes roared in less than 50 feet above the water and attacked with torpedoes, bombs, and parachute mines.

"The planes were so thick," said a seaman on the *Nathaniel Greene*, "they looked like a flock of geese." To Ensign George Robbins of the *William T. Barry* they looked more like "many blackbirds skimming the water."

The convoy put up a furious fire, and an estimated 15 planes were shot down, although in the excitement of battle gunners were prone to overestimate their success. The *William T. Barry* claimed three, the *Elihu Yale*, *William W. Gerhard*, and *George Davis* each claimed two, and the *George W. McCrary* and *David Stone* each claimed one.

Torpedoes seemed to fill the sea, and at least five of them just missed the *James G. Blaine*. The *Ezra Meeker* and *Anne Bradstreet* had several near misses. Two torpedoes missed the *William T. Barry* by inches; two more missed the *Francis W. Pettygrove*, but a third hit her engine room, and she was towed to Gibraltar and beached, a complete loss. Despite the large number of torpedoes launched, there was only one hit. The Germans blamed their poor luck on the Americans; the crew of a bomber fished out of the water complained that they were confused and disrupted by the intense fire from the Liberty ships.

The *William G. Gerhard* was not so lucky next time. On 21 September, loaded with ammunition, she was torpedoed off Salerno, caught on fire, blew up, and broke in two. One section sank, the other was sent down by gunfire.

□

One of the most costly engagements of the war in the Mediterranean and one seldom mentioned in World War II histories, occurred at the Italian port of Bari, on the Adriatic coast, the night of 2 December 1943. At that time the British 8th Army was pushing the enemy back along the coast, and 30 freighters and tankers were at the brilliantly illuminated docks in Bari, discharging ammunition, bombs, gasoline, and other supplies needed in the drive north.

About 2030, aircraft engines were heard, and winches stopped as stevedores searched the moonlit sky. Guns on all the ships were manned, and gunners waited for the command to open fire; ships at Bari were instructed not to fire on attacking aircraft until a designated gun ashore opened the action by firing tracers. The next moment parachute flares lit the harbor and the planes were overhead. On the *John Bascom*, Ensign Kay Vesole decided they had waited long enough and said to Captain Heitman, "It looks to me like it's time to start shooting."

Heitman agreed: "Start firing."

The *Bascom*'s guns let go, and in a second or so half a hundred guns poured shells into the sky as the first stick of bombs hit the Norwegian freighter *Lom*. She rolled over and sank with her crew of 23 men. The *Samuel Tilden*, which had just arrived at Bari, had a bomb go down her stack and explode in the engine room. Incendiaries set fire to her cargo of gasoline and ammunition. Men went overboard to escape the flames.

Direct bomb hits made raging infernos of the *John L. Motley* and *Joseph Wheeler*. Crewmen on the *John Bascom* tried to fight fire on the *Motley*, until the *Bascom* had a stick of bombs walk up her deck from stern to bow, with hits in number five hold, the boat deck, and number three hold. Officers and men rescued the wounded, got the only serviceable lifeboat into the water, and pulled away. By that time the harbor was filled with wreckage and flaming oil burned many men as they tried to swim away from wrecked ships.

Just as the *Bascom* boat reached the quay, the *John Motley* and the *John Harvey* both exploded. The terrific blast lifted the stern of the nearby *Lyman Abbott* out of the water and rolled her on her port side with decks ripped open. The *Joseph Wheeler*, hit at the same time as the *Motley*, blew up next, and the British *Fort Athabaska*, beside her and carrying two captured 1,000-pound German rocket bombs, caught fire, blew up, and sank. Forty-four men out of her crew of 56 were killed.

By that time, ships still afloat along the quay were burning fiercely, and violent explosions shook the air every few seconds. The little British freighter *Devon Coast*, untouched during the battle, had a stick of bombs miss her, and as she rolled and pitched in the resulting explosion, a last bomb made a direct hit. She went down, and the attack was over.

The battle at Bari lasted 20 minutes. Seventeen ships were sunk or damaged beyond all repair: *Testbank, Devon Coast, Fort Athabaska,* and *Lars Kruse* (British); *Barletta, Frasinone,* and *Cassola* (Italian); *John Bascom, John L. Motley, Joseph Wheeler, John Harvey,* and *Samuel Tilden* (American Libertys). Damaged ships were the *Lyman Abbott* (American Liberty); *Christa, Fort Lajoie,* and *Brittany Coast* (British); *Odysseus* (Dutch); and *Vest* (Norwegian).

The next day, with messboys filling in as able seamen, the crew of the *Lyman Abbott* managed to right her enough to get underway for emergency repairs. Searchers probing the wrecked American Libertys found 38 bodies; 150 men were missing from those five ships. The only men to survive out of the *Joseph Wheeler* crew had been ashore when the battle began. The shattered hulls were eventually removed, and the port of Bari is now filled with peaceful trade and commerce. But it will be a long time before the survivors of the "Battle of Bari" forget it.

☐

Although the raid at Bari was one of the worst disasters of the war in terms of ships and material lost, the *Paul Hamilton* produced a larger casualty list to become the most costly Liberty ship disaster, in terms of human life, in all of World War II. The ship was making her fifth voyage, as part of a huge convoy, UGS38, when it was attacked by 23 German bombers near sunset on 20 April 1944.

As was frequently the custom, in addition to her load of high explosives and bombs, the ship carried enough troops to bring the total on-board complement to 498 men. The bombers came in low; men on the bridge of the British tanker, *Athelchief*, looked down on one as it went by. Her gunners set it on fire, but it launched its torpedo less than 150 feet from the *Paul Hamilton*. Immediately after the torpedo hit the *Hamilton*, a violent explosion threw debris and dense black smoke high in the air. When the smoke cleared, there was no sign of the ship. Not one of the 498 men survived.

Several months later, in an amazing switch in the vagaries of war, another Liberty ship, the *Augustus Thomas*, carrying a cargo of ammunition and gasoline and 548 men in the Philippines, was hit and set on fire by a dive-bomber. Not a man was hurt.

Merchant shipping in the port of Bizerte and the surrounding seas was especially subject to attack. German airfields were nearby, and the narrow waters made hunting easy for submarines. Fortunately, because the waters were narrow, many damaged ships were towed to port, beached, or salvaged. A submarine torpedo blew the rudder off the *Pierce Soule* near Bizerte on 23 August 1943, but a Navy tug towed her in for repairs. On 12 September 1943, only 25 miles out of Bizerte, the *William B. Travis* was hit by a submarine torpedo but managed to make Bizerte under her own power, with a 36-foot-long hole in her side.

The *Richard Olney*, one of three ships in a convoy escorted by British corvettes and armed trawlers, was torpedoed on 22 September 1943. The engine was knocked off its foundation, the engine room flooded, and two men were killed; but the *Olney* stayed afloat and was towed to Bizerte.

What with submarines, dive-bombers, and mines, a cruise aboard a merchant ship in the Mediterranean was not like the ads in the *National Geographic* used to describe it. The *Nathaniel Greene* had just left Mostagonem, Algeria, to join a passing convoy, MDS8, when German bombers attacked. Her gunners shot down one plane before three torpedoes hit, killing four crewmen. The ship was beached at Salmanda, a total loss. The *James Russell Lowell* was torpedoed off Bizerte, abandoned, then reboarded, and towed to Algiers. The *Daniel Chester French* was "just passing through," as the expression goes, en route from Norfolk to the Persian Gulf, but a submarine sent her down near Bizerte with 37 casualties. The *John S. Copley* was torpedoed 15 miles off Oran but limped into port. When the *Hiram S. Maxim* was bombed between Oran and Algiers, her crew abandoned ship and were picked up by the Liberty ships *Harry Lane* and *Leslie W. Shaw*. The *Maxim* was towed to Algiers where her cargo was discharged.

The *William S. Rosecrans*, riding out a gale at Naples on 6 January 1944, was sunk while at anchor by a mine, but there were no casualties.

The *William B. Woods*, carrying 400 American troops and ammunition, was torpedoed, blew up, and sank with the loss of more than a hundred men. Survivors were picked up by the British cruiser *Arethusa*.

The results were very different when the Norwegian Liberty ship *Christian Michelsen* hit a mine the evening of 26 September 1943, 75 miles west of Bizerte. The ship blew up and sank in 42 seconds, no small wonder, considering that she carried 8,000 tons of ammunition and bombs. Out of a crew of 49, there were only three survivors. One man on the stern gun platform was thrown to the deck and knocked out, but regained consciousness as the vessel went under. The other two, asleep in their quarters at the stern, ran on deck and jumped overboard. All three were picked up by a British armed trawler.

Not all the hazards met by Liberty ships were of German origin. Officers and crew of the *Alexander H. Stevens*, on one of her Anzio supply runs, found that U. S. Army stevedores at Bizerte had nonchalantly loaded tanks atop a cargo of shells and hand grenades without securing them. There were tense moments when the tanks began walking back and forth over the ammunition in rough weather, and First Mate Wayne Kirkland led the deck crew below to lash them down before they set off the "firecrackers." On another run, the *Stevens* carried an even more disconcerting cargo—a load of 300 "psychos," soldiers who had broken down under combat.

One of the most tragic incidents of the war in the Mediterranean involved the *Benjamin Contee* which, under a bright, full moon on the night of 16 August 1943, sailed from Bone, Algeria, for Oran, carrying 1,800 Italian prisoners and 26 British prisoner guards. Only 23 minutes out of port, German bombers attacked with torpedoes, one of which blew a hole 50 feet wide and 21 feet deep between number one and number two holds. The hundreds of shouting, screaming Italian prisoners, filled with panic, broke out to the open deck and rushed the lifeboats, but did not know how to launch them. Fortunately, there were two Italian-speaking men in the crew, and on orders from the captain, they circulated among the wildly milling prisoners, assuring them that the vessel was in no immediate danger of sinking. The panic subsided and the *Contee* returned to Bone under her own power, but many prisoners were killed in their mad scramble. The *Contee* later became a blockship at Normandy.

☐

Expecting to be bombed was bad enough, but being told when to expect it was considerably worse. As the *Edward Bates* passed Gibraltar on 31 January 1944 in a 54-ship convoy bound for Italy, her captain heard this disconcerting news on a German-English broadcast: "A 54-ship convoy is now passing Gibraltar. It will be attacked within a few hours." That evening, as predicted, torpedo-bombers hit the convoy. The *Bates*, not yet one day in the Med, was only one of the victims.

The year before, the *Samuel Parker*, known to her crew as the *Fightin' Sam*, shuttled around the Mediterranean for six months and collected 140 shell and shrapnel holes in her hull and superstructure during that time. She was the first vessel to be named a "gallant ship of the merchant marine" in World War II, and Captain Elmer J. Stull, Chief Mate N. K. Storkersen, and Able Seaman Fred Anderson all won Merchant Marine Distinguished Service Medals for leadership and heroism in combat.

During the entire war period, a total of 413 merchant ships—1,740,250 tons—were sunk in the Mediterranean by enemy action. No American ships were sunk after June, 1944, and only 30 merchant ships of all Allied nations were sunk in those waters that year. The Germans had sustained such heavy U-boat losses there that Grand Admiral Doenitz gave up trying to replenish submarine forces by way of the "gut," the narrow and shallow seagate at Gibraltar. U. S. Army bombers sank five submarines during a raid at Toulon on 6 August, the few remaining U-boats were destroyed by planes and surface craft, and the submarine threat ceased to exist. As the U. S. Army drove toward Berlin, ships finally sailed the once-more peaceful Med with little to fear from the enemy. But along the African shores, and at the bottom of that sea, were the hulks of hundreds of merchantmen and men-of-war, who had helped to make it so.

Anyone could become an Armed Guard gunner, but the way to become a veteran Armed Guard gunner was to keep both eyes open and one finger on the trigger. Alert gunners could sometimes drive off a bomber or force a submarine down, and if a torpedo was sighted in time, good shooting could destroy it before it hit the ship.

8

THE
PERSIAN
GULF

By the winter of 1942, the Allied powers were faced with an overwhelming logistical problem, that of supplying Russian forces with the munitions needed to resist German attack along a vast front. The situation was complicated by bitter weather conditions in the North Atlantic and limited port facilities in northern Russia. There was urgent need for an alternative or supplement to the Murmansk-Archangel supply line with better weather conditions and a reduction in the intense air, surface, and submarine harassment that was decimating the North Russian convoys. New supply routes by way of the Persian Gulf provided a possible solution to the problem, but they offered primitive port facilities and the lack of good transportation from the Gulf to the Russian border.

Except for the British-built port of Basra in Iraq, shipping facilities were archaic. The Shah of Persia had built a railroad to the Russian border but, not trusting his neighbors, had purposely made it of different gauge than connecting lines in Russia and Iraq.

American engineers sent out to the Persian Gulf to survey the available facilities were quickly followed by construction crews that built docks, roads, railroads, and terminals for handling a vast flow of supplies for the hard-pressed Russians. Soon after port improvements started, the United States began to send a fleet of ships on the long run to the Gulf. They carried every conceivable kind of war and industrial equipment, vital supplies without which the Russians would have collapsed and World War II would have had an entirely different ending.

The Mediterranean at that time was still closed to Allied shipping, so ships had to take the long way around, as they did in the days of the Portuguese and Spanish trade to the Far East several centuries earlier. Three routes were followed. Ships from U. S. East Coast and Gulf ports sailed to Trinidad, then crossed the South Atlantic, rounded the Cape of Good Hope, and sailed up the east coast of Africa through the Indian Ocean and the Arabian Sea. The second route was from Panama down the Pacific coast of South America, eastward around Cape Horn and across the South Atlantic to the Cape of Good Hope, then across the Indian Ocean as before. The third route was from Panama across the South Pacific and around South Australia to Fremantle, then across the Indian Ocean to the Bay of Bengal and the Arabian Sea. It was impossible to convoy ships over such a long route, so they proceeded individually.

Ships sailing to the Persian Gulf used the once-primitive Iranian ports of Khorramshahr, Bandar Shapur, Bushire, and Ahwaz, which had been modernized with quays, rail spurs, and truck-marshalling yards. Big over-the-road convoys ran from the Shatt-Al-Arab area to the Russian border where American drivers, who were not allowed to cross the border, were relieved by Russians. Basra was used mainly by British vessels.

In 1942 and through part of 1943, the Iranian ports were unable to handle the vast flood of incoming supplies from the American arsenal. During the period October, 1942, to February, 1943, the average turnaround for ships there was 55 days. During the first five months of 1943, 59 ships stayed 40 days or more; 46 stayed 50 or more days; 33 were there at least 60 days; 22 ships waited 70 days or more; and nine ships languished in the Gulf area for 80 long days. Three unfortunate freighters waited three months for cargo discharge, and one forgotten crew totaled up 124 days before they slipped their lines and headed down the Gulf toward home.

The supply routes to the British in North Africa and to the Russians in the Persian Gulf were harassed by both German and Japanese submarines. Many ships were sunk in the Arabian Sea, the Indian Ocean, and especially in the Mozambique Channel, a favorite hunting ground for submarines.

An indication of both increased cargo traffic and submarine activity in that theatre is shown by the fact that in 1941 only 20 Allied merchant vessels of all kinds, totaling 73,155 tons, were sunk by enemy action in the entire Indian Ocean. In 1942 the score leaped to 205 ships, a total of 724,485 tons. It dropped to 82 ships in 1943, 50 in 1944, and to only three in 1945.

Among the first American Liberty ships to make the Persian Gulf run were the *Francis L. Lee, Ralph Izzard, Jonathan Grout,* and *Abraham Lincoln.* The *Izzard* had sailed from Philadelphia in October, 1942, and had been waiting to unload for three months when the *Grout* arrived.

The *Francis L. Lee* sailed from the East Coast in August, 1942, and took the Cape Horn route by way of the Panama Canal. Luckier than most ships at that stage of the war, she laid at anchor only two weeks in the Shatt-Al-Arab before proceeding to Khorramshahr for discharge. Then came a long trip to Rio de Janeiro for orders, thence to British Guinea for bauxite. She returned home almost a year after starting her initial loading in June of 1942.

The *Jonathan Grout* reached the Shatt-Al-Arab in March, 1943, 80 days out of New York. From Panama on, she sailed without escort and had sighted but one other vessel between Panama and Fremantle.

In the Indian Ocean, British naval forces warned the *Jonathan Grout* to be alert for enemy surface raiders and submarines. The next night lookouts saw a bluish flare, too bright to be a falling star. It was assumed to be a signal from a German or Japanese submarine, and the guns were manned. The next day, Captain Foster called his crew together for a talk that began with "We are in dangerous waters," and ended with "If we meet the enemy between here and our destination we will man our guns until the last shell is fired."

But the *Jonathan Grout,* more fortunate than other ships, sighted no enemy vessels as she plodded on toward the Shatt-Al-Arab, where the Tigris and Euphrates Rivers meet and the fabled garden of Eden once grew. The crew, with imagination working overtime, could almost smell beer, wine, and exotic perfumes, hear the sharp tinkle of glasses, and see the dark-eyed belly dancers that made things lively "east of Suez," according to the movies.

Finally, the afternoon of 3 March, they saw what appeared to be treetops on the distant horizon; but the trees turned out to be the masts of anchored ships, and there was no port or city to be seen. The *Jonathan Grout* anchored, far from the Persian shore, among three other American Libertys, several British ships, and a Norwegian. One vessel signalled the discouraging news that she had been there since 19 January and added, "Hope you have cigarettes."

But the *Jonathan Grout* had a high priority cargo of aviation supplies and ammunition and two days later went up to Abadan, where for two weeks cargo was discharged by barefooted laborers who knocked off work to rummage through the slop buckets when they were carried out on deck after each meal.

At Abadan, the crew of the *Jonathan Grout* watched other Liberty ships come and go; the *Benjamin Goodhugh*, *Will Rogers*, *William Patterson*, and *Timothy Pickering*, which met a tragic end during the invasion of Sicily.

Later, the *Jonathan Grout* steamed a few miles farther upstream to the American-built port of Khorramshahr, where she completed off-loading, then moved to Basra in Iraq and loaded thousands of aerial bombs for Suez. The bombs, of course, had merely been stockpiled in Iraq. There was a saying among old hands sailing to that part of the world that the Persian Gulf exported only three things: dates, oil, and syphilis.

The *Abraham Lincoln* left New Orleans on her maiden voyage on 14 January 1943, transitted the Panama Canal, and reached Fremantle, Australia, on 28 February. She stopped only long enough for fuel and freshwater and a brief run ashore for the crew. One man, full of Australian beer, jumped overboard and tried to swim back and rejoin the Fremantle "sheilas" as the ship got under way. "Manned a lifeboat," said the ship's log, "rescued the man, hoisted the boat aboard, and proceeded out to sea."

The *Lincoln* reached the Shatt-Al-Arab on 22 March, proceeded to Abadan, and began discharging cargo four days later. By 15 April, the cargo was discharged and the vessel was chartered by the British Ministry of War Transport to haul stockpiled war materials from Basra to Suez.

□

Some ships didn't make it to the Gulf. The ammunition-laden American steamer *La Salle* was one of those routed across the South Atlantic and around the Cape of Good Hope, but she never arrived at her destination, becoming one of the mystery ships of World War II. *La Salle* was probably the victim of a submarine that also failed to return, for no clue to the vessel's fate was obtained from German submarine records after the war. The Armed Guard officer, Lieutenant (junior grade) Carl F. Zeidler, had resigned as mayor of Milwaukee in order to enter the Navy.

The *George Gipp*'s second voyage took her from Philadelphia and Norfolk to the Persian Gulf in November of 1943. With the Mediterranean open then, she had a much shorter voyage by way of Suez. She left Norfolk on 14 November and was back on 8 March, steaming 9,491 miles at an average speed of 11.5 knots.

The *Anne Hutchinson* was en route home from the Middle East when she was torpedoed near Port Elizabeth on 26 October 1942. The torpedo broke the ship's back, and the crew abandoned her. A South African minesweeper and a tug tried to salvage the wreck but, like two ants trying to lug off a cube of sugar, they found the job too much for them, so they dynamited the half-severed sections apart. The after section sank, but they towed the forward part to Port Elizabeth.

The *Pierce Butler* was off Durban on 20 November, headed toward Suez with 9,787 tons of military cargo, when a U-boat put two torpedoes into her. She sank within 30 minutes. After abandoning ship and being questioned by the submarine's officers, the crew spent some hours in the boats before being picked up by HMS *Fortuna* and taken to Durban.

The enemy was not the only danger ships faced on the Persian Gulf run, as the crew of the *Richard Stockton* could well testify. En route from the Persian Gulf to Capetown, this ship ran into a storm during which 125-mile-an-hour winds "pushed the ship around like a toy," blew the paint off the deckhouses, poured water down the stack, and produced a good many prayers. Said an officer, not irreverently: "Every one of us who believed in God was praying during those hours for our deliverance and salvation. Our ship," he added, "miraculously came through."

Liberty ships met many strange experiences on their trips to far corners of the world, but one of the most unique had a touch of the Arabian Nights about it for it involved a man who went for a ride on a magic carpet. The man was Second Cook Helmar Schmidt of the *Richard D. Spaight*, which, on 10 March 1943, was in the Mozambique Channel between Madagascar and Africa.

Early in the evening Schmidt was relaxing on a mattress he had placed atop a forward hatch and was talking to Messman William J. O'Brien when a torpedo hit the ship right beneath them. The blast blew the hatches off the ship and threw the two men higher than the masts. O'Brien was never seen again but Schmidt and his mattress were hurled over the ship and into the sea. The mattress landed still right side up and Schmidt was still on top of it. One of the lifeboats picked him up later, unhurt.

The *Spaight* was struck by another torpedo, but the submarine had to surface and put more than two dozen shells into the ship before she finally went down. All hands were saved except for the unfortunate messman, and after a four day voyage the lifeboats landed safely on the coast of Africa.

The Mozambique Channel and the approaches to Durban were favorite hunting grounds for U-boats. The *Harvey Scott* was only a few hours out of Durban on 3 March 1943 en route to the Persian Gulf in an 11-ship convoy, when a submarine got her. There were no fatalities. Just two days later, the *James Stephens* was torpedoed in approximately the same area, broke in two, and sank. Survivors were picked up by the British ships *Norwich City* and *Nigeria*. One man was lost. The ship carried a strangely assorted cargo of empty beer bottles, empty ammunition cases, and damaged propellers.

The next loss was the *William King*, en route from Bahrein with 18,000 barrels of oil. She was torpedoed by the *U51* on 6 June 1943. Captain Owen H. Reed was taken aboard the submarine, which later delivered him to a prisoner-of-war camp in Java. Six men were lost; the survivors were picked up after three days by a British patrol ship and landed in Africa.

The *Alice F. Palmer* was torpedoed and shelled on 10 July, but all hands were saved. The *William Ellery* was hit 20 days later but made port under her own power. The *Lyman Stewart* was torpedoed on 7 September but not badly damaged. She managed to get off 15 rounds from the 4-inch stern gun, firing in the general direction from which the torpedoes had come, without seeing the submarine. No more attacks were made, and the ship continued on her way.

A more determined submarine got the *Robert Bacon* in the Mozambique Channel on the night of 13–14 July 1943. At about 2330 a torpedo just missed, but a second hit the port side, forward. After the crew abandoned ship, the submarine made another hit. Shortly after midnight a third torpedo blasted the vessel. She sank in ten minutes, taking five of the crew with her.

An unwary U-boat almost ended its career when it sent a torpedo into the *Cornelia Spencer* on 21 September and then surfaced at the indiscreet distance of only 100 yards, probably intending to finish the job with shells. But the *Spencer's* gunners were eager for action and forced the U-boat to crash-dive almost as soon as it broke the surface. An hour later the discomfited raider put another torpedo into the *Spencer*. The after magazine exploded, killed two of the gunners, and destroyed the rudder and propeller. The *Spencer* floated until a third torpedo sent her to the bottom.

Crewmen lost no time in abandoning the *Elias Howe* after she was torpedoed and set on fire on 24 September. The ship was carrying explosives, and 15 minutes after being hit she blew up—"disappeared before the flash and smoke of the explosion had cleared away." Two men were killed in the engine room.

The *Henry Knox* was sunk by a Japanese submarine as she headed up across the Indian Ocean, en route from Fremantle to the Persian Gulf, with 8,200 tons of supplies for the Russians, including tanks, P-39 fighter planes, and a thousand tons of gunpowder. The night of 19 June 1943 a torpedo hit in number three hold, the gunpowder blew up, and the entire ship shook from the concussion. The forward holds erupted with balls of fire that shot higher than the masts. A rain of blazing debris killed and wounded men trying to release the boats.

The flaming cordite fell all over the ship, ignited the deck cargo, blistered paint, and set the boat falls on fire. The boats fell into the sea as the falls burned through. Main engine controls jammed and the ship gradually stopped, sinking slowly by the bow. Men jumped over the sides and boarded life rafts or the three boats that drifted free.

The submarine circled, then approached, and survivors were questioned by a young officer who spoke good English. The submarine's crew was dressed in clean khaki shorts, V-necked blouses, and sandals and appeared quite excited about sinking a valuable ship and cargo.

The Japanese wanted to know the name of the ship, the port from which it had sailed, whether it had stopped in Australia, how many airplanes were in the cargo, and whether the crew had seen any battleships in New York. The Americans tried to be as evasive as possible in their answers. The Japanese then inspected one of the boats, took the charts, mast, and sail, and left. The men were not harmed. All 41 survivors out of the crew of 67 men eventually rowed their boats to the Maldives, from which the last group reached Colombo on 27 July.

The *Jose Navarro* was torpedoed between Aden and Colombo on the night after Christmas of 1943. The torpedo blasted a big hole in the bow, and the *Navarro* settled almost to the level of the main deck, forward. All hands, including 83 American soldiers, got off. But there was a touch of pathos to the scene, because the ship had a deckload of mules that had to be left behind. Early the next morning, the captain, chief engineer, and 28 volunteers reboarded the vessel to see if she could proceed under her own power, but they judged her too unseaworthy for this and left her again. All 166 men were picked up by the *Rajputana* of the Indian Navy and landed at Cochin. A plane searched the area two days later to find only pieces of flotsam where the ship went down. That same day, the *Robert F. Hoke* was torpedoed off Somalia but remained afloat and was towed to Aden.

Many a lonely soldier in the Persian Gulf Command never received his 1943 Christmas mail because some 500 bags of it went down when the *Albert Gallatin*, en route from Aden to Bandar Shapur, was sunk by a submarine on 1 January 1944. After the ship had been abandoned, there was a violent explosion, then she broke in two forward of the mainmast and sank. Moments later, survivors were amazed to see the bow pop back to the surface, float for a while, and go down again. About 15 minutes after the ship had sunk, there was an exceptionally violent explosion in the water that was heard aboard the HMS *Britannia* six miles away. There was speculation that the tremendous delayed blast was caused by some unusually powerful explosive in the cargo of which captain and crew were unaware. All 71 of the men aboard survived.

The crew of the *Walter Camp* was also lucky as she steamed from Aden toward Colombo on 25 January 1944. A submarine torpedo sent her down in 15 minutes, with a cargo of barges, steel, truck bodies, cranes, and earth-moving machinery. All hands were picked up by HMS *Danae* and landed at Aden.

A Liberty ship operated by the government of China, the *Chung Cheng*, was the victim of a German submarine just before midnight on 3 February 1944, while bound from Chochin, India, to Aden with 8,350 tons of ilmenite. Besides a merchant crew of 29 Chinese and an Armed Guard contingent of 27 Americans, the *Chung Cheng* was carrying eleven U. S. and four Chinese merchant marine officers. Like many other ships that were torpedoed while carrying cargoes of heavy ore, the *Chung Cheng* sank so quickly that all of the boats could not be launched. Twenty men were lost.

Japanese submarines were active in the Indian Ocean area in 1944, and one of them got the *Richard Hovey*, homeward bound from India, on 29 March. After the crew abandoned ship, the Japanese pursued their accustomed practice of shooting at the survivors and running down the lifeboats. Either their aim was bad or their heart was no longer in their work, for only four crewmen were lost in this sadistic endeavor.

Many more men would have been lost, however, if John Drechsler, a junior assistant engineer, had not been able to fashion a primitive still and make 60 gallons of fresh water for the 38 men who spent 16 days in a life boat under a torrid equatorial sun before being rescued by the British Liberty ship *Samuta*. The other boat, with 25 men, was picked up after only three days by another British Liberty, the *Samcalia*.

□

The Liberty *Jean Nicolet* also met a Japanese submarine, but with much more tragic results. She was homeward bound down the Arabian Sea on 2 July 1944 with a merchant crew of 41, an Armed Guard contingent of 28, and an Army and civilian passenger list of 30, many of them men returning home after two or more years in the Persian Gulf.

The first torpedo hit in number two hold and the second in number four. The vessel took a heavy starboard list. All hands abandoned ship safely in four lifeboats and two rafts.

The submarine soon surfaced and began shelling the deserted hulk. After firing ten or twelve rounds at the ship, the raider circled around the wreck to the rafts and lifeboats, and an officer on the conning tower shouted to them through a megaphone:

"All come here!"

The first boat to approach the submarine contained about 25 merchant seamen, Navy gunners, civilians, and soldiers. As they climbed aboard their life preservers were snatched from them. Japanese sailors also took their watches, wallets, and shirts and shoes.

The survivors were then prodded with bayonets onto the forward deck, where they were ordered to kneel and their hands were tied behind them with wire, lines, and strips of clothing. William Musser, a messboy who did not kneel fast enough, was shot in the back and thrown over the side. So began a night-long orgy of torture and murder.

One by one, the boats and rafts were ordered to the submarine. A machine gun was trained on each boat as it came alongside. Men were clubbed with lengths of pipe and cut with knives and bayonets.

When Lieutenant Deale, the Navy Armed Guard officer and five of his gunners tried to paddle away on a tiny doughnut raft, the Japanese turned on a searchlight and then opened fire. A man was hit and fell over the side, but the others flattened themselves on the raft, and the searchlight was soon cut off, the Japanese evidently assuming they had been killed.

The men lay as still as they could while the submarine circled the slowly sinking ship and listened to the screams and cries of their comrades. As the night wore on, men succumbed to wounds and beatings and were shoved off the submarine into the sea. Others were forced to run a gauntlet of clubs, pistols, knives, and pieces of pipe. When Charles Pyle, the first assistant engineer, hesitated, a sailor hit him on the head with the butt of a pistol. Another kicked him in the back and sent him reeling through the line of yelling, flailing seamen, until he stumbled over the side into the sea. The cold water revived him and he paddled away, struggling to free his hands. He was about to give up when Able Seaman Stuart Vanderhurst hoisted him head first onto a floating hatchboard.

Vanderhurst had slid off the bow of the submarine and swam away unnoticed earlier in the night. His wrists had not been tightly fastened and he freed them with a clasp knife the Japanese had overlooked.

By then the submarine was almost indistinct, marked by the glow from its hatches and lights carried by crewmen as they moved up and down the deck. The cries of the captives gradually diminished as they were beaten unconscious, one by one, or kicked overboard.

About dawn, when a distant aircraft was heard, the submarine hurriedly submerged, leaving several survivors still on its deck to flounder in the sea and drown but for a Navy gunner who, like Vanderhurst, had secreted a knife in his trousers, cut his own bonds, and then freed the others who were still afloat.

Minutes later, a Catalina patrol plane flew overhead, made a few lazy circles and left. It returned several hours later to drop life preservers and food. Some 30 hours later the frigate *Huxac* of the Indian Navy picked up the 23 survivors of the 99 men on the *Jean Nicolet*.

□

As prosaic merchant ships plodded up the trade routes where a "quinquireme of Ninevah" once carried "ivory, apes and peacocks," it would have been only fitting that one of them carried something more exotic than jeeps, mules, and C-rations. Such a ship was the *John Barry*, a most unlikely looking treasure ship as she steamed across the Arabian Sea in August of 1944. But securely crated and locked in her holds was a fortune more fabulous than even Ali Babi and his forty thieves could have hoped for—$26 million in silver bullion.

On 28 August a submarine put two torpedoes into the *John Barry*. The sea flooded two holds, the ship's back broke, and she went down in 1,000 fathoms of water. All but two of her crew were rescued by the Dutch tanker *Sunetta* and another Liberty, the *Benjamin Bourn*. Somewhere in the Arabian Sea one of the richest treasures of all time waits, well protected by a mile of saltwater, for the future technique that may enable salvage crews to bring it up.

Even more intriguing than the treasure in the *John Barry* was the mystery in her. What need could there have been, among all the military supplies sent to the Russians, for $26 million in silver? Why was such a fortune shipped in an unescorted, 10-knot Liberty ship? The answers will probably remain hidden among other unexplained mysteries of World War II.

By the time World War II ended, the little-known Persian Gulf run had become a vast shipping operation. More than 30,000 American service troops were stationed in the various Gulf ports to handle the food, ammunition, and military equipment bound for Russia. Hundreds of American engineers and workmen had modernized Persian Gulf ports with docks, roads, and other facilities.

Shipping losses in the Persian Gulf run were lumped together with all other parts of the Indian Ocean, so the number of Liberty ships sunk while on definite runs to the Gulf is not easily ascertained. In the first three years of the war, only 45 ships were sunk in the entire theatre. But in 1942, the year Liberty ships started on the Persian Gulf run, 205 ships were sunk. All together, 385 ships were sunk in the Indian Ocean. More than a few of them were the hard-working Libertys.

Dragging their white wakes behind them, the convoys plodded across peaceful looking waters where death might strike at any moment. At 275 miles a day, it took a long time to go anywhere, but anywhere a convoy went, there was certain to be a Liberty ship or so going with it. There is one here, at the left end of the five-ship row of a convoy heading west across the Pacific in September of 1942.

9

THE

PACIFIC

The largest battleground of World War II was the Pacific Ocean, which spreads across nearly half the globe. There the United States Navy and the Imperial Japanese Navy fought the battles that made headlines: Coral Sea, Midway, Guadalcanal, Leyte, Okinawa. At the same time, in minor actions extending from Southern California to the Aleutians and from Australia to the Ryukyu Islands, torpedoes, bombs, and suicide planes left the wrecks of many merchant ships to testify to the widespread toll of war in that vast sea.

For the merchant marine, the sea war reached to the very shores of the United States when raiding Japanese submarines torpedoed or shelled several vessels along the West Coast. The tanker *Emidio* lost five men when she was shelled and torpedoed by the Japanese submarine *18* some 18 miles off Crescent City, California, on 20 December 1941. She was the first ship sunk in American coastal waters in World War II.

The great American counteroffensive in the Pacific, involving incredible logistic support, would have been impossible without the use of a vast merchant fleet, a great percentage of which was composed of Liberty ships. By 1944 hun-

dreds of these ships were streaming across the Pacific, delivering millions of tons
of food, ammunition, guns, and other military supplies. They took part in all the
landings after Guadalcanal. Many Liberty ships and hundreds of merchant sailors
were lost getting their cargoes across that vast ocean area.

The first Liberty ship sunk in the Pacific was the *John Adams*, carrying 2,000
tons of gasoline, torpedoed the night of 5 May 1942 near New Caledonia. "A
rumbling explosion shook the ship," a survivor reported. "Lights went out.
Things that weren't bolted down fell and tumbled all over the place." Five Navy
gunners were killed. The rest of the crew, 45 in all, abandoned ship.

The next day a Greek ship found the *John Adams* still afloat and, hoping to
tow her into port, sent a boarding party on board. They found the midships deckhouse gutted by fire and the ship's cat purring on the bow. After a heavy explosion in number three hold, they left as quickly as they could, and the ship sank
soon afterward.

The next Liberty lost was the *William Dawes*. She was en route from Adelaide
to Brisbane, Australia, on 21 July 1942 when a torpedo exploded in her after
magazine, blew the stern off, killed three men, and injured four others. But she
refused to sink until HMAS *Southhampton* sent her down with gunfire.

The *Samuel Gompers* was torpedoed by a Japanese submarine on 20 January
1943 near New Caledonia. That torpedo, too, must have hit the magazine in the
stern; the after gun platform was under water in little more than a minute and
within five minutes the *Gompers* went down. Heavy seas capsized two boats on
launching, but one was righted and manned. All but one of the 16 men in the
captain's boat were injured in varying degrees. Two boats reached New Caledonia
after rowing and sailing for a week; one was picked up by *PT111* after two
weeks.

On their return voyages, Libertys often carried raw materials for war production and civilian needs. The *Peter H. Burnett* was not long out of Newcastle, Australia, with 18,154 bales of wool and 123 bags of mail when, on 22 January 1943,
a torpedo hit in number five hold. It blew the hatch covers off and threw bales of
wool on the deck and into the sea.

All hands abandoned ship except for the Armed Guard officer, the Army communications liaison officer, two cadets, and the engineers, who remained aboard
hoping to get a shot at the submarine. But the raider, probably assuming one
hit would sink its victim, disappeared. The *Burnett* was towed to Sydney, where
most of the cargo was salvaged.

Only a couple of weeks later, on 9 February 1943, the *Starr King* was en route to New Caledonia from Sydney when a submarine periscope was sighted, but it disappeared as soon as the guns were manned. After several hours, the gunners were relieved from battle stations and all hands relaxed. The following morning either the same submarine or another fired four torpedoes at the *Starr King*, two of which were hits. HMAS *Warramonga* tried to tow the vessel into port, but she gradually settled and went down in mid-afternoon.

The *William Williams* fared better on 2 May when a torpedo put a hole 40 feet long and 30 feet wide in her port side. The crew abandoned ship, but when the submarine did not come back to finish the job, most of them reboarded her, got up steam, and sailed her to Suva with the help of the USS *Catalpa*.

Just two weeks later, the *William K. Vanderbilt*, en route from Vila Efate to Suva, was hit by two torpedoes. Only one man was lost, although the submarine surfaced and machine gunned the lifeboats. Unlike other incidents of this kind, the machine-gunning seemed to be more a taunt than a deliberate attempt to eliminate survivors, for the submarine soon disappeared.

For some reason, Japanese submarines had numerous chances to finish off ships crippled by torpedo explosions but left without doing so, perhaps to conserve torpedoes, figuring the victim was a helpless hulk and would be of no further war use.

One such ship was the *Matthew Lyon*, torpedoed between Guadalcanal and Espiritu Santo. Despite a 35-foot-long hole in number three hold, the *Matthew Lyon* reached Espiritu Santo under her own power. There were no fatalities, and injuries were limited to a few cuts and bruises.

In a similar attack two days later, the *H. M. DeYoung*, en route to Espiritu Santo with road scrapers, cranes, trucks, and other heavy equipment, took a torpedo in the engine room that killed the watch below. She was towed to Nukualofa, Tongatabu, by the tanker *Quebec*.

A Japanese plane, one of three mistaken for friendly Navy torpedo-bombers, hit the *George H. Himes* at Koli Point, Guadalcanal, on 11 October 1943, while she was discharging cargo. The *Himes* was beached by the USS *Menominee*, and most of the cargo was salvaged. There was no loss of life. The *John H. Couch* was hit in the same attack.

Army commanders faced with severe logistical headaches fell in love with Libertys when they appeared in the South Pacific in 1942; so much so that they began commandeering them whenever they could for intratheatre, island-to-island shuttle services. Some became emergency troopships, being equipped with field kitchens, trough latrines flushed by fire hoses, and not much more in the way of accommodations. Each ship carried 900 men, most of whom had to sleep on bare decks.

"Passage on a Liberty ship," an Army general stated, "serves well as preparation for the hardships that lie ahead." Or, as the troops were apt to put it, "You spend a couple of weeks in the troop compartment of a Liberty, and you'll fight anyone to get ashore!"

Despite protestations by the WSA, the Army always had a number of these ships on island shuttles; and had as many as 11 serving troop ships in January of 1943. Many more Libertys worked for the Navy, and dozens of them were commissioned in the Navy* as cargo vessels. One of these ships may have been the fictional USS *Reluctant,* made famous in the novel, *Mr. Roberts,* by Thomas Heggen. Ports in the Pacific were given secret code names, such as *Echo, Fold,* and *Epic,* which Heggen paraphrased most appropriately as he described the routine of a cargo ship in the backwaters of the war:

"For the most part, it stayed on its regular run from Tedium to Apathy and back, about five days each way. It made an occasional trip to Monotony. . . ."

While some cargo ships in the Pacific experienced brief moments of action, for most of them the war varied between Tedium and Monotony. Gunners on the *José C. Barbosa* would have welcomed the sight of a Zero to break the boredom of unexciting "milk-runs" to South Pacific supply bases. Her maiden voyage, starting at San Francisco, lasted nine months and took her to Espiritu Santo, Milne Bay, Buna, Longemak, Lae, Biak, Hollandia, and Seadler Island.

The maiden voyage of the *Benjamin Franklin* involved an uneventful delivery of 10,000 tons of bombs, fuses, rations, trucks, gasoline, road graders, flour, Army cots, asphalt, lime, and nitrate to Vila in the New Hebrides. She returned by way of Antofogasta, Chile, for a cargo of ore. The only break in the routine came when a fireman did not report on the 4-to-8 watch. "A thorough search was made," said the ship's log. "Various members of the crew were questioned as to when the man was last seen and why he might want to jump overboard. He was not found."

When it came to long trips, sailors liked to tell about a Liberty ship that hauled a cargo of barbed wire around the South Pacific for six months until, finding no

* See Appendix C.

one to accept it, the disgusted captain finally headed back to the West Coast where it was discovered that the wire should have gone to Italy.

This story, true or not, was probably not greatly exaggerated. The *James Buchanan,* on her maiden voyage to the South Pacific in 1943, carried a deckload of PT-boats, equipment for a complete PT base, and 200 men of a PT squadron, riding in troop quarters in number two hold. The cargo was consigned to Pago Pago, but no one there would accept it. Not intending to roam the South Pacific like the Ancient Mariner, the skipper had the cargo unloaded and piled neatly on the waterfront. Two years later, most of it was still there, eloquent testimony to the waste and confusion of war. No one ever asked him what became of it.

Some anonymous poet on the *James Buchanan* penned a tribute to the military supply confusion and titled it *The New Guinea Theme Song.*

> Things ARE as snafu as they seem,
> Confusion and chaos reign supreme,
> So chuck it back aboard and we're on our way
> To Manus, Finsch and Milne Bay.
> Where we'll drop the hook and wait some more,
> Maybe then they'll know the score.
> But it's odds on end—ten to one at best,
> That they're as screwed up as the rest.
> And we'll sit around for a month or so
> With our spirits drooping and our morale low.

But all was not boredom aboard the *Buchanan.* Early in 1943 she was unloading bombs and ammunition at Noumea, New Caledonia. As First Mate Harland Soetan remembered it, the dock was piled with ammunition when a sling load was suddenly ignited. It exploded, setting off a pile of charges for fragmentation bombs.

"I was standing on the dock when it started," he recalled. "Chunks of metal began zooming past me like a scrap iron barrage. I flopped down on the dock, expecting to be chopped up by flying steel. Navy longshoremen jumped off the ship into the water. A sailor was sitting on a staging overside of a ship next to us when a big piece of metal almost cut him in half."

Peter Tregeboff, the ship's purser, took a fire hose into a hold when fragments of hot steel started a fire, and braved a hail of flying metal to let go all forward lines so the vessel could maneuver out of the dock into the harbor. Fortunately, the explosion was confined. There was no calamity such as that at Hells Point on Guadalcanal where she was scheduled to load ammunition a few days later. The ship arrived at Guadalcanal on the night of the explosion.

Explosions were not uncommon when ships were handling ammunition. The *Juan Cabrillo* was at the Nickle Dock, Noumea, on 1 November 1943, when ammunition exploded on the pier. Two of her Armed Guard were killed and three seriously wounded. Lieutenant (junior grade) Glen L. Davis, the Armed Guard officer, suffered a broken hip and other injuries.

Another ammunition explosion, far more spectacular and costly, rocked the San Francisco Bay area the night of 17 July 1944, as the Liberty ship *E. A. Bryan* and the Victory ship *Quinault Victory* loaded ammunition at the Port Chicago Annex of the Mare Island Navy Yard. There was an estimated 10,000 tons of ammunition in the ships or on the docks when a blinding flash filled the sky and two blasts shook buildings from Sacramento to San Jose. A plane flying 7,000 feet above Port Chicago was peppered by flying debris and made an emergency landing at Fairfield. Windows were knocked out 50 miles away. The town of Port Chicago, a mile away, was almost eradicated. In ten seconds the two ships, the dock, an ammunition train, a locomotive, and two Coast Guard boats vanished, and with them went 327 men. Only 25 bodies were ever recovered.

□

Typical of many another Liberty ship peregrination was the ten-month voyage of the *Clarence H. Matson*, which started from San Francisco in March of 1944. With Milne Bay, New Guinea, as a "home port," she shuttled to bases and forward supply areas all over the southwest Pacific. In another wartime snafu, the *Matson* unloaded a cargo at Hollandia and then picked it all up again on her next trip. More disgusted than the ship's crew were the sweating Army troops who had handled the same 6,000 tons of heavy cargo twice.

Wartime snafus did not end instantly the day the war ended, and the crew of the *Ada Rehan* spent eleven months learning this the hard way. The ship left San Francisco in August 1945, bound for New Orleans, but was diverted to Iquique, Chile, to load nitrates for Alexandria, Egypt. Before she reached Alexandria, she was again diverted to Tripoli, where she blundered into a minefield and was saved only by a plane that spotted her predicament and guided her out. The captain had a nervous breakdown and turned the ship over to the first mate. At Port Said the crew refused to work but finally agreed to sail the ship on to Khorramshahr, Iran.

There they adopted a vodka-drinking ape named Chippy. A few days out, bound for Ceylon, Singapore, and Shanghai, three women and a young child were discovered on board, smuggled out of Iran. Relations between captain and crew reached the boiling point. Then Chippy disappeared, with the skipper blaming the crew and the crew blaming the skipper for such monkey business. By the time the ship reached Shanghai, nine men had deserted and nine aliens had been picked up along the way to replace them. From Shanghai, the ship sailed for New Caledonia, where she picked up 21 homesick soldiers who had been stranded there, and headed for San Francisco. But again she was diverted and wound up in New York instead, on 5 July 1946, after an 11-month voyage "to everywhere."

The *Uriah M. Rose* spent a year as an island-hopper and once at Biak waited five weeks to discharge cargo. No Japanese were ever seen, but an Armed Guard gunner shot a shipmate while cleaning a revolver and another was seriously injured trying to dissect a souvenir shell.

Another island-hopper was the *Moina Michael;* her maiden voyage out of New Orleans lasted nine months, and despite the fact that she went to Manus, Hollandia, Biak, Finschaffen, Leyte, Mindoro, and Luzon, her Armed Guard officer reported, almost regretfully, "no enemy action."

The *Velva Lockwood* was another Liberty that always seemed to just miss the action. In the invasion of Normandy she had to report "no contact with the enemy." Then she reached Leyte Gulf in April, 1945, and waited 33 days for orders.

□

Such inactivity, together with long, boring trips inevitably led to friction and general erosion in crew morale. The Armed Guard officer was taken off one ship because of his proclivity for fighting with the master, a rough-spoken "square-head" who was a capable mariner but not very adept at shipboard diplomacy or wardroom etiquette. The Armed Guard officers, many of them young business executives and college graduates, were unable to understand the rough-hewn and often self-schooled type of prewar merchant ship master and this could lead to friction, especially when there was a complete lack of the battle action that most of them desired.

On one ship ill-feeling between the Armed Guard and merchant crew culminated in a wild fight with bottles of ink from the ship's cargo. The battle surged into the saloon, which from then on was known as the "leopard skin room."

Shuttle runs could have their lighter moments. Cargo unloading operations on one ship increased greatly in tempo when SeaBee cargo-handlers learned that liquor for an officers' club was stowed in one hold. The captain posted officers to make sure that the liquor would reach the club, but when the hold was almost bare and the liquor had still not come up, he ordered an investigation which showed, too late, that the SeaBees had merely transferred the liquor into empty ammunition cases. These were "accidentally" dropped into the harbor, from whence they were fished out by cooperating landing craft.

Long delays in discharging were common for Libertys on Pacific runs. The *Ada Rehan* waited 28 days to unload at Humboldt Bay, Hollandia, in 1944, because of the lack of dock space. She also lay at anchor for long periods at Finschafen, Maffin Bay, Morotai, and other ports waiting to discharge or load. Her Armed Guard officer, Lieutenant (junior grade) Christianson, reported that morale was much impaired because "little or no attempt is made to forward Armed Guard or merchant marine mail as it arrives in New Guinea, although the Army and Navy enjoy excellent mail service. This situation," he added, "is the cause of much dissatisfaction."

□

If there had been boredom and seeming lack of purpose in these island runs, it all ended when the merchant ships joined convoys for the invasion of the Philippines at Leyte in October, 1944. In two weeks, Libertys and other merchant ships delivered 30,000 troops and 500,000 tons of supplies to Leyte, fighting off almost continuous air attacks. They were credited with shooting down at least 107 enemy planes in the ten weeks after D-Day. Much of this shooting was done by merchant seamen who took the places of Navy gunners killed or injured in air attacks.

In the initial Leyte landing, the *Adoniram Judson* distinguished herself by not only delivering urgently needed aircraft landing mats and aviation gasoline for the captured field at Tacloban but also providing the principal air cover there for several days. The *Judson* was honored for her fighting abilities by being named a "Gallant Ship of the Merchant Marine," joining a select company of ships so cited by the Maritime Commission for outstanding service under combat conditions.

The crew of the *Judson* was virtually sitting on dynamite, for her holds contained 3,000 barrels of high-octane gasoline. She anchored at San Pedro Bay on 22 October under a full moon—and a heavy attack by fighters and bombers. Three Zeros were beaten off by 20-millimeter fire; the 3-inch gun kept the high-level bombers at a safe distance, and as soon as the attack was over Army troops began discharging her cargo.

This is a typical entry from the ship's log:

> "Jap Zero making run on the stern. Aft three-inch gun opened fire and forced him away at 1,500 yards ... Jap plane coming in on the stern. At 3,000 yards opened barrage and plane swerved off to starboard ... two Jap bombers overhead at medium altitude. Poor visibility. Dropped strings of bombs inshore near MacArthur's headquarters ... two Jap bombers port side at 5,000 yards. Barrage diverted them."

The crew was on continuous alert at Tacloban. The Navy gunners ate and slept at the guns, while the merchant crew carried ammunition, loaded the 20-millimeter magazines, and helped to man the lighter armament.

The *Adoniram Judson* was credited by the WSA with being the first merchant ship to actually dock in the Philippines after the invasion, although the *David Dudley Field* claimed to have been the first American freighter to return to the islands. To celebrate this historic event, the *Field*'s gunners shot down several enemy attackers and claimed three "probables." But the ship paid a heavy price for its good shooting when a suicide bomber crashed into the after gun tub and severely wounded several men.

The *Marcus Daly* was another fighting freighter honored as a "Gallant Ship" for her role in the invasion at Leyte. Two of her crew, killed trying to save wounded shipmates, were posthumously awarded the Merchant Marine Distinguished Service Medal. "This ship," said the WSA, "was under constant air attack for several days and was credited with shooting down several planes." Merchant seamen assisted in manning the guns. General MacArthur commended the *Marcus Daly* for saving the dock area from serious damage or destruction:

> For six days and nights, her guns, manned by a skillful and courageous crew, defeated vigorous attacks by enemy planes in a series of heroic actions. In December of 1944, she again engaged enemy bombers

and suicide planes and emerged victorious. The stark courage of her gallant crew against great odds caused her name to be perpetuated as a Gallant Ship.

On her second voyage to the Philippines, with 1,100 troops on board, the *Marcus Daly* was again attacked by Japanese planes. Able Seaman Alvin R. Crawford was killed instantly. Able Seaman Richard G. Matthiesen was severely wounded but managed to drag two men clear of a fire. He died soon after.

The *Thomas Nelson,* anchored with some 20 other ships at Dulag Bay on 20 November, had 633 Army troops and hundreds of tons of ammunition still on board when a suicide plane roared through a barrage of 20-millimeter fire and crashed on deck. Its bomb exploded on impact, killing 140 soldiers, Navy gunners, and merchant seamen.

The USS *Sonoma,* a small Navy tanker, was tied up alongside the *Augustus Thomas* when Japanese twin-engine bombers raided the anchorage early in the morning of 24 October. The men on the *Sonoma* would just as soon have been somewhere else at that moment, for the *Thomas* carried 3,000 tons of ammunition plus 1,000 drums of aviation gasoline.

One bomber, hit by antiaircraft fire, dived on the ship with both engines on fire, hit the stack of the *Sonoma,* and bounced against the *Thomas.* Its bombs blew a hole in the side of the *Thomas* and set the *Sonoma* ablaze from stem to stern. The *Thomas* had 548 men on board at the time, but amazingly, no one was killed.

A suicide plane hit the *Benjamin Ide Wheeler* on 27 October, and a gasoline fire in number five hold turned the bulkhead of number four hold red-hot. Despite the possibility that the ship might blow up, crewmen poured water into the hold to prevent the spread of the flames and to cool drums of fuel that had not yet caught fire. When a man fell into an adjoining hold, Cadet John Allen Wilson went down into this potential inferno, hot from the nearby fire and filled with steam, put a line around the helpless sailor, and helped hoist him to safety on the open deck. The *Wheeler* sat at Leyte for 76 days, an immobile hulk for most of that time.

Each ship at Leyte had a different story. The *Wilbur C. Atwater* logged 165 air raids and alerts during her stay in the Gulf but came out without harm. The *W. B. Ayer* towed an LCI into Leyte Gulf and then laid there for over a month without firing a gun. The *Jeremiah Daly* had many casualties when a kamikaze hit her just forward of the bridge. There was also heavy loss of life on the *Gilbert Stuart* on 18 November when a kamikaze hit a 20-millimeter gun tub. Although they could have jumped overboard and probably escaped the deadly impact, the gun crew fired at the oncoming plane until it crashed on top of them.

Six crewmen were injured when a bomb hit the *William S. Ladd*, completely wrecking the engine room and starting fires that gutted the ship. The *Otis Skinner* had a suicide plane crash through the main deck and explode in the 'tween deck, blasting a 35-foot-long hole in the hull, but no one was killed or injured, and she returned to the United States under her own power for repairs. The *Floyd Spencer*, approaching Leyte on her maiden voyage, was attacked by a Japanese torpedo-bomber, but Captain Simpson Blackwood maneuvered to evade the torpedo, and *Spencer*'s gunners splashed the bomber.

The *Matthew P. Deady* had just arrived at Tacloban on 3 November when several Japanese raiders bombed and strafed the shipping. Gunners on the *Juan Cabrillo* knocked down a plane headed directly for their ship, but it burst into flames and crashed into the *Deady*, killing four of the Armed Guard. Twenty-two soldiers were killed when the exploding plane set off a load of liquid acetylene. Arthur F. Maxam, an ordinary seaman on the *Deady*, received the Merchant Marine Meritorious Service Medal for heroic action in leading a group of volunteers into a blazing hold full of carbide and other inflammable cargo, an action that probably saved their ship. On 12 November another suicide plane missed the *Deady* and splashed into the bay nearby. Three more kamikazes were splashed by that ship, which claimed a total of six planes killed during 44 raids at Tacloban.

More than 400 troops had been off-loaded from the *Alexander Majors* when ten Japanese planes raided Dulag harbor at Leyte. A single-engine fighter, despite the fire of every gun that could bear, crashed into the mainmast, severed it ten feet above the deck, and then exploded and showered the deckhouse and the forward part of the ship with gasoline and bits of metal. Her crew, with the aid of foamite brought aboard by a Navy LCI, brought the fire under control. Two crewmen were killed; several gunners were badly wounded.

When a bomber hit the *Morrison R. Waite*, the explosion started a fire in a load of Army trucks. Able Seaman Anthony Martinez went below and rescued several Army longshoremen, then dove overboard and saved two soldiers who had been blown into the water. Twenty-one men were killed and 43 more were wounded. The *Antoine Saugrain* beat off several of 35 bombers during one raid on Leyte. Almost all of her Navy gunners were wounded, and merchant seamen manned the guns until the ship was hit and sunk by an aerial torpedo. The *Alcoa Pioneer*'s merchant crew also manned the guns after most of the Navy gunners had been killed or wounded.

The *Mary Kinney* claimed five kills at Leyte, as did the *Charlotte Cushman*. The *Laurence Gianella, Sidney H. Short, Clarence Darrow,* and *John W. Foster* claimed two each. Captain James Blaisdell of the *Mary Kinney* received the Merchant Marine Distinguished Service Medal for his organization and leadership in that ship's protection and defense.

□

Pacific beachheads took a toll of 44 merchant ships, most of them Libertys, which were sunk by kamikazes, bombers, shellfire, or torpedo attack. Many others were seriously damaged but were not listed as total losses.

For the merchant marine, the Mindoro landings in the Philippines were the most expensive in terms of ships and men. More merchant mariners lost their lives at Mindoro, according to the War Shipping Administration, than did members of the Armed Forces taking part in the D-Day invasion.

A convoy that left Leyte on 27 December for Mindoro had two especially tragic and spectacular losses. A dive-bomber hit the ammunition-laden *John Burke*, and the ship disappeared in a blast so devastating that when the smoke cleared away there was not even a handful of floating debris to mark where the ship and her 68 men had been. The *Lewis Dyche*, also loaded with ammunition, was hit by a kamikaze at Magrin Bay on 4 January. The ship and her crew of 71 were completely disintegrated.

The *Francisco Morazon* was the only one of four Liberty ships in this particular convoy to make the trip without being sunk or damaged. Lieutenant John J. Hartley, the Armed Guard officer, credited their survival to the "unceasing alertness of my men and the wonderful cooperation from the merchant crew. We fired ten tons of ammunition, all of which the merchant crew passed to us. . . . The men never left their gun positions from the time we sailed from Leyte till we arrived off Mindoro 72 hours later . . . we knocked down six planes and hit three others."

Brigadier General W. C. Dunkel of the West Visayan Task Force commended Captain John J. Brady and the officers and crew of the *Francisco Morazon* for "outstanding performance of duty. . . . The *Francisco Morazon*, with a cargo of bombs and other ammunition, maintained full efficiency and a well disciplined ship's crew and guncrew despite its perilous cargo."

At Mindoro the *Juan de Fuca* was fired at by Japanese surface ships, strafed by fighter planes, and blasted by an aerial torpedo. Captain Charles Robbins and his crew beached the ship before she sank, then helped to salvage the *John M. Clayton*, another Liberty that had been torpedoed and bombed.

The *James H. Breasted* narrowly missed being hit by fire from the same Japanese task force that shelled the *Juan de Fuca*, then was sunk in a bombing attack; but not before landing 600 Army troops without a single injury to passengers or crew.

In the same operation the *Hobart Baker* was sunk by an aerial torpedo while carrying a load of steel landing mats. The *Chief Charlot*, luckier, shot down a Japanese transport plane taking paratroops to Mindoro.

The *David F. Barry* escaped an ammunition explosion by the heroic action of 27-year-old J. F. Parker, an oiler. When fire broke out in a hold, presumably because of the carelessness of cargo-handlers, Parker took a heaving line into the hold and made it fast around an ignited smoke bomb so that the potentially explosive "fuse," laying among 25 tons of gelatin, percussion caps, and TNT, could be hoisted out and thrown over the side.

At Luzon, the *Edward N. Westcott* fired on a bomber headed directly for the ship and blew the plane to pieces, but the engine catapulted over the vessel, smashed two cargo booms, and finally crashed amidships. Six merchant seamen and seven members of the Armed Guard were wounded.

In mid-afternoon of New Year's Day, 1945, the *Floyd W. Spencer* was attacked by a torpedo-bomber, that dropped its torpedo at 1,800 yards. At 1,000 yards all of the ship's 20-millimeters that could bear opened up and splashed the plane. The torpedo missed by 20 feet. The *Gus Darnell*, not quite so lucky, was hit by an aerial torpedo but did not sink. She was patched up and became a floating storehouse for Army supplies in the Philippines.

Bad weather was welcome, in a way, because it kept the kamikazes at their home bases, but it slowed up the war in other ways. The *Juan Cabrillo*'s log noted that heavy swells in Lingayan Gulf made it difficult to handle cargo, and there were many days when it was too rough for landing craft to come alongside.

There were 500 Army troops and 2,500 tons of vehicles and gasoline in drums aboard the *Kyle V. Johnson* as she steamed toward Lingayan Gulf on 12 January

1945, in a 100-ship convoy about evenly divided between ships and LSTs. At 0130 the convoy was attacked by six or more planes, one of which crashed into the starboard side of the *Johnson* at number three hatch. The engine plowed through the hull-plating into a 'tween decks crowded with troops and thence into the lower hold.

Said a survivor: "There was a blinding flash and an explosion so heavy it blew the steel hatch beams higher than the flying bridge." The ship dropped out of convoy to fight the fire, extinguished the flames, and then rejoined the fleet, but with 129 men killed and many injured.

□

Far from the headline-making battles of the central and southwest Pacific, Liberty ships also helped fight a much lesser-known campaign of the Pacific war, the defense of Alaska and the recapture of the Aleutians from the Japanese. The war in the Aleutians had as much tedium and as many snafus as any other, but it went on in mists, fog, ice, cold, and howling williwaws and was overshadowed in history by the strategically decisive battles of Midway and the Philippine Sea.

Except for the occasional mention of Dutch Harbor, Adak, or Attu in war communiques, the Alaskan Theatre was as hazy in the minds of most Americans as if it was on the moon. And so it seemed to the thousands of GIs sent to the cold, wet, barren Aleutians, where the campaign ended with an almost comic opera invasion of an island where the enemy had decamped and disappeared. That dismal land, wrote Samuel Eliot Morison, "might well be called the Theater of Military Frustration . . . sailors, soldiers and aviators alike regarded an assignment to this region of almost perpetual mist and snow as little better than penal servitude."

The Alaskan run was no short haul. It was 1,700 miles and 8 days from Seattle to the closest port at Dutch Harbor—the same as from Halifax, Nova Scotia, to Kingston, Jamaica—and hundreds of miles more out to Amchitka and Kiska.

When the Alaskan buildup was accelerated in 1942, the territory had half a dozen ports capable of handling Liberty-type ships, and some of them were closed part of the year. Seward was the principal port. In the spring of 1943, the Army built a new port at Whittier on Prince William Sound, with a large pier to handle Liberty ships and a branch rail line to the Alaskan Railroad some 50 miles away.

Within a year this port was handling 55,000 tons of cargo a month. A dozen other new ports were built plus new or expanded facilities at Adak, Shemya, Amchitka, Massacre Bay, and Kiska. The Army built a breakwater and pier at Shemya that was handling 76,000 tons of cargo a month by 1944.

Port facilities for two Liberty-sized ships were developed at Amchitka, where the peak load hit 63,000 tons in September of 1943. By April of 1943, Adak was the busiest port in Alaska, handling as much as 130,000 tons of cargo a month.

A typical Liberty in the Alaskan shuttle was the *John Paul Jones*, which spent more than a year hauling thousands of tons of cargo to Kodiak, Ketchikan, Dutch Harbor, Seward, Woman's Bay, and Pleasant Island. The *Jonathan Harrington* became known as the "Kodiak Express," making many voyages to the inhospitable Aleutians and the Bering Sea, including one call at Point Barrow, the extreme northern tip of Alaska.

Another Liberty, the *Daniel L. Lamont*, logged more than a dozen trips between Seattle and Port Townsend, and northern ports of Seward, Skagway, Cordova, Dutch Harbor, Adak, Cold Bay, False Pass, Squaw Harbor, and Attu.

The inhospitable weather conditions in the Alaska run are shown by the log of the *Samuel D. Ingham*, operating out of Seattle in 1943.

> Feb. 10—Vessel rolling heavily. Wind force 6.
> Feb. 11—Snow squalls. Very rough sea. Wind force 7-8.
> Feb. 12—Wind force 7. Overcast with rain and rough sea.
> Feb. 19—Freezing weather. Snow storm.
> March 1—Rough head sea. Thick rain and mist. Very poor visibility.
> Mar. 26—Wind hauled from SE to SW, reaching hurricane force with
>   rain squals. Reduced speed to 50 rpm. Driving rain and snow.

A particularly vicious storm in the Alaskan area proved what some people had claimed about Liberty ships—that the welding was not always of high quality and sometimes let a ship come apart at the seams—but the aftermath of the affair proved that welding was, on the other hand, the best way there was of putting her back together.

The *Alexander Baranoff*, delivered by Permanente Metals Corporation of Richmond, California, on 17 April 1943, was soon thereafter turned over to the Russians under Lend-Lease and renamed *Valeri Chkaluv*. She had made several uneventful trips between the West Coast and Siberia with food and war supplies when she was caught in a terrific storm. During the third day of the storm, under the hammering of tremendous seas, a crack developed in the forward part of the ship and spread, foot by foot, until, after 48 hours, with a boom like the roar of a cannon, the *Valeri Chkaluv* broke completely in two.

All of the crew except one were in the after portion when the bow broke away. Another Russian ship, this one commanded by a woman, Captain Anna Schetinina, responded to the *Chkaluv*'s SOS, but huge seas prevented a rescue.

By the time a U. S. Navy destroyer and two tugs arrived on the scene, the two sections of the ship were still floating, ten miles apart. As the weather moderated, both ends were captured and towed to North Vancouver, British Columbia, where they were welded together. Then, as good as new, or perhaps even better, the ship went back under the American flag with her original name of *Alexander Baranoff* and sailed on through the war.

On 11 December 1943 the *Chief Washakie* was 10 miles off Cape Cheerful, in anything but cheerful weather—a northeast gale with 50- to 60-mile winds and seas as high as 40 feet. About 2215 what sounded like a heavy explosion startled all hands, and immediately the ship went down by the bow. First Mate Otto Karbbe rolled out of his bunk and ran to the wheelhouse.

"We discovered within a few minutes," he reported, "that the hull had cracked at number three hatch and in the 'tween decks below. There was a two-inch-wide crack across the deck from the hatch to the rail. When I went down the access hatch into number three hold to investigate I saw the deck beams cracked and sagging. I got out quick."

The crippled ship limped 30 miles into Makushin Bay, where SeaBees spent several weeks welding stiffeners over her ruptured plates so she could return to Seattle. Heavy seas soon broke the temporary stripping and she put into Dutch Harbor for more patching. Eventually, in Seattle, she was strengthened with longitudinal girders and heavier deck straps, and went on to become one of the most endurable of the Liberty fleet. In 1970, as the SS *Chena* of the Alaska Steamship Company, she was still operating to and from Alaska.

The winters of 1943 and 1945 were among the worst on record in Alaskan waters. It was common for ships to report winds of 75 to 100 knots and seas from 40 to 50 feet high. The *John P. Gaines*, on her second voyage, broke up about 40 miles south of Cherikoff Island on 27 November 1943 and went down with the loss of 11 lives. The *John Burke*, in the same area at the same time, experienced no trouble. That ship made nine voyages to Alaska; then, on her

10th voyage, to the Philippines, she was lost with all hands off Mindoro on 28 December 1944.

After the *John Straub* sank in Alaskan waters in April of 1944 with a loss of 15 men, there was a great hue and cry that the Liberty ship was a poor product of shipbuilding, although survivors reported that faulty construction "was not a factor in the sinking" and that, as a matter of fact, the sea was smooth and the night clear at the time of the accident.

Much of the criticism came from politicos and editors who didn't know a strake from a rudder post and who, indeed, probably couldn't distinguish a Liberty from a Victory or a C2. Their clamor was soon deflated, however, when an investigation revealed that the ship's loss was not, as first hastily assumed, caused by weakened deck plates and sea action, but rather the result of a violent underwater explosion.

□

Unlike the Germans who frequently offered cigarettes and sailing directions, the Japanese had a sadistic habit of harassing the survivors of torpedoed ships. The first vessel experiencing this savagery in the Pacific was the SS *Donerail*, a New Zealand-operated vessel flying the Panamanian flag, en route from Suva, Fiji, to Vancouver with a load of sugar and pineapple. The submarine that torpedoed her then surfaced and used its deck gun to send about 20 shells into the hulk while the crew and passengers were abandoning ship. Sixteen men were killed by this shelling and most of the rest were wounded. The surviving 24 set out in a riddled lifeboat for a 38-day voyage during which 16 of them died of wounds or starvation. Those who finally reached Japanese-held Tarawa were taken prisoner.

On 30 October 1944, the Liberty ship *John A. Johnson* was steaming from San Francisco toward Honolulu with food, explosives, and a deckload of trucks. That area of the Pacific was not considered particularly hazardous then, and the ship was running alone, although lookouts were posted and the gun crew was ready for action. The weather was clear, with scattered clouds, heavy swells and a three-quarter moon.

No one saw the submarine, or the torpedo that struck at number three hold. The ship was making a heavy roll at the time, and the explosion at the turn of the bilge was fatal. The crew abandoned ship, and as the last man left the ship she broke in two.

All hands escaped safely in two lifeboats and a raft. About half an hour after the ship was abandoned, the submarine surfaced and began shelling the two sections of the wreck, by then about a quarter of a mile apart. After a few rounds, the forward section blew up in a thunderous blast, with flames shooting hundreds of feet into the air. The after section was set on fire.

Finished with its target practice, the raider then turned on the lifeboats. One boat, with 28 men on board, was about 200 yards from the submarine when it surfaced. It was a big one—at least 300 feet long—with several American flags painted on the conning tower. The captain was dressed in a white uniform, and the crewmen were laughing and shouting as they fired into the wrecked ship.

When the submarine headed toward the boat, with the evident intention of ramming, the men jumped over the side and swam out of the way. A searchlight was turned on and several Japanese fired on the survivors with pistols and a machine gun. After the raider passed, the men could hear a number of their ship-mates crying for help, but there was nothing they could do.

They climbed back into the boat, but jumped out again when the submarine made another try at ramming, the sailors shouting "Banzai!" as they went by. This time, however, there was no firing. When the submarine finally headed off toward the other castaways the men climbed back into the lifeboat, but several of them had been shot or drowned.

The raft, with 17 men aboard or clinging to grab-ropes, was silhouetted by the burning ship and provided a perfect target for the gunners on the submarine. A machine gun fired several bursts at it and the submarine tried to ram, but twice a heavy sea rolled up just in time to carry the raft free. The third time the sub-marine sank the raft. Three men were killed by machine-gun fire as it passed. Then, after one attempt to ram the other boat, the submarine disappeared into the darkness.

Survivors were spotted the next morning by a Pan American Airways clipper, which directed the USS *Argus* to the scene. Ten men were killed by gunfire or drowned during the night of terror.

□

Obviously, a ship alone in the empty ranges of the Pacific looked suspiciously on any other vessel appearing over the horizon. As the *Juan Cabrillo* headed from San Francisco toward New Zealand on her maiden voyage in October, 1942, lookouts saw "a large, suspicious-looking ship on the horizon." Lieutenant (junior grade) William Canberry sent his gun crews to battle stations. There were tense moments, for German raiders were thought to be operating in those waters. Officers thumbed through their ship-recognition manuals, inspecting the ship through their glasses and trying to determine whether she was friend or foe.

And then as the gunners swung the 4-inch gun toward the target, the percussion hand-lever struck the telescope light switch and accidentally fired the gun. If there had been suspense before, there was twice as much in the following moments as all hands waited to see where the shell would hit. They were much relieved when, as the official report puts it, "the shell hit short and astern of the other ship, now some 8½ miles distant." They never did identify her.

While the toughest part of the Pacific War for Liberty ships was in Philippine waters, there were occasional actions in many other far-flung parts of that vast ocean. On Christmas Day of 1944, the *Robert J. Walker* was off the coast of Australia when a torpedo took off her propeller and destroyed the steering engine. The submarine, evidently chary of expending any more torpedoes than necessary, waited around for the ship to sink. When a second torpedo was seen about two hours later, gunners blew it up only a hundred yards from the ship. The submarine then tried a third shot that hit, despite a rain of 20-millimeter shells directed at it. The crew escaped without casualties and was picked up by HMAS *Quickmatch*. Despite two torpedoes, the *Robert J. Walker* did not sink and had to be sent to the bottom by the destroyer's guns.

For every ship that was attacked by planes or submarines, there were a dozen that uneventfully carried out their unromantic task of cargo delivery. The *Henry D. Thoreau* spent a year in the South Pacific under charter to the Australian government, running between Sydney and Port Moresby, Milne Bay, and other supply bases. She carried troops, bulldozers, gasoline, cement for airfield construction, cigarettes and beer. At one time, the *Thoreau* received 1,500 Australian troops right from the *Queen Mary* and carried them to New Guinea. Everyone of them was "a bloke from Tobruk," just back from three years of service in North Africa, and deserved a better fate than being crowded aboard a ten-knot Liberty ship for a slow trip to the jungles of New Guinea.

The *Stephen Crane* was the object of a mysterious air attack which no one ever explained. While at anchor at New Guinea, an airplane—apparently an American P38—approached the ship at low altitude. When the "friendly" P38 roared over the ship it dropped a bomb close alongside. Shrapnel from the blast killed an Army officer and wounded 24 men. All guns opened fire immediately and sent the plane down in flames. There was no way of knowing whether they had shot down a confused American pilot, or an enterprising Japanese who had somehow "borrowed" a P38.

It was in New Guinea, too, that heroic action saved the *John C. Calhoun*. This Liberty was discharging ammunition into another ship that caught fire and became a roaring inferno. Flames leaped between the two ships and set the *Calhoun* on fire. Her crew braved the flames to cut the mooring lines, shifted the ship to a safer anchorage, and extinguished the flames before they could reach 300 barrels of aviation gasoline.

Many Liberty ships added dramatic sea rescues to their routine war work in the Pacific. The *Edwin T. Meredith* was one of several Navy and merchant vessels that answered the SOS when the troopship *Cape San Juan,* carrying 1,429 soldiers, merchant seamen, and naval gunners, was sunk. The *Meredith* picked up 443 men. Even a Pan American Airways clipper landed in the open sea to rescue 40 survivors.

Two Army airmen whose plane crashed in the western Pacific were saved by the *John Howard Payne*. The ship was 75 miles away when it picked up a radio report of the crash, but it hurried at top speed to the scene. After several hours of searching, flares and then a yellow raft were sighted. Although a high sea was running, the *Payne* picked up the two men, one injured, and radioed the freighter *Whirlwind,* also in the vicinity, which transferred two medical corpsmen to the Liberty to care for the fliers. Two other men in the plane were never found, although the *Payne* and other ships searched for many hours.

The Pacific was no match for the North Atlantic when it came to bad weather, but there were times when it kicked up its heels and belied its gentle reputation.

The *Henderson Luelling,* westbound in February 1945, ran into such a bad storm that all hands had to be called to secure the deck cargo. A wave tore the tail assembly off an airplane, threw it against Seaman Roy Snell, and broke his leg. Despite this injury, Snell crawled to a shipmate who had been pinned against the bulwark, freed him, and dragged him to safety.

☐

Liberty ships saw their last action of the Pacific War during the invasion of Okinawa, where the Japanese launched hundreds of suicide planes at naval ships and transports in a desperate but futile attempt to delay the hour of final defeat.

At least 2,000 kamikazes, plus conventional bombers, attacked the invasion fleet, sinking 36 warships and damaging 368. A number of merchant ships were also sunk or damaged. Libertys helped to carry some of the 182,821 assault troops landed on Okinawa, plus a large share of the 746,850 tons of supplies and the 503,555 tons of vehicles.

One of these, the *William B. Allison,* was hit by an aerial torpedo while at anchor at Nakagusuku Wan, shortly after breakfast on 24 May 1945. The blast tore a hole 30 feet deep and 18 feet wide in the port side, demolished the machinery spaces and killed two men on watch below. A Navy gunner was killed and six crewmen injured. After temporary repairs made on the spot, the *Allison* was towed to Kerama Retto.

There were only 13 Navy gunners on the *Uriah M. Rose* when it arrived at Nagakusuku in May of 1945, but what they lacked in numbers they made up for in sharpshooting enthusiasm. With the help of the merchant crew, they shot down at least two enemy planes and claimed "assists" on six others.

On 3 June, the ship's gunners shot a wing off a kamikaze that was an estimated 2,000 yards away and headed straight for the ship. At one time during their stay at Okinawa, they manned their guns for 14 straight hours.

An interview with survivors of the *Josiah Snelling* made by Lieutenant E. M. Harris, Jr., USNR, described how she was crash-dived by a suicide plane at Nakagusuku on 27 May:

> Shortly before 2300 hours a Japanese plane was seen approaching from the North East, taking every advantage of clouds and haze for cover. Port .20 millimeters and three inch 50 aft gun opened fire. At about 2300 this plane broke through the overcast 5,000 feet off the port quarter. Two rounds of three inch 50 fire were seen to burst below the plane and between it and the ship. The plane winged over and dropped into a power dive directly for the midships house of the vessel. All guns except numbers one and five .20 millimeters firing. The attacking plane held a steady course for the ship's top deck. At 2301 it struck at number one hold, coming in at an angle between number two gun tub and the foremast. The plane sheared off numbers one and two port cargo booms and number two port mast stay of steel cable and demolished both forward winches. The plane then went through the deck plates at the after coaming of number one hold and exploded, bursting into flames on the cargo (sacks of cement) in the bottom of number one hold. The explosion blew the gunners out of numbers one and two .20 millimeter tubs down onto the main deck.

Miraculously, no one was killed in this attack, although the gunners could have touched the plane as it roared past them. About a dozen Navy men, merchant crewmen, and Army stevedores were injured.

The last Liberty ship damaged by the enemy in the Pacific War was the victim of an unusual and unexpected attack. The *Mary Livermore* was unloading at Nakagusuku the evening of 27 May, when lookouts saw a seaplane taxiing on the water for takeoff a mile or so away. It was reported to be an American floatplane of a type called the Kingfisher.

Perhaps two minutes later, the same plane was sighted in the air, headed straight for the ship. Before a single shot could be fired, it struck a boom, bounced off and crashed into a 20-millimeter gun tub on the starboard side, then caromed into the air and, with a roar of exploding fuel and flame, crashed into the chartroom and the captain's quarters. A bomb exploded and wrecked the bridge, lifeboats and accommodations on the boat deck.

Eleven men, including four of the Armed Guard, were killed and several were seriously injured in this strange attack. There wasn't enough left of the plane to determine if it really had been an American Kingfisher or a Japanese plane camouflaged to look like one.

After temporary repairs at Okinawa, the *Mary Livermore* sailed to San Francisco under her own power and continued a seagoing career that lasted 25 years. She later sailed as the *Concord, World Leader,* and *Myrto,* and finally went to the shipbreakers on Taiwan in 1968 as the *Pacmoon.*

□

Probably the most unusual cargo carried to a Pacific beachhead was delivered to Okinawa by the *William R. Davies*—a consignment of 2,500 homing pigeons and their Signal Corps handlers. The ship had plenty of other cargo, too, and it took 22 days to discharge it, during which time the crew went to battle stations 72 times and shot down one kamikaze, with another "probable." The records fail to show what happened to the pigeons.

The ship's most exciting moment came during a night air raid when the anchorage was blacked out and all hands were scanning the sky for suicide planes. Just as the first kamikaze reached the target zone, the deck cargo-lights were accidently flashed on, turning the vessel into a brightly lit target. The lights were quickly doused, but not before some fumble-thumb on the ship was soundly cursed by all vessels in the vicinity.

Not long after that, the Pacific War was over. Japanese sea and air power was a thing of the past, and cargo lights bloomed out on cargo ships whenever and wherever they were needed.

As some of the hard-working Libertys then joined in the jubilant task of bringing the victorious troops home again, General Douglas MacArthur paid this tribute to merchant seamen in the Pacific war:

> They have brought us our lifeblood and they had paid for it with some of their own. I saw them bombed off the Philippines and in New Guinea ports. When it was humanly possible, when their ships were not blown out from under them by bombs or torpedoes, they have delivered their cargoes to us who needed them so badly. In war it is performance that counts.

In other places ships were sunk by storm, collision, and the enemy, but at Normandy the Allies sank their own ships on purpose to form "Mulberries," artificial breakwaters put down to protect offloading operations. The Liberty ships shown here are not afloat, but sitting hard and fast on the bottom. They never moved again.

10

NORMANDY
THE
BIGGEST
BEACHHEAD

In the winter and spring of 1944, south-
ern England became a huge armed camp and staging area for the most massive
seaborne assault the world had ever seen, the Allied invasion of France. Operation Overlord, under the supreme command of General Dwight D. Eisenhower,
was planned to land the First United States Army on "Omaha" and "Utah"
beaches in Normandy. The invasion fleet of thousands of naval vessels, merchant
ships, and landing craft carried out pre-invasion minesweeping, and shore bombardment, and the actual landing of an assault force of 176,000 men and 20,000
vehicles. The vast armada moved out of ports all along the English coast and
first units appeared off the Normandy beaches early in the morning of 6 June.
Among them were the ubiquitous Liberty ships.

The logistics involved were vast in scope. The tremendous job the merchant
ships did in supporting the troops was a vital factor in making the invasion a
success. Once ashore, troops needed mountains of ammunition, food, guns, and
equipment to keep fighting. Hundreds of ships—a large number of them Libertys
—maintained a supply shuttle between England and the French coast after the
initial landings, and later to Cherbourg, Antwerp, and other captured ports as
soon as they could be reopened. In the first 20 days after D-Day, the shuttle ships

delivered 189,000 vehicles and 1,703,000 men, plus food, fuel, shells, and other supplies of every conceivable description, from typewriters and telephones to bombs, beds and bandages. But no freighter could unload without harbor facilities, and all harbors on the French coast were held by the Germans. The solution, proposed by the British, was to build artificial harbors, called "Mulberries," protected by breakwaters called "Gooseberries."

The Mulberry artificial harbor was one of the most imaginative achievements in the history of the war. More than 20,000 British workmen were employed in building their components, and on D-Day a great fleet of towboats of many nationalities, escorted by ships of the Royal Navy, moved them the 100 miles across the English Channel. These prefabricated harbors consisted of a breakwater formed by sunken ships, 150 ponderous concrete caissons, and a series of floating piers connected to the shore by miles of floating bridges and roadways. It was estimated that 8,000 yards of breakwater blockships would be needed, so Allied merchant and naval fleets were scoured for vessels that could be expended for such use. Seventy-six ships, including seven Liberty ships, were selected for this important sacrifice. Four obsolete British warships were also sunk.

The blockships arrived at the beachheads at various scheduled times commencing on D-Day, took their appointed positions, and were scuttled by dynamite charges in the holds. The SS *James Iredell,* a veteran of the Mediterranean campaign, was one of the first. The *Matt W. Ransom* followed soon after, with German 88s trying vainly to send her down before she was properly positioned. The *Benjamin Contee* was also the target of 88s, but she was put in position by tugs, scuttled and sent to the bottom as planned.

Other Libertys used as Mulberries were the *Artemus Ward, George S. Wasson, George M. Childs,* and *James W. Marshall.* American ships so used also included several "Hog Islanders;" *Sahale, Kofresi, Alcoa Leader,* and *Exford.* Still other veterans of the prewar merchant marine, products of the world War I shipbuilding program, were the *West Nilus, West Grama, Courageous, Galveston, Illinoian* and *Robin Gray.* Two concrete freighters built at Tampa were consigned to the blockship line and sunk there on their maiden voyages.

Some 800 merchant seamen volunteered to sail the doomed blockships from English ports. As the Normandy beaches were protected by German mines, heavy artillery, and, supposedly, bomber fleets, it was the conviction of almost everyone involved in Operation Overlord that the Germans would make every effort to sink the blockships before they could be positioned and scuttled. Nevertheless, both Mulberries were completed in five days.

Another group of Libertys, called "accommodation ships," were loaded in the United States, hauled their cargo to England, then went on to France. The *Thomas Johnson* served as a Mulberry accommodation ship. The *George B. Woodward* so served at Omaha Beach, as the *Bernard Carter* did at Utah Beach. The *Eleazer Wheelock* became the base for the Naval Officer in Command at Omaha Beach, the *Thomas B. Robertson* served in the same fashion at Utah Beach.

Following the operation, Admiral Sir Bertram H. Ramsey, Allied naval commander-in-chief, commended the U. S. War Shipping Administration as follows:

> Operations in which 32 United States merchant ships participated have been brought to an extremely successful conclusion. This reflects the greatest credit to the officers and men who manned these vessels. Particular praise is due to the engine room staffs for their tenacity and devotion to duty; especially in the case of those ships which had to be positioned under enemy shellfire. The result of their efforts is already bearing fruit and the shelters they provided are of great benefit to the Army.
>
> It is requested that you will convey to all the officers and men concerned my high appreciation of the valuable services they have rendered to the Allied cause.

⊔

The English Channel was so filled with ships during the first few days of the invasion that one felt every ship in the world must be there. That was the way it seemed to Captain Heinrich Kronke, of the SS *Cyrus H. McCormick,* as he described the scene.

> The Channel is the busiest thoroughfare in the world. Craft of every description are traversing it day and night and often there doesn't seem to be enough room to squeeze another ship through. The astonishing thing is how it all can be done in such safety, for we all feel that we are as safe as we would be walking up Market Street. Now and then there are planes making a fuss, but they do not hit anything.

The *Charles Willson Peale* was in a 40-ship convoy on D-Day, and her Armed Guard officer, Ensign R. A. Dolen, noted that they were escorted "by the combined forces of the Allied navies." He also noted the reassuring presence of fleets of Allied aircraft: "Thunderbolts, Spitfires, Typhoons, Mustangs and others all too numerous to mention."

The invasion fleet of 4,266 ships and landing craft was supported by more than

700 warships, from battleships to cruisers, destroyers, minesweepers, and torpedoboats. This armada of warships included six British and American battleships; two monitors; two cruisers; 119 destroyers and destroyer escorts; 113 sloops, frigates, and corvettes; 80 patrol boats; and about 400 torpedo boats, small gunboats, and minesweepers.

Overwhelming Allied sea and air superiority kept ship losses much below the point that planners had anticipated, but merchant ships did not go unscathed. The channel was not quite as safe as Market Street. A number of Libertys, including the *Matthew Goldsboro* and the *William L. Marcy*, were hit by artillery fire but were not put out of action.

One of the heaviest D-Day losses occurred on the British Liberty ship *Sambut,* which was hit by long-range German artillery located at Calais. The effect of these heavy caliber hits was both mystifying and tragic.

Shortly before the first shell hit, officers on the bridge saw two geysers of water several hundred feet from the ship, but before they realized what was happening and could take evasive action a second shell (later determined to be at least 12-inch) burst on the port side just above the engine room. There was no report of casualties, the hit did not seem to have damaged the vessel substantially, and the *Sambut* continued on. Less than 30 seconds later, another shell hit on the port side forward of the bridge, again there being no evidence of serious damage from the shell itself. But in a minute or so fire broke out in a deckload of gasoline cans, and before fire hoses could be manned, the forward part of the vessel was an inferno.

Fifteen minutes after the first hit, the *Sambut* was abandoned. Crew and passengers left in two lifeboats and 30 rafts while several landing craft hurried up to take men over the side from scramble nets. Unfortunately, 130 troops were drowned in this unusual disaster, probably because they were not able to inflate their life preservers in an emergency, either through excitement or because of defective equipment.

On her first trip to Omaha Beach, the *Enoch Train* carried complete motor combat equipment for 485 men of the U. S. 90th Division. Off the beach, gunners on various Liberty ships and LSTs opened fire on suspicious aircraft in conditions of poor visibility and learned later that they had shot down four friendly planes. After several shuttle trips, the ship loaded at Southampton, in November 1944, then sat for a month with engines on standby waiting for orders before she was finally instructed to discharge at Antwerp. In Antwerp one of the ship's gunners, Clarence A. Cox, was in the Rex Theater when it was hit by a V-2 rocket. Cox escaped with a sprained shoulder and a bad case of shock, although scores of people were killed or wounded.

□

Within six weeks after the initial Normandy landing, 30 Allied divisions had been put ashore with hundreds of thousands of tons of equipment. More than 150 ships were assigned to a shuttle service, ferrying supplies from English ports to the beachheads and, later, to the captured ports of Antwerp, Ghent, Rotterdam, and Le Havre.

The *David Starr Jordan* was a typical shuttle ship. She made deliveries to Omaha and Utah Beaches from Swansea, Cardiff, and Belfast and experienced numerous and varied adventures in the process. Three days after D-Day she collided with the *George E. Badger*, but no great damage was done. Soon after arriving at Omaha Beach that night a 20-millimeter shell landed on the foredeck and exploded, injuring several soldiers. The log for 25 July 1944 noted: "Vessel attacked by enemy planes. Ship bombed and strafed. Two soldiers killed and eleven injured. One Armed Guard suffered severe wounds. Ship's gunnery officer wounded."

Often as not, these shuttle runs were more routine than exciting. In October the ship spent two very uncomfortable weeks at anchor in rough seas off the French coast waiting for orders to discharge cargo.

Off Utah Beach on 27 August 1944, the *Jordon* took on coal from the collier *Baron Ruthven*. Like a number of other Libertys, she had coal-burning galley ranges and had to "coal ship" from time to time so the crew could eat.

Enemy shore bombardment and air attack was more spectacular, but less dangerous, than underwater mines, which accounted for most of the merchant ship casualties during the invasion.

The terrific destructive force of a mine was described by survivors of the *Charles W. Eliot*, mined the morning of 28 June 1944 about four miles off Juno Beach. The ship had just finished unloading its cargo.

> At 0550 an explosion occurred under the after part of number three hold, causing the vessel to rise up into the air and to shake violently. Two or three seconds later a second violent explosion occurred under the stern. Hull plates cracked open—the explosion blew hatch covers and beams out of number four and five hatches to a height of 300 feet and caused the vessel to break just aft of number five hatch. Fragments of steel and ballast were blown several hundred feet into the air. One hatch beam landed on the boat deck . . . quarters in the midships houses

were wrecked ... wash bowls were knocked off the walls ... numbers
three, four and five holds were flooded.

Despite the flying hatch beams and the general havoc wrought by the blast
inside the ship, there were no fatalities, although a number of men were injured.

When a mine exploded on the after port side of the *Francis C. Harrington*, the
blast sprung four sections of the propeller shaft and wrecked most of the auxiliary
machinery, such as pumps and dynamos.

Inspired by Chief Engineer Leonard W. Valentine, the black gang worked for
five days in the half-flooded engine room and shaft alley, sometimes up to their
necks in water, to remove shattered bearings, straighten the shaft, and repair the
machinery enough so that the vessel could discharge its cargo and return to
England under its own power. For his "skill, ingenuity and stout determination"
in salvaging the *Francis C. Harrington*, Chief Engineer Valentine was awarded
the Merchant Marine Distinguished Service Medal.

Just after unloading 500 troops and their equipment, the *Charles Morgan* was
hit by a bomb in number five hold and settled to the bottom in 33 feet of water.
Chief Engineer Sidney Scott and Chief Steward Robert McChain searched the
ship for injured men and left only after the Navy declared her a derelict. They
later led a salvage party back on board to obtain valuable equipment.

Many casualties had been expected from aerial bombing, but this danger
proved almost negligible, so great was Allied air superiority. In the first six days
after D-Day, ships landed 326,000 men, 54,000 vehicles, and 104,000 tons of
supplies. About 200 ships of all kinds arrived daily at the artificial harbors.
Winston Churchill said of the cargo-hauling operations: "The Merchant Navy
played an outstanding part. Their seamen cheerfully accepted all the risks of war
and weather and their staunchness and fidelity played an impressive part in the
vast enterprise."

The *Wolcott* spent four months on the Normandy shuttle, carrying everything
from ammunition to crated oranges. A large percentage of the latter disappeared
before the ship reached Normandy. She first anchored off Normandy the morning
of 7 June. Soon after that her log noted: "Unknown transport sank some distance
off our starboard side." The next day the log read: "Tremendous fire from ships
around us directed at enemy aircraft. Fired at plane overhead. Naval ships
shelling coast. Slight swells. Fair and clear." The fair and clear weather didn't
last long. By 19 June, seas were so rough that no cargo could be unloaded, and
for the next five days she had to go slow ahead on the engine to keep headed into
the seas and reduce the wild rolling.

During 13 months of shuttle service between England and France, from February 1944 to April 1945, the *Samuel Colt* delivered a huge amount of war freight and made two rescues. On one cross-channel trip, the crew spotted a plane about to make an emergency landing. The *Colt* headed for the spot at top speed and picked up an RAF pilot, floating in his Mae West. His flying companions circled the area until they were sure he was safe, then dipped their wings in "thanks" as they left. While steaming up the Bristol Channel in a heavy fog, this same ship picked up an SOS from a sinking British collier and rescued 36 of the survivors.

During the *Dan Beard*'s first trip to Omaha Beach on 9 June, cargo discharge was delayed for 24 hours because the captain refused a demand for food by sailors manning two LCTs. The landing craft left the ship and did not show up again until ordered to continue the unloading.

The *Dan Beard* was either torpedoed or mined in October of 1944 while bound from Barry, Wales, to Belfast. In rough seas whipped up by 40-knot winds, there was "a terrific vibration amidships, followed immediately by the ship's back breaking just forward of the house." Within five minutes she broke in two. Heavy casualties resulted when one boat was swamped by the heavy seas and capsized. In all, 17 merchant seamen and 12 Navy gunners lost their lives.

Mines or acoustic torpedoes accounted for four Liberty ships in a 20-ship convoy en route from Southampton to Utah Beach on 29 June 1944. The *H. G. Blasdel* was hit, managed to return to England, was beached at Southampton, and declared to be a total loss. The ship had 509 men on board at the time, including 436 American troops. Most of them were taken off safely by LST326, but there still were many casualties.

The *James A. Farrell*, hit just a few minutes later, was towed to Spithead and was also written off as a total loss. Four soldiers were killed and 45 injured when heavy, steel hatch beams fell into the troop quarters. At the same time, the *John A. Treutlen* was either mined or torpedoed, with a number of injuries to merchant crewmen and Armed Guard men. While LST336 was taking the injured from the *Treutlen*, a violent explosion under the bow of the *Edward M. House* sent water mixed with gravel and shells from the ocean bottom shooting 200 feet into the air. Still able to continue on her way, this Liberty, under command of Captain Austin Fithian, discharged her troops and cargo at Utah Beach before returning to England for repairs.

The master of the British Liberty ship *Samlong* was high in his praise of his ship after an "extremely violent" explosion under the engine room, while at anchor two miles off Juno Beach on 3 August, killed the men on watch below. "Not one piece of welding [beyond the impact area] on this ship cracked or broke," he reported. After the ship was towed to England and drydocked, it was ascertained that the damage was done by an acoustic torpedo. The SS *Fort Lac La Ronge* was damaged by another acoustic torpedo.

The *William L. Marcy* was at anchor six miles off Juno Beach on 7 August, empty and awaiting convoy, when it was hit by a torpedo, probably of the acoustic type. The *Marcy* was towed to England and beached. Her only fatality was a British Army sergeant.

On the following day, an explosion damaged the Normandy-bound *Ezra Meeker*. The Canadian corvette *Regina* came up, supervised the disembarkation of her crew into an LST, and directed the rigging of a towline between the LST and the damaged ship so it might be towed to port and its 5,800 tons of trucks and other cargo might be saved.

Just as the LST started to get the freighter under way, the *Regina* blew up in a tremendous explosion that killed many of her crew. A German U-boat had bagged both ships. Sixty-five survivors from the *Regina*, covered with fuel and suffering from injuries and shock, were rescued by American landing craft, some of whose sailors jumped overboard to save the exhausted Canadians.

The *Jonas Lie* was torpedoed and sunk on 9 January 1945, as was the *George Hawley* on 21 January while en route from Cherbourg to Cardiff. Two of the *Hawley*'s engine room watch were killed, the rest were rescued by the *Wiley Wakeman*. The *Hawley* was towed to port.

The *Robert L. Vann*, proceeding in a single-column convoy through a swept channel en route from Antwerp to the Thames, broke in two and sank after hitting a mine off Ostend on 1 March. Several men were injured but there were no fatalities.

Also returning from Antwerp on 22 March was the *Charles D. McIver*, which hit a mine and sank in shallow water. The explosion, typical of those caused by mines, threw men flat on the deck, blasted typewriters loose from their desks and threw them against bulkheads, ripped radiators from walls, and tore doors from their hinges.

Just a day prior to this, the *James Eagen Layne* was torpedoed en route from Barry, Wales, to Ghent, and although HMS *Flaunt* and *Atlas* towed her to Whitesand Bay and beached her, she was written off as a total loss. The same day the *John R. Park* was torpedoed nine miles off Lizard Head and sank several hours later but without any casualties.

The *Solomon Juneau,* torpedoed on 9 April on the way from Ghent to the Thames; was towed to Dover and beached. Two Armed Guard gunners were killed when a torpedo exploded under the stern. The British Liberty *Samida* was hit shortly before that.

The *Will Rogers,* in a seven-ship convoy bound from Liverpool toward Antwerp, was torpedoed on the afternoon of 12 April. In her holds was a strange cargo: 2,764 tons of airfield landing mats and several hundred tons of doughnut flour. The ship was beached at Holyhead and later towed to Liverpool for repairs.

Twenty-three-year-old Captain Jean Patrick, one of the youngest shipmasters in the merchant marine, had command of the *Francis Asbury* when she hit a mine off Ostend on 3 December 1944. Exploding under the engine room, the mine broke the vessel's back with a blast so violent that machinery blown out of the engine spaces severely wounded and scalded Chief Engineer Justice, who had been asleep in his room on the boat deck. The second and third assistant engineers, Francis Rack and Frederick Williams, risked their lives to get the Chief out of his shattered room and into a lifeboat, where he died soon afterward. They were later awarded the Merchant Marine Distinguished Service Medal for their efforts. Ten of the merchant crew and seven Armed Guard men were lost.

The last Liberty to be put out of service through enemy action in the European theater of operations was the *Horace Binney,* which struck a mine 8 May 1945, about 30 miles from Ostend. The explosion broke the vessel's back, after which it was towed to Deal and beached. There were no casualties.

Despite mines, bombs, and storms, the shuttle ships kept cargo flowing across the channel. In the first 109 days after D-Day, they put ashore 2,500,000 troops, 500,000 vehicles, and 17,000,000 tons of ammunition, food, and other supplies. The *George Dewey* made 12 shuttle runs to Omaha and Utah Beaches and Rouen. The *Peale* made seven shuttle trips. The *Robert L. Vann* was sunk by a mine but there were no casualties. The *Dan Beard* saw the nearby *Ezra Weston* "rise out of the water" after a mine explosion and sink in minutes. The *William Tyler Page* rescued six survivors of an LST blown apart by a mine.

It is a tribute to the designers, builders, and crews of the Libertys that most of them hit by mines stayed afloat and were able to return to port, although few ships that hit mines were salvaged and put back in service. A mine explosion caused so much structural damage to the keel and lower hull of a vessel, which required expensive and time-consuming repairs in busy shipyards, that most vessels so damaged were written off as "total constructive losses."

A bomb or mine hit usually classed a ship as TCL—total constructive loss—because the damage was too extensive for economical repair. A "stateside hit" was one which left the ship able to return home for repairs. The *Allegan* (AK225), shown here with repair staging rigged, got her stateside hit at Okinawa on 3 June 1945 when a kamikaze ripped open the starboard bow.

11

LIBERTYS
IN THE
ARMY
AND
NAVY

The simple, uncomplicated design of the Liberty ship made it highly adaptable to conversion for special requirements, and by the time the war ended a couple of hundred of them, in at least a dozen configurations, had joined the Army and Navy. Their military employment ranged from hospital ships to freshwater distilling plants, with the most of them, actually, doing exactly what they had been built for in the first place, carrying cargo.

Naval conversions of EC2 hulls resulted in the following numbers and classifications of ships: 10 AG (miscellaneous), 66 AK (cargo), 4 AKN (net cargo), 11 AKS (general stores issue), 6 AR (ship repair), 10 ARG (internal combustion engine repair), 2 ARV (aircraft repair), 1 AVS (aviation supply), 2 AW (distilling ship), and 21 IX (unclassified, usually tankers). After World War II, another 16 EC2 hulls were converted to YAGR (radar picket ships). The Army converted six EC2s to hospital ships for operation by the Army Transport Service, and another six to aircraft repair ships. Such ships were usually given new names honoring Army officers. Another 14 ships were converted to mule carriers, but not given new names, possibly because no one could think of anything appro-

173

priate, yet polite. And a total of 220 ships were altered, but not taken over or named by the Army, to carry from 300 to 500 troops or prisoners of war.

The need for the POW ships was an unexpected development of Allied victory in North Africa and the near-embarrassing flood of German and Italian captives. A fleet of Liberty ships—eventually, more than 200 of them—were hurriedly given makeshift conversion that enabled them to carry nearly 75,000 prisoners to the United States. The military prisoners had to rough it, with C-rations, rationed water, and rationed bunks. Some of the first conversions were done so hurriedly there was no time to install bunks, and they slept on bedrolls or bare decks. Prisoners were quartered belowdecks behind wire barricades. Each ship also carried about 40 armed guards, a doctor, and three enlisted medical assistants.

Not all the POWs were unhappy over the way the war ended for them. As a shipload of prisoners pulled away from the dock in a Mediterranean port, one of them shouted to the American soldiers left behind: "You guys are going to Berlin, but we're going to Brooklyn!"

The conversion for use as hospital ships involved the most extensive alterations in any Liberty ship hull. The cargo holds were turned into 44 hospital wards by installing additional decks and bulkheads through nearly three-fourths of the length of the ship. The ships were provided with necessary operating rooms, laboratories, and medical support facilities for 600 bed patients, and with berthing and messing arrangements for the medical personnel to care for that many patients.

Army hospital ships were the *Blanche F. Sigman, Dogwood, Jarret M. Huddleston, John J. Meany, St. Olaf,* and *Wisteria.* The *St. Olaf* was commissioned in the Army under her original Maritime Commission name. *Dogwood* was originally the *George Washington Carver,* and *Wisteria* was built as the *William Oslar.* The *John J. Meany,* built as *Zebulon E. Vance,* honored an officer killed in North Africa. In 1946 the ship was again altered, that time to carry war brides from Europe, and resumed her original name. The *Blanche F. Sigman,* originally *Stanford White,* honored an Army nurse, and the *Jarrett M. Huddleston,* originally *Samuel F. B. Morse,* honored an Army surgeon, both killed in Italy. The *St. Olaf,* decommissioned as an Army hospital ship in 1945, had a short career as a transport, carrying as many as 1,000 troops and 147 women and children.

Troop-ship duty was somewhat like spending a month in Grand Central Station, and one such trip was nearly enough for Second Mate Bob Seager of the *Ponce de Leon.* At Le Havre in December 1945 the ship was loaded right to the overhead with men from the 20th Air Force, en route home from the China-India-Burma theater. Practically every one of them was seasick all the way across, and by the time they entered the Chesapeake Capes, the ship had an air about her that discouraged even the seagulls. But worse, heavy weather had set her leaking like a sieve, and the Coast Guard boarding officer refused to clear her to sail to Baltimore, saying she "was unseaworthy for Chesapeake Bay operations."

"That's funny," said Captain Freddie Larson. "She crossed the North Atlantic all right."

The Army-converted mule carriers were an unexpected usage of Liberty ships in a highly mechanized war, where ships loaded down to the marks with jeeps, tanks, trucks, and locomotives were a common sight. Nevertheless, a lot of mules were either imported into overseas theaters or deported from the United States, depending on how one felt about mules. Conversion to this unglamorous duty cost about $317,000 per ship.

Ships so converted were the *Alcée Fortier, Charles W. Wooster, Cyrus W. Field, F. J. Luckenbach, Henry Dearborn, John J. Crittenden, Zona Gale, José Navarro, Joshua Hendy, Peter Silvester, Samuel H. Walker, Santiago Iglesias, William J. Palmer,* and *William S. Halstead*. A shipload of mules varied from 320 to 699 animals because, contrary to all expectations, Texas mules were smaller than Missouri mules. Their stalls, adjustable to fit various sizes, were built athwartships as it was found that mules, unlike people, were more liable to be seasick when they rode fore-and-aft.

The Army aircraft repair ships, with their commissioned and original names, were: *Brig. Gen. Alfred J. Lyon (Nathaniel Scudder), Brig. Gen. Asa N. Duncan (Richard O'Brien), Brig. Gen. Clinton W. Russell (Robert W. Bingham), Maj. Gen. Herbert A. Dargue (Rebecca Lukens), Maj. Gen. Robert Olds (Daniel E. Garrett),* and *Maj. Gen. Walter R. Weaver (Thomas LeValley)*.

□

The work involved in converting a Liberty to naval use varied according to her naval classification. All such ships had to carry larger crews, for increased gun batteries, communications, radar, and round-the-clock cargo-handling or repair work. The AKs had their boom capacities increased to 50 tons, and each had berthing facilities for 15 officers and 222 men. Their cargo capacity was about 400,000 cubic feet, as compared to the original Liberty capacity of

499,000, but they had to carry more provisions, water, fuel, and ammunition. The AGs were fitted to carry 28 officers and 899 enlisted men. An AK could carry only 15 officers and 180 men, but had space and refrigerating equipment for 219,018 cubic feet of refrigerated cargo. The IX conversions—tankers— carried the smallest crews, with less than a hundred officers and men, but had tank capacity for 63,000 barrels of fuel oil. The tankers that became freshwater distilling plants could carry 33,600 barrels of water.

The YAGR conversions, after World War II, when time and money was in better supply, resulted in ships that no wartime sailor could have imagined. The *Picket* (*James F. Harrell*), a typical YAGR, carried 14 officers and 167 enlisted men. Part of her capacious cargo spaces had been changed into radar spotting, tracking, and communications centers where batteries of radarscopes were manned day and night to pick up and follow the movements of aircraft. The *Picket* and her sister ships remained on ocean stations for 30 days at a time. With hull space to spare, one hold was equipped as a gym and recreation hall, with volleyball and basketball courts, a boxing ring, weight-lifting and table tennis rooms, hobby shops, and an archery range. Another hold was made into a theater and lecture hall with a capacity for 250 people. Tanks holding 6,000 gallons of water ballast provided more stability and minimized rolling.

Liberty ships commissioned in the Navy were usually renamed, following the long-established system of specific categories of names for each type of ship. Several dozen cargo ships were named for stars and constellations, ranging from *Acubens* to *Zaniah*. As the brighter and better-known star names had been used years earlier for ships such as *Altair, Canopus, Spica,* and *Vega,* the new cargo ships carried names very few people had ever heard and even fewer could pronounce. Because most prominent stars were named centuries ago by middle-eastern astronomers, the U. S. Navy had a lot of ships with Arabian names, such as *Arkab, Kochab,* and *Azimech.*

Another group of 22 ships, designated IX, were named for a whole menagerie of animals, again ranging from one end of the alphabet to the other, *Antelope* to *Zebra.* A dozen or so repair ships were named for islands. About three dozen ships, possibly because they were marked for transfer to the Navy before completion, were given their Navy names in the star, animal, or island group at launching, instead of the usual famous person name in the Maritime Commission system. The 16 postwar radar picket ships were given names indicative of their mission—*Scanner, Tracer,* and *Watchman,* for example.

While most Navy Libertys spent much of their time in dreary base-support and supply runs, somewhat after the fashion of the *Reluctant* in *Mr. Roberts*, there were moments of excitement for some of them. A typical tanker, the *Camel* (*William H. Carruth*), was commissioned in November, 1943 and decommissioned in 1946, during which time she served as a floating fuel farm in the Marshalls and at Eniwetok, Saipan, and Okinawa. *Camel* and her seven officers and 95 men pumped over 73,000,000 gallons of fuel and aviation gas to ships of the fleet as their contribution to winning the war in the Pacific.

At Saipan, in August, 1944, two Japanese sneaked aboard, then went over the side when they were discovered. One was killed by a guard. The survivor said that all they wanted was to surrender and get out of the war.

Camel's big day came on 6 April 1945, in the opening phase of the invasion of Okinawa, when a massed attack by Japanese suicide planes sank two U. S. ships and damaged at least two dozen more. No one knows how many planes were shot down that day, but the *Camel* got two of them.

Another Liberty tanker, the *Caribou* (*Nathaniel B. Palmer*) spent only 22 months in the Navy but in that time she serviced 847 ships, from battlewagons to spitkids, with more than 70,000,000 gallons of fuel oil. There were the fighting ships that made headlines, but without the hard-working tankers the headlines would have been greatly reduced. The *Caribou*, not a fighting ship at all, once found herself in the exact middle of a very lively battle. At Leyte on 27 November she was pumping oil to a battleship on one side and a destroyer on the other when an air attack came in. Not one of the three ships could move, but half a dozen others steamed around them in a circle and put up an antiaircraft barrage that kept the attackers away, while shooting down 14 of the enemy planes.

A couple of the Navy's Libertys saw more action before they joined the Navy than afterward. The *Zebra* (*Matthew Lyon*), while wearing her original name, was torpedoed on 11 August 1943 en route from Guadalcanal to Espirito Santo. She was patched up, pressed into service as a net cargo ship, and then, after a complete repair job, commissioned in the Navy on 27 February 1944. The *Antelope* (*J. H. DeYoung*) while still a merchantman, was torpedoed by a Japanese submarine near Noumea, New Caledonia, in August of 1943. After being taken over by the Navy, she was used for storage until returned to the Maritime Commission at Subic Bay in March, 1948. She was then sold to the Asia Development Corporation of Shanghai for scrap, but may well have sailed for some years after that under the Chinese flag.

The net cargo ships, *Indus, Sagittarius, Tuscana,* and *Zebra,* had especially tedious jobs, helping to build big steel fences in the seas around advance bases as protection against submarine torpedoes. These ships had extra-heavy capacity booms and winches, cutaway bulwarks and builtup hatches that made them efficient net layers. The *Sagittarius* (originally named *J. Fred Essary* for a former president of the National Press Club in Washington), could carry enough gear to put down nearly three and a half miles of net. At Okinawa she helped lay more than five miles of net.

Tutuila (Arthur P. Gorman), was typical of the fleet of internal combustion engine repair ships whose mission was to service the Navy's vast armada of landing craft, minesweepers, tugs, and other small craft powered by everything from five-horsepower outboards to diesel plants of 6,000 horsepower or more. She was commissioned on 8 April 1944 and, from the Solomon Islands to Taku, China, serviced more than 1,800 ships. She was decommissioned in July 1945, reactivated for the Korean War, and later served in Viet Nam from 1966 to 1971. The last EC2 in the U.S. Navy, she was decommissioned in February, 1972.

The *Samar* was commissioned only two months before the war ended, but found plenty of work; a typical day found her doing jobs for 26 different ships. The varied tasks of ARG repair crews included overhauling fire extinguishers and repairing refrigeration units, galley ranges, navigational instruments, typewriters, radios, clocks, gyro compasses, engines, evaporators, and pumps. They also did major welding and had busy printing shops.

A general stores issue ship carried as many as 8,000 different items and acted as a combination floating supermarket and hardware store for the fleet. They could be picked out of any fleet anchorage by the number of small boats clustered around, waiting for some storekeeper or supply officer to do their "shopping." That they got around was indicated by the service career of the *Acubens* which, between July 1944 and March 1946, issued stores at Hollandia, Leyte, Subic Bay, Davao, Tarakan, and Manila.

For every sailor who took part in a World War II battle, there were a dozen or more involved in logistics, repairs, transportation, and supply, providing the materials and services that made the fighting possible. Unglamorous though these jobs were much of the time, they were all vital to the winning of the war. So, too, were the supply and service ships. They met little excitement and their bored crews had few opportunities to win battle stars for their campaign ribbons, but they were always ready to fight when the chance came.

Few ships of any class responded more admirably in their first combat action than the *Celeno* (*Redfield Proctor*) commissioned in January of 1943. While unloading at Guadalcanal on 16 June 1943, *Celeno* was attacked by a "swarm" of Japanese dive bombers—so many, in fact, that no accurate tally was ever made. This was partly because the crew was so busy shooting they had no time for counting. After three near-misses, a bomb made a direct hit on the after five-inch gun platform and knocked it out of action. The rudder was damaged so the ship could only steam in wide circles.

Another bomb hit in number five hold started fires, and shrapnel from near-misses set fire to the deck cargo of diesel oil and gasoline. Fire and damage control parties worked with guns chattering and banging around them as the Japanese continued determined efforts to sink the ship. When the attack finally ceased, *Celeno* was credited with shooting down six planes, a record that would have done credit to a battleship. She had 15 men killed and 19 wounded in the battle.

The damaged ship was beached at Lunga Point; cargo offloaded, water pumped out, and sufficient repairs made for a tow to Espiritu Santo. The ship was later towed back to San Francisco, given a complete repair job, and then returned to the Pacific war in 1944.

The crew of the *Sabik* (*William Becknell*), found that their duty was not entirely boresome either. The *Sabik* was converted to carry 1,000 passengers and general cargo. In addition to the regular crew of 113, she carried 40 more men in boat crews to operate eight LCMs and LCVPs. The *Sabik* made the usual inter-island shuttle runs and then took part in the invasion of the Philippines. Her gunners knocked down a kamikaze at Tacloban and a few days later at Dulag shared credit with other ships for getting another. The *Sabik* logged 20 air raids while in Leyte Gulf.

Almost as exciting as the air raids was the trip the *Sabik* made from Efate to Noumea, with a pretty American Red Cross nurse, Virginia Davis, on board. Long before the *Ladies Home Journal* urged its readers to "never underestimate the power of a woman," Miss Davis proved the point and accomplished what the officers of the *Sabik* had never been able to do. As soon as Miss Davis came aboard, according to the ship's history, "all hands suddenly blossomed out in clean khakis and dungarees."

The *Livingston* (*Josiah D. Whitney*) could carry 1,000 men. In 73 interisland voyages during which she sailed 64,978 miles, she carried a total of 100,000 men, including soldiers, sailors, marines, government employees, and Japanese prisoners of war. In the same time her cargo-handlers loaded, and then unloaded, enough candy bars, cigarettes, filing cabinets, Quonset huts, jeeps, tanks, and airplanes to total 200,000 tons.

In all that assorted cargo there may have been a rabbit's foot to account for *Livington*'s close escape at Tinian. There, completely undetected, a lone Japanese plane sneaked in, dropped a torpedo only 100 yards from the ship, and disappeared into the clouds before anyone could fire a gun. But there was no explosion —the torpedo went completely under the ship and came up on the other side, a clean miss.

The *Serpens* (*Benjamin N. Cordoza*) was one of the Navy's ships that carried a complete U. S. Coast Guard crew. Her career was short and her end was spectacular. On 29 January 1945 the ship was anchored off Lunga Point, Guadalcanal, loading bombs, when she was suddenly and completely destroyed by an explosion. There had been eight officers, 188 men, and 57 Army stevedores on board at the time. The only survivors were two officers and eight men who had just left the ship. One of them vividly described the ship's last minute:

> As we headed shoreward in the personnel boat the sound and concussion of the explosion suddenly reached us and as we turned we witnessed the awe-inspiring death drama unfold before us. As the report of screeching shells filled the air and the flash of tracers continued, the water throughout the harbor splashed as the shells hit. We headed our boat in the direction of the smoke and as we came into closer view of what had once been a ship, the water was filled only with floating debris, dead fish, torn lifejackets, lumber and other unidentifiable objects. The smell of death and fire and gasoline and oil was evident and nauseating. This was sudden death and horror, unwanted and unasked for, but complete.

At the time of the Solomons campaign, Japanese submarines had not been cleared from the sea, and the slow cargo ships were an easy target for them. On 23 June 1943 the RO-103 got two ships in the same convoy as it sailed from Guadalcanal to Espiritu Santo; the *Aludra* (*Robert T. Lincoln*), and the *Deimos* (*Chief Ouray*). The *Aludra* sank several hours later and the *Deimos*, with her after holds flooded, was sunk by gunfire from the destroyer *O'Bannon*.

The varied duties of a cargo ship were illustrated by the service of the *Alnitah* (*John A. Logan*). Like many AKs, she was fitted to carry 1,000 troops, 3,500 tons of general cargo, and a crew of 250. On her first trip she carried 1,150 men of the 12th SeaBees from Port Hueneme, California, to Espiritu Santo. During the rest of the war she sailed all over the Pacific Ocean, from New Zealand to Okinawa. One cargo consisted of 425 tons of freight, $50,000 in silver coins, 2,020 bags of mail, 16 Army nurses, 16 Army dogs, and 246 other military passengers. During her Pacific service, the *Alnitah* carried out 53 different missions, in which she spent 288 days at sea, steamed 70,371 miles, anchored 105 times in 34 different ports, and carried 32,286 tons of cargo and 34,715 passengers, including Fiji infantry scouts and 900 Gilbert Island natives.

There were so many Navy Libertys, and most of them were so busy with dull dreary routine jobs exactly like every other one was, that any small claim to superiority or distinction was eagerly seized upon. The *Sterope* made 22 ports and invasion beachheads in 24 months. The *Mona Island* logged 180 air raids and air alerts while she was at Okinawa. The *Wildcat*, one of two ships equipped to make fresh water, acted as "water boy" to a grand total of 1,500 thirsty ships. But her big claim to fame was that, with a crew of less than a hundred officers and men, her softball team took on the team from the mighty *Missouri,* which had nearly 30 times as many people, and beat them.

The *Wildcat* had more than good softball players in her crew. Someone aboard that ship, in a brief paragraph prepared for her ship's history, paid a fitting tribute to hundreds of men who served in the armada of auxiliary craft that backed up the fighting fleets, seldom won any medals, hardly ever met the enemy, but contributed significantly to the final victory:

> The *Wildcat* fought an enemy more cruel and dangerous to men than the Japanese—monotony, sameness and invariable routine. The mission of this ship was not glamorous, her task seldom dangerous; no headlines were captured for the folks back home; nobody on board became a hero, unless doing a job with a minimum of complaining and soldiering and a maximum of loyalness, cheerfulness and diligence can be said to make a man a hero. If so, the *Wildcat* had its share.

Only the name of the ship has to be changed to make such praise fit any one of the many Libertys that served the armed forces in World War II.

Home from the wars, a fleet of Liberty ships are berthed in the National Fleet Reserve at Astoria, Oregon. This photograph, made in 1957, shows 162 ships. The EC2 had all the individuality of any assembly line product; like a Model T or a DC 3, any one looked exactly like all the others in the family.

12

PEACETIME
OPERATIONS

When the end of World War II made great numbers of Liberty ships available for charter or purchase at nominal prices and revived world trade produced an abundance of cargo at high rates, the American merchant marine acquired a large and temporarily prosperous portion of tramp shipping; a trade that had for years been monopolized by the British, Greeks, Norwegians, and other Europeans, and had not been seen under the American flag for many decades.

However, shipping operators of other nations were not slow in building up their war-depleted fleets. Anyone with shipping know-how was almost certain to parlay one Liberty ship into a fleet or a fortune in the immediate postwar years, when there was American foreign aid or private cargoes for almost anything that could float.

Foreign merchant fleets still being short of ships and with profitable cargoes available for any kind of a vessel, American-flag tramps, mostly Libertys, carried millions of tons of relief cargoes to Europe and Asia and, later, great quantities of rehabilitation cargoes sent overseas by the Economic Cooperation Administration.

Accordingly, after World War II, Liberty ships sailed the seas under many names and many flags. They were to be seen in ports all over the world, and no new paint scheme or name could hide the fact that, whether they sailed under the Greek, Italian, French, or Panamanian flag, they were still the same ugly ducklings and expendables—U. S.-built Libertys.

The price of Liberty ships was set at approximately 35 percent of construction cost to help Allies who had experienced heavy ship losses. For the faster C-types, reserved mostly for American purchasers, prices ranged up to 87 percent of construction costs. By the time the Ship Sales Act expired in January, 1951, American operators had purchased 831 war-built ships, including 130 Libertys, at a total price of some $80 million. Foreign buyers, up to that time, had purchased 1,113 vessels. Most of them were EC2s, but the total included 98 Victory ships, 46 C1 types, a few C2 types, and some coastal freighters, tankers, and miscellaneous types. Foreign and American buyers had spent $425 million for Liberty ships by the time the Act expired. American firms showed little interest in Libertys until other types had all been sold. Profits to be made during the Korean War sparked their interest, however, and they snapped up 91 Libertys from reserve fleets before the 15 January 1951 deadline for ship purchases.

The value of Libertys held up amazingly well for two decades. Fluctuations in world tonnage requirements set the price, and during periods of intense tonnage demands, such as the 1956 Suez Canal crisis and the Korean War, a Liberty sold for as much as $2 million.

In typical sales during 1955, the *Hoosier State* (*Hugh J. Kilpatrick*)* was sold by American owners for American-flag operation and brought $500,000. The *Resolute* (*George H. Thomas*) went from the Panamanian to the Danish flag for $740,000. The *Marit* (*W. B. Ayers*), operating under the Norwegian flag, fetched $820,000 when sold to Greek owners for operation under the Panamanian flag. The American *Hawaiian Forester* (*George E. Waldo*) brought $450,000; she later was named *C. R. Musser* and *Reliance Serenity*. The *Polarusoil* (*Lafcadio Hearn*) was sold from American- to Panamanian-flag operation for $550,000. One of the lowest prices—$480,000—was brought by the *Sulphur*

---

* During their peacetime careers, Liberty ships were usually given new names when their ownership changed. Some ships had as many as nine names before they were scrapped. In this chapter, ships are usually referred to by their last, or latest name; all prior names appear in parentheses with the original name first and others in chronological order following. Where the name used in the text is not the last name, its place in the sequence is indicated by an ellipsis.

Mines (*Casper S. Yost*), which was still only $20,000 less than she had cost in 1946.

Again, in 1961, anticipating heavy grain shipments to Europe, sellers of Liberty ships demanded high prices. Several sold for more than $350,000, and one vessel went for over $400,000. Large wheat shipments boosted prices in 1963, forcing buyers to pay up to $300,000 for these aging tramps. By contrast, a slump in bulk cargo movements in mid-1958 dropped prices as low as $275,000. Such sharp fluctuations reflected the precarious nature of tramp shipping for amateurs and were one reason why so many American firms came and went in the business in the postwar years. Lower prices involved in American transactions reflected the shrinking demand for American-flag tramp ships, tramping being the only employment for Libertys not converted to special uses.

By June of 1947 there were more than 1,200 American tramp ships on the seas, as many as in the entire deep-sea merchant marine in 1939. Many of them were being operated by neophytes in the shipping business who had entered the industry to get the "fast buck" that was available as long as ships were scarce, cargoes were plentiful, and rates were high. Most operators had a minimum investment to make, as tramps could be chartered at roughly $8,000 a month rather than purchased from the U. S. Maritime Commission.

The number of American-flag tramps, and this included 500 engaged only in the coal and grain trade between the U. S., Europe, and the Middle East, had dropped to 950 by February of 1948. The decline was caused by higher government charter rates, foreign competition, and higher operating expenses. Always complicated by the intricacies of international currency, national preferences, international trade agreements, politics, and fast-changing cargo trends, not to mention the intense competition of shipowners wise in the ways of tramp operation, this highly specialized branch of the maritime business suffered a steady decline after 1948 as far as the American flag was concerned. Except for government-sponsored foreign aid cargoes and war shipments, there would have been little employment for even a small fleet of American tramps.

☐

Most of the American companies were newcomers to the shipping industry, at least as far as corporate structure was concerned and, in more than a few cases, as far as management and know-how was concerned. Their advent in the industry was made possible by foreign aid, the requirement that government-owned cargoes must move in American ships, and the availability of good vessels at reasonable prices. Most of them dropped out of the shipping business when competition increased.

The James W. Elwell Company of New York, which once owned the famous clipper *Glory of the Seas,* went back into ship-owning in 1951 with the *Thunderbird (Charles D. Lanham)*, chartered for the grain trade to India. The *Thunderbird* was sold, transferred foreign (*Watling, New Kailing*), and scrapped at Hong Kong in 1962.

The Mar-Trade Corporation, for many years an agent for Greek and Panamanian ships, entered the shipping business in 1948 with six vessels, including four Liberty tankers: *John Stagg, Sanford B. Dole, John H. Marion,* and *Andrew Marschalk.*

During the last days of the Ship Sales Act, these firms bought one ship each: Advance Steamship Company, Alliance Steamship Company, American Steamship Company, Arc Steamship Company, Capehorn Steamship Company, Excelsior Steamship Company, General Steamship Company, Kea Steamship Company, Kurz and Company, Muguel J. Ossoria, and Saxon Steamship Company. These firms bought two, usually tankers: Eastern Seaways, Hess Incorporated, Mercador Trading Company, Metro Steamship Company, Pacific Cargo Carriers, and Paco Tankers. The American Pacific Steamship Company bought three.

American tramp ship operators attempted to obtain a government subsidy during the forties and fifties, but without success and without encouragement from subsidized and unsubsidized berth line operators, whose regularly scheduled ships also carried a large percentage of government-sponsored freight.

Tramp operators told Congressional committees that it cost them an average of $928 a day to operate a Liberty ship compared to the average cost of $457 a day for British ships and even lower figures for Norwegian, Greek, Italian, and other ships. Foreign-owned Libertys under the Panamanian flag, they said, could operate at 66 percent of American costs. There was a similar cost differential in later years when hundreds of Libertys operated under flags of convenience provided by Panama, Lebanon, Liberia, and Cyprus.

According to a U. S. Maritime Commission study in 1949, it cost an American operator about $46,000 to operate a Liberty ship for a 50-day voyage, while a similar vessel under British registry could make the same voyage for $22,872.

□

Liberty ships helped to rebuild the war-shattered merchant fleets of all European allies, the ships being sold for a fixed price of $500,000 under the Ship Sales Act of 1946. Although the German merchant marine, under the Potsdam Agreement, was not allowed to rebuild until a few years after the war, surplus Libertys were transferred to Italy as early as 1946–47. Some buyers considered the price tag of $500,000 rather stiff, but as ships were scarce and shipyards were just resuming commercial production, they did not haggle over the cost. As it worked out, the price was nominal, and most ships quickly earned their purchase price.

Of a group of 106 ships, mostly Libertys, sold by the U. S. government in March of 1947, 23 went to Greek operators such as Michael Kulukundis, Nicholas Goulandris, E. J. Chandris, and the Livanos brothers. From an initial allotment of 100 to Greek buyers, vessels were distributed to operators according to the amount of tonnage under their control before the war.

Typical of them was the SS *San Lorenzo* (*John LaFarge, Sea Life, Andros Lion*), flying the Liberian flag, owned by a Greek firm, and trading in the Pacific between the U. S., Japan, and Korea, carrying scrap metal to the Far East and returning with cargoes of steel and plywood. In 20 years of war and peace, this freighter had seen most of the world's ports and had carried almost every kind of cargo that could be loaded into a ship. When she called at San Diego in 1964, Captain Nicolas Protopapas of Piraeus said her engine was still as efficient and reliable as it was during World War II.

"We averaged 10½ knots, fully-loaded, on the trip from Pusan, Korea, to San Diego," he reported, proudly. "Some days we made as many as eleven knots! When a ship is 20 years old you can't ask for more than that."

Another Greek-owned ship, the *Aktis,* sailed under the Lebanese flag. Originally built for the British under Lend-Lease as the *Samgaudie* (*Norah Moller, Statesman*), she had logged enough peacetime miles to have gone many times around the world. In one year, the *Aktis* had carried grain from Russia to South America, more grain from South America to Germany, newsprint from Canada to Brazil, scrap iron from Baltimore to Japan, and plywood from Korea to California.

Typical of many Greek merchant sailors, Captain Dimitrios M. Koukounas of the *Archandros* (*Samtyne, Argentine Transport, . . . , Zephyr*) went to sea in 1947 and spent more than 20 years in Liberty ships. "I have been on eleven ships," he said in 1967. "All of them have been Liberty ships. They have taken me to ports all over the world. Name them. I have been there. Me and my Liberty ships."

Ships such as these repaid the original investment many times over. After World War II Liberty ships made fortunes for many a shipping entrepreneur who was astute enough to purchase cheap ships in an era of high freight rates. It was not unusual for a Liberty to completely repay her purchase cost in only a few trips.

Captain Menelaus Pappas, master of the *Ektor* (*Jesse Cottrell, Seaqueen, Caribsea, Holy Star, Symphony*), was one of many Greek shipmasters who praised the wartime expendables. "Still she goes . . ." he said, ". . . 22 years after the war and still she goes. With no cargo, she can go eleven knots, as good as when she was new." At that time, the *Ektor* had seen 23 years of continuous service.

Vessels in this same group were purchased by the Italian, Norwegian, and Netherlands governments and by private operators, including the Danish East Asiatic Company and Lorentzen Rderi Company of Norway. The Scindia Navigation Company of India bought the *Benito Juarez* and an Italian firm acquired the *Hiram Bingham, James Rolph*, and *Ada Rehan*.

A *Fortune* magazine survey in 1953 described how Greek shipping tycoons had expanded their maritime enterprises after the war, the initial impetus coming from Libertys acquired through the Ship Sales Act of 1946. Stavros Niarchos had 34 ships, many of them Libertys, under the Greek, Liberian, Panamanian, Honduran, and British flags. They were owned by an assortment of corporations with headquarters in Bermuda, London, Paris, Hamburg, and Zurich. Stavros Livanos had 70 ships and Manuel Kulukundis owned 60, including many EC2s. Other Liberty ship owners were Pericles Callimanopulos, Andrew Vergottis, and the Embiricos, Pateros, and Goulandris families.

Liberty ships also played an important role in rebuilding the French merchant marine after the war. The French Messageries Maritimes, whose motor ship *Marechal Joffre* had become the USS *Rochambeau* in World War II, acquired *Les Gileries* (*Royal S. Copeland*), *Nantes* (*William S. Young*), *Ovennax* (*Wilbur O. Atwater*), *Saint Nazaire* (*Emma Willard*), *Vercors* (*Benjamin H. Latrobe*), *Grenoble* (*Henry George*), *Biancon* (*John Colter*), *Courseulles* (*Will M. Hays*), *Falaise* (*Carl G. Barth*), *Mortain* (*Stephen Johnson Field*), *Saint Valery* (*George W. Campbell*), *Auray* (*Uriah M. Rose*), *Sainte Mere Eglise* (*Stephen Girard*), *Beauvais* (*John Lawson*), *Saint Marcouf* (*John Robert Gordon*), *Le Verdon* (*Victor Herbert*), and *Strasbourg* (*John B. Lennon*).

Many Libertys joined Britain's war-shattered merchant fleet. One of the largest and most famous lines under the Red Ensign, the Ellerman Company, used them to reinstate its far-flung services after the war, and as late as 1953 still had eleven: *City of Chelmsford* (*Lionel Copley, Sambrake*), *City of Colchester* (*Samlea*), *City of Doncaster* (*Emma Lazarus, Samara*), *City of Ely* (*James Blair, Samarina*), *City of Leeds* (*Samcrest*), *City of Lichfield* (*Samuel H. Ralston, Samois*), *City of Newport* (*William R. Cox, Samtweed*), *City of Portsmouth* (*Henry Van Dyke, Samhain*), *City of Shrewsbury* (*Ben H. Miller*), *City of St. Albans* (*Frederick Banting*), and *City of Stafford* (*Samtorch*).

The newly independent India, in order to enter the shipping business, purchased 110,000 tons of surplus Libertys, almost the equivalent of its entire deepsea fleet in 1940. Among the last Libertys in the world used as commercial carriers, were World War II veterans still sailing along the coast of India 25 years after the war ended, shuttling grain between grain-carrying supertankers and ports with insufficient draft to accommodate them, such as Bombay, Calcutta, Madras, and Chittagong. Most of them were Greek-owned, with Greek officers and Indian crews. Hired at very low rates on a daily charter basis, they eked out a bare living, staving off that final trip to a wreckers yard.

In addition to these and other sales abroad, a number of Lend-Lease Libertys were held by the Russians who declined to return them after the war.* Such ships, unlike those loaned to the British, never reverted to the American flag, and the United States was not reimbursed for their use. One of them, the *Kolkhoznik* (*Charles Wilkes*), carried a cargo of arms from Russia to Cuba during the "missile crisis" of 1962.

Besides selling off servicable ships, the U. S. Maritime Administration, in the fifties, offered for sale the wrecks of hundreds of ships that had been sunk during the war. Some were hulks deep in the sea; others were cargo-laden vessels a relatively few feet below the surface. The offer had few takers, as the hazards of salvaging a sunken ship were so great that even large salvage firms shied clear of these jobs. The list of ships available for salvage included the *George W. Norris*, wrecked on Tenega Shima Island, Japan; the *John Couch*, lying under a few fathoms at Guadalcanal, and the *Christopher Newport*, hundreds of feet deep in the Barents Sea.

☐

---

* See Appendix D.

In their new lease on life, the wartime Liberty ships plied the peacetime cargo routes under many names. The *Willard R. Johnson*, from launching in 1945 to scrapping in 1967, had been, in turn, the *Neptunus, Apollo, Evimar, Theokeetor, Riverhead*, and *Maru*. The *Sanford B. Dole*, a 1943 Liberty tanker later became the *Giraffe, Sanford B. Dole* again, *Eileen, Peapendar, Ragnar Haess, Ocean Daphne*, and *Orient Lake*. She was converted to a dry-cargo ship in 1949 and was eventually scrapped in Japan.

Another ship with many names was the *George L. Baker*. After the war she was sold to the Dutch and became the *Kamerlingh Onnes*. In later changes of ownership, she was *Tonini, Texel, Southern Cross*, and finally the *Mindanao Merchant*.

The *James Cook* was sold to Greek owners and renamed *Antipolis* in 1957, *Andros City* in 1960, *Thermaikos* in 1963, *Calliope* in 1965, and *Vancalt* in 1966. In 1967 she was scrapped as *Michiko*.

Changes of name usually followed transfer of the ship to a new owner or a change in corporate structure for the same owner. Frequently, owners incorporated each of their vessels as a separate legal entity for financial or political reasons. Changing a ship's name is not done capriciously, for it costs from $700 to $2,000 for the necessary official documentation, advertising the intent for change of name, legal fees, and rewriting the mortgage agreements.

In some cases it must have been difficult for a ship to remember her latest name or who she worked for. The *Cyrus Holliday* became, in turn, the *Chrysanthy, Rhapsody*, and *Fos*. The *Charles Porter Low* continued her peacetime career as the *Northern Traveller, Teng*, and *Tieh Chiao*. The *Samjack* was sold to Alfred Holt and Company in 1947 for the Blue Funnel Line and renamed *Tudeus*. Next she went to the Glen Line as the *Glensburg*. In 1960 she hoisted the Liberian Flag as *Jucar*, the name under which she was scrapped in Japan in 1967. The *Efdemon* had been, in turn, the *Thomas Hendricks, Robert Fruin*, and *Amsteldiep* before she was sold to Taiwan wreckers in 1967 for $145,000.

Many Libertys survived wartime operations and escaped the wreckers, only to find a watery grave after long and profitable service. The *San Nicola* (*William H. Kendrick, Judge Bland, Athenian, Andros Citadel*) sank in 1967 with a full load of scrap metal while bound from the West Coast of the United States to Formosa.

In 1964, the *Grammatiki* (*George A. Marr*) was bound from Portland, Oregon, for Keelung, Formosa, with a cargo of scrap metal when she began leaking halfway between the West Coast and Honolulu. Pumps were unable to handle flooding, and the ship sent out an SOS answered by the American steamer *Cotton State* and the British freighter *Roland*. They took off the crew of 29 just before the ship sank.

Numerous Liberty ships appeared on Lloyd's casualty list during the latter years of their service as they succumbed to accidents of one kind or another all over the seven seas:

> The Liberian Liberty ship *Universal Trader*, originally *the Edward K. Collier*, aground in latitude 06 degrees, 24 minutes, north; longitude 81 degrees, 47 minutes east, has broken in two.
>
> The Panamanian Liberty ship *Enosis* (*Otto Mears, Napoli, Posillipo, Federica Costa, Bianca, Bice Costa*) went aground in latitude 07 degrees, 52 minutes north, longitude 98 degrees, 56 minutes east after reporting fire in her number five and possibly number four holds. She had a cargo of coal.
>
> Greek Liberty ship *Odysion* sank approximately 300 miles from Walvis Bay. Crew rescued.

The *Odysion* was originally the *Ezra Cornell*, which had been the French SS *Isigny* from 1947 to 1965 before being sold to Greek owners, the Northern Marine Corporation of Monrovia. The dramatic end of her career, as witnessed by the crew of the Belgian tanker *Fina America* on 23 December 1967 while the ship was bound from the Persian Gulf to Antwerp, was reported in *Marine News*, journal of the World Ship Society.

> The tanker sighted a derelict about 300 miles west of Walvis Bay, South Africa, a vessel which was obviously an American-built Liberty and riding very deep in the water. Through the glasses they could identify the V (I want assistance) code pennant flying from the signal halyards but there was no sign of life on board. It being a clear, fine day, with a moderate sea, the tanker's captain, B. Diricq, stopped his ship and sent a motorboat in charge of the second mate to see if there was anyone on board the vessel in need of help.
>
> The boarding party found no sign of life on the derelict ... the Greek S. S. *Odysion*. During this time, the British tanker *British Realm* came up ... saying it had been abandoned and that the crew had been picked up by the Liberian tanker *Marilou*.
>
> Even while the boarding party was leaving the derelict for their motorboat, they heard a deep rumbling sound from inside the deserted vessel and a geyser of water shot out of number three hold, tossing

hatch covers high in the air. These were the final death throes for the *Odysion* and so quickly did she go down after that—no more than ten seconds—that the second mate and an able seaman found themselves swimming among the debris of the sunken ship. Fortunately, both men were wearing life preservers.

In September of 1967, the senior deputy chairman of Lloyds, Paul Dixey, said that Liberty ships as a whole were being used for the transport of scrap, metal ores and grain "where operation is marginal, maintenance minimal and profit frequently insufficient to provide reserve even for survey expenses." Rough usage, according to Dixey, weakened the ships through the holing of transverse bulkheads by scrap metal; by lack of painting and preservation of metal in critical areas; and by severe corroding of plates at the waterline because of poor maintenance. He charged that many ships were operating with deficiencies that would never pass the more stringent classification agencies such as Lloyds. The casualty list for that year showed that insurors were hit hard by widespread accidents and losses to EC2s all over the world.

Rough usage helped speed the end for many such ships. The SS *Grand* (*Walter Husband, Ivybank, Winona, Kondor*) sailed from San Francisco for Yokohama in 1966, loaded down to her marks with scrap metal, and broke up during heavy weather. Of her crew of 44, 21 drowned. The *Maria Despina* (*Washington Allston, Thorbecke, Lutterkerk*), flying the Lebanese flag, also broke up when she went aground outside Alexandria in March of 1966.

It was a bad year for the aging EC2s. The *White Mountain* (*Mary Bickerdyke*), operating under the Liberian flag, collided with the British *Funabashi* in February, near Singapore, and capsized while *Funabashi* was beached. The Liberian *Pensacola* (*John Leckie*) sank that same month in Mona Passage in the Caribbean when leaks developed and pumps were unable to handle the flooding.

Another Liberian Liberty, the *Rockport* (*Wilfred R. Belevue, Edison Mariner, Ionnis Daskalelis*), foundered in February in the North Pacific when her hull split on a voyage from Vancouver to Japan. The *Elias Dayfas II* (*Raymond Clapper, Thrylos, Master Nicky, T. J. Stevenson*) was en route from Galveston to Vietnam on 5 July 1966 when leaks developed off Yucatan. She was taken in tow by the tanker *Sea Pioneer*, but fire broke out and she sank.

The Lebanese *Suerte* (*Lionel Copley, Sambrake, City of Chelmsford, San George*) went aground near Halifax in January of 1962, was adjudged unfit for further use, and was towed 250 miles out to sea and scuttled. No one explained why a vessel that could survive such a tow was not taken to a scrap yard or repaired instead of being sunk. The *Faro* (*James Fenimore Cooper*) went aground near Tokyo Bay during a storm in January of 1966. The *Lampsis* (*J. D. Ross*), owned by the Proteus Shipping Company of Greece, sank in the same month about 600 miles off Bermuda. The Lebanese *Alheli* (*Henry Dodge*) developed leaks on a trans-Atlantic trip and sank two days after being abandoned about 900 miles east of Bermuda in April of 1968.

After 20 years of service, some weak and leaky hulls could take no more. Such was the *Marcar* (*George H. Thomas, Aristarchos, Resolute, Cape Palmas*), a Liberian Liberty that went down in the harbor of St. Vincent, Cape Verde Islands. Leaks on a trans-Atlantic voyage also spelled the end of the *Orione* (*Jesse Billingsley*), which arrived at Fayal in February of 1969 in an unseaworthy condition, was towed to Vigo, and then was sold to Italian shipbreakers. The *Conchita* (*Samconon*) developed leaks on a voyage from Mormugao, India, to Poland and sank in July of 1967 about 300 miles southwest of the Seychelles.

Throughout the year Lloyds reported many Liberty ship casualties. The Liberian *Demetrios* (*Charles Paddock, Kenneth H. Stevenson, Skiathos*) was abandoned by her crew in a sinking condition on 12 July near Diego Juarez. The *Leftric* (*Jacob H. Gallagher*), flying the Lebanese flag, went aground at Mormugao, hit a breakwater, broke in two, and became a total loss.

The Panamanian SS *Pinguino* (*George Gamblin*) foundered 90 miles from Rio de Janeiro in 1967 but all hands were saved. The Liberian *Thimars* (*Oakley Wood, Keystone State, Georges Fribourg, Magallanes, Alexander S.M.*) was a total loss when she went aground near Sarawak in 1967. A 1966 casualty was the *Zaneta* (*Sara Teasdale, California Sun, Hera, Leotric, Oradour*), which started to leak in the Arabian sea and was abandoned on 19 June.

Libertys that had managed to avoid serious accidents for two decades were afflicted with an epidemic of engine room fires and explosions in 1967. The *Kostis A. Georgilis* (*Samconstant*) had such an accident in November of 1967 and was beached on Cocos Island in the Indian Ocean. The Liberian-flag *California Sun* (*Henry C. Wallace, Trocadero, Percy Jordan*) had an engine room explosion and fire in November, 1967, which gutted the ship.

Hardy survivors of wartime convoy routes and beachheads, Libertys often went down through old age and neglect. The *Omega* (*Thomas H. Sumner*) was abandoned by her crew on 13 November 1966, after the hull cracked at sea. The *Tegean* (*James W. Fannin*) went aground that month near Halifax and became a total loss. The *Elenik* (*Johns Hopkins*) broke in two and foundered on 29 September 1966 about eight miles from Thevenard Island, Western Australia. The *Ionnis K.* (*Samsoaring*) was abandoned after going aground off Vung Tau in January of 1968.

□

More than a few Liberty ships sank under dubious circumstances in times of falling freight rates or when insurance was pushed so unreasonably high as to make it unprofitable to operate with low-paying cargoes. There have been a number of Liberty ships, sunk or stranded, for which insurance firms were reluctant to pay claims.

Owners of some ships that sank under wholly legitimate circumstances spent large sums of money for legal fees in trying to collect insurance claims on their vessels, and some were unsuccessful in their claims. Said one Liberty shipowner:

> In some circumstances, marine underwriters have taken the position that no 'insured peril' had transpired even though the ship may be sitting on the bottom, be stranded on a reef, or be towed in, gutted by fire. By taking this position, they throw the burden of proving an 'insured peril' upon the owner. In other words, the claim itself is not denied, but the underwriters conveniently ignore the fact that a casualty has occurred. The only recourse to the assured is to bring suit against the underwriters, which is a very costly affair and is quite often an exercise in futility. In one case in London, the owners carried their suit all the way to the House of Lords. The suit was ultimately decided in the owners' favor, but legal fees and expenses were almost as much as the insured valuation of the ship. With marine underwriters faring very poorly in recent years on all classes of insured tonnage, including newly built, high-value ships, underwriters have at times abused the owners of relatively low valued warbuilt tonnage by refusing to admit claim through denial of peril. Numerous legitimate total losses and constructive total losses have been settled through negotiation as 'compromised' total losses at considerably less than policy value, because the time and legal expenses involved in collecting under litigation were utilized as discount leverage by underwaters against owners of Liberty ship tonnage.

Whatever the reason for their loss, the hulks of many EC2s can still be seen around the world, and some of them will probably last for many years. The *White*

Eagle (*George Weems, Myken, Cavolid, Cocle*) ran hard and fast on San Clemente Island off the California coast in what most mariners would describe as fair weather. For many months she sat serenely on the rocks, exactly as if she were at a pier, ready to sail as soon as the cargo was loaded and the hatches battened down. She will probably be there for years to come. The *Francis Preston Blair* went aground on Saumarez Reef, off Queensland, Australia, in July of 1945, and twenty five years later appeared in good condition, sitting on an even keel as if she was in a graving dock.

Some Liberty ships escaped all the perils of the sea, only to be abandoned when their owners were overcome by financial difficulties. One such ship was the *Valiant Enterprise* (*Harold T. Andrews, Bassa, Spiro Makris, Robertville*) owned by the Enterprise Steamship Company, an American corporation. She became the "ghost ship" of Colombo after she entered that port in 1960 and was held for unpaid harbor dues and other debts. By 1966 so much water had collected in her holds from rain and leaks that alarmed officials, afraid she might sink inside the port, had her towed six miles away from the harbor area. She lay at anchor there for many more months, until she was finally sold to Japan for scrapping.

In a similar case of abandonment, 15 crewmen of the scrap iron-laden *Protostatis* (*John Philip Sousa, Erato, Paxiarchis*) were marooned when their Greek-owned, Panamanian-registered freighter went aground on Wolfe Island in the St. Laurence River in November of 1965. Her owner, Marcus Lemos of London, told the Canadian government that he was abandoning the ship. After most of the officers left for home, the first mate and 15 penniless crewmen remained on board the hulk without pay, living without light or heat, far from their homes in Greece.

Attorney George Speal of Kingston, Ontario, took an interest in their plight, saw that townspeople supplied them with food, and arranged for them to receive back pay and transportation to Greece. The ship was later refloated, taken to Toronto and sold; then towed to Spain for scrapping.

☐

Some Libertys became mysteries of the sea, joining the long line of ships that left port never to return. In 1948 the *Samkey* with a crew of 40 men left England for Havana, made a routine position report off the Azores, and was never heard of again. No exceptionally heavy weather was reported from the area at the time, and the chance of hitting a floating World War II mine in that region was most remote. Explosion or fire was the most likely explanation, but whatever her fate, it came so suddenly that the radio operator sent no SOS. The ship was listed at Lloyds as "presumed lost and missing with all hands."

A more gruesome mystery involved the SS *Pomona* (*John Carroll, Solmar, Kronviken*), a Liberty owned by Brazilians, flying the Liberian flag, and carrying a crew of Norwegians, West Indians, Spaniards, and Finns when she left Norway for the Caribbean in October of 1943 under the command of Captain Jacob Natvig.

The *Pomona* had been at sea only a few days when one of the Finns went berserk and had to be subdued. They landed him in Bilbao, Spain. Then there were bloody fights and drunken binges among the crew. A seaman jumped overboard but was recovered, half drowned. En route to California, one seaman tried to commit suicide and another threatened to cut the captain's throat with a knife.

A few days after leaving San Pedro with scrap iron for Taiwan in May of 1964, Captain Natvig was seen drinking with Chief Steward Ander Baardsen. Two days later, First Mate Alf Olsen went to the Captain's cabin to find him in his bunk with his skull smashed and a bloody fireaxe on the deck beside him. Olsen took command and sailed the ship to Honolulu. While the "hell ship" headed for port, edgy crewmen slept with lights burning and walked warily along decks and passageways, for they knew there was a maniacal killer loose among them.

At Honolulu there was an investigation, purely routine. No one was likely to be punished, because the crime had been committed on the high seas beyond American jurisdiction, and Liberian authorities were half the world away.

The investigation produced no clues. Crewmen could offer no reason as to why anyone would kill the captain; indeed he had been rarely seen on deck throughout the trip, leaving the ship's navigation and operation to the first mate. There were no fingerprints on the axe. No members of the crew were arraigned or charged, although two Norwegian detectives flew to Honolulu and took Baardsen back to Oslo with them. When authorities eventually released the vessel and the time came for it to clear for the Orient, most of the crew refused to sail and demanded release from the ship's articles on the grounds that their lives were in danger. A new crew was hired, and the *Pomona* sailed with a Chinese crew, Norwegian officers, and a Brazilian radio operator. By that time the "hell ship" had become a jinx ship as well—100 miles out of Honolulu, there was a fire in the engine room and the 33 crewmen abandoned ship. They later returned on board, put out the fire, and rode the ill-fated *Pomona* back to Honolulu at the end of a towline.

☐

In the 18 months after the start of the Korean War in 1950, more than 600 ships, including many Libertys, were withdrawn from reserve fleets. At that time, it cost about $100,000 to reactivate a Liberty ship and another $50,000 to lay her up again when her emergency usefulness was over. When Egypt closed the Suez Canal in 1956, more than 200 ships were taken out of reserve fleets to meet increased shipping demands. No Libertys were withdrawn from the mothball fleets for the Vietnam War, although all laid-up Victory ships were placed in service. At one time, more than 175 of them were operating on the Vietnam shuttle from American ports.

☐

During the 1950s, the U. S. Maritime Administration experimented with different methods of powering Liberty ships to give them more speed. The idea was to possibly upgrade a number of them for more profitable peacetime use as well as for greater transport potential in time of war. As part of this program, the *John Sergeant,* a former World War II POW ferry, became the first large ocean-going vessel to be powered with a gas turbine. Her conventional propeller was replaced by a controllable-pitch propeller. A new bow lengthened the hull by 25 feet. After several voyages, the alteration was deemed successful, but no more ships received this treatment.

Another experiment was made when the *Benjamin Chew* was given a steam turbine, which boosted her speed to 15.3 knots on a trans-Atlantic test trip. The *Thomas Nelson* was equipped with a diesel engine, and the *William Patterson* was powered with a free-piston gas turbine. All four ships were prototypes and no other conversions were made.

To make them more competitive with newer ships and large, new carriers specially designed for the bulk-cargo trades, many Libertys were jumboized—lengthened by cutting the ship in two and inserting a 70-foot section between number two and three holds. The additional space enabled a vessel to carry up to 1,500 more tons of cargo with about two feet less draft.

While most Liberty ships were jumboized when it came to conversion, the *Janet Lord Roper* went the other way. She was shortened—a 30-foot section aft of the engines was cut out to accommodate her to limited berths in ports at which her owners wanted to operate. This ship honored a woman who served for many years at the Seamens Church Institute in New York City. Beloved of seamen, Janet Lord Roper became the aide and confidante of seafarers of many nationalities, to whom she was known affectionately as "Mother Roper."

A special conversion job turned two war-blasted Libertys into one ship, the Italian *Boccadasse*, owned by Maritime Industriale of Genoa. She was built by welding together the bow section of the *Nathaniel Bacon* and the stern section of the *Bert Williams*. The *Boccadasse* was 30 feet longer than the regular EC2 and could carry close to 11,000 tons of cargo instead of the usual 10,000. The 30-foot stretch required additional strengthening with steel girders welded lengthwise inside the hull.

A proposal for improving Libertys and making them more commercially competitive was developed in 1953 by the Gibbs Engineering Company, which determined after extensive studies that the vessel's amidships and after body sections were suitable for higher speeds. By modifying the forward third of the ship with finer lines, increasing the length, and adding more power, engineers predicted the enlarged Liberty could do 18 knots and still maintain an economical fuel consumption. The proposal was submitted to the Senate Subcommittee on Maritime Subsidies and to the Maritime Administration, but nothing further came of it. By then most Libertys were already 10 years old, and another two years would have been required for engineering and conversion work.

In 1961 the Weyerhaeuser Lumber Company altered six Liberty ships at a cost of about one million dollars each to carry an additional 275,000 board-feet of lumber on voyages from the American West Coast to the East Coast. Additional space was provided by removing some bulkheads and deeptanks. Holds were altered for the use of forklift trucks. Crew quarters were greatly improved.

What was probably the world's last fleet of Liberty ships in commercial service was still being operated in 1970 by the Alaska Steamship Company, with six ships sailing between Seattle and Alaskan ports. They were the *Chena* (*Chief Washakie*), *Fortuna* (*Samuel R. Cobb, Volunteer State*), *Iliamna* (*Edmond Mallet*), *Nadina* (*William G. Lee, Dorian Prince*), *Nenana* (*Felix Riesenberg*), and *Tonsina* (*Arthur P. Fairfield, Seacoronet, Chung Ting, Adm. Arthur P. Fairfield*). That these ships were still sailing, twenty-five years after the last Liberty was built, was due to a program of thorough upkeep and maintenance. All were strengthened structurally for work in ice and the rough weather usual in North Pacific and Bering Sea service. The *Chena*, with 320 voyages to Alaskan waters, and the *Nadina*, with 340 such voyages, demonstrated the long life potential of a ship, given proper care. But by the end of 1971, all six ships were laid up.

The *Chena* went through the severe earthquake that struck Alaska in 1964 with only minor damage. She was tied up at Valdez when the quake struck and completely demolished the dock, killing 25 men. The ship rolled 50 degrees, struck bottom, then was lifted on top of the dock wreckage, but with engines on the line immediately succeeded in backing clear.

□

Unique among hundreds of sister ships was the *Arthur M. Huddell*, which had been especially altered to load and lay a flexible gasoline pipeline (*PLUTO*) across the English Channel for the Normandy landings. Laid up for some years, she was chartered by the American Telephone and Telegraph Company to help transport a submarine cable between the continental United States, Hawaii, and the arctic area where the Distant Early Warning (DEW) Line was being built.

The *Lt. Gen. Samuel D. Sturgis* (*Charles H. Cugle*) became the world's first floating nuclear power station, with a uranium core reactor producing ten million watts of electricity, the normal electrical needs of a city of 25,000. The plant was designed by the Martin Company of Baltimore. Alterations to the ship were made by the Alabama Drydock and Shipbuilding Company at Mobile.

Renamed to honor a former chief of the Army Engineer Corps, *Sturgis* (MH-1A; M for mobile, H for high power, 1A for prototype) can be towed to distant military bases and can provide power for a year, saving on fuel and overseas transport. The reactor and steam generator are housed in a 350-ton, watermelon-shaped steel container located amidships in a 212-foot-long section spliced to the bow and stern sections after the original midships area had been cut away.

More than 800 tons of concrete and 600 tons of lead and polyethylene shielding surround the steel container in a four-foot thick protective layer to prevent radiation. The inner bottom was greatly strengthened, and a thick collision barrier was built to protect the reactor in case of ramming. The plant carries a 15-man crew, and galley, laundry, recreation room, repair and maintenance shop, and a sewage disposal system.

A number of EC2s were sold by the Maritime Commission for nontransportation use. The *Harold L. Winslow* became a combination pier, warehouse, and cold storage plant at Nikiska, Alaska, and the *Thomas Hartley*, one of the "lost convoy" to Russia in 1942, became a floating platform for a 200-ton derrick at Seattle, Washington.

During the bumper grain crops of the early 1950s, Libertys mothballed in reserve fleets provided emergency storage for surplus grain and saved millions of tons from rotting in the fields. In July of 1953, when the U. S. had a 700,000,000 bushel surplus, wheat valued at $2.25 a bushel was stored in 75 Libertys in the Hudson River, 50 in the James River, and many others at Astoria, Oregon. Three years later, a total of 330 Libertys were loaded with wheat. Each ship held 225,000 bushels, enough to make 15 million loaves of bread.

The *John Brown* served for many years in the New York City public school system. Permanently tied up at a Hudson River pier, the nautical schoolship trained thousands of youngsters in basic skills of the deck, engine, and steward departments, and many of them later found careers in the merchant marine.

The *Michael Moran*, named for the founder of the Moran Towing and Transportation Company, made five voyages, including a circumnavigation of the world, in the two years before she was laid up at New Orleans in 1946. In 1958 she was taken out of the mothball fleet, towed into the Atlantic, and used as a target for new Navy missiles.

Another unusual use for Liberty ships was proposed by Harvard professors Leslie Silverman and Melvin W. First in 1963. They sought a $350,000 federal grant to study converting them into floating incinerators for big coastal cities such as Boston, which has to dispose of 1,000 tons of waste every day. They proposed three deck-mounted rotary incinerators on each ship at an estimated conversion cost of $1.25 million per ship. The grant was not approved.

□

Probably the biggest headlines ever made by any Liberty ship came out of Texas City, Texas, the morning of 16 April 1947. There, berthed only 700 feet from the Monsanto chemical plant, the French-owned Liberty ship *Grancamp* (*Benjamin R. Curtis*) had loaded 800 tons of ammonium nitrate fertilizer when longshoremen discovered a fire in the hold. Few of the dockworkers, crewmen, or others who gathered to fight the fire or watch it had any idea that ammonium nitrate could become violently explosive because of the action of heat.

Moored nearby were the *High Flyer* and another Liberty, *Willson B. Keene*, while overhead two light planes circled, carrying photographers. An hour after the fire was discovered the *Grancamp* blew up in "one tremendous thunder clap" heard more than 100 miles away.

The two planes, knocked out of the sky, splashed into the harbor along with debris of all kinds, including huge jagged chunks of ship plating and fittings. The *High Flyer* was destroyed and the *Willson B. Keene* was blasted into an almost unrecognizable hulk. Moments later the entire Monsanto plant blew up, taking with it adjoining plants, buildings, and warehouses. In the series of explosions, more than 400 people were killed.

Twenty three years later, another Liberty ship made more, if not bigger head-lines. The *LeBaron Russel Briggs* was also the subject of radio and TV coverage, protests, demonstrations, and court actions, and was featured in *Time* magazine for two weeks running. When she finally terminated her public career by a spec-tacular plunge to the bottom of the ocean on 18 August 1970, some 265 miles east of Daytona Beach, Florida, photos of her end made front pages across the country. The long controversy over the *Briggs* commenced when the U. S. Army announced plans to scuttle her with a load of extremely deadly chemical nerve gas.

That was not the first time a Liberty ship had been used to dispose of surplus chemicals or ammunition. In fact, between 1958 and 1970, eight other ships had so been used, but increasing interest in ecology and ocean pollution, plus the fact that the chemicals had to be moved to a seaport by rail through populated areas, combined to arouse great public controversy of the *Briggs* and her deadly cargo.

The deep-sea disposal of surplus ammunition in the U. S. commenced in 1958, although the Germans tried it first in 1946 when the *Arthur Sewall* sailed from Bremerhaven with a load of ammunition and chemicals and was scuttled at sea. The American disposal plan, termed Operation Chase for "cut holes and sink 'em" involved some 60,000 tons of chemicals, ammunition, and over-age or obso-lete ordnance material. It began when the *William C. Ralston* was sunk off San Francisco in 1956, with 6,500 tons of mustard gas and lewisite. The *John F. Shafroth*, with nearly 10,000 tons of dangerous cargo, was sent down off the Golden Gate in 1964. That year the *Joseph N. Dinand* also took a load of obso-lete ammunition to the bottom. The *Santiago Iglesias* was sent down in 1965 and the *Isaac Van Zandt* in 1966 with more ammunition.

In 1967 the *Robert Louis Stevenson* was loaded with 2,000 tons of ammunition and towed to the Aleutian Islands, where her cargo was to be exploded by remote control after she was sunk. Through some error she got away, was lost in the fog, and went down with the ammunition still intact. In subsequent disposal operations the *Michael James Monahan* was sunk in 1967 and the *Frederick E. Williamson* in 1970.

The problem with the *LeBaron Russel Briggs* was that everyone wanted to make certain that she reached the bottom with her cargo still intact. The gas was packed in 418 concrete and steel coffins and the ship was sent down in 16,000 feet of water. The Navy monitored the operation and verified that all the containers reached the bottom unbroken.

At the end of World War II, a number of Libertys were adapted by the WSA for repatriation of troops from overseas. The first of these conversions was the *Edward Richardson,* with accommodations for 498 passengers. "What a ride!" said a delighted sergeant. "Nothing to do but sleep and relax. The best meals I've had since the Army got me." One man gained 15 pounds while aboard.

Sergeants might not have had such an enjoyable trip on the *Thomas W. Bickett,* which hauled 743 members of the Headquarters, Fourth Army Corps, to New York in October of 1945. The passenger list included 14 colonels, 15 lieutenant colonels, 28 majors, and 33 captains.

To tired combat veterans, going home on freighters was like a vacation at the Hilton. They were fed fresh milk, eggs, fruit, vegetables, pie and ice cream. A menu for one day was: Lunch: chicken soup, beef stew, tomatoes, egg salad, pie, and coffee. Dinner: chicken and rice, string beans, green salad, strawberry sundae, and a half-pint of fresh milk. And steak twice a week.

The *Otto Mears,* converted into a troopship in four days under plans prepared by Lieutenant Colonel C. H. Davidson, carried 534 GIs from Manila to San Francisco. Three holds were converted into troop quarters with triple deck bunks on wooden frames. Officers slept in canvas cots. Nine field ranges on the forward deck provided three meals a day for all hands. The conversion was an example of ingenuity and imagination, saving thousands of dollars in shipyard costs and weeks of time.

Most unusual of all the Liberty "troop" ships were those employed by the Army Memorial Service to return to the United States the bodies of servicemen buried overseas. Each ship could carry 6,000 caskets.

□

Unnumbered American service men and merchant men sailed or rode Liberty ships during World War II, but it is probable that the Libertys carried more Japanese passengers than all others combined. During the war Japan had scattered "colonizers" in occupied territory all across the Pacific, and once the war was over they had to be sent home. A hurriedly set up Naval Shipping Control Authority for the Japanese merchant marine was given 104 Libertys and some LSTs and other merchant type ships to do the job, and Japanese crews were trained to handle the ships. In less than a year, 5,700,000 Japanese were returned to their native land, several million of them packed in the ubiquitous Libertys.

In addition to combat troops, casualties, and Japanese colonizers, many Libertys returning from Europe in 1946 and 1947 carried war brides. The ships had no regular passenger accommodations, but quarters vacated by the Armed Guard and Army cargo security officers provided some space for women who had been waiting many months for transportation.

One of the first Libertys to end her career in peacetime operations was the *Byron Darnton*. Outward-bound from the Firth of Clyde on 17 March 1946, she ran aground on Sandra Island and was badly battered by heavy seas. All hands were removed in safety, including the crew of 39 and 13 assorted passengers, among them a war bride and seven Norwegian girls bound for the United States on college scholarships.

Despite the sale of a great number of Liberty ships to the United States and foreign buyers in the immediate postwar years, and the scrapping of a large number that had been war-damaged, the reserve fleets held hundreds of idle ships up until 1960 when a large-scale scrapping program was begun. By 1963, 543 EC2s had been sold, mostly for scrap.*

Scrap prices varied tremendously according to world demand. Although the U. S. Maritime Administration in 1967–68 sold many Libertys to wreckers for as little as $45,000, foreign buyers were paying much more for overage EC2s. In April of 1968, Chinese Nationalist buyers paid $140,000 for the Liberian flag SS *African Princess* (*Samearn, Clarepark, Argolib*). This British "Sam" Liberty had earned her initial cost many times over and finally sold for almost a third of what similar ships had brought 22 years before.

□

* As of May 1970 the reserve fleets still held 469 Liberty ships; 6 Army hospital ships, 73 Navy cargo ships and other types, and 390 general cargo ships, in the Hudson and James Rivers on the East Coast, at Mobile and Beaumont, Texas, in the Gulf, and in Suisun Bay and Olympia on the West Coast. Over 250 have been scrapped since then; by 1972 there were no Libertys in the Hudson River, or at Olympia.

The demise of the EC2 was speeded in 1966 when British and American insurance firms inaugurated a 37½ percent penalty charge on each $100 of insured cargo for Libertys and other war-built ships. Appleton Cox, American insurance underwriter, told his customers: "Because of unfavorable experience we have had in recent years on wartime-built vessels we have come to the conclusion that we cannot continue to pass these vessels without additional premium." Many of the 42 ships totally lost in 1964 were Libertys.

One former Liberty owner explained the end of the Liberty ship this way:

> High insurance rates were part of the death blow for the Liberty ship, but it was just plain old age and hard service that killed off most of them. It got to the point where even foreign flag Libertys being operated at minimum expense were costing more to maintain than they were able to earn. Prolonging the useful life of a ship is a continual process of repair and replacement that almost amounts to rebuilding over a period of years. There wasn't enough money operating EC2s to make the repairs that keep a ship safe and efficient. They just came to the end of the road, operationally.

With wreck and ruin fast depleting the once vast fleets of Libertys, no greater tribute could be paid to their usefulness than the attempt by shipyards all over the world to design and build a replacement. More than 30 different designs have been offered as "Liberty ship replacements" for the 700 or so ships gradually forced off the seas after 1957 by high insurance rates, cost of maintenance, and increased competition from larger, faster bulk carriers for their "bread and butter" cargoes of fertilizers, lumber, coal, scrap metal, and grain.

A Japanese "Freedom" freighter was built and sold by Ishikawajima-Harima Heavy Industries as a Liberty successor. First of this class was the *Chian Captain*, a vessel of 14,700 deadweight tons, measuring 465 feet overall, with diesel engines aft. Extensive use of automation in the engine room allows the ship to operate with a crew of 28.

A group of German shipyards also offered an updated version of the Liberty: a 14,500-ton ship measuring 457 feet overall and capable of 15 knots with diesel power. Like her wartime predecessor, this ship is all-welded and designed for large-scale prefabrication.

Britain's replacement for the wartime Liberty is the SD14, the first of which, the *Mimis N. Papalios*, was launched at Sunderland in November of 1967. The

Papalios is 462 feet overall and has a beam of 67 feet, and her diesel engines give a speed of 14 knots, loaded. Her deadweight tonnage is 12,400; her cost one million pounds, a very moderate sum for a vessel of such size these days. Many ships of this class have been sold to Greek and other buyers.

Nicholas Papalios, president of Aegis Shipping Company and owner of the first SD14, described her as "an economical, medium-sized cargo ship which will take us through not only the good days but also the bad ones." Papalios and many other shipowners, whose fleets and fortunes prospered with the wartime Liberty, hope their replacements will have the same versatility, earning power, and durability. Plus, of course, the same reputation for service earned by the wartime immortals.

□

In October of 1958 a rusty veteran of the seas was towed up the Patapsco River at Baltimore. The ship was coming back to be scrapped at the same place where she had been launched with cheers and fanfare some 17 years earlier. Faded letters on her bow spelled out a name that deserved to be remembered along with that of *Half Moon* and *Flying Cloud* in the annals of the sea: *Patrick Henry*. She was the first of the great Liberty fleet that had sailed the dangerous sea lanes of World War II and that had left a legacy of heroism and courage, of hard work, and of service in war and peace, that has seldom been equalled in the history of man's endeavors on the sea.

The *Patrick Henry* deserved a better fate than the scrap pile; at least she should have been preserved as a maritime museum, a monument to the men and women who built the Libertys and the seamen who sailed them, and a tribute to the greatest single shipbuilding effort the world has ever seen.

But *Patrick Henry* was not quite the last of the line. Scattered along the trade routes of the world a few time-scarred Libertys still plod their ten-knot courses. When the last one of them finally meets the Atlantic gale or Pacific reef that breaks her back, it will be time again for John Masefield's fitting requiem: ". . . earth will not see such ships as these again."

APPENDIX A. Hull Number Sequence

Hull No.	Name	Hull No.	Name
1	J. L. M. Curry	48	William Patterson
2	John Marshall	49	Luther Martin
3	Henry Clay	50	William Wirt
4	Arthur Middleton	51	Reverdy Johnson
5	Alexander H. Stephens	52	John H. B. Latrobe
6	Thomas Heyward	53	Richard II. Alvey
7	Judah P. Benjamin	54	John P. Poe
8	Jefferson Davis	55	Bernard Carter
9	Thomas Lynch	56	John Carter Rose
10	Joel Chandler Harris	57	Andrew Hamilton
11	Nathaniel Bacon	58	Benjamin Chew
12	Israel Putman	59	William Tilghman
13	Joseph Wheeler	60	Jared Ingersoll
14	Patrick Henry	61	William Rawle
15	Charles Carroll	62	Horace Binney
16	Francis Scott Key	63	John Sergeant
17	Roger B. Taney	64	John C. Frémont
18	Richard Henry Lee	65	Thomas Paine
19	John Randolph	66	Benjamin Franklin
20	American Mariner	67	John Paul Jones
21	Christopher Newport	68	Paul Revere
22	Carter Braxton	69	Daniel Boone
23	Samuel Chase	70	Robert Morris
24	George Wythe	71	Samuel Adams
25	Benjamin Harrison	72	Nathan Hale
26	Francis L. Lee	73	Zebulon Pike
27	Thomas Stone	74	Henry Knox
28	Richard Bland	75	Abraham Clark
29	George Calvert	76	William Floyd
30	Thomas Nelson	77	John Langdon
31	John Witherspoon	78	Caleb Strong
32	Robert Treat Paine	79	Paine Wingate
33	St. Olaf	80	James Monroe
34	Esek Hopkins	81	F. A. C. Muhlenberg
35	Peter Minuit	82	John B. Ashe
36	Alexander Macomb	83	Egbert Benson
37	Henry St. G. Tucker	84	Isaac Coles
38	Eleazor Wheelock	85	Stephen Johnson Field
39	Thomas Ruffin	86	Joseph McKenna
40	William Johnson	87	William M. Stewart
41	Richard Bassett	88	Willis Van Devanter
42	Oliver Ellsworth	89	Francis Parkman
43	Theodore Foster	90	John Fiske
44	James Gunn	91	George Bancroft
45	John Henry	92	James Ford Rhodes
46	Samuel Johnston	93	William H. Prescott
47	William MacLay	94	Hinton R. Helper

Hull No.	Name	Hull No.	Name
95	Sam Houston	148	William Hooper
96	Davy Crockett	149	Daniel Morgan
97	Matthew Maury	150	Francis Marion
98	Winfield Scott	151	Charles C. Pinckney
99	Michael J. Stone	152	John Cropper
100	David S. Terry	153	William Moultrie
101	Benjamin Bourn	154	Thomas Sumter
102	Daniel Carroll	155	Jeremiah Van Rensselaer
103	Nicholas Gilman	156	Artemus Ward
104	Samuel Griffin	157	Hugh Williamson
105	Thomas Hartley	158	William R. Davie
106	Daniel Hiester	159	William Gaston
107	Benj. Huntington	160	William A. Graham
108	John Laurance	161	James K. Polk
109	Samuel Livermore	162	Alexander Martin
110	Houston Volunteers	163	Richard D. Spaight
111	A. P. Hill	164	Samuel Ashe
112	James Longstreet	165	Banjamin Williams
113	Jos. E. Johnston	166	James Turner
114	J. E. B. Stuart	167	Nathaniel Alexander
115	John B. Hood	168	David Stone
116	Big Foot Wallace	169	Benjamin Smith
117	Amelia Earhart	170	Meriwether Lewis
118	Champ Clark	171	Star of Oregon
119	Joseph T. Robinson	172	William Clark
120	William C. C. Claiborne	173	Robert Gray
121	T. L. Jackson	174	John Barry
122	Thomas B. Robertson	175	Thomas Jefferson
123	Abraham Baldwin	176	John Hancock
124	Theodoric Bland	177	Philip Livingston
125	Benjamin Contee	178	John Jay
126	George Gale	179	Thomas MacDonough
127	Wm. B. Giles	180	William Dawes
128	Jonathan Grout	181	Philip Schuyler
129	Daniel Huger	182	George Clymer
130	George Leonard	183	James Wilson
131	Andrew Moore	184	John Hart
132	Josiah Parker	185	Henry W. Longfellow
133	Thomas Scott	186	Edgar Allan Poe
134	Joshua Senney	187	Nathaniel Hawthorne
135	Thos. Sinnickson	188	John G. Whittier
136	Jonathan Sturges	189	William Cullen Bryant
137	Jonathan Trumbull	190	James Russell Lowell
138	John Vining	191	Henry D. Thoreau
139	Alexander White	192	Ralph Waldo Emerson
140	Henry Wynkoop	193	James Whitcomb Riley
141	Samuel Jordon Kirkwood	194	Oliver Wendell Holmes
142	Abraham Lincoln	195	Walt Whitman
143	Pat Harrison	196	Mark Twain
144	Leonidas Polk	197	Washington Irving
145	Zebulon B. Vance	198	James Fenimore Cooper
146	Nathanael Greene	199	Thomas Bailey Aldrich
147	Virginia Dare	200	Bret Harte

Hull No.	Name	Hull No.	Name
201	*John Davenport*	254	*George Taylor*
202	*John Winthrop*	255	*William Whipple*
203	*Thomas Hooker*	256	*Oliver Wolcott*
204	*Ethan Allen*	257	*Francis Lewis*
205	*Josiah Bartlett*	258	*John Morton*
206	*William King*	259	*George Read*
207	*John Carver*	260	*Roger Sherman*
208	*William Bradford*	261	*Richard Stockton*
209	*William Brewster*	262	*Matthew Thornton*
210	*Lou Gehrig*	263	*William Williams*
211	*Daniel Webster*	264	*Eli Whitney*
212	*William Pierce Frye*	265	*Stephen F. Austin*
213	*Hannibal Hamlin*	266	*William B. Travis*
214	*John Sullivan*	267	*Mirabeau B. Lamar*
215	*John Chandler*	268	*Theo. Sedgwick*
216	*John Holmes*	269	*Thomas T. Tucker*
217	*Joseph Hewes*	270	*Jeremiah Wadsworth*
218	*John Penn*	271	*James Bowie*
219	*John C. Calhoun*	272	*Thomas J. Rusk*
220	*Edward Rutledge*	273	*Lambart Cadwalader*
221	*Abel Parker Upshur*	274	*James Madison*
222	*William Hawkins*	275	*William L. Smith*
223	*Thomas Pinckney*	276	*Stephen C. Foster*
224	*Roger Williams*	277	*Albert Gallatin*
225	*John Drayton*	278	*Oliver Hazard Perry*
226	*James B. Richardson*	279	*Elbridge Gerry*
227	*Paul Hamilton*	280	*Rufus King*
228	*Henry Middleton*	281	*Abiel Foster*
229	*Alexander Hamilton*	282	*Benjamin Goodhue*
230	*Robert Fulton*	283	*John Hathorn*
231	*Stephen A. Douglas*	284	*Edwin Markham*
232	*John Dickinson*	285	*George Matthews*
233	*Fisher Ames*	286	*John Page*
234	*Robert G. Harper*	287	*James Schureman*
235	*Samuel Moody*	288	*Peter Silvester*
236	*John Sevier*	289	*John Steele*
237	*Jonathan Edwards*	290	*George Thacher*
238	*Anne Hutchinson*	291	*Juan Cabrillo*
239	*John Harvard*	292	*Junipero Serra*
240	*Elihu Yale*	293	*John A. Sutter*
241	*James Otis*	294	*Richard Henry Dana*
242	*John Adams*	295	*William F. Cody*
243	*Kit Carson*	296	*Robert F. Stockton*
244	*Zachary Taylor*	297	*Starr King*
245	*Anthony Wayne*	298	*Leland Stanford*
246	*Timothy Pickering*	299	*Francis Drake*
247	*Stephen Hopkins*	300	*Peter H. Burnett*
248	*Samuel Huntington*	301	*Thomas McKean*
249	*William Ellery*	302	*William Paca*
250	*Lewis Morris*	303	*Benjamin Rush*
251	*John Wise*	304	*Joseph Stanton*
252	*George Ross*	305	*John Walker*
253	*James Smith*	306	*Pierce Butler*

Hull No.	Name	Hull No.	Name
307	Tristram Dalton	423	George Westinghouse
308	Jonathan Elmer	424	John Bartram
309	William Few	425	G. H. Corliss
310	William Grayson	426	Richard March Hoe
311	John Mitchell	427	Elihu Thomson
312	John W. Brown	428	George B. Seldon
313	Charles Brantley Aycock	429	Nathaniel Bowditch
314	William Blount	430	Charles M. Conrad
315	Wade Hampton	431	John B. Floyd
316	Richmond Mumford Pearson	432	Joseph Holt
317	David G. Farragut	433	John M. Schofield
318	Mayo Brothers	434	John A. Rawlins
319	William Harper	435	George W. McCrary
320	Pierre Soulé	436	Alexander Ramsey
321	Irvin MacDowell	437	Robert T. Lincoln
322	George B. McClellan	438	William C. Endicott
323	Joseph Hooker	439	Redfield Proctor
324	Ambrose E. Burnside	440	Robert E. Peary
325	Peter J. McGuire	441	David Gaillard
326	Philip H. Sheridan	442	Henry J. Raymond
327	David Bushnell	443	William G. McAdoo
328	John Fitch	444	Leslie M. Shaw
329	James Rumsey	445	George B. Cortelyou
330	John Stevens	446	Frederick Jackson Turner
331	Samuel F. B. Morse	447	Joseph G. Cannon
332	Cyrus H. McCormick	448	George Rogers Clark
333	James G. Blaine	449	Louis Joliet
334	Herman Melville	450	Samuel de Champlaiń
335	Julia Ward Howe	451	John A. Logan
336	Anne Bradstreet	452	Père Marquette
337	John Trumbull	453	John M. Palmer
338	Richard Hovey	454	Richard Yates
339	Emily Dickinson	455	Nancy Hanks
340	Eugene Field	456	Edward P. Costigan
341	James Oglethorpe	457	Sieur Duluth
342	George Handley	458	Richard Henderson
343	James Jackson	459	Benjamin Bonneville
344	George Walton	460	Charles Wilkes
345	Lyman Hall	461	Justin S. Morrill
346	John Milledge	462	Thomas Kearns
347	Robert Toombs	463	Vitus Bering
348	Robert M. T. Hunter	464	Dan Beard
349	Crawford W. Long	465	Jane A. Delano
350	John C. Breckinridge	466	John R. Park
351	Button Gwinnett	467	James B. Hickok
352	Felix Grundy	468	Hiram S. Maxim
353	George Vancouver	469	William B. Ogden
354	Elias Howe	470	David Dudley Field
418	James B. Francis	471	Charles P. Steinmetz
419	Richard Jordan Gatling	472	David Starr Jordan
420	John James Audubon	473	Jacques Laramie
421	John F. Appleby	474	Lucy Stone
422	Charles M. Hall	475	Frances E. Willard

Hull No.	Name	Hull No.	Name
476	*Betsy Ross*	529	*Nathaniel Currier*
477	*Abigail Adams*	530	*James Ives*
478	*Elizabeth Blackwell*	531	*Thomas Corwin*
479	*S. Hall Young*	532	*James Guthrie*
480	*J. H. Kinkaid*	533	*Howell Cobb*
481	*Alexander Baranoff*	534	*Hugh McCulloch*
482	*Sheldon Jackson*	535	*Matthew Lyon*
483	*Edward Rowland Sill*	536	*George D. Prentice*
484	*Joaquin Miller*	537	*William A. Jones*
485	*Lew Wallace*	538	*Homer Lea*
486	*O. Henry*	539	*Anson Burlingame*
487	*F. Marion Crawford*	540	*Louis Hennepin*
488	*Joseph Rodman Drake*	541	*Josiah Snelling*
489	*William Dean Howells*	542	*George Washington Carver*
490	*John Howard Payne*	543	*Cornelius Gilliam*
491	*Andrew Furuseth*	544	*George H. Williams*
492	*Moses Rogers*	545	*Matthew P. Deady*
493	*William K. Vanderbilt*	546	*Jason Lee*
494	*James J. Hill*	547	*Marcus Whitman*
495	*John Rutledge*	548	*John McLoughlin*
496	*William Cushing*	549	*Jesse Applegate*
497	*John Blair*	550	*George Abernathy*
498	*Robert H. Harrison*	551	*Joseph Lane*
499	*John McLean*	552	*Harvey W. Scott*
500	*Noah H. Swain*	553	*James W. Nesmith*
501	*Samuel F. Miller*	554	*John C. Ainsworth*
502	*David Davis*	555	*William P. McArthur*
503	*Morrison R. Waite*	556	*Eugene Skinner*
504	*Melville W. Fuller*	557	*Daniel H. Lownsdale*
505	*Stanley Matthews*	558	*Elijah White*
506	*David J. Brewer*	559	*Harry Lane*
507	*Pierre Laclède*	560	*George Chamberlin*
508	*Frederic Remington*	561	*Jonathan Harrington*
509	*Walter Colton*	562	*William H. Seward*
510	*J. Sterling Morton*	563	*Gideon Welles*
511	*George H. Dern*	564	*Edwin M. Stanton*
512	*Key Pittman*	565	*Cleveland Abbe*
513	*Chief Ouray*	566	*Andrew Carnegie*
514	*George S. Boutwell*	567	*Pierre S. Dupont*
515	*Benjamin H. Bristow*	568	*James Duncan*
516	*William Windom*	569	*George H. Thomas*
517	*Charles J. Folger*	570	*William S. Rosecrans*
518	*Charles S. Fairchild*	571	*Henry Villard*
519	*John G. Carlisle*	572	*Samuel Seabury*
520	*Lyman J. Gage*	573	*Mark Hanna*
521	*William H. Aspinwall*	574	*Henry George*
522	*Grenville M. Dodge*	575	*Edward Everett*
523	*Julien Dubuque*	576	*James McNeill Whistler*
524	*Acloniram Judson*	577	*Salmon B. Chase*
525	*John G. Nicolay*	578	*Stephen Girard*
526	*Edward Bates*	579	*Henry Dearborn*
527	*Josiah B. Grinnell*	580	*James B. Stephens*
528	*Henry H. Richardson*	581	*Joseph N. Teal*

Hull No.	Name	Hull No.	Name
582	Tabitha Brown	635	Jane Addams
583	Alexander Graham Bell	636	Clara Barton
584	Thomas A. Edison	637	William Ellery Channing
585	Samuel Colt	638	Wendell Phillips
586	John Deere	639	Felipe De Neve
587	Charles Goodyear	640	Samuel Gompers
588	Elmer A. Sperry	641	Horace Greeley
589	John P. Holland	642	Henry Ward Beecher
590	S. M. Babcock	643	James Gordon Bennett
591	Charles Gordon Curtis	644	Joseph Pulitzer
592	James B. Eads	645	Malcolm M. Stewart
593	Samuel Parker	646	George A. Custer
594	Joseph Gale	647	George G. Meade
595	Peter Skene Ogden	648	Booker T. Washington
596	Joseph L. Meek	649	Fitz-John Porter
597	Samuel J. Tilden	650	James B. McPherson
598	Abner Doubleday	651	Samuel Heintselman
599	George W. Goethals	652	John Sedwick
600	William T. Sherman	653	William Lloyd Garrison
601	Frank B. Kellogg	654	Smith Thompson
602	Carl Schurz	655	Joseph Story
603	Henry Barnard	656	Gabriel Duval
604	John S. Copley	657	Henry Baldwin
605	Charles Willson Peale	658	Brockholst Livingston
606	Edwin Booth	659	Thomas Johnson
607	Joseph Jefferson	660	Philip B. Barbour
608	Richard Mansfield	661	Peter V. Daniel
609	John Burke	662	Samuel Nelson
610	Jim Bridger	663	Robert C. Grier
611	Ezra Meeker	664	Benjamin R. Curtis
612	Sacajawea	665	Marion McKinley Bovard
613	Chief Washakie	666	Stephen M. White
614	William E. Borah	667	William Raton
615	M. M. Guhin	668	Lincoln Steffens
616	Lindley M. Garrison	669	Hubert Howe Bancroft
617	John W. Weeks	670	James W. Marshall
618	Stephen B. Elkins	671	George Chaffey
619	Daniel S. Lamont	672	Frank Joseph Irwin
620	Alexander J. Dallas	673	Helen Hunt Jackson
621	Richard Rush	674	Abel Stearns
622	Samuel D. Ingham	675	Benjamin Ide Wheeler
623	George W. Campbell	676	Amos G. Throop
624	William J. Duane	677	William Mulholland
625	Thomas Ewing	678	Gaspar De Portolá
626	Walter Forward	679	Luis Arguollo
627	Franklin MacVeagh	680	Sebastían Vizcáino
628	George M. Bibb	681	King S. Woolsey
629	Robert J. Walker	682	Archbishop Lamy
630	William M. Meredith	683	John Bidwell
631	Ewing Young	684	Louis McLane
632	Peter Cartwright	685	Hugh S. Legare
633	Brigham Young	686	James Buchanan
634	Horace Mann	687	John M. Clayton

Hull No.	Name	Hull No.	Name
688	William L. Marcy	741	Clark Mills
689	Lewis Cass	742	Benjamin H. Latrobe
690	Jeremiah S. Black	743	Simon Willard
691	Elihu B. Washburne	744	Colin P. Kelly, Jr.
692	Harrison Gray Otis	745	William C. Gorgas
693	Joseph H. Hollister	746	Lawton B. Evans
694	Phoebe A. Hearst	768	William P. Fessenden
695	Zane Grey	769	Winslow Homer
696	Pio Pico	770	John Murray Forbes
697	John Drake Sloat	771	Augustine Heard
698	Carlos Carrillo	772	Edward Preble
699	William B. Young	773	Calvin Coolidge
700	George E. Hale	774	John A. Dix
701	Thomas East	775	Walter E. Ranger
702	Samuel P. Langley	776	Noah Webster
703	James Robertson	777	Eliphalet Nott
704	William J. Worth	778	Isaac Sharpless
705	Howard Stunsbury	779	Timothy Dwight
706	Robert Stuart	780	Ezra Cornell
707	William Dunbar	781	Francis Amasa Walker
708	George C. Yount	782	Joseph Warren
709	Solomon Juneau	783	Emma Willard
710	Edmand Fanning	784	William Phips
711	Phineas Banning	785	Charles Sumner
712	Edmund Randolph	786	Asa Gray
713	Edward Livingston	787	Mary Lyon
714	Josiah Royce	788	Henry Wilson
715	Daniel Drake	789	Charles W. Eliot
716	Benjamin Lundy	790	Harriet Beecher Stowe
717	Theodore Dwight Weld	791	Eugene Hale
718	Theodore Parker	792	Robert Treat
719	James G. Birney	793	George Cleeve
720	Lydia M. Child	794	Jacob H. Gallinger
721	Rachel Jackson	795	Sylvester Gardiner
722	Maria Mitchell	796	Robert Jordan
723	Margaret Fuller	797	Robert Rogers
724	William B. Allison	798	Ezra Weston
725	Ansel Briggs	799	Josiah Quincy
726	Alice F. Palmer	800	William Sturgis
727	James M. Goodhue	801	Thomas W. Hyde
728	Henry H. Sibley	802	George F. Patten
729	Henry M. Rice	803	William Pepperell
730	John S. Pillsbury	804	Thomas B. Reed
731	Knute Nelson	805	Joshua L. Chamberlain
732	James B. Weaver	806	Jeremiah O'Brien
733	Simon Newcomb	807	John A. Poor
734	Amy Lowell	808	Harry A. Garfield
735	William G. Gargo	809	Arthur L. Perry
736	William James	810	Nelson Dingley
737	Jacques Cartier	811	James Bowdoin
738	Stanford White	812	Henry Jocelyn
739	Benjamin N. Cardozo	813	Bartholomew Gosnold
740	James Hoban	814	Ferdinando George

Hull No.	Name	Hull No.	Name
815	John Mason	868	Penelope Barker
816	Anna Howard Shaw	869	Alexander Lillington
817	Tobias Lear	870	Richard Caswell
818	William H. Todd	871	Pocahontas
819	John N. Robins	872	Christopher Gadsden
820	Cyrus H. K. Curtis	873	Betty Zane
821	William Dewitt Hyde	874	James J. Pettigrew
822	Thomas Clyde	875	Daniel H. Hill
823	Park Holland	876	George Davis
824	Peregrine White	877	Walter Raleigh
825	Enoch Train	878	John Harvey
826	William Blackstone	879	Robert Howe
827	John Fairfield	880	Nathaniel Macon
828	William Eustis	881	John Wright Stanly
829	John Armstrong	882	Francis Nash
830	William H. Crawford	883	Ephraim Brevard
831	James Barbour	884	George E. Badger
832	John H. Eaton	885	Flora MacDonald
833	Joel R. Poinsett	886	James Sprunt
834	John Bell	887	Matt W. Ransom
835	John C. Spencer	888	Furnifield M. Simmons
836	James M. Porter	889	Edward B. Dudley
837	William Wilkins	890	Willie Jones
838	Fitzhugh Lee	891	James Moore
839	Jubal A. Early	892	Alfred Moore
840	Richard S. Ewell	893	Woodrow Wilson
841	George E. Pickett	894	William D. Pender
842	William N. Pendleton	895	William D. Moseley
843	Moses Austin	896	David L. Swain
844	Benito Jaurez	897	Jonathan Worth
845	David G. Burnet	898	Matthew T. Goldsboro
846	James S. Hogg	899	Elisha Mitchell
847	Jane Long	900	Christopher Gale
848	James B. Bonham	901	William L. Davidson
849	James W. Fannin	902	Walker Taylor
850	Anson Jones	903	Roger Moore
851	Frederick L. Dau	904	Robert Rowan
852	James E. Haviland	905	Thomas W. Bickett
853	Edward Burleson	906	Horace Williams
854	Lorenzo DeZavala	907	José Bonifacio
855	Benjamin R. Milam	908	Thomas L. Clingman
856	Sidney Sherman	909	David Caldwell
857	John Mary Odin	910	Waigstill Avery
858	Mary Austin	911	Cornelia P. Spencer
859	E. A. Peden	912	Walter Hines Page
860	Collis P. Huntington	913	Benjamin Hawkins
861	Cornelius Harnett	914	Ralph Izard
862	Henry Bacon	915	James Caldwell
863	Abner Nash	916	Caesar Rodney
864	Joseph Alston	917	Nicholas Biddle
865	Paul Hamilton Hayne	918	George Weems
866	Marshall Elliott	919	Grace Abbott
867	James Iredell	920	Cardinal Gibbons

Hull No.	Name	Hull No.	Name
921	*Thomas Sim Lee*	974	*William Pepper*
922	*Cotton Mather*	975	*Silas Weir Mitchell*
923	*Will Rogers*	976	*Joseph Leidy*
924	*Daniel Chester French*	977	*William W. Gerhard*
925	*Daniel Willard*	978	*John Morgan*
926	*Thaddeus Kosciuszko*	979	*James R. Randall*
927	*Pearl Harbor*	980	*William H. Webb*
928	*Lord Delaware*	981	*Samuel Bowles*
929	*James Woodrow*	982	*Stevenson Taylor*
930	*Willard Hall*	983	*Elbert Hubbard*
931	*Woodbridge N. Ferris*	984	*John E. Schmeltzer*
932	*William McKinley*	985	*Charles A. McAllister*
933	*Thomas R. Marshall*	986	*John L. Motley*
934	*Andrew G. Curtin*	987	*Haym Salomon*
935	*Molly Pitcher*	988	*Frederick Douglass*
936	*Horace Gray*	989	*Thomas F. Bayard*
937	*Samuel Blatchford*	990	*Conrad Weiser*
938	*Henry B. Brown*	991	*John M. T. Finney*
939	*George Shiras*	992	*Louisa M. Alcott*
940	*Rufus W. Peckham*	993	*William Tyler Page*
941	*William R. Day*	994	*Joseph H. Nicholson*
942	*Mahlon Pitney*	995	*Thomas Nelson Page*
943	*Louis D. Brandeis*	996	*James McCosh*
944	*Nathan Clifford*	997	*Albert C. Ritchie*
945	*George Sharswood*	998	*George W. Woodward*
946	*Henry L. Benning*	999	*Charles Bulfinch*
947	*Johns Hopkins*	1000	*Samuel McIntyre*
948	*Thomas Cresap*	1001	*Pierre L'Enfant*
949	*James W. Denver*	1002	*Edward L. Grant*
950	*Henry Gilbert Costin*	1003	*Robert J. Collier*
951	*John Gallup*	1004	*Joshua W. Alexander*
952	*Clifford D. Mallory*	1005	*John A. Donald*
953	*William H. Welch*	1006	*William H. Jackson*
954	*William Osler*	1007	*Janet Lord Roper*
955	*Howard A. Kelly*	1008	*Nathan Towson*
956	*William S. Halsted*	1009	*Robert Erskine*
957	*Franklin P. Mall*	1010	*John Wanamaker*
958	*John Howland*	1011	*John Stevenson*
959	*William H. Wilmer*	1012	*George M. Cohan*
960	*John J. Able*	1013	*George H. Pendleton*
961	*Santiago Iglesias*	1014	*George W. Childs*
962	*John Banvard*	1015	*Robert Eden*
963	*Edward N. Hurley*	1016	*James A. Farrell*
964	*Charles M. Schwab*	1017	*José Marti*
965	*Charles Piez*	1018	*Crosby S. Noyes*
966	*Bernard N. Baker*	1019	*Louis Marshall*
967	*Winfred L. Smith*	1020	*Townsend Harris*
968	*Bushrod Washington*	1021	*George Vickers*
969	*Levi Woodbury*	1022	*John W. Powell*
970	*William Strong*	1023	*Black Hawk*
971	*Joseph P. Bradley*	1024	*Robt. M. Lafollette*
972	*Ward Hunt*	1025	*Walter Q. Gresham*
973	*John Woolman*	1026	*Richard Olney*

Hull No.	Name	Hull No.	Name
1027	Robert Bacon	1104	George Eastman
1028	Philander C. Knox	1105	Cyrus W. Field
1029	Lucius Q. C. Lamar	1106	Isaac Babbitt
1030	James McHenry	1107	Charles E. Duryea
1031	Samuel Dexter	1108	Benjamin Holt
1032	Roger Griswold	1109	Oliver Evans
1033	Timothy Bloodworth	1110	Elisha Graves Otis
1034	Elias Boudinot	1111	Knute Rockne
1035	Aedanus Burke	1112	James J. Corbett
1036	Thomas Fitzsimons	1113	Walter Camp
1037	Henry Groves Connors	1114	Hobart Baker
1038	William M. Evarts	1115	Christy Mathewson
1039	F. T. Frelinghuysen	1116	George Gipp
1040	Tarleton Brown	1117	Matthew B. Brady
1041	Henry S. Foote	1118	Edward A. MacDowell
1042	James E. Howard	1119	Joseph Smith
1043	Charles Henderson	1120	Tecumseh
1044	Robert Lowry	1121	John L. Sullivan
1045	George Poindexter	1122	Geronimo
1046	John A. Quitman	1193	Ponce De León
1047	John Sharp Williams	1194	John Gorrie
1048	Julien Poydras	1195	Francis Asbury
1049	Richard M. Johnson	1196	John J. Crittenden
1050	Joseph N. Nicollet	1197	Sidney Lanier
1051	Langdon Cheves	1198	Robert Y. Hayne
1052	Nicholas Herkimer	1199	Richard Montgomery
1053	Casimir Pulaski	1200	John Philip Sousa
1054	Hamlin Garland	1201	Henry Watterson
1055	Andrew Pickens	1202	George Dewey
1056	William L. Yancey	1203	William Byrd
1057	George Whitefield	1204	Rufus C. Dawes
1058	Joseph E. Brown	1205	Thomas Sully
1059	Dudley M. Hughes	1206	Dwight W. Morrow
1060	Jerome K. Jones	1207	John S. Mosby
1061	Hoke Smith	1208	Grant Wood
1062	William Black Yates	1209	Edward M. House
1063	James H. Couper	1210	Harvey Cushing
1064	Joseph Habersham	1211	William G. Sumner
1065	Joseph H. Martin	1212	Peter Stuyvesant
1066	Robert Fechner	1213	James Screven
1067	Charles C. Jones	1214	Napoleon B. Broward
1068	Florence Martus	1215	Arthur M. Huddell
1069	Charles H. Herty	1216	Owen Wister
1070	John E. Ward	1217	Elizabeth C. Bellamy
1071	Edwin L. Godkin	1218	John White
1072	A. Frank Lever	1219	Royal S. Copeland
1073	Thomas Wolfe	1220	John Einig
1074	Louis A. Godey	1221	Edwin G. Weed
1099	Luther Burbank	1222	Andrew Trunbull
1100	George M. Pullman	1223	William A. Richardson
1101	Wilbur Wright	1224	William T. Coleman
1102	William Thornton	1225	William Kent
1103	Glenn Curtiss	1226	John Muir

Hull No.	Name	Hull No.	Name
1227	*Philip Kearny*	1525	*John Hay*
1228	*Thomas Hart Benton*	1526	*Dwight L. Moody*
1229	*Lyman Beecher*	1527	*Peter Zenger*
1230	*Francis Preston Blair*	1528	*Harriet Hosmer*
1231	*Mark Hopkins*	1529	*Duncan U. Fletcher*
1232	*Andrew D. White*	1530	*Dolly Madison*
1233	*Sebastian Cermeno*	1531	*Robert Lansing*
1234	*Peter Donahue*	1532	*Victor Herbert*
1235	*Sun Yat Sen*	1533	*Julius Rosenwald*
1236	*Henry Durant*	1534	*Mary Ball*
1237	*Jack London*	1535	*John Barton Payne*
1457	*William Coddington*	1536	*Frederic C. Howe*
1458	*John Clarke*	1537	*William B. Wilson*
1459	*Samuel Gorton*	1538	*Sarah J. Hale*
1460	*James De Wolf*	1539	*Nathan B. Forrest*
1461	*Lyman Abbott*	1540	*Stephen R. Mollory*
1462	*Moses Brown*	1541	*Edgar E. Clark*
1489	*James M. Wayne*	1542	*Walter L. Fleming*
1490	*William B. Woods*	1543	*Salvador Brau*
1491	*Joseph R. Lamar*	1544	*Harold T. Andrews*
1492	*Thomas Todd*	1545	*Russell Sage*
1493	*Robert Trimble*	1546	*William W. Loring*
1494	*John Catron*	1547	*Minnie M. Fiske*
1495	*John McKinley*	1548	*John W. Griffiths*
1496	*John A. Campbell*	1549	*Augustus St. Gaudens*
1497	*John M. Harlan*	1550	*John M. Brooke*
1498	*Howell E. Jackson*	1551	*Rebecca Lukens*
1499	*Edward D. White*	1552	*James A. Bayard*
1500	*Horace H. Lurton*	1553	*Mary Cassatt*
1501	*Henry W. Grady*	1554	*Michael Pupin*
1502	*James W. Grady*	1555	*Cyrus Hamlin*
1503	*Frederick Bartholdi*	1556	*Henry Bergh*
1504	*John B. Gordon*	1557	*John Carroll*
1505	*Edward P. Alexander*	1558	*Jonathan P. Dolliver*
1506	*Robert Battey*	1559	*James Harlan*
1507	*Patrick H. Morrissey*	1560	*Robert Lucas*
1508	*Joe C. S. Blackburn*	1561	*Edwin T. Meredith*
1509	*John B. Lennon*	1562	*Maria Sanford*
1510	*George G. Crawford*	1563	*Christopher C. Andrews*
1511	*David B. Johnson*	1564	*Leonidas Merritt*
1512	*Howard E. Coffin*	1565	*Floyd B. Olson*
1513	*R. Ney McNeeley*	1566	*Irving M. Scott*
1514	*Benjamin H. Hill*	1567	*Joseph S. Emery*
1515	*Joseph M. Terrell*	1568	*George Berkeley*
1516	*Robert R. Livingston*	1569	*Adolph Sutro*
1517	*Samalness*	1570	*John W. Mackay*
1518	*Isaac Shelby*	1571	*James W. Nye*
1519	*E. Kirby Smith*	1572	*William W. Mayo*
1520	*Newton D. Baker*	1573	*John Lind*
1521	*John Bascom*	1574	*Ole E. Rolvaag*
1522	*William J. Bryan*	1575	*John T. McMillan*
1523	*Joseph M. Medill*	1576	*Fremont Older*
1524	*Elihu Root*	1577	*Conrad Kohrs*

Hull No.	Name	Hull No.	Name
1578	Stephen Crane	1631	William H. McGuffey
1579	William Beaumont	1632	William Carson
1580	John H. Rosseter	1633	Carles H. Windham
1581	Henry Dodge	1634	Juan Flaco Brown
1582	John S. Sargent	1635	Thaddeus S. C. Lowe
1583	Charles Robinson	1636	Miguel Hidalgo
1584	Increase A. Lapham	1637	Josiah D. Whitney
1585	Clarence King	1638	William M. Gwin
1586	William Prouse	1639	Mark Keppel
1587	M. H. De Young	1640	Wiley Post
1588	John E. Wilkie	1641	George Gershwin
1589	John Ross	1642	General Vallejo
1590	John Whiteaker	1643	Andrew Rowan
1591	Sam Jackson	1644	Thomas Hill
1592	Owen Summers	1645	Edward W. Scripps
1593	Arthur Riggs	1646	Benjamin D. Wilson
1594	Lot Whitcomb	1647	José Sepulveda
1595	Morton M. McCarver	1648	Ignace Paderewski
1596	Hall J. Kelley	1649	Charles Lummis
1597	John W. Cullen	1650	Jedediah S. Smith
1598	Nathaniel J. Wyeth	1651	Josiah Nelson Cushing
1599	Henderson Luelling	1652	John Burroughs
1600	E. H. Harriman	1653	Charles Crocker
1601	Cushing Eells	1654	John S. Casement
1602	James Harrod	1655	P. T. Barnum
1603	Christopher Greenup	1656	Thomas Oliver Larkin
1604	Amos Kendall	1657	Juan Bautisto de Anza
1605	Belva Lockwood	1658	Lyman Stewart
1606	Kenneth A. J. MacKenzie	1659	John Alden
1607	Lucretia Mott	1660	Clarence Darrow
1608	Pierre Gibault	1661	Charles D. Poston
1609	Benjamin H. Grierson	1662	Josiah Earl
1610	Elijah P. Lovejoy	1663	Franklin K. Lane
1611	Graham Taylor	1664	James H. McClintock
1612	Albert B. Cummins	1665	Jacob S. Mansfeld
1613	James W. Grimes	1666	David E. Hughes
1614	George L. Baker	1667	Billy Mitchell
1615	Chief Joseph	1668	James Shields
1616	Henry W. Corbett	1669	Eugene B. Daskam
1617	George Flavel	1670	Andrew T. Huntington
1618	John H. Couch	1671	D. W. Harrington
1619	George H. Flanders	1672	William F. MacLennan
1620	Francis W. Pettygrove	1673	Wilfred Grenfell
1621	Henry Failing	1674	Florence Crittenton
1622	B. F. Shaw	1675	Joseph Priestley
1623	Simon Bolivar	1676	Stephen T. Mather
1624	Louis Agassiz	1677	Frank Springer
1625	Edward Bellamy	1678	Finley Peter Dunne
1626	Cass Gilbert	1679	Marina Raskova
1627	Gouverneur Morris	1680	Charles A. Warfield
1628	Gilbert Stuart	1681	Stephen Vincent Benet
1629	De Witt Clinton	1682	Stephen H. Long
1630	Richard Harding Davis	1683	Anson P. K. Safford

Hull No.	Name	Hull No.	Name
1684	*William R. Nelson*	1737	*John Stagg*
1685	*Jacob Riis*	1738	*Jacob Thompson*
1686	*John J. Ingalls*	1739	*Tobias E. Stansbury*
1687	*Billy Sunday*	1740	*Lafcadio Hearn*
1688	*Granville Stuart*	1741	*David Holmes*
1689	*Zona Gale*	1742	*William E. Pendleton*
1690	*Brand Whitlock*	1743	*Irwin Russell*
1691	*Vernon L. Kellogg*	1744	*Henry L. Ellsworth*
1692	*Francis G. Newland*	1745	*Reginald A. Fessenden*
1693	*Ambrose Bierce*	1746	*William Crompton*
1694	*James Fergus*	1747	*Juan de Fuca*
1695	*William N. Byers*	1748	*Francisco Coronado*
1696	*Joshua Hendy*	1749	*John Cabot*
1697	*Marcus Daly*	1750	*Moses Cleaveland*
1698	*John Constantine*	1751	*Joseph Henry*
1699	*William F. Vilas*	1752	*Laura Keene*
1700	*Myron T. Herrick*	1753	*Walter Reed*
1701	*Ring Lardner*	1754	*Russell A. Alger*
1702	*Horace Wells*	1755	*Edwin L. Drake*
1703	*Winfield S. Stratton*	1756	*Thomas U. Walter*
1704	*James Lick*	1757	*Thorstein Veblen*
1705	*Floyd Bennett*	1758	*John T. Holt*
1706	*David Belasco*	1759	*Arunah S. Abell*
1707	*John S. Bassett*	1760	*Joshua Thomas*
1708	*Joseph A. Holmes*	1761	*William S. Thayer*
1709	*Luther S. Kelly*	1762	*David Devries*
1710	*Charles N. McGroarty*	1763	*Henry Van Dyke*
1711	*Thomas M. Cooley*	1764	*James M. Gillis*
1712	*John Evans*	1765	*Lionel Copley*
1713	*Frank D. Phinney*	1766	*Mathew Brush*
1714	*William H. Allen*	1767	*Holland Thompson*
1715	*Melville E. Stone*	1768	*John W. Garrett*
1716	*Henry V. Alvarado*	1769	*Peter Cooper*
1717	*George Inness*	1770	*Tench Tilghman*
1718	*H. G. Blasdel*	1771	*James Blair*
1719	*Thomas C. Power*	1772	*Emma Lazarus*
1720	*William Matson*	1773	*Charles C. Long*
1721	*Brander Matthews*	1774	*William Smallwood*
1722	*William Keith*	1775	*James T. Earle*
1723	*Joseph K. Toole*	1776	*John H. Hatton*
1724	*Jeremiah M. Daily*	1777	*Orville P. Taylor*
1725	*Mary Patten*	1778	*Marie M. Meloney*
1726	*Hiram Bingham*	1779	*Tutuila*
1727	*William D. Burnham*	1780	*Heywood Broun*
1728	*Antoine Saugrain*	1781	*Philip F. Thomas*
1729	*Stephen W. Kearny*	1782	*Caleb C. Wheeler*
1730	*James Rowan*	1783	*Hawkins Fudske*
1731	*Richard Moczowski*	1784	*Henry Lomb*
1732	*Edward Sparrow*	1785	*George Uhler*
1733	*John McDonogh*	1786	*Patrick C. Boyle*
1734	*George W. Kendall*	1787	*Margaret Brent*
1735	*Mary Ashley Towsend*	1788	*Ben F. Dixon*
1736	*Andrew Marshalk*	1789	*Francis Vigo*

Hull No.	Name	Hull No.	Name
1790	John J. McGraw	1844	Ben H. Miller
1791	Adolph S. Ochs	1845	Martha C. Thomas
1792	Nikola Tesla	1846	Louis C. Tiffany
1793	Franz Boas	1847	Carl Thusgard
1794	John Russell Pope	1848	Byron Darnton
1795	Horace Bushnell	1849	Melvil Dewey
1796	Joyce Kilmer	1850	Frederick Banting
1797	W. R. Grace	1851	Martin Van Buren
1798	Jesse Deforest	1852	Samtweed
1799	Lyon G. Tyler	1853	Samforth
1800	Adolph Lewisohn	1854	Howard T. Ricketts
1801	Edward Cook	1855	Robert G. Ingersoll
1802	Simon B. Elliott	1856	Ina Coolbirth
1803	George M. Shriver	1857	Cornelius Cole
1804	Stage Door Canteen	1858	Arthur P. Davis
1805	Cebu	1859	Augustus H. Garland
1806	Lewis Emery, Jr.	1860	Wyatt Earp
1807	Harold L. Winslow	1861	Edwin Joseph O'Hara
1808	J. Whitridge Williams	1862	James H. Robinson
1809	Edith Wharton	1863	William I. Kip
1810	W. Walter Husband	1864	Edwin Abbey
1811	U.S.O.	1865	Henry M. Robinson
1812	Jose Artigas	1866	George Kenny
1813	Priscilla Alden	1867	David R. Francis
1814	Theodore Roosevelt	1868	Thomas G. Masaryk
1815	Samuel M. Ralston	1869	Gutzon Borglum
1816	Edwin A. Robinson	1870	Joseph Reynolds
1817	Augustine Herman	1871	Victor F. Lawson
1818	Charles Scribner	1872	William Kelly
1819	Edward Bruce	1873	Frank Wiggins
1820	Israel J. Merritt	1874	Don Marquis
1821	Frank A. Vanderlip	1875	Joseph Francis
1822	John LaFarge	1876	Dwight B. Heard
1823	Jacob H. Schiff	1877	Albert P. Ryder
1824	John T. Clark	1878	Samson Occum
1825	Francis C. Harrington	1879	Albino Peres
1826	James Carroll	1880	John Goode
1827	Barbara Frietchie	1881	Henry C. Wallace
1828	Daniel Appleton	1882	Albert J. Berres
1829	Leo J. Duster	1883	Richard J. Cleveland
1830	Culebra Island	1884	Josiah G. Holland
1831	James C. Cameron	1885	Oscar F. Barrett
1832	Willis J. Abbott	1886	James Cook
1833	Hugh M. Smith	1887	Christopher L. Sholes
1834	Ross G. Marvin	1888	Orson D. Munn
1835	J. Fred Essary	1889	Alan Seeger
1836	A. J. Cermak	1890	Horace See
1837	Ammla	1891	Carlston Ellis
1838	Louis Kossuth	1892	Charlotte P. Gilman
1839	Israel Wheelen	1893	Morton Prince
1840	Hugh L. Kerwin	1894	Harvey W. Wiley
1841	Joshua B. Lippincott	1895	John H. Marion
1843	Frank R. Stockton	1896	John P. Altgeld

Hull No.	Name	Hull No.	Name
1897	*Paul Dunbar*	1950	*Erastus Smith*
1898	*Thomas H. Gallaudet*	1951	*José Navarro*
1899	*Schuyler Colfax*	1952	*Joshua A. Leach*
1900	*Sidney Howard*	1953	*Harvey C. Miller*
1901	*David Rittenhouse*	1954	*George W. Lively*
1902	*William H. Carruth*	1955	*Thomas W. Gregory*
1903	*Nathaniel B. Palmer*	1956	*Will R. Wood*
1904	*William Winter*	1957	*William M. Rayburn*
1905	*Cyrus K. Holliday*	1958	*L. H. McNelly*
1906	*Carl R. Gray*	1959	*Lucien B. Maxwell*
1907	*Sanford B. Dole*	1960	*Albert S. Burleson*
1908	*Nicholas Longworth*	1961	*Joseph H. Kibbey*
1909	*Charles T. Yerkes*	1962	*Oscar Chappell*
1910	*Ralph A. Cram*	1963	*J. S. Cullinan*
1911	*John J. Roebling*	1964	*Hugh Young*
1912	*Orland Loomis*	1965	*Matthew J. O'Brien*
1913	*Edward Paine*	1966	*Henry Austin*
1914	*Sylvester Pattie*	1967	*Joseph A. Brown*
1915	*Leopold Damrosch*	1968	*Robert F. Hoke*
1916	*Andrew A. Humphreys*	1969	*Sallie S. Cotton*
1917	*Joseph Goldberger*	1970	*John Owne*
1918	*Oscar S. Straus*	1971	*Philip Doddridge*
1919	*Thomas F. Cunningham*	1972	*John Grier Hibben*
1920	*Jean Baptiste Lemoyne*	1973	*Kemp P. Battle*
1921	*Albert G. Brown*	1974	*Robert Dale Owen*
1922	*Eliza Jane Nicholson*	1975	*John P. Mitchell*
1923	*Paul Tulane*	1976	*Charles D. McIver*
1924	*Horace H. Harvey*	1977	*John D. Morehead*
1925	*Charles A. Wickliffe*	1978	*Hannis Taylor*
1926	*William B. Bankhead*	1979	*Edward Richardson*
1927	*Judah Touro*	1980	*William T. Barry*
1928	*Mason L. Weems*	1981	*Lee S. Overman*
1929	*Opie Read*	1982	*Thomas J. Jarvis*
1930	*Leif Ericson*	1983	*Joseph Leconte*
1931	*J. C. W. Beckham*	1984	*Arthur Dobbs*
1932	*Norman O. Pedrick*	1985	*John Lawson*
1933	*Eugene W. Hilgard*	1986	*Hilary A. Herbert*
1934	*Leon Godchaux*	1987	*Hutchinson I. Cone*
1935	*Acubens*	1988	*Lawrence D. Tyson*
1936	*Sam Houston II*	1989	*David F. Houston*
1937	*George C. Childress*	1990	*John Merrick*
1938	*J. Pincknew Henderson*	1991	*Charles A. Dana*
1939	*George P. Garrison*	1992	*Clement Clay*
1940	*Oran M. Roberts*	1993	*Thomas W. Owen*
1941	*Robert T. Hill*	1994	*Richmond P. Hobson*
1942	*Frederick H. Newell*	1995	*Chatham C. Lyon*
1943	*John H. Reagan*	1996	*James I. McKay*
1944	*R. M. Williamson*	1997	*John N. Maffitt*
1945	*Jesse Billingsley*	1998	*George Durant*
1946	*Edwin W. Moore*	1999	*Augustus S. Merrimon*
1947	*George Bellows*	2000	*Montfort Stokes*
1948	*David Wilmot*	2001	*Thomas Pollock*
1949	*Samuel H. Walker*	2002	*John Branch*

Hull No.	Name	Hull No.	Name
2003	Cushman K. Davis	2056	Clinton Kelly
2004	George L. Shoup	2057	Edward D. Baker
2005	Ignatius Donnelly	2058	Samuel Lancaster
2006	Robert Newell	2059	John Jacob Astor
2007	Stanford Newel	2060	Charles M. Russell
2008	William G. Tvault	2061	Joseph Simon
2009	William H. Gray	2062	R. P. Warner
2010	Edward Eggleston	2063	Henry L. Abott
2011	Thomas A. Hendricks	2064	C. J. Jones
2012	Jonathan Jennings	2065	David Thompson
2013	George W. Julian	2066	Dunham Wright
2014	Henry S. Lane	2067	B. F. Irvine
2015	James Oliver	2068	David F. Barry
2016	Eric V. Hauser	2069	Thomas J. Walsh
2017	R. C. Brennan	2070	Peter Desmet
2018	Francis E. Warren	2071	James M. Clements
2019	George Davidson	2072	Edward N. Westcott
2020	Joseph C. Avery	2073	Charles A. Broadwater
2021	John Minto	2074	Joseph W. Folk
2022	Pleasant Armstrong	2075	James L. Breck
2023	Wilson P. Hunt	2076	Sidney Edgerton
2024	Ben Holladay	2077	Robert S. Bean
2025	Joel Palmer	2078	Nathaniel Crosby
2026	Thomas Nuttall	2079	John I. Nolan
2027	John A. Johnson	2080	Ben T. Osborne
2028	Ephraim W. Baughman	2081	James S. Lawson
2029	Edward Canby	2082	Midwest Farmer
2030	Samuel A. Worcester	2083	Victor C. Vaughn
2031	John F. Steffen	2084	William S. Ladd
2032	Thomas Condon	2085	Frederick Billings
2033	Simon Benson	2086	Anthony Ravalli
2034	Irving W. Pratt	2087	Edmund F. Dickins
2035	Nicholas J. Sinnott	2088	John F. Myers
2036	Henry L. Pittock	2089	David B. Henderson
2037	Felix Hathaway	2090	John M. Bozeman
2038	James Withycombe	2091	Thomas Howell
2039	Binger Hermann	2092	James D. Doty
2040	Donald MacLeay	2093	Prince L. Campbell
2041	Henry L. Hoyt	2094	Manasseh Culter
2042	Joseph Watt	2095	John G. Brady
2043	Delazon Smith	2096	Jean Nicolet
2044	Samuel K. Barlow	2097	W. B. Ayer
2045	John P. Gaines	2098	Charles Nordhoff
2046	William C. Lane	2099	John Reed
2047	David Douglas	2100	Vachel Lindsay
2048	George H. Himes	2101	Michael Casey
2049	J. D. Ross	2102	Murat Halstead
2050	James K. Kelly	2103	Henry Wells
2051	Thomas W. Symons	2104	James J. O. Kelly
2052	Willis C. Hawley	2105	Reinhold Richter
2053	George L. Curry	2106	William Sharon
2054	William Hume	2107	John G. North
2055	Anton M. Holter	2108	Simon Bamberger

Hull No.	Name	Hull No.	Name
2109	Cyrus T. Brady	2162	William S. Clark
2110	Samuel Brannon	2163	Samuel W. Williston
2111	Chief Charlet	2164	Edgar W. Nye
2112	Casper S. Yost	2165	Frank C. Emerson
2113	William J. Palmer	2166	John W. Foster
2114	Peter Cooper Hewitt	2167	Norman Hapgood
2115	Ethan A. Hitchcock	2168	Bernardo O'Higgins
2116	Mary Bickerdyke	2169	Norman E. Mack
2117	William W. Campbell	2170	Henry H. Blood
2118	Michael C. Kerr	2171	John Swett
2119	Harry Leon Wilson	2172	Vernon L. Parrington
2120	John W. Meldrum	2173	George K. Fitch
2121	Clyde L. Seavey	2174	Francis A. Wardwell
2122	William A. Coulter	2175	Kate Douglas Wiggin
2123	Louis Pasteur	2176	David Hewes
2124	William C. Ralston	2177	Ferdinand A. Silcox
2125	Lawrence Gianella	2178	Sara Teasdale
2126	George H. Powell	2179	James King
2127	José J. Acosta	2180	R. F. Peckham
2128	Heber M. Creel	2181	Peter Trumble Rowe
2129	Millen Griffith	2182	Keith Vawter
2130	Otis Skinner	2183	James G. Maguire
2131	John Sherman	2184	Robert Louis Stevenson
2132	Henry R. Schoolcraft	2185	Francisco N. Quinones
2133	Joseph E. Wing	2186	Ferdinand Westdahl
2134	Harriet Monroe	2187	William F. Empey
2135	Frank J. Cuhel	2188	Sumner I. Kimball
2136	Daulton Mann	2189	Robert L. Vann
2137	John Colter	2190	Jeremiah Chaplin
2138	Mary M. Dodge	2191	Elias H. Derby
2139	Emile Berliner	2192	Mary Wilkins Freeman
2140	Charles G. Coutant	2193	Omar E. Chapman
2141	John W. Hoyt	2194	George Popham
2142	Wayne MacVeagh	2195	J. Willard Gibbs
2143	Harmon Judson	2196	Barrett Wendell
2144	Henry M. Teller	2197	William Pitt Preble
2145	Jeremiah M. Rusk	2198	James Manning
2146	Benjamin H. Brewster	2199	Percy D. Haughton
2147	Charles E. Smith	2200	Robert R. Randall
2148	Charles Devens	2201	Mercy Warren
2149	Louis A. Sengteller	2202	Charles A. Young
2150	Donald M. Dickinson	2203	Peleg Wadsworth
2151	Augustus Thomas	2204	Bronson Alcott
2152	George Sterling	2205	Webb Miller
2153	William H. Moody	2206	George S. Wasson
2154	Henry C. Payne	2207	Edward Kavanagh
2155	George Von L. Myer	2208	George T. Angell
2156	James D. Phelan	2209	Eugene E. O'Donnell
2157	Otto Mears	2210	Samdon
2158	Frank Norris	2211	Edward H. Crockett
2159	Francis M. Smith	2212	Samythian
2160	Frank A. Munsey	2213	Susan Colby
2161	Frederic A. Eilers	2214	Samearn

Hull No.	Name	Hull No.	Name
2215	Renald Fernald	2268	Henry Adams
2216	Samannan	2269	George Coggeshall
2217	Washington Allston	2270	John Isaacson
2218	Samteviot	2271	Silvestre Escalante
2219	Sarah Orne Jewett	2272	George Clement Perkins
2220	Frederick W. Taylor	2273	Gilbert M. Hitchcock
2221	Samwye	2274	Henry White
2222	Samtyne	2275	Emmet D. Boyle
2223	Samstrae	2276	Alexander Woolcott
2224	Samderwent	2277	E. A. Christenson
2225	John Tripton	2278	Henry J. Waters
2226	Lorrin A. Thurston	2279	William E. Ritter
2227	Annie Oakley	2280	Joe Harris
2228	Henry M. Stanley	2281	Mello Franco
2229	E. H. Sothern	2282	William Allen White
2230	Paul Chandler	2283	Stephen Hopkins
2231	Jack Singer	2284	Cecil G. Sellers
2232	Charles Paddock	2285	Norman J. Colman
2233	Edward J. O'Brien	2286	William Sproule
2234	Julian W. Mack	2287	John L. Stoddard
2235	Allen C. Balch	2288	Frank H. Dodd
2236	Raymond T. Baker	2289	Mary Walker
2237	David A. Curry	2290	J. Maurice Thompson
2238	Oscar Underwood	2291	Walter Williams
2239	J. Frank Cooper	2292	Mary A. Livermore
2240	Robert L. Hague	2293	Alanson B. Houghton
2241	Joe Fellows	2294	Samuel G. French
2242	C. K. McClatchy	2295	Thomas Levalley
2243	Petter Lassen	2296	Josephine Shaw Lowell
2244	Martin Johnson	2297	Richard V. Oulahan
2245	William L. Sublette	2298	James H. Kimball
2246	William H. Ashley	2299	Stephen Furdek
2247	W. W. McCrackin	2300	Jean Ribaut
2248	Francis N. Blanchet	2301	LeBaron Russell Briggs
2249	Charles F. Amidon	2302	Howard Gray
2250	Joseph M. Carey	2303	H. H. Raymond
2251	Watson C. Squire	2304	T. A. Johnston
2252	Stephen C. Porter	2305	M. Michael Edelstein
2253	Abbot L. Mills	2306	William D. Bloxham
2254	Albert A. Michelson	2307	Nick Stoner
2255	Edmund G. Ross	2308	William E. Dodd
2256	Peter White	2309	J. H. Drummond
2257	J. Warren Keifer	2310	William L. Watson
2258	William H. Dall	2311	John R. McQuigg
2259	James H. Lane	2312	Carl E. Ladd
2260	William D. Hoard	2313	Pedro Menendez
2261	Francis W. Parker	2314	George Ade
2262	Alexander Majors	2315	Edward K. Collins
2263	Jan Pieterszoon Coen	2316	C. Francis Jenkins
2264	Augustin Daly	2317	Raymond V. Ingersoll
2265	James H. Breasted	2318	Benjamin F. Coston
2266	Walter Wyman	2319	William P. Duval
2267	John Roach	2320	Stepas Darius

Hull No.	Name	Hull No.	Name
2321	Alexander E. Brown	2374	Lunsford Richardson
2322	Chief Osceola	2375	Johan Printz
2323	Richard Halliburton	2376	Charles S. Haight
2324	Samuel G. Howe	2377	R. J. Reynolds
2325	Granville S. Hall	2378	Duncan L. Clinch
2326	Stephen Smith	2379	Abigail Gibbons
2327	Charles D. Walcott	2380	Charles W. Stiles
2328	Art Young	2381	Murray M. Blum
2329	Charles H. Marshall	2382	Laura Bridgman
2330	Ransom A. Moore	2383	Richard Randall
2331	Soter Ortynsky	2384	Edward R. Squibb
2332	Bjarne A. Lia	2385	John H. Hammond
2333	Wendell L. Willkie	2386	Albert K. Smiley
2334	Frederick E. Williamson	2387	Ira Nelson Morris
2335	Michael James Monohan	2388	George W. Norris
2336	Charles A. Draper	2389	Arthur M. Hulbert
2337	Rafael R. Rivera	2390	M. E. Comerford
2338	James W. Wheeler	2391	Felix Riesenberg
2339	Raymond Van Brogan	2391	Frederic A. Kummer
2340	William J. Riddle	2392	Robert J. Banks
2341	Dudley H. Thomas	2393	William F. Jerman
2342	John L. McCarley	2394	William Cox
2343	Vernon S. Hood	2395	George R. Poole
2344	Edwin D. Howard	2396	Harold O. Wilson
2345	Wesley W. Barrett	2397	James Bennett Moore
2346	Warren P. Marks	2398	Halton R. Carey
2347	Frank O. Peterson	2399	Harold Dossett
2348	Barney Kirschbaum	2400	Patrick S. Mahony
2349	Mary Cullom Kimbro	2401	Richard A. Van Pelt
2350	Samfairy	2402	Charles C. Randleman
2351	Samfoyle	2403	Roy James Cole
2352	Samfinn	2404	Patrick B. Whalen
2353	Samvigna	2405	Samclyde
2354	Samselbu	2406	William R. Cox
2355	Samleyte	2407	Samettrick
2356	Samaustral	2408	Samcree
2357	Samingoy	2409	Samfough
2358	Samlorian	2410	Sameveron
2359	Samoland	2411	Samtay
2360	Donald W. Bain	2412	Samnid
2361	Augustine B. McCanus	2413	Samouse
2362	James B. Duke	2414	Eloy Alfaro
2363	W. P. Few	2415	Samchess
2364	Alexander S. Clay	2416	Allegan
2365	F. Southall Farrar	2417	Samesk
2366	James W. Cannon	2418	Benjamin Schlesinger
2367	Frank Park	2419	Morris Hillquit
2368	Eugene T. Chamberlain	2420	Charles Morgan
2369	Thomas B. King	2421	John W. Gates
2370	P. Walton Moore	2422	Zaniah
2371	Neils Poulson	2423	Sabik
2372	Arthur J. Tyrer	2424	Harry Percy
2373	Cassius Hudson	2425	Rebecca Boone

Hull No.	Name	Hull No.	Name
2426	Charles Goodnight	2479	Raymond Clapper
2427	Andrew Briscoe	2480	Hugh J. Kilpatrick
2428	William M. Eastland	2481	Noah Brown
2429	José G. Benitez	2482	Hendrik Willem Van Loon
2430	Anna H. Branch	2483	Stephen Beasley
2431	Isaac Van Zandt	2484	Jasper F. Cropsey
2432	Ben Robertson	2485	William Crane Gray
2433	Samuel T. Darling	2486	Ethelbert Nevin
2434	Isaac S. Hopkins	2487	W. S. Jennings
2435	Samhorn	2488	Filipp Mazzei
2436	A. Mitchell Palmer	2489	Henry Hadley
2437	Samdart	2490	Alfred I. Dupont
2438	John E. Sweet	2491	Irvin S. Cobb
2439	Clark Howell	2492	Negley D. Cochran
2440	Earl Layman	2493	Anna Dickinson
2441	John A. Treutlen	2494	John Ringling
2442	Ben A. Ruffin	2495	Michael Dekovats
2443	William D. Hoxie	2496	John H. McIntosh
2444	Samcebu	2497	Jerry S. Foley
2445	Harry L. Glucksman	2498	Robert Mills
2446	Juliette Low	2499	Morris C. Feinstone
2447	Francis S. Bartow	2500	David L. Yulee
2448	Linn Boyd	2501	George E. Waldo
2449	Arkab	2502	Harald Torsvik
2450	James B. Aswell	2503	Frederic W. Galbraith
2451	Rufus E. Foster	2504	C. W. Post
2452	R. S. Wilson	2505	Junius Smith
2453	Seginus	2506	Isaac M. Singer
2454	George A. Marr	2507	Telfair Stockton
2455	Syrma	2508	Louis Bamberger
2456	John M. Parker	2509	Isaac Mayer Wise
2457	Cecil N. Bean	2510	Henry B. Plant
2458	Burias	2511	Walter M. Christiansen
2459	Kochab	2512	Grover C. Hutcherson
2460	Basilan	2513	Fred C. Stebbins
2461	Charles W. Wooster	2514	Harold A. Jordan
2462	W. C. Latta	2515	John Miller
2463	Andrew Stevenson	2516	James H. Courts
2464	William Wheelwright	2517	Fred Herrling
2465	Edwin A. Stevens	2518	Thomas L. Haley
2466	Alexander W. Doniphan	2519	Horace V. White
2467	Henry S. Sanford	2520	Elisha P. Ferry
2468	James L. Ackerson	2521	Lucius Fairchild
2469	Edward W. Bok	2522	Jane G. Swisshelm
2470	Melucta	2523	Henry T. Rainey
2471	Propus	2524	Thomas Crawford
2472	Edward A. Filene	2525	George P. McKay
2473	Richard K. Call	2526	Richard J. Oglesby
2474	August Belmont	2527	John Ball
2475	Arthur R. Lewis	2528	Segundo Ruiz Belvis
2476	George E. Merrick	2529	Frank B. Linderman
2477	James K. Paulding	2530	John B. Kendrick
2478	Thomas J. Lyons	2531	Simeon G. Reed

Hull No.	Name	Hull No.	Name
2532	Lewis L. Dyche	2585	Meyer London
2533	John Straub	2586	Morris Sigman
2534	Wilbur O. Atwater	2587	Samleven
2535	Isaac McCoy	2588	William D. Byron
2536	John W. Davis	2589	Samlyth
2537	Enos A. Mills	2590	Samstrule
2538	Henry Miller	2591	Saminver
2539	John Davey	2592	Thomas Donaldson
2540	John W. Searles	2593	Samlossie
2541	Meyer Lissner	2594	John L. Elliott
2542	Franklin H. King	2595	Leyte
2543	Ben B. Lindsey	2596	Samgaudie
2544	Sherwood Anderson	2597	Warren Delano
2545	Philip C. Shera	2598	Samaffric
2546	James W. Johnson	2599	Samconon
2547	John H. Quick	2600	Samethy
2548	Charles Fort	2601	Stephen W. Gambrill
2549	John Drew	2602	Sameden
2550	William Wolfskill	2603	Robert Ellis Lewis
2551	Hart Crane	2604	Samcolne
2552	Henry L. Gantt	2605	Samlea
2553	William Glackens	2606	Samshee
2554	Augustin Stahl	2607	Samjack
2555	Clarance H. Matson	2608	Samspelga
2556	James A. Wilder	2609	Samdonard
2557	Carole Lombard	2610	Samgallion
2558	A. B. Hammond	2611	Samneagh
2559	Elinor Wylie	2612	Edward B. Haines
2560	Henry E. Huntington	2613	Samhope
2561	John Dockweiler	2614	John H. Murphy
2562	Sherman O. Houghton	2615	Samsturdy
2563	Horatio Allen	2616	Lawrence J. Brengle
2564	Russell H. Chittenden	2617	Samdauntless
2565	I. N. Van Nuys	2618	Sverre Helmersen
2566	Ida M. Tarbell	2619	Samtrusty
2567	Frederick C. Hicks	2620	Deborah Gannett
2568	Grace R. Hebard	2621	Samconstant
2569	James B. Miller	2622	Francis D. Culkin
2570	Ralph Barnes	2623	Samfaithful
2571	Gabriel Franchere	2624	Samwinged
2572	William A. Henry	2625	Samloyal
2573	Grant P. Marsh	2626	Samfleet
2574	Narcissa Whitman	2627	Samglory
2575	Isaac I. Stevens	2628	James Kerney
2576	William I. Chamberlain	2629	Samsoaring
2577	Mary E. Kinney	2630	Samorest
2578	Harrington Emerson	2631	James D. Trask
2579	Elwood Mead	2632	Samfreedom
2580	Samuel V. Stewart	2633	Samtruth
2581	John W. Troy	2634	Mona Island
2582	Abigail S. Duniway	2635	Samtorch
2583	Edward Lander	2636	Samlistar
2584	Peter Moran	2637	Chourre

Hull No.	Name	Hull No.	Name
2638	Samspeed	2692	Henry T. Scott
2639	Samluzon	2693	Ovid Butler
2640	Samnegros	2694	Jay Cooke
2641	Samindoro	2695	Terry E. Stephenson
2642	Chung Tung	2696	Thomas F. Hunt
2643	Samtana	2697	George E. Goodfellow
2644	Samskern	2698	Justo Arosemena
2645	Samsylarna	2699	Samuel Gompers
2646	Samlamu	2700	Benjamin Warner
2647	Samuel F. B. Morse	2701	Seaman A. Knapp
2648	Dexter W. Fellows	2702	James Rolph
2649	Assistance	2703	Antonin Dvorak
2650	Oakley Wood	2704	Albert A. Robinson
2651	William S. Baer	2705	Richard B. Moore
2652	Sidney Wright	2706	Alexander Wilson
2653	William Hodson	2707	José C. Barbosa
2654	Mary Pickersgill	2708	Alexander Mitchell
2655	Joseph B. Eastman	2709	J. C. Osgood
2656	Walter Kidde	2710	Frank H. Evers
2657	George R. Holmes	2711	James Oliver Curwood
2658	Diligence	2712	Edward G. Acheson
2660	Edward A. Savoy	2713	Francis Wilson
2661	Vincent Harrington	2714	Claus Spreckles
2662	Appanoose	2715	David Lubin
2663	S. Wiley Wakeman	2716	Frank J. Sprague
2664	Hecla	2717	Jean P. Chouteau
2665	Frederick W. Wood	2718	Julia L. Dumont
2666	Webster	2719	Robert G. Cousins
2667	S. M. Shoemaker	2720	George B. Porter
2668	Palawan	2721	William Ford Nichols
2669	Alexander V. Fraser	2722	Lillian Wald
2670	Frederick H. Baetjer	2723	George Luks
2671	Jesse Cottrell	2724	William Vaughn Moody
2672	William Libbey	2725	Oliver Kelley
2673	Benjamin Peixotto	2726	Abram S. Hewitt
2674	Dutiful	2727	William Peffer
2675	George M. Verity	2728	Ada Rehan
2676	Charles G. Glover	2729	Uriah M. Rose
2677	John Hanson	2730	John W. Burgess
2678	Charles A. McCue	2731	Moses G. Farmer
2679	Milan R. Stefanik	2732	Alfred C. True
2680	Kermit Roosevelt	2733	William B. Leeds
2681	Faithful	2734	Francisco Morazan
2682	Hooper Island	2735	William D. Boyce
2683	Samar	2736	W. B. Rodgers
2684	George Crile	2737	Carl B. Eielson
2685	Ralph T. O'Neil	2738	Alice H. Rice
2686	George B. McFarland	2739	Elwood Haynes
2687	William H. Clagett	2740	Nathan S. Davis
2688	José Pedro Varela	2741	Morgan Robertson
2689	Samuel I. Cobb	2742	John Hope
2690	Edward P. Ripley	2743	Daniel G. Reid
2691	Charles J. Colden	2744	Cornelius Vanderbilt

Hull No.	Name	Hull No.	Name
2745	*James Devereux*	2798	*Milton B. Medary*
2746	*John H. Thomas*	2799	*Ferdinand R. Hassler*
2747	*Percy E. Foxworth*	2800	*O. L. Bodenhamer*
2748	*Carl G. Barth*	2801	*Frederick Von Steuben*
2749	*Edwin C. Musick*	2802	*Floyd W. Spencer*
2750	*Sara Bache*	2803	*Milton H. Smith*
2751	*Hans Heg*	2804	*E. G. Hall*
2752	*Franz Sigel*	2805	*Robert F. Broussard*
2753	*Arthur A. Penn*	2806	*Ancil F. Haines*
2754	*Allen Johnson*	2807	*George Pomutz*
2755	*George A. Pope*	2808	*Am Mer Mar*
2756	*Joseph J. Kinyoun*	2809	*Sieur de LaSalle*
2757	*Juan Pablo Duarte*	2810	*Isaac Delgado*
2758	*John F. Shafroth*	2811	*Christian Bergh*
2759	*Cleveland Forbes*	2812	*Alfred J. Evans*
2760	*Sidney H. Short*	2813	*Katharine B. Sherwood*
2761	*E. A. Bryan*	2814	*J. Rufino Barrios*
2762	*Henry M. Stephens*	2815	*Thomas P. Leathers*
2763	*Willet M. Hays*	2816	*Jagger Seam*
2764	*Edward E. Hale*	2817	*Ales Hrdlicka*
2765	*Charles John Seghers*	2818	*Benjamin Silliman*
2766	*William J. Gray*	2819	*King Hathaway*
2767	*Amerigo Vespucci*	2820	*Cybele*
2768	*George Middlemas*	2821	*Hecuba*
2769	*Robert D. Carey*	2822	*Joseph Weydemeyer*
2770	*H. Weir Cook*	2823	*Gratia*
2771	*Louis Weule*	2824	*Sewanee Seam*
2772	*José M. Morelos*	2825	*Hesperia*
2773	*Benjamin Waterhouse*	2826	*Helena Modjeska*
2774	*William Schirmer*	2827	*Martin Behrman*
2775	*J. S. Hutchinson*	2828	*William H. Kendrick*
2776	*Edward S. Hough*	2829	*Andreas Honcharenko*
2777	*E. A. Burnett*	2830	*Nachman Syrkin*
2778	*Wallace R. Farrington*	2831	*James Eagan Layne*
2779	*Louis Sloss*	2832	*Herrin Seam*
2780	*Toussaint L'Ouverture*	2833	*Carl Zachary Webb*
2781	*Louis Sullivan*	2834	*Benjamin A. Fisher*
2782	*Lucien Labaudt*	2835	*William W. McKee*
2783	*James A. Drain*	2836	*Lasalle Seam*
2784	*Thomas F. Flaherty*	2837	*John C. Preston*
2785	*Robert S. Abbott*	2838	*Darel M. Ritter*
2786	*Benjamin Carpenter*	2839	*Frank E. Spencer*
2787	*Charlotte Cushman*	2840	*Streator Seam*
2788	*Henry Meiggs*	2841	*Roy K. Johnson*
2789	*Mariscal Sucre*	2842	*Linton Seam*
2790	*Amasa Delano*	2843	*Donald S. Wright*
2791	*Frank Adair Monroe*	2844	*Redstone Seam*
2792	*Cyrus Adler*	2845	*Laurence J. Gallagher*
2793	*George W. Alther*	2846	*Jewell Seam*
2794	*Robert W. Bingham*	2847	*Merrimac Seam*
2795	*Collin McKinney*	2848	*Jellico Seam*
2796	*Walker D. Hines*	2849	*Bon Air Seam*
2797	*Alcée Fortier*	2850	*Glamorgan Seam*

Hull No.	Name	Hull No.	Name
2851	Sewell Seam	2913	Robert Henri
2852	Beckley Seam	2914	Keith Palmer
2853	Pocahontas Seam	2915	George Steers
2854	Eagle Seam	2916	John Gibbons
2855	Powellton Seam	2917	Thomas Say
2856	Chilton Seam	2918	Daniel E. Garrett
2857	Banner Seam	2919	Christopher S. Flanagan
2858	Roda Seam	2920	John Ireland
2859	Imboden Seam	2921	Henry M. Robert
2860	Freeport Seam	2922	Sul Ross
2861	Mingo Seam	2923	Julius Olsen
2862	Pittsburg Seam	2924	Felipi Debastrop
2863	Jacob Sloat Fassett	2925	Richard O'Brien
2864	Richard Upjohn	2926	O. B. Martin
2865	William G. Lee	2927	Henry D. Lindsley
2866	Ruben Dario	2928	Minor C. Keith
2867	Benjamin Brown French	2929	Nicholas D. Labadie
2868	Stephen Leacock	2930	Arthur St. Clair
2869	Charles A. Keffer	2931	Rufus Choate
2870	Risden Tyler Bennett	2932	Gus W. Darnwell
2871	Alexander R. Shepard	2933	Eleazar Lord
2872	James Swan	2934	Juan N. Seguin
2873	Martha Berry	2935	Betram G. Goodhue
2874	Frank P. Walsh	2936	Oliver Loving
2875	Floyd Gibbons	2937	Andrew W. Preston
2876	Jones Lie	2938	Nathaniel Scudder
2877	John P. Harris	2939	John B. Hamilton
2878	Richard Coulter	2940	Nathaniel Silsbee
2879	Addie Bagley Daniels	2941	Robert Watchorn
2880	William H. Edwards	2942	Tomas Guardia
2881	Joseph Murgas	2943	Laura Drake Gill
2882	Milton J. Foreman	2944	Angus McDonald
2883	Joseph S. McDonagh	2945	Wynn Seale
2884	Josiah Tattnell	2946	T. E. Mitchell
2885	Moina Michael	2947	Carlos J. Finlay
2886	Robert Parrot	2948	Kyle V. Johnson
2887	Josiah Cohen	2949	Jacob A. Westervelt
2888	Rudolph Kauffmann	2950	Robert S. Lovett
2889	James H. Price	2951	Ida Straus
2890	William L. McLean	2952	Thomas Bulfinch
2891	Edward J. Berwind	2953	Lorado Taft
2892	William W. Seaton	2954	Howard L. Gibson
2893	Mack Bruton Bryan	2955	Thomas Eakins
2894	William Terry Howell	2956	Robert E. Clarkson
2895	William Leory Gable	2957	Irving Babbitt
2896	Harry Kirby	2958	Michael J. Owens
2897	Arlie Clark	2959	Edward G. Janeway
2898	Thomas W. Murray	2960	Herbert D. Croly
2908	John G. Tod	2961	Frederic E. Ives
2909	Charles J. Finger	2962	Walter Wellman
2910	Morris Sheppard	2963	Richard J. Hopkins
2911	Katherine L. Bates	2964	J. D. Yeager
2912	Jacob Perkins	2965	Johnny Appleseed

Hull No.	Name	Hull No.	Name
2966	*Paul Bunyan*	3019	*George Eldridge*
2967	*Anson Mills*	3020	*Samadang*
2968	*Robert Neighbors*	3021	*Samsuva*
2969	*Francis B. Ogden*	3022	*Samidway*
2970	*Edwin S. Nattleton*	3023	*Hadley F. Brown*
2971	*Pontus H. Ross*	3024	*Samsmola*
2972	*Clarence Roberts*	3025	*George Hawlcy*
2973	*Otis E. Hall*	3026	*John Chester Kendall*
2974	*Charles L. McNary*	3027	*Joseph I. Kemp*
2975	*Cyril G. Hopkins*	3028	*Joseph Squires*
2976	*I. B. Perrine*	3029	*Joseph Augustin Chevalier*
2977	*Paul David Jones*	3030	*William Leavitt*
2978	*Will B. Otwell*	3031	*Miaoulis*
2979	*Jacob Chandler Harper*	3032	*Harriet Tubman*
2980	*Harold D. Whitehead*	3033	*Ernest W. Gibson*
2981	*Clyde Austin Dunning*	3034	*Thomas H. Sumner*
2982	*James Kyron Walker*	3035	*Joseph C. Lincoln*
2983	*Walter Frederick Kraft*	3036	*Aram J. Pothier*
2984	*William R. Lewis*	3037	*George L. Farley*
2985	*William Asa Carter*	3038	*Andrew J. Newbury*
2986	*James Roy Wells*	3039	*Augustus P. Loring*
2987	*William K. Kamaka*	3040	*B. Charney Vladeck*
2988	*Daniel L. Johnston*	3041	*James Sullivan*
2989	*Lloyd S. Carlson*	3042	*Lot M. Morill*
2990	*Russell R. Jones*	3043	*Joseph N. Dinand*
2991	*John Martin Miller*	3044	*Harold I. Pratt*
2992	*Wallace M. Tyler*	3045	*Edward E. Spafford*
2993	*William W. Johnson*	3046	*Marcus H. Tracy*
2994	*Bernard L. Rodman*	3047	*Thomas Bradlee*
2995	*Leonardo L. Romero*	3048	*William Tyler*
2996	*Willard R. Johnson*	3049	*George N. Seger*
2997	*Samuel L. Jeffery*	3050	*Michael Moran*
2998	*Clifford E. Ashby*	3051	*Archibald R. Munsfield*
2999	*Alfred L. Baxley*	3052	*Galen L. Stone*
3000	*Francis E. Siltz*	3053	*William Lyon Phelps*
3001	*Charles H. Lanham*	3054	*C. H. M. Jones*
3002	*Mark A. Davis*	3055	*Ferdinand Gagnon*
3003	*Edward N. Hinton*	3056	*Robert B. Forbes*
3004	*Stanton H. King*	3057	*Frank P. Reed*
3005	*Samsperrin*	3058	*Michael Anagnos*
3006	*Arthur Sewall*	3059	*Elijah Cobb*
3007	*Samdaring*	3060	*Loammi Baldwin*
3008	*Par Benjamin*	3061	*James T. Fields*
3009	*Samderry*	3062	*Robert R. McBurney*
3010	*Lillian Nordica*	3063	*Edward L. Logan*
3011	*Belgian Tenacity*	3064	*Charles Tufts*
3012	*Elijah Kellog*	3065	*Kenyon L. Butterfield*
3013	*Charles Dauray*	3066	*Abraham Rosenberg*
3014	*Samadre*	3067	*Wilson B. Keene*
3015	*Sambanka*	3068	*Iolanda*
3016	*Raymond B. Stevens*	3069	*Winthrop L. Marvin*
3017	*Samwake*	3070	*Belle Isle*
3018	*Samoresby*	3071	*Liguria*

Hull No.	Name	Hull No.	Name
3072	*Belgian Unity*	3108	*Ernest L. Dawson*
3073	*Coasters Harbor*	3109	*Oliver Westover*
3074	*Edmond Mallet*	3110	*Elias Reisberg*
3075	*Matthew Sneehan*	3111	*William H. Lane*
3076	*Frederick Bouchard*	3112	*Allen G. Collins*
3077	*Thomas F. Meagher*	3113	*John Robert Gordon*
3078	*Joseph Lee*	3114	*Leif M. Olson*
3079	*Bert Williams*	3115	*Harold H. Brown*
3080	*Cuttyhunk Island*	3116	*Stanley R. Fisher*
3081	*Calvin Austin*	3117	*Charles H. Shaw*
3082	*Joshua Slocum*	3118	*Frederick Austin*
3083	*Julia P. Shaw*	3119	*Melville Jacoby*
3084	*Paul Buck*	3120	*Frank Gilbreth*
3085	*Avery Island*	3121	*Cornelius Ford*
3086	*F. Scott Fitzgerald*	3122	*Jesse H. Metcalf*
3087	*Ezra Meech*	3123	*Nelson W. Aldrich*
3088	*Indian Island*	3125	*Robert W. Hart*
3089	*William A. Dobson*	3126	*J. Howland Gardner*
3090	*Leon S. Merrill*	3127	*Samuel R. Aitken*
3091	*Francis A. Retka*	3128	*Lorenzo C. McCarthy*
3092	*Kent Island*	3129	*Cardinal O'Connell*
3093	*Alfred E. Smith*	3130	*Tom Treanor*
3094	*T. S. Gold*	3131	*Walter F. Perry*
3095	*William Bevan*	3132	*Albert M. Boe*
3096	*Charles N. Cole*	3137	*James G. Squires*
3097	*George A. Lawson*	3138	*James F. Harrell*
3098	*James A. Butts*	3139	*Claude Kitchin*
3099	*Richard D. Lyons*	3140	*Francis J. Ogara*
3100	*George N. Drake*	3141	*Frank Flowers*
3101	*Clarence F. Peck*	3142	*Edwin H. Duff*
3102	*Lawrence T. Sullivan*	3143	*Joseph F. Connolly*
3103	*Joseph Carrigan*	3144	*Walter E. Schwenk*
3104	*Donald H. Holland*	3145	*Charles H. Cuglo*
3105	*Wilfred R. Bellevue*	3146	*Robert F. Burns*
3106	*Fred F. Joyce*	3147	*Edward W. Burton*
3107	*Elwin F. Knowles*	3148	*Ora Ellis*
			2,695 total

APPENDIX B. Alphabetical Listing

Hull No.	Name	Hull No.	Name
2558	A. B. Hammond	229	Alexander Hamilton
1072	A. Frank Lever	620	Alexander J. Dallas
1836	A. J. Cermak	869	Alexander Lillington
2436	A. Mitchell Palmer	36	Alexander Macomb
111	A. P. Hill	2262	Alexander Majors
2253	Abbot L. Mills	162	Alexander Martin
221	Abel Parker Upshur	2708	Alexander Mitchell
674	Abel Stearns	2871	Alexander R. Shepard
281	Abiel Foster	436	Alexander Ramsey
477	Abigail Adams	2364	Alexander S. Clay
2379	Abigail Gibbons	2669	Alexander V. Fraser
2582	Abigail S. Duniway	2466	Alexander W. Doniphan
598	Abner Doubleday	139	Alexander White
863	Abner Nash	2706	Alexander Wilson
123	Abraham Baldwin	2276	Alexander Woolcott
75	Abraham Clark	2732	Alfred C. True
142	Abraham Lincoln	3093	Alfred E. Smith
3066	Abraham Rosenberg	2490	Alfred I. Dupont
2726	Abram S. Hewitt	2812	Alfred J. Evans
524	Adoniram Judson	2999	Alfred L. Baxley
1935	Acubens	892	Alfred Moore
2728	Ada Rehan	726	Alice F. Palmer
2879	Addie Bagley Daniels	2738	Alice H. Rice
1800	Adolph Lewisohn	2416	Allegan
1791	Adolph S. Ochs	2235	Allen C. Balch
1569	Adolph Sutro	3112	Allen G. Collins
1035	Aedanus Burke	2754	Allen Johnson
1889	Alan Seeger	2808	Am Mer Mar
2293	Alanson B. Houghton	2790	Amasa Delano
2254	Albert A. Michelson	1693	Ambrose Bierce
2704	Albert A. Robinson	324	Ambrose E. Burnside
1612	Albert B. Cummins	117	Amelia Earhart
997	Albert C. Ritchie	20	American Mariner
1921	Albert G. Brown	2767	Amerigo Vespucci
277	Albert Gallatin	1837	Ammla
1882	Albert J. Berres	676	Amos G. Throop
2386	Albert K. Smiley	1604	Amos Kendall
3132	Albert M. Boe	734	Amy Lowell
1877	Albert P. Ryder	2806	Ancil F. Haines
1960	Albert S. Burleson	2829	Andreas Honcharenko
1879	Albino Peres	1916	Andrew A. Humphreys
2797	Alcée Fortier	2427	Andrew Briscoe
2817	Ales Hrdlicka	566	Andrew Carnegie
481	Alexander Baranoff	1232	Andrew D. White
2321	Alexander E. Brown	491	Andrew Furuseth
583	Alexander Graham Bell	934	Andrew G. Curtin
5	Alexander H. Stephens	57	Andrew Hamilton

233

Hull No.	Name	Hull No.	Name
3038	Andrew J. Newbury	771	Augustine Heard
1736	Andrew Marshalk	1817	Augustine Herman
131	Andrew Moore	1859	Augustus H. Garland
1055	Andrew Pickens	3039	Augustus P. Loring
1643	Andrew Rowan	1999	Augustus S. Merrimon
2463	Andrew Stevenson	1549	Augustus St. Gaudens
1670	Andrew T. Huntington	2151	Augustus Thomas
1222	Andrew Trunbull	3085	Avery Island
2937	Andrew W. Preston	3040	B. Charney Vladeck
2944	Angus McDonald	2067	B. F. Irvine
2493	Anna Dickinson	1622	B. F. Shaw
2430	Anna H. Branch	2857	Banner Seam
816	Anna Howard Shaw	1827	Barbara Frietchie
336	Anne Bradstreet	2348	Barney Kirschbaum
238	Anne Hutchinson	2196	Barrett Wendell
2227	Annie Oakley	813	Bartholomew Gosnold
725	Ansel Briggs	2460	Basilan
539	Anson Burlingame	2852	Beckley Seam
850	Anson Jones	3011	Belgian Tenacity
2967	Anson Mills	3072	Belgian Unity
1683	Anson P. K. Safford	3070	Belle Isle
2086	Anthony Ravalli	1605	Belva Lockwood
245	Anthony Wayne	2442	Ben A. Ruffin
1728	Antoine Saugrain	2543	Ben B. Lindsey
2055	Anton M. Holter	1788	Ben F. Dixon
2703	Antonin Dvorak	1844	Ben H. Miller
2662	Appanoose	2024	Ben Holladay
3036	Aram J. Pothier	2432	Ben Robertson
682	Archbishop Lamy	2080	Ben T. Osborne
3051	Archibald R. Mansfield	844	Benito Jaurez
2449	Arkab	107	Benj. Huntington
2897	Arlie Clark	2834	Benjamin A. Fisher
2328	Art Young	459	Benjamin Bonneville
156	Artemus Ward	101	Benjamin Bourn
2753	Arthur A. Penn	2867	Benjamin Brown French
1984	Arthur Dobbs	2786	Benjamin Carpenter
2372	Arthur J. Tyrer	58	Benjamin Chew
809	Arthur L. Perry	125	Benjamin Contee
1215	Arthur M. Huddell	1646	Benjamin D. Wilson
2389	Arthur M. Hulbert	2318	Benjamin F. Coston
4	Arthur Middleton	66	Benjamin Franklin
1858	Arthur P. Davis	282	Benjamin Goodhue
2475	Arthur R. Lewis	2146	Benjamin H. Brewster
1593	Arthur Riggs	515	Benjamin H. Bristow
3006	Arthur Sewall	1609	Benjamin H. Grierson
2930	Arthur St. Clair	1514	Benjamin H. Hill
1759	Arunah S. Abell	742	Benjamin H. Latrobe
786	Asa Gray	25	Benjamin Harrison
2649	Assistance	913	Benjamin Hawkins
2474	August Belmont	1108	Benjamin Holt
2264	Augustin Daly	675	Benjamin Ide Wheeler
2554	Augustin Stahl	716	Benjamin Lundy
2361	Augustine B. McCanus	739	Benjamin N. Cardozo

Hull No.	Name	Hull No.	Name
2673	*Benjamin Peixotto*	1847	*Carl Thusgard*
664	*Benjamin R. Curtis*	2833	*Carl Zachary Webb*
855	*Benjamin R. Milam*	698	*Carlos Carrillo*
303	*Benjamin Rush*	2947	*Carlos J. Finlay*
2418	*Benjamin Schlesinger*	1891	*Carlston Ellis*
2818	*Benjamin Silliman*	2557	*Carole Lombard*
169	*Benjamin Smith*	22	*Carter Braxton*
2700	*Benjamin Warner*	1053	*Casimir Pulaski*
2773	*Benjamin Waterhouse*	2112	*Casper S. Yost*
165	*Benjamin Williams*	1626	*Cass Gilbert*
55	*Bernard Carter*	2373	*Cassius Hudson*
2994	*Bernard L. Rodman*	1805	*Cebu*
966	*Bernard N. Baker*	2284	*Cecil G. Sellers*
2168	*Bernardo O'Higgins*	2457	*Cecil N. Bean*
3079	*Bert Williams*	118	*Champ Clark*
2935	*Betram G. Goodhue*	2073	*Charles A. Broadwater*
476	*Betsy Ross*	1991	*Charles A. Dana*
873	*Betty Zane*	2336	*Charles A. Draper*
116	*Big Foot Wallace*	2869	*Charles A. Keffer*
1667	*Billy Mitchell*	985	*Charles A. McAllister*
1687	*Billy Sunday*	2678	*Charles A. McCue*
2039	*Binger Hermann*	1680	*Charles A. Warfield*
2332	*Bjarne A. Lia*	1925	*Charles A. Wickliffe*
1023	*Black Hawk*	2202	*Charles A. Young*
2849	*Bon Air Seam*	313	*Charles Brantley Aycock*
648	*Booker T. Washington*	999	*Charles Bulfinch*
1690	*Brand Whitlock*	1067	*Charles C. Jones*
1721	*Brander Matthews*	1773	*Charles C. Long*
200	*Bret Harte*	151	*Charles C. Pinckney*
633	*Brigham Young*	2402	*Charles C. Randleman*
658	*Brockholst Livingston*	15	*Charles Carroll*
2204	*Bronson Alcott*	1653	*Charles Crocker*
2458	*Burias*	1976	*Charles D. McIver*
968	*Bushrod Washington*	1661	*Charles D. Poston*
351	*Button Gwinnett*	2327	*Charles D. Walcott*
1848	*Byron Darnton*	3013	*Charles Dauray*
2316	*C. Francis Jenkins*	2148	*Charles Devens*
3054	*C. H. M. Jones*	1107	*Charles E. Duryea*
2064	*C. J. Jones*	2147	*Charles E. Smith*
2242	*C. K. McClatchy*	2249	*Charles F. Amidon*
2504	*C. W. Post*	2548	*Charles Fort*
916	*Caesar Rodney*	2140	*Charles G. Coutant*
1782	*Caleb C. Wheeler*	2676	*Charles G. Glover*
78	*Caleb Strong*	2426	*Charles Goodnight*
3081	*Calvin Austin*	587	*Charles Goodyear*
773	*Calvin Coolidge*	591	*Charles Gordon Curtis*
920	*Cardinal Gibbons*	3145	*Charles H. Cuglo*
3129	*Cardinal O'Connell*	1069	*Charles H. Herty*
2737	*Carl B. Eielson*	3001	*Charles H. Lanham*
2312	*Carl E. Ladd*	2329	*Charles H. Marshall*
2748	*Carl G. Barth*	3117	*Charles H. Shaw*
1906	*Carl R. Gray*	1633	*Charles H. Windham*
602	*Carl Schurz*	1043	*Charles Henderson*

Hull No.	Name	Hull No.	Name
2691	*Charles J. Colden*	2972	*Clarence Roberts*
2909	*Charles J. Finger*	2439	*Clark Howell*
517	*Charles J. Folger*	741	*Clark Mills*
2765	*Charles John Seghers*	3139	*Claude Kitchin*
2974	*Charles L. McNary*	2714	*Claus Spreckles*
1649	*Charles Lummis*	1992	*Clement Clay*
430	*Charles M. Conrad*	565	*Cleveland Abbe*
422	*Charles M. Hall*	2759	*Cleveland Forbes*
2060	*Charles M. Russell*	952	*Clifford D. Mallory*
964	*Charles M. Schwab*	2998	*Clifford E. Ashby*
2420	*Charles Morgan*	2056	*Clinton Kelly*
3096	*Charles N. Cole*	2981	*Clyde Austin Dunning*
1710	*Charles N. McGroarty*	2121	*Clyde L. Seavey*
2098	*Charles P. Steinmetz*	3073	*Coasters Harbor*
2232	*Charles Paddock*	744	*Colin P. Kelly, Jr.*
965	*Charles Piez*	2795	*Collin McKinney*
1583	*Charles Robinson*	860	*Collis P. Huntington*
518	*Charles S. Fairchild*	1577	*Conrad Kohrs*
2376	*Charles S. Haight*	990	*Conrad Weiser*
1818	*Charles Scribner*	911	*Cornelia P. Spencer*
785	*Charles Sumner*	1857	*Cornelius Cole*
1909	*Charles T. Yerkes*	3121	*Cornelius Ford*
3064	*Charles Tufts*	543	*Cornelius Gilliam*
789	*Charles W. Eliot*	861	*Cornelius Harnett*
2380	*Charles W. Stiles*	2744	*Cornelius Vanderbilt*
2461	*Charles W. Wooster*	922	*Cotton Mather*
460	*Charles Wilkes*	349	*Crawford W. Long*
605	*Charles Willson Peale*	1018	*Crosby S. Noyes*
2787	*Charlotte Cushman*	1830	*Culebra Island*
1892	*Charlotte P. Gilman*	1601	*Cushing Eells*
1995	*Chatham C. Lyon*	2003	*Cushman K. Davis*
2111	*Chief Charlet*	3080	*Cuttyhunk Island*
1615	*Chief Joseph*	2820	*Cybele*
2322	*Chief Osceola*	2975	*Cyril G. Hopkins*
513	*Chief Ouray*	2792	*Cyrus Adler*
613	*Chief Washakie*	820	*Cyrus H. K. Curtis*
2856	*Chilton Seam*	332	*Cyrus H. McCormick*
2637	*Chourre*	1555	*Cyrus Hamlin*
2811	*Christian Bergh*	1905	*Cyrus K. Holliday*
1563	*Christopher C. Andrews*	2109	*Cyrus T. Brady*
872	*Christopher Gadsden*	1105	*Cyrus W. Field*
900	*Christopher Gale*	1671	*D. W. Harrington*
1603	*Christopher Greenup*	464	*Dan Beard*
1887	*Christopher L. Sholes*	1828	*Daniel Appleton*
21	*Christopher Newport*	69	*Daniel Boone*
2919	*Christopher S. Flanagan*	102	*Daniel Carroll*
1115	*Christy Mathewson*	924	*Daniel Chester French*
2642	*Chung Tung*	715	*Daniel Drake*
636	*Clara Barton*	2918	*Daniel E. Garrett*
2555	*Clarance H. Matson*	2743	*Daniel G. Reid*
1660	*Clarence Darrow*	875	*Daniel H. Hill*
3101	*Clarence F. Peck*	557	*Daniel H. Lownsdale*
1585	*Clarence King*	106	*Daniel Hiester*

Hull No.	Name	Hull No.	Name
129	*Daniel Huger*	1529	*Duncan U. Fletcher*
2988	*Daniel L. Johnston*	2066	*Dunham Wright*
149	*Daniel Morgan*	2674	*Dutiful*
619	*Daniel S. Lamont*	1876	*Dwight B. Heard*
211	*Daniel Webster*	1526	*Dwight L. Moody*
925	*Daniel Willard*	1206	*Dwight W. Morrow*
2838	*Darel M. Ritter*	2761	*E. A. Bryan*
2136	*Daulton Mann*	2777	*E. A. Burnett*
2237	*David A. Curry*	2277	*E. A. Christenson*
2089	*David B. Henderson*	859	*E. A. Peden*
1511	*David B. Johnson*	2804	*E. G. Hall*
1706	*David Belasco*	1600	*E. H. Harriman*
327	*David Bushnell*	2229	*E. H. Sothern*
909	*David Caldwell*	1519	*E. Kirby Smith*
502	*David Davis*	2854	*Eagle Seam*
1762	*David Devries*	2440	*Earl Layman*
2047	*David Douglas*	186	*Edgar Allan Poe*
470	*David Dudley Field*	1541	*Edgar E. Clark*
1666	*David E. Hughes*	2164	*Edgar W. Nye*
2068	*David F. Barry*	1809	*Edith Wharton*
1989	*David F. Houston*	710	*Edmund Fanning*
845	*David G. Burnet*	3074	*Edmond Mallet*
317	*David G. Farragut*	2087	*Edmund F. Dickins*
441	*David Gaillard*	2255	*Edmund G. Ross*
2176	*David Hewes*	712	*Edmund Randolph*
1741	*David Holmes*	2472	*Edward A. Filene*
506	*David J. Brewer*	1118	*Edward A. MacDowell*
896	*David L. Swain*	2660	*Edward A. Savoy*
2500	*David L. Yulee*	889	*Edward B. Dudley*
2715	*David Lubin*	2612	*Edward B. Haines*
1867	*David R. Francis*	526	*Edward Bates*
1901	*David Rittenhouse*	1625	*Edward Bellamy*
100	*David S. Terry*	1819	*Edward Bruce*
472	*David Starr Jordan*	853	*Edward Burleson*
168	*David Stone*	2029	*Edward Canby*
2065	*David Thompson*	1801	*Edward Cook*
1948	*David Wilmot*	2057	*Edward D. Baker*
96	*Davy Crockett*	1499	*Edward D. White*
1629	*De Witt Clinton*	3045	*Edward E. Spafford*
2620	*Deborah Gannett*	2010	*Edward Eggleston*
2043	*Delazon Smith*	2764	*Edward E. Hale*
2648	*Dexter W. Fellows*	575	*Edward Everett*
2658	*Diligence*	2712	*Edward G. Acheson*
1530	*Dolly Madison*	2959	*Edward G. Janeway*
1874	*Don Marquis*	2211	*Edward H. Crockett*
3104	*Donald H. Holland*	2891	*Edward J. Berwind*
2150	*Donald M. Dickinson*	2233	*Edward J. O'Brien*
2040	*Donald MacLeay*	2315	*Edward K. Collins*
2843	*Donald S. Wright*	2207	*Edward Kavanagh*
2360	*Donald W. Bain*	1002	*Edward L. Grant*
2341	*Dudley H. Thomas*	3063	*Edward L. Logan*
1059	*Dudley M. Hughes*	2583	*Edward Lander*
2378	*Duncan L. Clinch*	713	*Edward Livingston*

Hull No.	Name	Hull No.	Name
1209	Edward M. House	777	Eliphalet Nott
3003	Edward N. Hinton	1110	Elisha Graves Otis
963	Edward N. Hurley	899	Elisha Mitchell
2072	Edward N. Westcott	2520	Elisha P. Ferry
1505	Edward P. Alexander	1922	Eliza Jane Nicholson
456	Edward P. Costigan	478	Elizabeth Blackwell
2690	Edward P. Ripley	1217	Elizabeth C. Bellamy
1913	Edward Paine	588	Elmer A. Sperry
772	Edward Preble	2414	Eloy Alfaro
2384	Edward R. Squibb	3107	Elwin F. Knowles
1979	Edward Richardson	2739	Elwood Haynes
483	Edward Rowland Sill	2579	Elwood Mead
220	Edward Rutledge	2139	Emile Berliner
2776	Edward S. Hough	339	Emily Dickinson
1732	Edward Sparrow	1772	Emma Lazarus
2469	Edward W. Bok	783	Emma Willard
3147	Edward W. Burton	2275	Emmet D. Boyle
1645	Edward W. Scripps	825	Enoch Train
1816	Edwin A. Robinson	2537	Enos A. Mills
2465	Edwin A. Stevens	883	Ephraim Brevard
1864	Edwin Abbey	2028	Ephraim W. Baughman
606	Edwin Booth	1950	Erastus Smith
2749	Edwin C. Musick	2016	Eric V. Hauser
2344	Edwin D. Howard	3108	Ernest L. Dawson
1221	Edwin G. Weed	3033	Ernest W. Gibson
3142	Edwin H. Duff	34	Esek Hopkins
1861	Edwin Joseph O'Hara	2115	Ethan A. Hitchcock
1755	Edwin L. Drake	204	Ethan Allen
1071	Edwin L. Godkin	2486	Ethelbert Nevin
564	Edwin M. Stanton	1669	Eugene B. Daskam
284	Edwin Markham	2209	Eugene E. O'Donnell
2970	Edwin S. Nattleton	340	Eugene Field
1561	Edwin T. Meredith	791	Eugene Hale
1946	Edwin W. Moore	556	Eugene Skinner
83	Egbert Benson	2368	Eugene T. Chamberlain
983	Elbert Hubbard	1933	Eugene W. Hilgard
279	Elbridge Gerry	631	Ewing Young
2933	Eleazar Lord	780	Ezra Cornell
38	Eleazor Wheelock	3087	Ezra Meech
264	Eli Whitney	611	Ezra Meeker
1034	Elias Boudinot	798	Ezra Weston
2191	Elias H. Derby	81	F. A. C. Muhlenberg
354	Elias Howe	487	F. Marion Crawford
3110	Elias Reisberg	3086	F. Scott Fitzgerald
691	Elihu B. Washburne	2365	F. Southall Farrar
1524	Elihu Root	1039	F. T. Frelinghuysen
427	Elihu Thomson	2681	Faithful
240	Elihu Yale	639	Felipe De Neve
3059	Elijah Cobb	2924	Felipi Debastrop
3012	Elijah Kellog	352	Felix Grundy
1610	Elijah P. Lovejoy	2037	Felix Hathaway
558	Elijah White	2391	Felix Riesenberg
2559	Elinor Wylie	2177	Ferdinand A. Silcox

Hull No.	Name	Hull No.	Name
3055	*Ferdinand Gagnon*	2839	*Frank E. Spencer*
2799	*Ferdinand R. Hassler*	3141	*Frank Flowers*
2186	*Ferdinand Westdahl*	3120	*Frank Gilbreth*
814	*Ferdinando George*	2288	*Frank H. Dodd*
2488	*Filipp Mazzei*	2710	*Frank H. Evers*
1678	*Finley Peter Dunne*	2135	*Frank J. Cuhel*
233	*Fisher Ames*	2716	*Frank J. Sprague*
649	*Fitz John Porter*	672	*Frank Joseph Irwin*
838	*Fitzhugh Lee*	2158	*Frank Norris*
885	*Flora MacDonald*	2347	*Frank O. Peterson*
1674	*Florence Crittenton*	3057	*Frank P. Reed*
1068	*Florence Martus*	2874	*Frank P. Walsh*
1565	*Floyd B. Olson*	2367	*Frank Park*
1705	*Floyd Bennett*	1843	*Frank R. Stockton*
2875	*Floyd Gibbons*	1677	*Frank Springer*
2802	*Floyd W. Spencer*	1873	*Frank Wiggins*
475	*Frances E. Willard*	2542	*Franklin H. King*
3091	*Francis A. Retka*	1663	*Franklin K. Lane*
2174	*Francis A. Wardwell*	627	*Franklin MacVeagh*
781	*Francis Amasa Walker*	957	*Franklin P. Mall*
1195	*Francis Asbury*	1793	*Franz Boas*
2969	*Francis B. Ogden*	2752	*Franz Sigel*
1825	*Francis C. Harrington*	2513	*Fred C. Stebbins*
2622	*Francis D. Culkin*	3106	*Fred F. Joyce*
299	*Francis Drake*	2517	*Fred Herrling*
3000	*Francis E. Siltz*	2161	*Frederic A. Eilers*
2018	*Francis E. Warren*	2391	*Frederic A. Kummer*
1692	*Francis G. Newland*	1536	*Frederic C. Howe*
3140	*Francis J. O'Gara*	2961	*Frederic E. Ives*
26	*Francis L. Lee*	508	*Frederic Remington*
257	*Francis Lewis*	2503	*Frederic W. Galbraith*
2159	*Francis M. Smith*	3118	*Frederick Austin*
150	*Francis Marion*	1050	*Frederick Bunting*
2248	*Francis N. Blanchet*	1503	*Frederick Bartholdi*
882	*Francis Nash*	2085	*Frederick Billings*
89	*Francis Parkman*	3076	*Frederick Bouchard*
1230	*Francis Preston Blair*	2567	*Frederick C. Hicks*
2447	*Francis S. Bartow*	988	*Frederick Douglass*
16	*Francis Scott Key*	2334	*Frederick E. Williamson*
1789	*Francis Vigo*	2670	*Frederick H. Baetjer*
2261	*Francis W. Parker*	1942	*Frederick H. Newell*
1620	*Francis W. Pettygrove*	446	*Frederick Jackson Turner*
2713	*Francis Wilson*	851	*Frederick L. Dau*
1748	*Francisco Coronado*	2801	*Frederick Von Steuben*
2734	*Francisco Morazan*	2220	*Frederick W. Taylor*
2185	*Francisco N. Quinones*	2665	*Frederick W. Wood*
2160	*Frank A. Munsey*	2860	*Freeport Seam*
1821	*Frank A. Vanderlip*	1576	*Fremont Older*
2791	*Frank Adair Monroe*	888	*Furniford M. Simmons*
601	*Frank B. Kellogg*	425	*G. H. Corliss*
2529	*Frank B. Linderman*	656	*Gabriel Duval*
2165	*Frank C. Emerson*	2571	*Gabriel Franchere*
1713	*Frank D. Phinney*		

Hull No.	Name	Hull No.	Name
3052	Galen L. Stone	544	George H. Williams
678	Gaspar De Portolá	342	George Handley
1642	General Vallejo	3025	George Hawley
646	George A. Custer	1717	George Inness
3097	George A. Lawson	2173	George K. Fitch
2454	George A. Marr	1866	George Kenny
550	George Abernathy	1614	George L. Baker
2314	George Ade	2053	George L. Curry
2755	George A. Pope	3037	George L. Farley
445	George B. Cortelyou	2004	George L. Shoup
322	George B. McClellan	130	George Leonard
2686	George B. McFarland	2723	George Luks
2720	George B. Porter	628	George M. Bibb
428	George B. Seldon	1012	George M. Cohan
91	George Bancroft	2768	George Middlemas
1947	George Bellows	1100	George M. Pullman
1568	George Berkeley	1803	George M. Shriver
1937	George C. Childress	2675	George M. Verity
708	George C. Yount	285	George Matthews
29	George Calvert	3100	George N. Drake
671	George Chaffey	3049	George N. Seger
560	George Chamberlin	1939	George P. Garrison
793	George Cleeve	2525	George P. McKay
2272	George Clement Perkins	1045	George Poindexter
182	George Clymer	2807	George Pomutz
2269	George Coggeshall	2194	George Popham
2684	George Crile	2657	George R. Holmes
536	George D. Prentice	2395	George R. Poole
2019	George Davidson	259	George Read
876	George Davis	448	George Rogers Clark
1202	George Dewey	252	George Ross
1998	George Durant	514	George S. Boutwell
884	George E. Badger	2206	George S. Wasson
2697	George E. Goodfellow	945	George Sharswood
700	George E. Hale	939	George Shiras
2476	George E. Merrick	2915	George Steers
841	George E. Pickett	2152	George Sterling
2501	George E. Waldo	2208	George T. Angell
1104	George Eastman	254	George Taylor
3019	George Eldridge	290	George Thacher
802	George F. Patten	1785	George Uhler
1617	George Flavel	353	George Vancouver
1510	George G. Crawford	1021	George Vickers
647	George G. Meade	2155	George Von L. Myer
126	George Gale	2793	George W. Alther
1641	George Gershwin	623	George W. Campbell
1116	George Gipp	1014	George W. Childs
511	George H. Dern	599	George W. Goethals
1619	George H. Flanders	2013	George W. Julian
2048	George H. Himes	1734	George W. Kendall
1013	George H. Pendleton	1954	George W. Lively
2126	George H. Powell	435	George W. McCrary
569	George H. Thomas	2388	George W. Norris

Hull No.	Name	Hull No.	Name
998	*George W. Woodward*	2896	*Harry Kirby*
344	*George Walton*	2445	*Harry L. Glucksman*
542	*George Washington Carver*	559	*Harry Lane*
918	*George Weems*	2119	*Harry Leon Wilson*
423	*George Westinghouse*	2424	*Harry Percy*
1057	*George Whitefield*	2551	*Hart Crane*
24	*George Wythe*	1953	*Harvey C. Miller*
1122	*Geronimo*	1210	*Harvey Cushing*
563	*Gideon Welles*	552	*Harvey W. Scott*
2273	*Gilbert M. Hitchcock*	1894	*Harvey W. Wiley*
1628	*Gilbert Stuart*	1783	*Hawkins Fudske*
2850	*Glamorgan Seam*	0987	*Haym Salomon*
1103	*Glenn Curtiss*	2128	*Heber M. Creel*
1627	*Gouverneur Morris*	2664	*Hecla*
919	*Grace Abbott*	2821	*Hecuba*
2568	*Grace R. Hebard*	673	*Helen Hunt Jackson*
1611	*Graham Taylor*	2826	*Helena Modjeska*
2573	*Grant P. Marsh*	1599	*Henderson Luelling*
1208	*Grant Wood*	2482	*Hendrik Willem Van Loon*
2325	*Granville S. Hall*	2268	*Henry Adams*
1688	*Granville Stuart*	1966	*Henry Austin*
2823	*Gratia*	938	*Henry B. Brown*
522	*Grenville M. Dodge*	2510	*Henry B. Plant*
2512	*Grover C. Hutcherson*	862	*Henry Bacon*
2932	*Gus W. Darnwell*	657	*Henry Baldwin*
1869	*Gutzon Borglum*	603	*Henry Barnard*
1718	*H. G. Blasdel*	1556	*Henry Bergh*
2303	*H. H. Raymond*	2154	*Henry C. Payne*
2770	*H. Weir Cook*	1881	*Henry C. Wallace*
3023	*Hadley F. Brown*	3	*Henry Clay*
1596	*Hall J. Kelley*	2927	*Henry D. Lindsley*
2398	*Halton R. Carey*	191	*Henry D. Thoreau*
1054	*Hamlin Garland*	579	*Henry Dearborn*
213	*Hannibal Hamlin*	1581	*Henry Dodge*
1978	*Hannis Taylor*	1236	*Henry Durant*
2751	*Hans Heg*	2560	*Henry E. Huntington*
2502	*Harald Torsvik*	1621	*Henry Failing*
2143	*Harmon Judson*	574	*Henry George*
2514	*Harold A. Jordan*	950	*Henry Gilbert Costin*
2980	*Harold D. Whitehead*	1037	*Henry Groves Connors*
2399	*Harold Dossett*	2170	*Henry H. Blood*
3115	*Harold H. Brown*	528	*Henry H. Richardson*
3044	*Harold I. Pratt*	728	*Henry H. Sibley*
1807	*Harold L. Winslow*	2489	*Henry Hadley*
2396	*Harold O. Wilson*	442	*Henry J. Raymond*
1544	*Harold T. Andrews*	2278	*Henry J. Waters*
790	*Harriet Beecher Stowe*	812	*Henry Jocelyn*
1528	*Harriet Hosmer*	74	*Henry Knox*
2134	*Harriet Monroe*	2063	*Henry L. Abbott*
3032	*Harriet Tubman*	946	*Henry L. Benning*
2578	*Harrington Emerson*	1744	*Henry L. Ellsworth*
692	*Harrison Gray Otis*	2552	*Henry L. Gantt*
808	*Harry A. Garfield*	2041	*Henry L. Hoyt*

Hull No.	Name	Hull No.	Name
2036	Henry L. Pittock	1702	Horace Wells
1784	Henry Lomb	906	Horace Williams
729	Henry M. Rice	2563	Horatio Allen
2921	Henry M. Robert	110	Houston Volunteers
1865	Henry M. Robinson	955	Howard A. Kelly
2228	Henry M. Stanley	1512	Howard E. Coffin
2763	Henry M. Stephens	2302	Howard Gray
2144	Henry M. Teller	2954	Howard L. Gibson
2788	Henry Meiggs	0705	Howard Stansbury
228	Henry Middleton	1854	Howard T. Ricketts
2538	Henry Miller	533	Howell Cobb
2132	Henry R. Schoolcraft	1498	Howell E. Jackson
1041	Henry S. Foote	669	Hubert Howe Bancroft
2014	Henry S. Lane	2480	Hugh J. Kilpatrick
2467	Henry S. Sanford	1840	Hugh L. Kerwin
37	Henry St. G. Tucker	1833	Hugh M. Smith
2523	Henry T. Rainey	534	Hugh McCulloch
2692	Henry T. Scott	685	Hugh S. Legare
1716	Henry V. Alvarado	157	Hugh Williamson
1763	Henry Van Dyke	1964	Hugh Young
571	Henry Villard	1987	Hutchinson I. Cone
1616	Henry W. Corbett	2976	I. B. Perrine
1501	Henry W. Grady	2565	I. N. Van Nuys
185	Henry W. Longfellow	2566	Ida M. Tarbell
642	Henry Ward Beecher	2951	Ida Straus
1201	Henry Watterson	1648	Ignace Paderewski
2103	Henry Wells	2005	Ignatius Donnelly
2274	Henry White	2859	Imboden Seam
788	Henry Wilson	1856	Ina Coolbirth
140	Henry Wynkoop	1584	Increase A. Lapham
2960	Herbert D. Croly	3088	Indian Island
334	Herman Melville	3068	Iolanda
2832	Herrin Seam	2387	Ira Nelson Morris
2825	Hesperia	321	Irvin MacDowell
1780	Heywood Broun	2491	Irvin S. Cobb
1986	Hilary A. Herbert	2957	Irving Babbitt
94	Hinton R. Helper	1566	Irving M. Scott
1726	Hiram Bingham	2034	Irving W. Pratt
468	Hiram S. Maxim	1743	Irwin Russell
1114	Hobart Baker	1106	Isaac Babbitt
1061	Hoke Smith	84	Isaac Coles
1767	Holland Thompson	2810	Isaac Delgado
538	Homer Lea	2575	Isaac I. Stevens
2682	Hooper Island	2506	Isaac M. Singer
62	Horace Binney	2509	Isaac Mayer Wise
1795	Horace Bushnell	2535	Isaac McCoy
936	Horace Gray	2434	Isaac S. Hopkins
641	Horace Greeley	778	Isaac Sharpless
1924	Horace H. Harvey	1518	Isaac Shelby
1500	Horace H. Lurton	2431	Isaac Van Zandt
634	Horace Mann	1820	Israel J. Merritt
1890	Horace See	12	Israel Putman
2519	Horace V. White	1839	Israel Wheelen

Hull No.	Name	Hull No.	Name
2709	J. C. Osgood	811	James Bowdoin
1931	J. W. Beckham	271	James Bowie
2049	J. D. Ross	686	James Buchanan
2964	J. D. Yeager	1831	James C. Cameron
114	J. E. B. Stuart	915	James Caldwell
2239	J. Frank Cooper	1826	James Carroll
1835	J. Fred Essary	1886	James Cook
2309	J. H. Drummond	2092	James D. Doty
480	J. H. Kinkaid	2156	James D. Phelan
3126	J. Howland Gardner	2631	James D. Trask
1	J. L. M. Curry	1460	James De Wolf
2290	J. Maurice Thompson	2745	James Devereux
1938	J. Pincknew Henderson	568	James Duncan
2814	J. Rufino Barrios	852	James E. Haviland
1963	J. S. Cullinan	1042	James E. Howard
2775	J. S. Hutchinson	2831	James Eagan Layne
510	J. Sterling Morton	3138	James F. Harrell
2257	J. Warren Keifer	198	James Fenimore Cooper
1808	J. Whitridge Williams	1694	James Fergus
2195	J. Willard Gibbs	92	James Ford Rhodes
1237	Jack London	719	James G. Birney
2231	Jack Singer	333	James G. Blaine
2949	Jacob A. Westervelt	2183	James G. Maguire
2979	Jacob Chandler Harper	3137	James G. Squires
794	Jacob H. Gallinger	643	James Gordon Bennett
1823	Jacob H. Schiff	44	James Gunn
2912	Jacob Perkins	532	James Guthrie
1685	Jacob Riis	2265	James H. Breasted
1665	Jacob S. Mansfeld	1063	James H. Couper
2863	Jacob Sloat Fassett	2516	James H. Courts
1738	Jacob Thompson	2298	James H. Kimball
737	Jacques Cartier	2259	James H. Lane
473	Jacques Laramie	1664	James H. McClintock
2816	Jagger Seam	2889	James H. Price
1552	James A. Bayard	1862	James H. Robinson
3098	James A. Butts	1559	James Harlan
2783	James A. Drain	1602	James Harrod
1016	James A. Farrell	740	James Hoban
2556	James A. Wilder	1996	James I. McKay
2450	James B. Aswell	867	James Iredell
848	James B. Bonham	530	James Ives
2362	James B. Duke	1112	James J. Corbett
592	James B. Eads	494	James J. Hill
418	James B. Francis	2104	James J. O. Kelly
467	James B. Hickok	874	James J. Pettigrew
650	James B. McPherson	343	James Jackson
2569	James B. Miller	2050	James K. Kelly
226	James B. Richardson	2477	James K. Paulding
580	James B. Stephens	161	James K. Polk
732	James B. Weaver	2628	James Kerney
831	James Barbour	2179	James King
2397	James Bennett Moore	2982	James Kyron Walker
1771	James Blair	2468	James L. Ackerson

Hull No.	Name	Hull No.	Name
2075	James L. Breck	465	Jane A. Delano
1704	James Lick	635	Jane Addams
112	James Longstreet	2522	Jane G. Swisshelm
2071	James M. Clements	847	Jane Long
1764	James M. Gillis	1007	Janet Lord Roper
727	James M. Goodhue	60	Jared Ingersoll
836	James M. Porter	546	Jason Lee
1489	James M. Wayne	2484	Jasper F. Cropsey
274	James Madison	2694	Jay Cooke
2198	James Manning	1920	Jean Baptiste LeMoyne
996	James McCosh	2096	Jean Nicolet
1030	James McHenry	2717	Jean P. Chouteau
576	James McNeil Whistler	2300	Jean Ribaut
80	James Monroe	1650	Jedediah S. Smith
891	James Moore	8	Jefferson Davis
341	James Oglethorpe	2848	Jellico Seam
2015	James Oliver	2190	Jeremiah Chaplin
2711	James Oliver Curwood	1724	Jeremiah M. Daily
241	James Otis	2145	Jeremiah M. Rusk
979	James R. Randall	806	Jeremiah O'Brien
703	James Robertson	690	Jeremiah S. Black
2702	James Rolph	155	Jeremiah Van Rensselaer
1730	James Rowan	270	Jeremiah Wadsworth
2986	James Roy Wells	1060	Jerome K. Jones
329	James Rumsey	2497	Jerry S. Foley
190	James Russell Lowell	549	Jesse Applegate
846	James S. Hogg	1945	Jesse Billingsley
2081	James S. Lawson	2671	Jesse Cottrell
287	James Schureman	1798	Jesse DeForest
1213	James Screven	3122	Jesse H. Metcalf
1668	James Shields	2846	Jewell Seam
253	James Smith	610	Jim Bridger
886	James Sprunt	484	Joaquin Miller
3041	James Sullivan	1508	Joe C. S. Blackburn
2872	James Swan	2241	Joe Fellows
1775	James T. Earle	2280	Joe Harris
3061	James T. Fields	10	Joel Chandler Harris
166	James Turner	2025	Joel Palmer
2366	James W. Cannon	833	Joel R. Poinsett
949	James W. Denver	2375	Johan Printz
849	James W. Fannin	1496	John A. Campbell
1502	James W. Grady	774	John A. Dix
1613	James W. Grimes	1005	John A. Donald
2546	James W. Johnson	2027	John A. Johnson
670	James W. Marshall	451	John A. Logan
553	James W. Nesmith	807	John A. Poor
1571	James W. Nye	1046	John A. Quitman
2338	James W. Wheeler	434	John A. Rawlins
193	James Whitcomb Riley	293	John A. Sutter
183	James Wilson	2441	John A. Treutlen
2038	James Withycombe	242	John Adams
929	James Woodrow	1659	John Alden
2263	Jan Pieterszoon Coen	829	John Armstrong

Hull No.	Name	Hull No.	Name
82	*John B. Ashe*	2758	*John F. Shafroth*
431	*John B. Floyd*	2031	*John F. Steffen*
1504	*John B. Gordon*	827	*John Fairfield*
2939	*John B. Hamilton*	90	*John Fiske*
115	*John B. Hood*	328	*John Fitch*
2530	*John B. Kendrick*	2095	*John G. Brady*
1509	*John B. Lennon*	519	*John G. Carlisle*
2527	*John Bull*	525	*John G. Nicolay*
962	*John Banvard*	2107	*John G. North*
174	*John Barry*	2908	*John G. Tod*
1535	*John Barton Payne*	188	*John G. Whittier*
424	*John Bartram*	951	*John Gallup*
1521	*John Bascom*	2916	*John Gibbons*
0834	*John Bell*	1880	*John Goode*
0683	*John Bidwell*	1194	*John Gorrie*
497	*John Blair*	1972	*John Grier Hibben*
2002	*John Branch*	52	*John H. B. Latrobe*
609	*John Burke*	1618	*John H. Couch*
1652	*John Burroughs*	832	*John H. Eaton*
554	*John C. Ainsworth*	2385	*John H. Hammond*
350	*John C. Breckinridge*	1776	*John H. Hatton*
219	*John C. Calhoun*	1895	*John H. Marion*
64	*John C. Frémont*	2496	*John H. McIntosh*
2837	*John C. Preston*	2614	*John H. Murphy*
835	*John C. Spencer*	2547	*John H. Quick*
1749	*John Cabot*	1943	*John H. Reagan*
1557	*John Carroll*	1580	*John H. Rosseter*
56	*John Carter Rose*	2746	*John H. Thomas*
207	*John Carver*	176	*John Hancock*
1494	*John Catron*	2677	*John Hanson*
215	*John Chandler*	184	*John Hart*
3026	*John Chester Kendall*	239	*John Harvard*
1458	*John Clarke*	878	*John Harvey*
2137	*John Colter*	283	*John Hathorn*
1698	*John Constantine*	1525	*John Hay*
152	*John Cropper*	45	*John Henry*
1977	*John D. Morehead*	216	*John Holmes*
201	*John Davenport*	2742	*John Hope*
2539	*John Davey*	490	*John Howard Payne*
586	*John Deere*	958	*John Howland*
232	*John Dickinson*	2079	*John I. Nolan*
2561	*John Dockweiler*	2920	*John Ireland*
697	*John Drake Sloat*	2270	*John Isaacson*
225	*John Drayton*	960	*John J. Able*
2549	*John Drew*	1196	*John J. Crittenden*
984	*John E. Schmeltzer*	1686	*John J. Ingalls*
2438	*John E. Sweet*	1790	*John J. McGraw*
1070	*John E. Ward*	1911	*John J. Roebling*
1588	*John E. Wilkie*	2059	*John Jacob Astor*
1220	*John Einig*	420	*John James Audubon*
1712	*John Evans*	178	*John Jay*
421	*John F. Appleby*	2594	*John L. Elliott*
2088	*John F. Myers*	2342	*John L. McCarley*

Hull No.	Name	Hull No.	Name
986	John L. Motley	1589	John Ross
2287	John L. Stoddard	1794	John Russell Pope
1121	John L. Sullivan	495	John Rutledge
1822	John LaFarge	1707	John S. Bassett
77	John Langdon	1654	John S. Casement
108	John Laurance	604	John S. Copley
1985	John Lawson	1207	John S. Mosby
1573	John Lind	730	John S. Pillsbury
2090	John M. Bozeman	1582	John S. Sargent
1550	John M. Brooke	652	John Sedwick
687	John M. Clayton	63	John Sergeant
1497	John M. Harlan	236	John Sevier
453	John M. Palmer	1047	John Sharp Williams
2456	John M. Parker	2131	John Sherman
433	John M. Schofield	1737	John Stagg
991	John M. T. Finney	289	John Steele
2	John Marshall	330	John Stevens
2991	John Martin Miller	1011	John Stevenson
857	John Mary Odin	2533	John Straub
815	John Mason	214	John Sullivan
1733	John McDonogh	2171	John Swett
1495	John McKinley	1824	John T. Clark
499	John McLean	1758	John T. Holt
548	John McLoughlin	1575	John T. McMillan
1990	John Merrick	2225	John Tripton
346	John Milledge	337	John Trumbull
2515	John Miller	138	John Vining
2021	John Minto	312	John W. Brown
311	John Mitchell	2730	John W. Burgess
978	John Morgan	1597	John W. Cullen
258	John Morton	2536	John W. Davis
1226	John Muir	2166	John W. Foster
770	John Murray Forbes	1768	John W. Garrett
1997	John N. Maffitt	2421	John W. Gates
819	John N. Robins	1548	John W. Griffiths
1970	John Owne	2141	John W. Hoyt
1896	John P. Altgeld	1570	John W. MacKay
2045	John P. Gaines	2120	John W. Meldrum
2877	John P. Harris	1022	John W. Powell
589	John P. Holland	2540	John W. Searles
1975	John P. Mitchell	2581	John W. Troy
54	John P. Poe	617	John W. Weeks
286	John Page	305	John Walker
67	John Paul Jones	1010	John Wanamaker
218	John Penn	1218	John White
1200	John Philip Sousa	1590	John Whiteaker
2311	John R. McQuigg	202	John Winthrop
466	John R. Park	251	John Wise
19	John Randolph	31	John Witherspoon
2099	John Reed	973	John Woolman
2494	John Ringling	881	John Wright Stanly
2267	John Roach	2965	Johnny Appleseed
3113	John Robert Gordon	947	Johns Hopkins

Hull No.	Name	Hull No.	Name
237	*Jonathan Edwards*	976	*Joseph Leidy*
308	*Jonathan Elmer*	2250	*Joseph M. Carey*
128	*Jonathan Grout*	1523	*Joseph M. Medill*
561	*Jonathan Harrington*	1515	*Joseph M. Terrell*
2012	*Jonathan Jennings*	86	*Joseph McKenna*
1558	*Jonathan P. Dolliver*	2881	*Joseph Murgas*
136	*Jonathan Sturges*	3043	*Joseph N. Dinand*
137	*Jonathan Trumbull*	1050	*Joseph N. Nicollet*
897	*Jonathan Worth*	581	*Joseph N. Teal*
2776	*Jones Lie*	971	*Joseph P. Bradley*
113	*Jos E. Johnston*	1675	*Joseph Priestley*
1812	*José Artigas*	644	*Joseph Pulitzer*
907	*José Bonifacio*	1491	*Joseph R. Lamar*
2707	*José C. Barbosa*	1870	*Joseph Reynolds*
2429	*José G. Benitez*	488	*Joseph Rodman Drake*
2127	*José J. Acosta*	1567	*Joseph S. Emery*
2772	*José M. Morelos*	2883	*Joseph S. McDonagh*
1017	*José Marti*	2061	*Joseph Simon*
1951	*José Navarro*	1119	*Joseph Smith*
2688	*José Pedro Varela*	3028	*Joseph Squires*
1647	*José Sepulveda*	304	*Joseph Stanton*
1967	*Joseph A. Brown*	655	*Joseph Story*
1708	*Joseph A. Holmes*	119	*Joseph T. Robinson*
864	*Joseph Alston*	2074	*Joseph W. Folk*
3029	*Joseph Augustin Chevalier*	782	*Joseph Warren*
2655	*Joseph B. Eastman*	2042	*Joseph Watt*
2020	*Joseph C. Avery*	2822	*Joseph Weydemeyer*
3035	*Joseph C. Lincoln*	13	*Joseph Wheeler*
3103	*Joseph Carrigan*	2296	*Josephine Shaw Lowell*
1058	*Joseph E. Brown*	1952	*Joshua A. Leach*
2133	*Joseph E. Wing*	1841	*Joshua B. Lippincott*
3143	*Joseph F. Connolly*	1696	*Joshua Hendy*
1875	*Joseph Francis*	805	*Joshua L. Chamberlain*
447	*Joseph G. Cannon*	134	*Joshua Senney*
594	*Joseph Gale*	3082	*Joshua Slocum*
1917	*Joseph Goldberger*	1760	*Joshua Thomas*
693	*Joseph H. Hollister*	1004	*Joshua W. Alexander*
1961	*Joseph H. Kibbey*	527	*Josiah B. Grinnell*
1065	*Joseph H. Martin*	205	*Josiah Bartlett*
994	*Joseph H. Nicholson*	2887	*Josiah Cohen*
1064	*Joseph Habersham*	1637	*Josiah D. Whitney*
1751	*Joseph Henry*	1662	*Josiah Earl*
217	*Joseph Hewes*	1884	*Josiah G. Holland*
432	*Joseph Holt*	1651	*Josiah Nelson Cushing*
323	*Joseph Hooker*	132	*Josiah Parker*
3027	*Joseph I. Kemp*	799	*Josiah Quincy*
607	*Joseph Jefferson*	714	*Josiah Royce*
2756	*Joseph J. Kinyoun*	541	*Josiah Snelling*
1723	*Joseph K. Toole*	2884	*Josiah Tattnell*
596	*Joseph L. Meek*	1796	*Joyce Kilmer*
551	*Joseph Lane*	1657	*Juan Bautisto de Anza*
1983	*Joseph LeConte*	291	*Juan Cabrillo*
3078	*Joseph Lee*	1747	*Juan de Fuca*

Hull No.	Name	Hull No.	Name
1634	Juan Flaco Brown	1930	Leif Ericson
2934	Juan N. Seguin	3114	Leif M. Olson
2757	Juan Pablo Duarte	298	Leland Stanford
839	Jubal A. Early	1829	Leo J. Duster
7	Judah P. Benjamin	1934	Leon Godchaux
1927	Judah Touro	3090	Leon S. Merrill
2718	Julia L. Dumont	2995	Leonardo L. Romero
3083	Julia P. Shaw	1564	Leonidas Merritt
335	Julia Ward Howe	144	Leonidas Polk
2234	Julian W. Mack	1915	Leopold Damrosch
523	Julien Dubuque	444	Leslie M. Shaw
1048	Julien Poydras	969	Levi Woodbury
2446	Juliette Low	485	Lew Wallace
2923	Julius Olsen	689	Lewis Cass
1533	Julius Rosenwald	1806	Lewis Emery, Jr.
292	Junípero Serra	2532	Lewis L. Dyche
2505	Junius Smith	250	Lewis Morris
461	Justin S. Morrill	2595	Leyte
2698	Justo Arosemena	3071	Liguria
2175	Kate Douglas Wiggin	3010	Lillian Nordica
2813	Katharine B. Sherwood	2722	Lillian Wald
2911	Katherine L. Bates	668	Lincoln Steffens
2914	Keith Palmer	616	Lindley M. Garrison
2182	Keith Vawter	2448	Linn Boyd
1973	Kemp P. Battle	2842	Linton Seam
1606	Kenneth A. J. MacKenzie	1765	Lionel Copley
3092	Kent Island	2989	Lloyd S. Carlson
3065	Kenyon L. Butterfield	3060	Loammi Baldwin
2680	Kermit Roosevelt	2953	Lorado Taft
0512	Key Pittman	928	Lord Delaware
2819	King Hathaway	3128	Lorenzo C. McCarthy
681	King S. Woolsey	854	Lorenzo DeZavala
243	Kit Carson	2226	Lorrin A. Thurston
731	Knute Nelson	3042	Lot M. Morill
1111	Knute Rockne	1594	Lot Whitcomb
2459	Kochab	210	Lou Gehrig
2948	Kyle V. Johnson	1074	Louis A. Godey
1958	L. H. McNelly	2149	Louis A. Sengteller
1740	Lafcadio Hearn	1624	Louis Agassiz
273	Lambart Cadwalader	2508	Louis Bamberger
1051	Langdon Cheves	1846	Louis C. Tiffany
2836	LaSalle Seam	943	Louis D. Brandeis
2382	Laura Bridgman	540	Louis Hennepin
2943	Laura Drake Gill	449	Louis Joliet
1752	Laura Keene	1838	Louis Kossuth
2845	Laurence J. Gallagher	1019	Louis Marshall
1988	Lawrence D. Tyson	684	Louis McLane
2125	Lawrence Gianella	2123	Louis Pasteur
2616	Lawrence J. Brengle	2779	Louis Sloss
3102	Lawrence T. Sullivan	2781	Louis Sullivan
746	Lawton B. Evans	2771	Louis Weule
2301	LeBaron Russell Briggs	992	Louisa M. Alcott
1981	Lee S. Overman	1959	Lucien B. Maxwell

Hull No.	Name	Hull No.	Name
2782	*Lucien Labaudt*	2349	*Mary Cullom Kimbro*
2521	*Lucius Fairchild*	2577	*Mary E. Kinney*
1029	*Lucius Q. C. Lamar*	787	*Mary Lyon*
1607	*Lucretia Mott*	2138	*Mary M. Dodge*
474	*Lucy Stone*	1725	*Mary Patten*
679	*Luis Arguello*	2654	*Mary Pickersgill*
2374	*Lunsford Richardson*	2289	*Mary Walker*
1099	*Luther Burbank*	2192	*Mary Wilkins Freeman*
49	*Luther Martin*	1928	*Mason L. Weems*
1709	*Luther S. Kelly*	1766	*Mathew Brush*
720	*Lydia M. Child*	887	*Matt W. Ransom*
1461	*Lyman Abbott*	1117	*Matthew B. Brady*
1229	*Lyman Beecher*	1965	*Matthew J. O'Brien*
345	*Lyman Hall*	97	*Matthew Maury*
520	*Lyman J. Gage*	545	*Matthew P. Deady*
1658	*Lyman Stewart*	3075	*Matthew Sneehan*
1799	*Lyon G. Tyler*	898	*Matthew T. Goldsboro*
2390	*M. E. Comerford*	262	*Matthew Thornton*
1587	*M. H. De Young*	318	*Mayo Brothers*
615	*M. M. Guhin*	2281	*Mello Franco*
2305	*M. Michael Edelstein*	2470	*Melucta*
2893	*Mack Bruton Bryan*	1849	*Melvil Dewey*
942	*Mahlon Pitney*	1715	*Melville E. Stone*
645	*Malcolm M. Stewart*	3119	*Melville Jacoby*
2094	*Manasseh Culter*	504	*Melville W. Fuller*
1697	*Marcus Daly*	2201	*Mercy Warren*
3046	*Marcus H. Tracy*	170	*Meriwether Lewis*
547	*Marcus Whitman*	2847	*Merrimac Seam*
1787	*Margaret Brent*	2541	*Meyer Lissner*
723	*Margaret Fuller*	2585	*Meyer London*
722	*Maria Mitchell*	3031	*Miaoulis*
1562	*Maria Sanford*	3058	*Michael Anagnos*
1778	*Marie M. Meloney*	2118	*Michael C. Kerr*
1679	*Marina Raskova*	2101	*Michael Casey*
665	*Marion McKinley Bovard*	2495	*Michael deKovats*
2789	*Mariscal Sucre*	2958	*Michael J. Owens*
3002	*Mark A. Davis*	99	*Michael J. Stone*
573	*Mark Hanna*	2335	*Michael James Monohan*
1231	*Mark Hopkins*	3050	*Michael Moran*
1639	*Mark Keppel*	1554	*Michael Pupin*
196	*Mark Twain*	2082	*Midwest Farmer*
866	*Marshall Elliott*	1636	*Miguel Hidalgo*
2873	*Martha Berry*	2679	*Milan R. Stefanik*
1845	*Martha C. Thomas*	2129	*Millen Griffith*
2827	*Martin Behrman*	2798	*Milton B. Medary*
2244	*Martin Johnson*	2803	*Milton H. Smith*
1851	*Martin Van Buren*	2882	*Milton J. Foreman*
2292	*Mary A. Livermore*	2861	*Mingo Seam*
1735	*Mary Ashley Towsend*	1547	*Minnie M. Fiske*
858	*Mary Austin*	2928	*Minor C. Keith*
1534	*Mary Ball*	267	*Mirabeau B. Lamar*
2116	*Mary Bickerdyke*	2885	*Moina Michael*
1553	*Mary Cassatt*	935	*Molly Pitcher*

Hull No.	Name	Hull No.	Name
2634	*Mona Island*	500	*Noah H. Swain*
2000	*Montfort Stokes*	776	*Noah Webster*
2741	*Morgan Robertson*	2169	*Norman E. Mack*
2499	*Morris C. Feinstone*	2167	*Norman Hapgood*
2419	*Morris Hillquit*	2285	*Norman J. Colman*
2910	*Morris Sheppard*	1932	*Norman O. Pedrick*
2586	*Morris Sigman*	2926	*O. B. Martin*
503	*Morrison R. Waite*	486	*O. Henry*
1595	*Morton M. McCarver*	2800	*O. L. Bodenhamer*
1893	*Morton Prince*	2650	*Oakley Wood*
843	*Moses Austin*	1574	*Ole E. Rolvaag*
1462	*Moses Brown*	42	*Oliver Ellsworth*
1750	*Moses Cleaveland*	1109	*Oliver Evans*
2731	*Moses G. Farmer*	2725	*Oliver Kelley*
492	*Moses Rogers*	2936	*Oliver Loving*
2102	*Murat Halstead*	194	*Oliver Wendell Holmes*
2381	*Murray M. Blum*	3109	*Oliver Westover*
1700	*Myron T. Herrick*	256	*Oliver Wolcott*
2830	*Nachman Syrkin*	278	*Oliver Hazard Perry*
455	*Nancy Hanks*	2193	*Omar E. Chapman*
1214	*Napoleon B. Broward*	1929	*Opie Read*
2574	*Narcissa Whitman*	3148	*Ora Ellis*
1539	*Nathan B. Forrest*	1940	*Oran M. Roberts*
944	*Nathan Clifford*	1912	*Orland Loomis*
72	*Nathan Hale*	1888	*Orson D. Munn*
2740	*Nathan S. Davis*	1777	*Orville P. Taylor*
1008	*Nathan Towson*	1962	*Oscar Chappell*
146	*Nathanael Greene*	1885	*Oscar F. Barrett*
167	*Nathaniel Alexander*	1918	*Oscar S. Straus*
1903	*Nathaniel B. Palmer*	2238	*Oscar Underwood*
11	*Nathaniel Bacon*	2973	*Otis E. Hall*
429	*Nathaniel Bowditch*	2130	*Otis Skinner*
2078	*Nathaniel Crosby*	2157	*Otto Mears*
529	*Nathaniel Currier*	2693	*Ovid Butler*
187	*Nathaniel Hawthorne*	1592	*Owen Summers*
1598	*Nathaniel J. Wyeth*	1216	*Owen Wister*
880	*Nathaniel Macon*	1655	*P. T. Barnum*
2938	*Nathaniel Scudder*	2370	*P. Walton Moore*
2940	*Nathaniel Silsbee*	79	*Paine Wingate*
2492	*Negley D. Cochran*	2668	*Palawan*
2371	*Neils Poulson*	3008	*Par Benjamin*
810	*Nelson Dingley*	823	*Park Holland*
3123	*Nelson W. Aldrich*	143	*Pat Harrison*
1520	*Newton D. Baker*	2404	*Patrick B. Whalen*
1908	*Nicholas Longworth*	1786	*Patrick C. Boyle*
917	*Nicholas Biddle*	1507	*Patrick H. Morrissey*
2929	*Nicholas D. Labadie*	14	*Patrick Henry*
103	*Nicholas Gilman*	2400	*Patrick S. Mahony*
1052	*Nicholas Herkimer*	3084	*Paul Buck*
2035	*Nicholas J. Sinnott*	2966	*Paul Bunyan*
2307	*Nick Stoner*	2230	*Paul Chandler*
1792	*Nikola Tesla*	2977	*Paul David Jones*
2481	*Noah Brown*	1897	*Paul Dunbar*

Hull No.	Name	Hull No.	Name
227	*Paul Hamilton*	2855	*Powellton Seam*
865	*Paul Hamilton Hayne*	2093	*Prince L. Campbell*
68	*Paul Revere*	1813	*Priscilla Alden*
1923	*Paul Tulane*	2471	*Propus*
927	*Pearl Harbor*	2017	*R. C. Brennan*
2313	*Pedro Menendez*	2180	*R. F. Peckham*
2203	*Peleg Wadsworth*	2377	*R. J. Reynolds*
868	*Penelope Barker*	1944	*R. M. Williamson*
2199	*Percy D. Haughton*	1513	*R. Ney McNeeley*
2747	*Percy E. Foxworth*	2062	*R. P. Warner*
452	*Père Marquette*	2452	*R. S. Wilson*
824	*Peregrine White*	721	*Rachel Jackson*
632	*Peter Cartwright*	2337	*Rafael R. Rivera*
1769	*Peter Cooper*	1910	*Ralph A. Cram*
2114	*Peter Cooper Hewitt*	2570	*Ralph Barnes*
2070	*Peter Dasmet*	914	*Ralph Izard*
1234	*Peter Donahue*	2685	*Ralph T. O'Neil*
300	*Peter H. Burnett*	192	*Ralph Waldo Emerson*
325	*Peter J. McGuire*	2330	*Ransom A. Moore*
35	*Peter Minuit*	3016	*Raymond B. Stevens*
2584	*Peter Moran*	2479	*Raymond Clapper*
288	*Peter Silvester*	2236	*Raymond T. Baker*
595	*Peter Skene Ogden*	2317	*Raymond V. Ingersoll*
1212	*Peter Stuyvesant*	2339	*Raymond Van Brogan*
2181	*Peter Trumble Rowe*	2425	*Rebecca Boone*
661	*Peter V. Daniel*	1551	*Rebecca Lukens*
2256	*Peter White*	439	*Redfield Proctor*
1527	*Peter Zenger*	2844	*Redstone Seam*
2243	*Petter Lassen*	1745	*Reginald A. Fessenden*
1028	*Philander C. Knox*	2105	*Reinhold Richter*
660	*Philip B. Barbour*	2215	*Renald Fernald*
2545	*Philip C. Shera*	51	*Reverdy Johnson*
1971	*Philip Doddridge*	2401	*Richard A. Van Pelt*
1781	*Philip F. Thomas*	2705	*Richard B. Moore*
326	*Philip H. Sheridan*	41	*Richard Bassett*
1227	*Philip Kearny*	28	*Richard Bland*
177	*Philip Livingston*	870	*Richard Caswell*
181	*Philip Schuyler*	2878	*Richard Coulter*
711	*Phineas Banning*	3099	*Richard D. Lyons*
694	*Phoebe A. Hearst*	163	*Richard D. Spaight*
306	*Pierce Butler*	53	*Richard H. Alvey*
1608	*Pierre Gibault*	2323	*Richard Halliburton*
507	*Pierre Laclède*	1630	*Richard Harding Davis*
1001	*Pierre L'Enfant*	458	*Richard Henderson*
567	*Pierre S. Dupont*	294	*Richard Henry Dana*
320	*Pierre Soule*	18	*Richard Henry Lee*
696	*Pio Pico*	338	*Richard Hovey*
2862	*Pittsburg Seam*	1883	*Richard J. Cleveland*
2022	*Pleasant Armstrong*	2963	*Richard J. Hopkins*
871	*Pocahontas*	2526	*Richard J. Oglesby*
2853	*Pocahontas Seam*	419	*Richard Jordan Gatling*
1193	*Ponce De León*	2473	*Richard K. Call*
2971	*Pontus H. Ross*	1049	*Richard M. Johnson*

Hull No.	Name	Hull No.	Name
608	*Richard Mansfield*	70	*Robert Morris*
426	*Richard March Hoe*	2968	*Robert Neighbors*
1731	*Richard Moczkowski*	2006	*Robert Newell*
1199	*Richard Montgomery*	2886	*Robert Parrot*
2925	*Richard O'Brien*	1516	*Robert R. Livingston*
1026	*Richard Olney*	3062	*Robert R. McBurney*
2383	*Richard Randall*	2200	*Robert R. Randall*
621	*Richard Rush*	797	*Robert Rogers*
840	*Richard S. Ewell*	904	*Robert Rowan*
261	*Richard Stockton*	2785	*Robert S. Abbott*
2864	*Richard Upjohn*	2077	*Robert S. Bean*
2297	*Richard V. Oulahan*	2950	*Robert S. Lovett*
454	*Richard Yates*	706	*Robert Stuart*
316	*Richmond Mumford Pearson*	1941	*Robert T. Hill*
1994	*Richmond P. Hobson*	437	*Robert T. Lincoln*
1701	*Ring Lardner*	347	*Robert Toombs*
2870	*Risden Tyler Bennett*	792	*Robert Treat*
3056	*Robert B. Forbes*	32	*Robert Treat Paine*
1027	*Robert Bacon*	1493	*Robert Trimble*
1506	*Robert Battey*	2794	*Robert W. Bingham*
663	*Robert C. Grier*	3125	*Robert W. Hart*
2769	*Robert D. Carey*	2941	*Robert Watchorn*
1974	*Robert Dale Owen*	1842	*Robert Wickliffe*
2956	*Robert E. Clarkson*	1193	*Robert Y. Hayne*
440	*Robert E. Peary*	1024	*Robt. M. LaFollette*
1015	*Robert Eden*	2858	*Roda Seam*
2603	*Robert Ellis Lewis*	17	*Roger B. Taney*
1009	*Robert Erskine*	1032	*Roger Griswold*
2805	*Robert F. Broussard*	903	*Roger Moore*
3146	*Robert F. Burns*	260	*Roger Sherman*
1968	*Robert F. Hoke*	224	*Roger Williams*
296	*Robert F. Stockton*	1834	*Ross G. Marvin*
1066	*Robert Fechner*	2403	*Roy James Cole*
230	*Robert Fulton*	2841	*Roy K. Johnson*
2719	*Robert G. Cousins*	1219	*Royal S. Copeland*
234	*Robert G. Harper*	2866	*Ruben Dario*
1855	*Robert G. Ingersoll*	2888	*Rudolph Kauffmann*
173	*Robert Gray*	1204	*Rufus C. Dawes*
498	*Robert H. Harrison*	2931	*Rufus Choate*
2913	*Robert Henri*	2451	*Rufus E. Foster*
879	*Robert Howe*	280	*Rufus King*
2392	*Robert J. Banks*	940	*Rufus W. Peckham*
1003	*Robert J. Collier*	1545	*Russell Sage*
629	*Robert J. Walker*	1754	*Russell A. Alger*
796	*Robert Jordan*	2564	*Russell H. Chittenden*
2240	*Robert L. Hague*	2990	*Russell R. Jones*
2189	*Robert L. Vann*	479	*S. Hall Young*
1531	*Robert Lansing*	590	*S. M. Babcock*
2184	*Robert Louis Stevenson*	2667	*S. M. Shoemaker*
1044	*Robert Lowry*	2663	*S. Wiley Wakeman*
1560	*Robert Lucas*	2423	*Sabik*
348	*Robert M. T. Hunter*	612	*Sacajawea*
2498	*Robert Mills*	1969	*Sallie S. Cotton*

Hull No.	Name	Hull No.	Name
577	*Salmon B. Chase*	2587	*Samleven*
1543	*Salvador Brau*	2355	*Samleyte*
95	*Sam Houston*	2636	*Samlistar*
1936	*Sam Houston II*	2358	*Samlorian*
1591	*Sam Jackson*	2593	*Samlossie*
3020	*Samadang*	2625	*Samloyal*
3014	*Samadre*	2639	*Samluzon*
2598	*Samaffric*	2589	*Samlyth*
1517	*Samalness*	2611	*Samneagh*
2216	*Samannan*	2640	*Samnegros*
2683	*Samar*	2412	*Samnid*
2356	*Samaustral*	2359	*Samoland*
3015	*Sambanka*	3018	*Samoresby*
2444	*Samcebu*	2630	*Samorest*
2415	*Samchess*	2413	*Samouse*
2405	*Samclyde*	2354	*Samselbu*
2604	*Samcolne*	2606	*Samshee*
2599	*Samconon*	2644	*Samskern*
2621	*Samconstant*	3024	*Samsmola*
2408	*Samcree*	2629	*Samsoaring*
3007	*Samdaring*	1878	*Samson Occum*
2437	*Samdart*	2638	*Samspeed*
2617	*Samdauntless*	2608	*Samspelga*
3009	*Samderry*	3005	*Samsperrin*
2224	*Samderwent*	2223	*Samstrae*
2210	*Samdon*	2590	*Samstrule*
2609	*Samdonard*	2615	*Samsturdy*
2214	*Samearn*	3021	*Samsuva*
2602	*Sameden*	2645	*Samsylarna*
2417	*Samesk*	2643	*Samtana*
2600	*Samethy*	2411	*Samtay*
2407	*Samettrick*	2218	*Samteviot*
2410	*Sameveron*	2635	*Samtorch*
2350	*Samfairy*	2619	*Samtrusty*
2623	*Samfaithful*	2633	*Samtruth*
2409	*Samfeugh*	1852	*Samtweed*
2352	*Samfinn*	2222	*Samtyne*
2626	*Samfleet*	2030	*Samuel A. Worcester*
1853	*Samforth*	71	*Samuel Adams*
2351	*Samfoyle*	164	*Samuel Ashe*
2632	*Samfreedom*	937	*Samuel Blatchford*
2610	*Samgallion*	981	*Samuel Bowles*
2596	*Samgaudie*	2110	*Samuel Brannon*
2627	*Samglory*	23	*Samuel Chase*
2613	*Samhope*	585	*Samuel Colt*
2435	*Samhorn*	622	*Samuel D. Ingham*
3022	*Samidway*	450	*Samuel de Champlain*
2641	*Samindoro*	1031	*Samuel Dexter*
2357	*Samingoy*	2647	*Samuel F. B. Morse*
2591	*Saminver*	331	*Samuel F. B. Morse*
2607	*Samjack*	501	*Samuel F. Miller*
2646	*Samlamu*	2294	*Samuel G. French*
2605	*Samlea*	2324	*Samuel G. Howe*

Hull No.	Name	Hull No.	Name
2699	Samuel Gompers	2652	Sidney Wright
640	Samuel Gompers	2809	Sieur de LaSalle
1459	Samuel Gorton	457	Sieur Duluth
104	Samuel Griffin	975	Silas Weir Mitchell
1949	Samuel H. Walker	2271	Silvestre Escalante
651	Samuel Heintselman	2531	Simeon G. Reed
248	Samuel Huntington	1802	Simon B. Elliott
2689	Samuel I. Cobb	2108	Simon Bamberger
597	Samuel J. Tilden	2033	Simon Benson
46	Samuel Johnston	1623	Simon Bolivar
141	Samuel Jordon Kirkwood	733	Simon Newcomb
2044	Samuel K. Barlow	743	Simon Willard
2997	Samuel L. Jeffery	654	Smith Thompson
2058	Samuel Lancaster	709	Solomon Juneau
109	Samuel Livermore	2331	Soter Ortynsky
1815	Samuel M. Ralston	33	St. Olaf
1000	Samuel McIntyre	1804	Stage Door Canteen
235	Samuel Moody	2007	Stanford Newel
662	Samuel Nelson	738	Stanford White
702	Samuel P. Langley	505	Stanley Matthews
593	Samuel Parker	3116	Stanley R. Fisher
3127	Samuel R. Aitken	3004	Stanton H. King
572	Samuel Seabury	171	Star of Oregon
2433	Samuel T. Darling	297	Starr King
2580	Samuel V. Stewart	2320	Stepas Darius
2163	Samuel W. Williston	231	Stephen A. Douglas
2353	Samvigna	618	Stephen B. Elkins
3017	Samwake	2483	Stephen Beasley
2624	Samwinged	276	Stephen C. Foster
2221	Samwye	2252	Stephen C. Porter
2212	Samythian	1578	Stephen Crane
1907	Sanford B. Dole	265	Stephen F. Austin
961	Santiago Iglesias	2299	Stephen Furdek
2750	Sara Bache	578	Stephen Girard
2178	Sara Teasdale	1682	Stephen H. Long
1538	Sarah J. Hale	247	Stephen Hopkins
2219	Sarah Orne Jewett	2283	Stephen Hopkins
1899	Schuyler Colfax	85	Stephen Johnson Field
2701	Seaman A. Knapp	2868	Stephen Leacock
1233	Sebastían Cermeno	666	Stephen M. White
680	Sebastían Vizcáino	1540	Stephen R. Mallory
2453	Seginus	2326	Stephen Smith
2528	Segundo Ruiz Belvis	1676	Stephen T. Mather
2824	Sewanee Seam	1681	Stephen Vincent Benet
2851	Sewell Seam	2601	Stephen W. Gambrill
482	Sheldon Jackson	1729	Stephen W. Kearney
2562	Sherman O. Houghton	982	Stevenson Taylor
2544	Sherwood Anderson	2840	Streator Seam
2076	Sidney Edgerton	2922	Sul Ross
1900	Sidney Howard	2188	Sumner I. Kimball
2760	Sidney H. Short	1235	Sun Yat Sen
1197	Sidney Lanier	2213	Susan Colby
856	Sidney Sherman	2618	Sverre Helmersen

Hull No.	Name	Hull No.	Name
795	*Sylvester Gardiner*	2091	*Thomas Howell*
1914	*Sylvester Pattie*	1982	*Thomas J. Jarvis*
2455	*Syrma*	2478	*Thomas J. Lyons*
2304	*T. A. Johnston*	272	*Thomas J. Rusk*
2946	*T. E. Mitchell*	2069	*Thomas J. Walsh*
121	*T. J. Jackson*	175	*Thomas Jefferson*
3094	*T. S. Gold*	659	*Thomas Johnson*
582	*Tabitha Brown*	462	*Thomas Kearns*
1040	*Tarleton Brown*	908	*Thomas L. Clingman*
1120	*Tecumseh*	2518	*Thomas L. Haley*
2507	*Telfair Stockton*	2295	*Thomas LeValley*
1770	*Tench Tilghman*	9	*Thomas Lynch*
2695	*Terry E. Stephenson*	1711	*Thomas M. Cooley*
926	*Thaddeus Kosciuszko*	179	*Thomas MacDonough*
1635	*Thaddeus S. C. Lowe*	301	*Thomas McKean*
268	*Theo. Sedgwick*	30	*Thomas Nelson*
717	*Theodore Dwight Weld*	995	*Thomas Nelson Page*
43	*Theodore Foster*	2026	*Thomas Nuttall*
718	*Theodore Parker*	1656	*Thomas Oliver Larkin*
1814	*Theodore Roosevelt*	2815	*Thomas P. Leathers*
124	*Theodoric Bland*	65	*Thomas Paine*
584	*Thomas A. Edison*	223	*Thomas Pinckney*
2011	*Thomas A. Hendricks*	2001	*Thomas Pollock*
2369	*Thomas B. King*	933	*Thomas R. Marshall*
804	*Thomas B. Reed*	39	*Thomas Ruffin*
122	*Thomas B. Robertson*	2917	*Thomas Say*
199	*Thomas Bailey Aldrich*	133	*Thomas Scott*
3047	*Thomas Bradlee*	921	*Thomas Sim Lee*
2952	*Thomas Bulfinch*	27	*Thomas Stone*
1719	*Thomas C. Power*	1205	*Thomas Sully*
822	*Thomas Clyde*	154	*Thomas Sumter*
2032	*Thomas Condon*	269	*Thomas T. Tucker*
531	*Thomas Corwin*	1492	*Thomas Todd*
2524	*Thomas Crawford*	1756	*Thomas U. Walter*
948	*Thomas Cresap*	905	*Thomas W. Bickett*
2592	*Thomas Donaldson*	1955	*Thomas W. Gregory*
2955	*Thomas Eakins*	801	*Thomas W. Hyde*
701	*Thomas East*	2898	*Thomas W. Murray*
625	*Thomas Ewing*	1993	*Thomas W. Owen*
989	*Thomas F. Bayard*	2051	*Thomas W. Symons*
1919	*Thomas F. Cunningham*	1073	*Thomas Wolfe*
2784	*Thomas F. Flaherty*	1757	*Thorstein Veblen*
2696	*Thomas F. Hunt*	135	*Thos. Sinnickson*
3077	*Thomas F. Meagher*	779	*Timothy Dwight*
1036	*Thomas Fitzsimons*	1033	*Timothy Bloodworth*
1868	*Thomas G. Masaryk*	246	*Timothy Pickering*
1898	*Thomas H. Gallaudet*	1739	*Tobias E. Stansbury*
3034	*Thomas H. Sumner*	817	*Tobias Lear*
1228	*Thomas Hart Benton*	3130	*Tom Treanor*
105	*Thomas Hartley*	2942	*Tomas Guardia*
6	*Thomas Heyward*	2780	*Toussaint L'Ouverture*
1644	*Thomas Hill*	1020	*Townsend Harris*
203	*Thomas Hooker*	307	*Tristram Dalton*

Hull No.	Name	Hull No.	Name
1779	*Tutuila*	2666	*Webster*
1811	*U. S. O.*	2333	*Wendell L. Willkie*
2729	*Uriah M. Rose*	638	*Wendell Phillips*
2100	*Vachel Lindsay*	2345	*Wesley W. Barrett*
1691	*Vernon L. Kellogg*	2534	*Wilbur O. Atwater*
2172	*Vernon L. Parrington*	1101	*Wilbur Wright*
2343	*Vernon S. Hood*	1640	*Wiley Post*
2083	*Victor C. Vaughn*	1673	*Wilfred Grenfell*
1871	*Victor F. Lawson*	3105	*Wilfred R. Bellevue*
1532	*Victor Herbert*	2978	*Will B. Otwell*
2661	*Vincent Harrington*	2763	*Willet M. Hays*
147	*Virginia Dare*	1956	*Will R. Wood*
463	*Vitus Bering*	923	*Will Rogers*
2097	*W. B. Ayer*	930	*Willard Hall*
2736	*W. B. Rodgers*	2996	*Willard R. Johnson*
2462	*W. C. Latta*	2122	*William A. Coulter*
2363	*W. P. Few*	3089	*William A. Dobson*
1797	*W. R. Grace*	160	*William A. Graham*
2487	*W. S. Jennings*	2572	*William A. Henry*
2247	*W. W. McCrackin*	537	*William A. Jones*
1810	*W. Walter Husband*	1223	*William A. Richardson*
315	*Wade Hampton*	2282	*William Allen White*
910	*Waigstill Avery*	2985	*William Asa Carter*
2796	*Walker D. Hines*	724	*William B. Allison*
902	*Walker Taylor*	1926	*William B. Bankhead*
2992	*Wallace M. Tyler*	2733	*William B. Leeds*
2778	*Wallace R. Farrington*	469	*William B. Ogden*
195	*Walt Whitman*	266	*William B. Travis*
1113	*Walter Camp*	1537	*William B. Wilson*
509	*Walter Colton*	1490	*William B. Woods*
775	*Walter E. Ranger*	699	*William B. Young*
3144	*Walter E. Schwenk*	1579	*William Beaumont*
3131	*Walter F. Perry*	3095	*William Bevan*
626	*Walter Forward*	1062	*William Black Yates*
2983	*Walter Frederick Kraft*	826	*William Blackstone*
912	*Walter Hines Page*	314	*William Blount*
2656	*Walter Kidde*	208	*William Bradford*
1542	*Walter L. Fleming*	209	*William Brewster*
2511	*Walter M. Christiansen*	1203	*William Byrd*
1025	*Walter Q. Gresham*	120	*William C. C. Claiborne*
877	*Walter Raleigh*	438	*William C. Endicott*
1753	*Walter Reed*	745	*William C. Gorgas*
2962	*Walter Wellman*	2046	*William C. Lane*
2291	*Walter Williams*	2124	*William C. Ralston*
2266	*Walter Wyman*	1632	*William Carson*
972	*Ward Hunt*	172	*William Clark*
2597	*Warren Delano*	1457	*William Coddington*
2346	*Warren P. Marks*	2394	*William Cox*
2217	*Washington Allston*	2485	*William Crane Gray*
197	*Washington Irving*	1746	*William Crompton*
2251	*Watson C. Squire*	189	*William Cullen Bryant*
2142	*Wayne MacVeagh*	496	*William Cushing*
2205	*Webb Miller*	2306	*William D. Bloxham*

Hull No.	Name	Hull No.	Name
2735	*William D. Boyce*	959	*William H. Wilmer*
1727	*William D. Burnham*	319	*William Harper*
2588	*William D. Byron*	222	*William Hawkins*
2260	*William D. Hoard*	2653	*William Hodson*
2443	*William D. Hoxie*	148	*William Hooper*
895	*William D. Moseley*	2054	*William Hume*
894	*William D. Pender*	2576	*William I. Chamberlain*
180	*William Dawes*	1863	*William I. Kip*
489	*William Dean Howells*	1522	*William J. Bryan*
821	*William DeWitt Hyde*	624	*William J. Duane*
707	*William Dunbar*	2766	*William J. Gray*
614	*William E. Borah*	2113	*William J. Palmer*
2308	*William E. Dodd*	2340	*William J. Riddle*
1742	*William E. Pendleton*	704	*William J. Worth*
2279	*William E. Ritter*	736	*William James*
249	*William Ellery*	10	*William Johnson*
637	*William Ellery Channing*	2987	*William K. Kamaka*
828	*William Eustis*	493	*William K. Vanderbilt*
295	*William F. Cody*	1722	*William Keith*
2187	*William F. Empey*	1872	*William Kelly*
2393	*William F. Jerman*	1225	*William Kent*
1672	*William F. MacLennan*	206	*William King*
1699	*William F. Vilas*	901	*William L. Davidson*
309	*William Few*	688	*William L. Marcy*
76	*William Floyd*	2890	*William L. McLean*
2721	*William Ford Nichols*	275	*William L. Smith*
735	*William G. Gargo*	2245	*William L. Sublette*
2865	*William G. Lee*	2310	*William L. Watson*
443	*William G. McAdoo*	1056	*William L. Yancey*
1211	*William G. Sumner*	3030	*William Leavitt*
2008	*William G. Tvault*	2895	*William Leory Gable*
159	*William Gaston*	2672	*William Libbey*
2553	*William Gluckens*	653	*William Lloyd Garrison*
310	*William Grayson*	3053	*William Lyon Phelps*
1714	*William H. Allen*	2428	*William M. Eastland*
2246	*William H. Ashley*	1038	*William M. Evarts*
521	*William H. Aspinwall*	1638	*William M. Gwin*
1902	*William H. Carruth*	630	*William M. Meredith*
2687	*William H. Clagett*	1957	*William M. Rayburn*
830	*William H. Crawford*	87	*William M. Stewart*
2258	*William H. Dall*	47	*William Maclay*
2880	*William H. Edwards*	1720	*William Matson*
2009	*William H. Gray*	932	*William McKinley*
1006	*William H. Jackson*	153	*William Moultrie*
2828	*William H. Kendrick*	677	*William Mulholland*
3111	*William H. Lane*	1695	*William N. Byers*
1631	*William H. McGuffey*	842	*William N. Pendleton*
2153	*William H. Moody*	954	*William Osler*
93	*William H. Prescott*	2319	*William P. Duval*
562	*William H. Seward*	768	*William P. Fessenden*
818	*William H. Todd*	555	*William P. McArthur*
980	*William H. Webb*	302	*William Paca*
953	*William H. Welch*	48	*William Patterson*

Hull No.	Name	Hull No.	Name
2727	*William Peffer*	977	*William W. Gerhard*
974	*William Pepper*	2993	*William W. Johnson*
803	*William Pepperell*	1546	*William W. Loring*
784	*William Phips*	1572	*William W. Mayo*
212	*William Pierce Frye*	2835	*William W. McKee*
2197	*William Pitt Preble*	2892	*William W. Seaton*
1586	*William Prouse*	2464	*William Wheelwright*
2406	*William R. Cox*	255	*William Whipple*
158	*William R. Davie*	837	*William Wilkins*
941	*William R. Day*	263	*William Williams*
2984	*William R. Lewis*	516	*William Windom*
1684	*William R. Nelson*	1904	*William Winter*
667	*William Raton*	50	*William Wirt*
61	*William Rawle*	2550	*William Wolfskill*
2651	*William S. Baer*	890	*Willie Jones*
2162	*William S. Clark*	2052	*Willis C. Hawley*
956	*William S. Halsted*	1832	*Willis J. Abbot*
2084	*William S. Ladd*	88	*Willis Van Devanter*
570	*William S. Rosecrans*	3067	*Wilson B. Keene*
1761	*William S. Thayer*	2023	*Wilson P. Hunt*
2774	*William Schirmer*	1703	*Winfield S. Stratton*
2106	*William Sharon*	98	*Winfield Scott*
1774	*William Smallwood*	967	*Winfred L. Smith*
2286	*William Sproule*	769	*Winslow Homer*
970	*William Strong*	3069	*Winthrop L. Marvin*
800	*William Sturgis*	127	*Wm. B. Giles*
1980	*William T. Barry*	931	*Woodbridge N. Ferris*
1224	*William T. Coleman*	893	*Woodrow Wilson*
600	*William T. Sherman*	1860	*Wyatt Earp*
2894	*William Terry Howell*	2945	*Wynn Seale*
1102	*William Thornton*	244	*Zachary Taylor*
59	*William Tilghman*	695	*Zane Grey*
3048	*William Tyler*	2422	*Zaniah*
993	*William Tyler Page*	145	*Zebulon B. Vance*
2724	*William Vaughn Moody*	73	*Zebulon Pike*
2117	*William W. Campbell*	1689	*Zona Gale*

2,695 Total Ships

APPENDIX C. Liberty Ships Commissioned in U.S. Navy*

Date	Hull number	Name	Maritime number	Name
4–21–44	AG68	Basilan (ex ARG12)	2460	Basilan
4–24–44	AG69	Burias (ex ARG13)	2458	Burias
12–22–43	AG70	Zaniah (ex AK120)	2422	Zaniah
1–1–44	AG71	Baham (ex AK122)	1217	Elizabeth C. Bellamy
11–15–44	AG73	Belle Isle	3070	Belle Isle
11–26–44	AG74	Coasters Harbor	3073	Coasters Harbor
12–7–44	AG75	Cuttyhunk Island	3080	Cuttyhunk Island
12–21–44	AG75	Avery Island	3085	Avery Island
12–30–44	AG77	Indian Island	3088	Indian Island
1–19–45	AG78	Kent Island	3092	Kent Island
7–8–61	AGTR1	Oxford	3127	Samuel R. Aitken
11–9–63	AGTR2	Georgetown	3125	Robert W. Hart
12–13–63	AGTR3	Jamestown	3126	J. Howland Gardner
10–31–42	AK70	Crater	420	John James Audubon
11–16–42	AK71	Adhara	425	G. H. Corliss
12–14–42	AK72	Aludra**	437	Robert T. Lincoln
11–23–42	AK73	Arided	500	Noah H. Swaine
12–1–42	AK74	Carina	502	David Davis
12–8–42	AK75	Cassiopeia	504	Melville W. Fuller
1–2–42	AK76	Celeno	539	Redfield Procter
1–18–43	AK77	Cetus	445	George B. Cortelyou
1–28–43	AK78	Deimos***	513	Chief Ouray
2–16–43	AK79	Draco	453	John M. Palmer
3–29–43	AK90	Albireo	525	John G. Nicolay
4–16–43	AK91	Cor Caroli	476	Betsy Ross
5–8–43	AK92	Eridanus	1099	Luther Burbank
5–25–43	AK93	Etamin (to IX173)	1106	Isaac Babbitt
5–10–43	AK94	Mintaka	725	Ansel Briggs
5–14–43	AK95	Murnim (S)	623	Brigham Young
5–11–43	AK96	Sterope	183	James Wilson
5–28–43	AK97	Serpens	739	Benjamin N. Cardoza
7–15–43	AK99	Bootes (S)	1656	Thomas O. Larkin
7–26–43	AK100	Lynx	1657	Juan Bautista de Anza
7–22–43	AK101	Lyra (S)	1555	Cyrus Hamlin
7–30–43	AK102	Triangulum	1669	Eugene B. Daskom
8–10–43	AK103	Sculptor	1671	D. W. Harrington
7–31–43	AK104	Ganymede (S)	1571	James W. Nye
8–17–43	AK105	Naos	1684	William R. Nelson
10–22–43	AK106	Caelum	1860	Wyatt Earp
8–25–43	AK107	Hyperion	1563	Christopher C. Andrews
11–23–43	AK108	Rotanin	1872	William Kelly

* Those ships still in Marad Reserve Fleets as of late 1971 are marked as follows: (S) Suisun Bay, California; (J) James River, Virginia; (B) Beaumont, Texas.
** Sunk 6–23–43.
*** Sunk 6–23–43

Date	Hull number	Name	Maritime number	Name
10–25–43	**AK109**	*Alioth* (to AVS4)	1730	*James Rowan*
10–29–43	**AK110**	*Alkes* (**J**)	1584	*Increase A. Lapham*
10–29–43	**AK111**	*Giansar*	625	*Thomas Ewing*
10–20–43	**AK112**	*Grumium* (to IX174)	443	*William B. McAdoo*
10–30–43	**AK113**	*Rutilicus* (**J**)	1643	*Andrew Rowan*
3–27–43	**AK114**	*Alkaid*	1211	*William G. Sumner*
3–17–44	**AK115**	*Crux*	1212	*Peter Stuyvesant*
11–25–43	**AK116**	*Alderamin*	1963	*J. S. Cullinan*
3–17–44	**AK117**	*Zaurak*	1964	*Hugh Young*
5–5–43	**AK118**	*Shaula*	1213	*James Screven*
5–17–44	**AK119**	*Matar*	1214	*Napoleon B. Broward*
See AG70	**AK120**	*Zaniah* (to AG70)	2422	*Zaniah*
12–29–43	**AK121**	*Sabik*	2423	*William Becknell*
1–1–44	**AK122**	*Baham* (to AG71)	1217	*Elizabeth C. Bellamy*
1–18–44	**AK123**	*Menkar*	1218	*John White*
10–29–44	**AK124**	*Azimech* (**J**)	1725	*Mary Patten*
11–1–43	**AK125**	*Lesuth*	1638	*William M. Gwin*
10–26–43	**AK126**	*Megrez* (**S**)	1642	*General Vallejo*
11–27–43	**AK127**	*Alnitah*	451	*John A. Logan*
10–25–43	**AK128**	*Leonis*	512	*Key Pittman*
6–14–44	**AK129**	*Phobos*	1961	*Joseph H. Kibby*
2–21–44	**AK130**	*Arkab* (**J**)	2449	*Warren Stone*
7–22–44	**AK131**	*Melucta*	2470	*Melucta*
6–12–44	**AK132**	*Propus*	2471	*Propus*
4–12–44	**AK133**	*Seginus*	2453	*Harry Toulmin**
3–21–44	**AK134**	*Syrma*	2455	*Syrma***
9–26–44	**AK135**	*Venus*	263	*William Williams*
1–4–44	**AK136**	*Ara* (**J**)	69	*Daniel Boone*
1–7–44	**AK137**	*Ascella*	708	*George C. Yount*
1–1–44	**AK138**	*Cheleb* (**S**)	520	*Lyman J. Gage*
1–14–44	**AK139**	*Pavo* (**J**)	846	*James F. Hogg*
1–14–44	**AK140**	*Situla*	1590	*John Whitaker*
11–14–43	**AK221**	*Kenmore* (ex AP162)	1664	*James H. McClintock*
11–10–43	**AK222**	*Livingston* (ex AP163)	1637	*Josiah D. Whitney*
11–8–43	**AK223**	*De Grasse* (ex AP164)	1598	*Nathaniel Wyeth*
11–10–43	**AK224**	*Prince Georges* (ex AP165)	426	*Richard March Hoe*
9–24–44	**AK225**	*Allegan*	2416	*Van Lear Black*
9–26–44	**AK226**	*Appanoose*	2662	*A. J. Cassatt*
2–15–44	**AKN1**	*Indus*	1814	*Theodore Roosevelt*
3–18–44	**AKN2**	*Sagittarius* (**J**)	1835	*J. Fred Essary*
3–28–44	**AKN3**	*Tuscana*	2406	*William R. Cox*
2–27–44	**AKN5**	*Zebra* (ex IX107) (**S**)	535	*Matthew Lyon*
7–15–44	**AKS5**	*Acubens*	1935	*Acubens*
5–2–44	**AKS6**	*Kochab*	2459	*Kochab*
2–7–44	**AKS7**	*Luna*	1528	*Harriet Hosmer*
3–4–44	**AKS8**	*Talita*	2012	*Jonathan Jennings*
3–31–44	**AKS9**	*Volans*	772	*Edward Preble*
11–14–44	**AKS10**	*Cybele*	2820	*Cybele*
11–20–44	**AKS11**	*Gratia*	2823	*Gratia*
4–21–25	**AKS12**	*Hecuba*	2821	*Hecuba*

* after decommissioning, operated commercially as *Harry Toulmin, Kehrea*
** after decommissioning, operated commercially as *Andres Almonaster, San Jorge*

Date	Hull number	Name	Maritime number	Name
4–1–45	AKS13	*Hesperia*(S)	2825	*Hesperia*
10–31–44	AKS14	*Iolanda*(S)	3068	*Iolanda*
11–20–44	AKS15	*Liguria*(S)	3071	*Liguria*
	AKV6	*Albert M. Boe*	3132	*Albert M. Boe*
	AKV7	*Cardinal O'Connell*	3129	*Cardinal O'Connell*
*	APB51	*DuPage*	617	*John W. Weeks*
*	AR17	*Assistance*(J)	2649	*Assistance*
*	AR18	*Diligence*(S)	2658	*Diligence*
5–9–45	AR19	*Xanthus*(J)	2664	*Hecla*
3–24–45	AR20	*Laertes*(S)	2674	*Dutiful*
4–28–45	AR21	*Dionysus*(B)	2681	*Faithful*
10–12–43	ARG2	*Luzon*	981	*Samuel Bowles*
11–6–43	ARG3	*Mindanao*	983	*Elbert Hubbard*
4–0–44	ARG4	*Tutuila***	1779	*Tutuila*
4–4–44	ARG5	*Oahu*	1782	*Caleb C. Wheeler*
4–15–44	ARG6	*Cebu*	1805	*Cebu*
5–19–44	ARG7	*Culebra Island*	1830	*Culebra Island*
8–17–44	ARG8	*Maui*	2595	*Leyte*
10–17–44	ARG9	*Mona Island*	2634	*Mona Island*
8–29–44	ARG10	*Palawan*	2668	*Palawan*
6–5–45	ARG11	*Samar*	2683	*Samar*
5–31–45	ARG16	*Kermit Roosevelt*	2680	*Kermit Roosevelt*
7–13–45	ARG17	*Hooper Island*	2682	*Hooper Island*
12–7–44	ARV1	*Chourre* (ex ARG14)	2637	*Chourre*
3–17–45	ARV2	*Webster* (ex ARG15)	2666	*Webster*
10–25–43	AVS4	*Allioth*	1730	*James Rowan*
2–17–44	AW1	*Stag* (ex IX128)	1732	*Norman O. Pedrick*
2–17–44	AW2	*Wildcat* (ex IX130)	1934	*Leon Godchaux*
See AKN5	IX107	*Zebra*	535	*Matthew Lyon*
10–4–43	IX109	*Antelope*	1587	*M.H. de Young*
11–18–43	IX111	*Armadillo*	1900	*Sidney Howard*
11–20–43	IX112	*Beagle*	1901	*David Rittenhouse*
11–22–43	IX113	*Camel*	1902	*William H. Carruth*
11–25–43	IX114	*Caribou*	1903	*Nathaniel B. Palmer*
11–26–43	IX115	*Elk*	1904	*William Winter*
11–29–43	IX116	*Gazelle*	1905	*Cyrus K. Holiday*
12–3–43	IX117	*Gemsbok*	1906	*Carl R. Gray*
12–12–43	IX118	*Giraffe*	1907	*Sanford B. Dole*
12–13–43	IX119	*Ibex*	1908	*Nicholas Longworth*
12–15–43	IX120	*Jaguar*	1909	*Charles T. Yerkes*
12–17–43	IX121	*Kangaroo*	1923	*Paul Tulane*
12–26–43	IX122	*Leopard*	1926	*William S. Bankhead*
1–9–44	IX123	*Mink*	1927	*Judah Touro*
1–28–44	IX124	*Moose*	1928	*Mason L. Weems*
1–6–44	IX125	*Panda*	1929	*Opie Read*
12–30–43	IX126	*Porcupine*	1930	*Leif Ericson*
2–1–44	IX127	*Raccoon*	1931	*J. C. W. Beckham*
2–17–44	IX128	*Stag* (to AW1)	1932	*Norman O. Pedrick*
1–14–44	IX129	*Whippet*	1933	*Eugene W. Hilgard*
2–17–44	IX130	*Wildcat* (to AW2)	1934	*Leon Godchaux*

* Lent to England, never commissioned USN.
** Last Liberty ship in U.S. Navy, stricken 2–21–72.

Date	Hull number	Name	Maritime number	Name
5–25–43	IX173	*Etamin* (ex AK93)	1106	*Isaac Babbitt*
10–20–43	IX174	*Grumium* (es AK112)	443	*William B. McAdoo*
5–24–45	IX223	*Triana*	2559	*Elinor Wiley*
	MSS–1*	*No name*	2445	*Harry L. Glucksman*
	YAG2*	*No name*	2337	*Rafael R. Rivera*
	YAG4*	*No name*	2338	*James W. Wheeler*
	YAG5*	*No name*	2344	*Edwin D. Howard*
	YAG6*	*No name*	2347	*Frank O. Peterson*
2–1–55	YAGR1	*Guardian*	3137	*James G. Squires*
3–5–55	YAGR2	*Lookout*	3139	*Claude Kitchin*
3–29–55	YAGR3	*Skywatcher*	2337	*Rafael R. Rivera*
4– –55	YAGR4	*Searcher*	2338	*James W. Wheeler*
1– –56	YAGR5	*Scanner*	2344	*Edwin D. Howard*
1–21–56	YAGR6	*Locator*	2347	*Frank O. Peterson*
2–8–56	YAGR7	*Picket*	3138	*James F. Harrell*
2–15–56	YAGR8	*Interceptor*	3147	*Edward W. Burton*
1–16–57	YAGR9	*Investigator*	2336	*Charles A. Draper*
2–6–57	YAGR10	*Outpost*	3140	*Francis J. O'Gara*
2–20–57	YAGR11	*Protector*	2346	*Warren P. Marks*
3–5–57	YAGR12	*Vigil*	2339	*Raymond Van Brogan*
4–7–58	YAGR13	*Interdictor*(S)	3142	*Edwin H. Duff*
5–29–58	YAGR14	*Interpreter*(S)	2341	*Dudley H. Thomas*
10–16–58	YAGR15	*Interrupter*(S)	2340	*William J. Riddle*
	renamed	*Tracer*, 9–4–59		
1–5–59	YAGR16	*Watchman*	2343	*Vernon S. Hood*
	YAG36	*no name*	2802	*Floyd W. Spencer*
	YAG37	*no name*	1121	*John L. Sullivan*
	YAG38	*no name*	2207	*Edward Kavanagh*
10–20–62	YAG39	*George Eastman***	1104	*George Eastman*
10–20–62	YAG40	*Granville S. Hall****	2325	*Granville S. Hall*

* not commissioned, but active
** Originally placed in service May 53
*** Originally placed in service 10–20–53. Completed as RA *Nelson Morris*

APPENDIX D. Ships transferred to Russia.* (Operational as of 1968.)

Original Name	Russian Name
Cass Gilbert	Stepan Razin
Charles E. Duryea	Ivan Polzunov
Charles Gordon Curtis	Sergei Kirov
Charles S. Fairchild	Krasnogvardeets
Charles Wilkes	Kolkhosnik
David Douglas	Baku
De Witt Clinton	Sevastopol
Edward Eggleston	Novorossisk
E. H. Harriman	Dekabrist
Emmet D. Boyle	Ingul
Elijah P. Lovejoy	Alexandr Suvorov
George Coggeshall	Sukhona
George E. Goodfellow	General Panfilov
George L. Shoup	Pskov
George Whitefield	Daryal
Gouverneur Morris	Ivan Kulubin
Graham Taylor	Mikhail Kutosov
Grant P. Marsh	Valery Chkalov
Haym Salomon	Karpaty
Henry J. Waters	Rodina
Henry L. Pittock	Askold
Henry W. Corbett	Alexandr Nevsky
Horace Bushnell	Pamyati Kirova
Irving W. Pratt	Nahodka
James Rolph	Alatau
Jay Cooke	Miklukho-Makalai
J. C. Osgood	Beshtau
John Langdon	Tbilisi
John Minto	Vitebsk
José J. Acosta	Khibini
José Sepulveda	Suchan
Joseph Watt	Erevan
Louis Agassiz	Emilian Pugachev
Mary Cassat	Odessa
Paul Dunbar	Byelgorod
Pleasant Armstrong	Uelen
Richard B. Moore	Mashuk
Robert G. Cousins	Avacha
Robert S. Abbott	Kamenets-Podolsk
Samlyth	Sajany
Samuel A. Worcester	Sovetskaya Gavan
Samuel P. Langley	Voikov
Sieur Duluth	Tungus
Thomas Nast	Jean Jaures
Thomas F. Flaherty	Volgograd
Thomas H. Gallaudet	Maikop
Thomas Nelson Page	Sikhote Alin
William D. Boyce	Malakhov Kurgan
William E. Ritter	Briansk
William G. T. Vault	Kuban
Willis C. Hawley	Dushambe

* Lend-Lease.

263

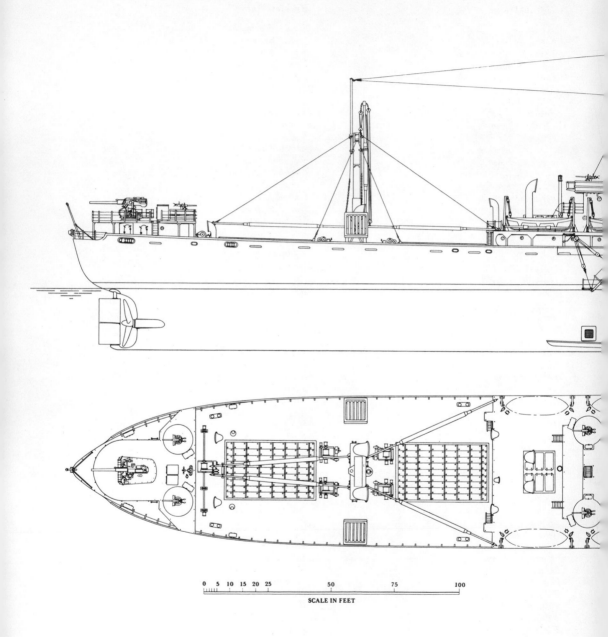

0   5   10 15 20 25   50   75   100

SCALE IN FEET

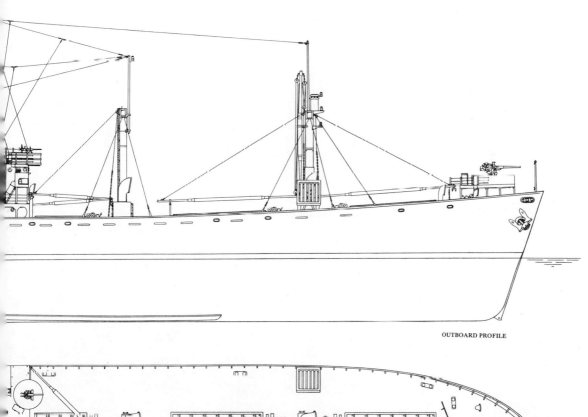

OUTBOARD PROFILE

OVERHEAD VIEW

265

APPENDIX E. Lines and Specifications

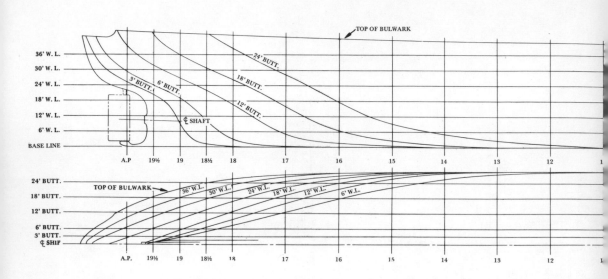

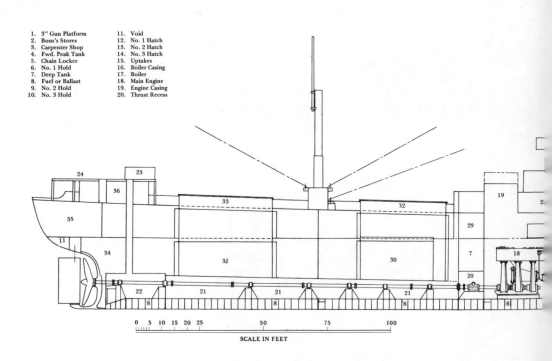

1. 3" Gun Platform
2. Bosn's Stores
3. Carpenter Shop
4. Fwd. Peak Tank
5. Chain Locker
6. No. 1 Hold
7. Deep Tank
8. Fuel or Ballast
9. No. 2 Hold
10. No. 3 Hold

11. Void
12. No. 1 Hatch
13. No. 2 Hatch
14. No. 3 Hatch
15. Uptakes
16. Boiler Casing
17. Boiler
18. Main Engine
19. Engine Casing
20. Thrust Recess

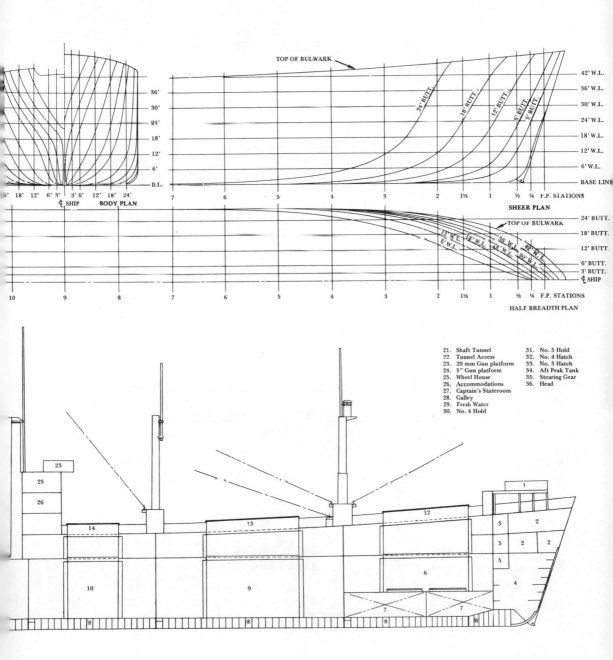

TOP OF BULWARK

42' W.L.
36' W.L.
30' W.L.
24' W.L.
18' W.L.
12' W.L.
6' W.L.
BASE LINE

24' BUTT.
18' BUTT.
12' BUTT.
6' BUTT.
3' BUTT.

36'
30'
24'
18'
12'
6'
D.L.

18' 12' 6' 3' 3' 6' 12' 18' 24'
₵ SHIP   BODY PLAN

7   6   5   4   3   2   1½   1   ½   ¼   F.P. STATIONS
SHEER PLAN

TOP OF BULWARK

24' BUTT.
18' BUTT.
12' BUTT.
6' BUTT.
3' BUTT.
₵ SHIP

10   9   8   7   6   5   4   3   2   1½   1   ½   ¼   F.P. STATIONS
HALF BREADTH PLAN

21. Shaft Tunnel
22. Tunnel Access
23. 20 mm Gun platform
24. 5" Gun platform
25. Wheel House
26. Accommodations
27. Captain's Stateroom
28. Galley
29. Fresh Water
30. No. 4 Hold

31. No. 5 Hold
32. No. 4 Hatch
33. No. 5 Hatch
34. Aft Peak Tank
35. Stearing Gear
36. Head

267

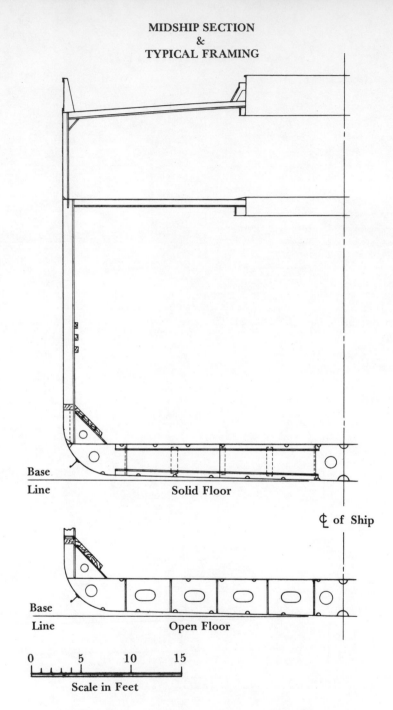

Base
Line   Solid Floor

₵ of Ship

Base
Line   Open Floor

0   5   10   15

Scale in Feet

Notes:
    Solid floors on every frame in engine room, under boiler
stools, under bulkheads and forward of 3/5 of length. Open
floors to longitudinals in way of thrust. Solid floors in
every fourth frame elsewhere.

268

GENERAL SPECIFICATIONS

PRINCIPAL DIMENSIONS

Length over all .... 441' 6"
Length between perpendiculars
   (25' 3¼" W.L.) .... 416'
Breadth molded .... 56' 10¾"
Breadth extreme .... 57'
Depth to upper deck, molded ..... 37' 4"
Depth to second deck, molded ..... 28' 7"
Draft .... 27' 9¼"
Displacement .... 14257 tons
   Light ship (approx.) .... 3337 tons
   Deadweight .... 10920 tons
   U.S. .... 7197 gr. t. ... 4309 net t.
   Panama .... 7223 gr. t. ... 5093 net t.
   Suez .... 7230 gr. t. ... 5399 net t.

MAIN ENGINE

Direct acting, condensing, three cylinder, triple expansion, developing 2500 horsepower at 76 RPM.
Engine size . bore 24½"-37"-70" . stroke 48"
Rated speed .... 11 knots

BOILERS

Two cross drum, sectional, sinuous header, straight tube type fitted with super heaters burning bunker "E" oil. Pressure: 220 PSI Temperature 450°F. Total heating surface 10,234 sq. ft.

CARGO CAPACITY (cu. ft.)

Compartment		Grain	Bale
Hold No. 1	Hold	41257	36083
	Tween decks	42924	39322
Hold No. 2	Hold	98860	92008
	Tween decks	46744	42630
Hold No. 3	Hold	68459	59793
	Tween decks	27970	23904
Hold No. 4	Hold	58841	52574
	Tween decks	35277	29689
Hold No. 5	Hold	58620	51571
	Tween decks	34570	30684
Deep tanks	No. 1 port	3639	2729
	No. 1 stbd	3639	3004
	No. 2 port	7473	5294
	No. 2 stbd	7473	5578
	No. 3 port	13674	12506
	No. 4 stbd	13188	12024
	total	562608	499573

ANCHORS

Two bower—8410 lbs. each, one stream—3195 lbs.

ANCHOR WINDLASS

Steam, minimum speed 30 FPM.

WARPING WINCH

Steam, minimum pull 2500 lb. at 75 FPM, maximum pull 26000 lb. at 75 FPM.

AUXILIARIES

Propeller	4-blade, 18'6" D., pitch 16'
Generators	3 DC type, 400 RPM, 167 amps, 120 V. 25KW each.
Evaporator	1, vertical submerged type, capacity 25 tons per 24 hours
Distiller	1, capacity 6000 gal. per 24 hours
Refrigeration system	1 compressor, Carrier model 7H5; meat room 15°F., dairy room 30°F., vegetable room 40°F., fish room 15°F., scuttle butt 5 gal. per hour at 40°F., 24 lbs. ice per freeze.

MASTS

(Height above bottom of keel plate)

Foremast .... Frame 39 .... 82' ¼"
Fixed mast .... Frame 68 .... 82' ¼"
Fixed mast .... Frame 134 .... 82" ¼"
Telescopic mast .. Frame 68 ....102' ¼"
Telescopic mast .. Frame 134 ....102' ¼"

CARGO WINCHES

Nine, 7" × 12" double geared for 5, 15, & 30 ton booms, capacity 10,000 lb. at 125 FPM, 5,000 lb. at 250 FPM. One 10½" × 12" double geared for 5 ton boom.

BOOMS

Ten 5-ton (55' at hatch 1 & 2, 47' at 3, 55' at 4 & 5)
One 30-ton (51' at hatch 2)
One 15-ton (51' at hatch 4)

TANK CAPACITY

Fuel oil .... 50792 gal. ..... 1818 tons
Fresh water .... 506272 gal. ..... 188 tons

STORES (cu. ft.)

Bosns. stores, 2nd deck, FP to Fr. 112 .. 3034
Bosns. stores, flat between 2nd and upper
   decks 3492
Cabin stores, 2nd deck, Fr. 88-106 4329
Linen locker 585
Bonded stores 186
Meat (refrigerated) 801
Fish (refrigerated) 173
Vegetables (refrigerated) 768
Dairy (refrigerated) 176

WATER BALLAST

98361 cu. ft. .... 2811 tons

Line drawings of a Liberty ship on the preceding pages are by Robert F. Sumrall.

Details of Liberty ship construction on following pages were photographed by the Mariners Museum, Newport News, Virginia. The model is the *Zebulon B. Vance*. The original ship was towed to Spain and scrapped in 1971.

A Bow view at waterline.

B Bow view, fo'c'sle arrangement.

C Bridge and superstructure, from aft.

D Bridge and superstructure, from forward.

E Forward cargo deck, from port side.

F After cargo deck, from port side

G Stern view, poop deck arrangement.

H Stern view, port side.

I Screw and rudder detail.

A Bow view at waterline.

B Bow view, fo'c'sle arrangement.

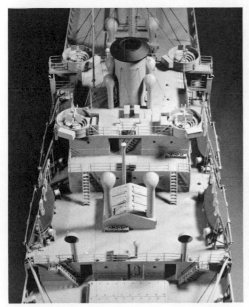

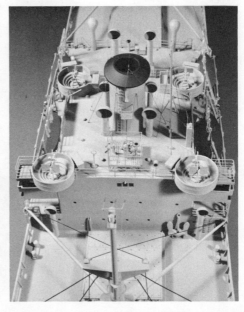

C Bridge and superstructure, from aft.

D Bridge and superstructure, from forward.

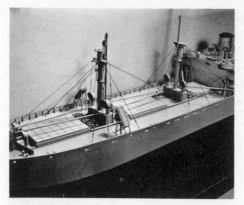

E Forward cargo deck, from port side.

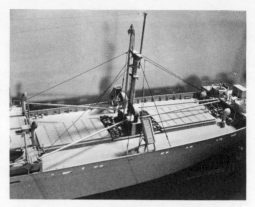

F After cargo deck, from port side.

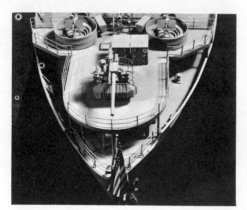

G Stern view, poop deck arrangement.

H Stern view, port side.

I Screw and rudder detail.

INDEX

273